Central Statistical Office

"Our mission is to improve decision making, stimulate research and inform debate within government and the wider community by providing a quality statistical service"

Social Trends 24

1994 Edition

D1630823

Editor:	JENNY CHURCH
Associate Editor:	CAROL SUMMERFIELD

Production team:	DAVID FRY
	STEPHEN DREWELL
	DUNCAN MILLARD
	CARLTON BROWN
	DAVID PENNY
	DAVID SHARP
	AKHTAR UZZAMAN
	STEVE WHYMAN
	AFUA DARKO

London: HMSO

Contents

Page

Page

Introduction

Social Trends draws together statistics from a wide range of government departments and other organisations to paint a broad picture of British society today, and how it has been changing. The 13 chapters each focus on a different social policy area, described in tables, charts and explanatory text. *Social Trends* is aimed at a very wide audience: policy-makers in the public and private sectors; market researchers; journalists and commentators; academics and students; schools; and the general public.

The editorial team always welcomes readers' views on how *Social Trends* could be improved. Please write to the Editor at the address shown below.

Article

Social Trends 24 contains an article, 'Characteristics of the bottom 20 per cent of the income distribution', by Nick Adkin of the Department of Social Security. This is based on the regular DSS analysis of Households Below Average Income.

New material and sources

To preserve topicality, almost a third of the 348 tables and charts in *Social Trends 24* are new compared with the previous edition. In all chapters, the source of the data is given below each table and chart. *Social Trends 24* also includes at the end of each chapter a list of references directing readers to other published sources of data (both government and non government). Those

using *Social Trends* as a first point of reference should find this particularly useful. Regional and local authority analyses of much of the information in *Social Trends* may be found in the CSO's publication *Regional Trends*.

Contributors

The Editor and Associate Editor wish to thank all colleagues in the Government Statistical Service and contributors in other organisations without whose help this publication would not be possible. Thanks also go to our Graphic Design Unit.

Appendix

The Appendix gives definitions and general background information, particularly on administrative structures and legal frameworks. Anyone seeking to understand the tables and charts in detail will find it helpful to read the corresponding entries in the Appendix in addition to the footnotes relevant to each table and chart. A full index to this edition is included following the appendix.

Social Statistics Section
Central Statistical Office
PO Box 1333
Millbank Tower
Millbank
London SW1P 4QQ

Symbols and conventions

Reference years. Where, because of space constraints, a choice of years has to be made, the most recent year or a run of recent years is shown together with past population census years (1981, 1971, 1961 etc) and sometimes the mid-points between census years (1976 etc). Other years may be added if they represent a peak or trough in the series in the table.

Rounding of figures. In tables where figures have been rounded to the nearest final digit, there may be an apparent discrepancy between the sum of the constituent items and the total as shown.

Billion. This term is used to represent a thousand million.

Provisional and estimated data. Some data for the latest year (and occasionally for earlier years) are provisional or estimated. To keep footnotes to a minimum, these have not been indicated; source departments will be able to advise if revised data are available.

Non-calendar years.
Financial year - eg 1 April 1991-31 March 1992 would be shown as 1991-92
Academic year - eg September 1991/July 1992 would be shown as 1991/92
Data covering more than one year - eg 1990, 1991 and 1992 would be shown as 1990-1992

Italics. Figures are shown in italics when they represent percentages.

Symbols. The following symbols have been used throughout *Social Trends*:
..	*not available*
.	*not applicable*
-	*negligible (less than half the final digit shown)*
0	*nil*

List of tables and charts

Numbers in brackets refer to similar items appearing in *Social Trends 24*

6: Expenditure

7: Health

Characteristics of the bottom 20 per cent of the income distribution

Nick Adkin

Department of Social Security

Introduction

This article looks at various characteristics of the individuals who made up the bottom 20 per cent (or bottom quintile) of the 1990-1991 household income distribution (the latest years for which data are available). The characteristics analysed are: economic status; family type; children; age of head of benefit unit; level and type of expenditure; share of total income; sources of income; occupation; access to consumer durables; amount of capital held; length of time in work; and type of housing.

By definition we are looking at the characteristics of 20 per cent of the United Kingdom population. This covers some 11.2 million people. It should not be assumed that all the people in the bottom quintile are poor or on low income. Such a definition would mean that 20 per cent (and only 20 per cent) of the population would always be poor or on low income. The selection of any particular section of the bottom of the income distribution is necessarily arbitrary; the results presented here therefore apply only to the bottom 20 per cent of the 1990-1991 Households Below Average Income (HBAI) income distribution. For a wider examination of the numbers below various levels of household income see the HBAI publication[1].

Background

An analysis of the characteristics of low income households was produced for the 1977 edition of *Social Trends*. The article 'The characteristics of low income households' by R Van Slooten and A G Coverdale of the then Department of Health and Social Security, was based on a new methodology developed to enable income comparisons to be made across all types of households. That work now stands as a foundation stone to the current official statistical series on low incomes in the United Kingdom: Households Below Average Income.

Although HBAI uses a different income concept from that derived for the 1977 article, the influence of the 1977 work is clear in HBAI. The equivalence scales presented in the article and the household definition of income it used are both important parts of the current HBAI series. This article is therefore more than a simple update of the 1977 piece. It incorporates the changes which have occurred in the definition of income due to changes in data collected and also changes to the benefits system since the 1977 article, which looked at the 1975 distribution of income. An article[2] in the Summer 1993 edition of *Statistical News* discussed in detail the recent history of official income statistics.

In addition, there is a greater understanding of the circumstances of people reporting low incomes since the HBAI analysis became the official series: as a consequence more interest has been shown in what very low incomes as measured in statistical series actually mean in terms of living standards. In particular it is questionable whether, for some groups such as the self-employed, income (in terms of profit and loss) is as meaningful an indicator as might have been hoped.

This article will first establish the definitions on which the HBAI analysis is based. Secondly there is a summary of the difficulties in assessing living standards from incomes. There then follows an examination of the socio-economic backdrop to the figures, which has a critical impact on the income distribution. This leads to the heart of the article: an analysis of the make up of the bottom 20 per cent of the income distribution. Finally a brief conclusion highlights the messages to be drawn from the article and looks at how the Department of Social Security is moving to improve further the quality of its income analyses.

The author would like to thank Matt Davies and Graeme Connor for their help in producing the anlyses contained in this article.

Household income: definitions

The definition of income used is weekly equivalised disposable household income. Details of how this measure is constructed can be found in the Annex at the end of this article. Fuller commentary on all definitional aspects of the HBAI series can be found in *Households Below Average Income - A Statistical Analysis 1979 to 1990/91* published by HMSO.

This definition gives us one measure of disposable income. But in HBAI two measures of disposable income are used: before housing costs (BHC) and after housing costs (AHC). (See Annex for definition of housing costs.) The two measures are used concurrently to capture the effect of housing costs on disposable income.

Why before and after housing costs?

To an extent housing costs are akin to a tax on an individual's disposable income, in that they can vary independently of any change in quality of housing obtained. This is particularly true in the case of owner occupiers who might have bought property at a time of moderate interest rates, only to see interest rates increase significantly - resulting in their housing costs also rising significantly. This increase in housing costs reduces the amount of income available to the household to spend as they wish. In such cases the AHC income measure may relate more closely than the BHC measure to changes in their actual standard of living.

In some cases the AHC measure can also be a poor indicator of living standards, since AHC income in part reflects a decision to spend more (or less) of BHC income on accommodation. If the same individuals had chosen to move to a more expensive property they would, on the AHC measure, have reduced their disposable income; but their standard of living may in fact be unchanged, as the better quality housing they have obtained offsets lower consumption of other items. So, to the extent that differences in housing costs reflect differences in quality of housing obtained, the AHC measure can give a distorted picture.

HBAI analyses are therefore routinely presented both BHC and AHC, without preferring one measure above the other; thereby acknowledging that each measure has strengths and weaknesses and neither alone would tell a sufficiently informed story. Exceptions have been made to this rule when presenting results in this article. Where there is an insignificant difference between BHC and AHC distributions only BHC is shown. In such cases presenting both breakdowns would provide no additional information.

Equivalisation and household income

The two income measures are calculated by accumulating all the components across all the individuals in the household. The level of income is then adjusted for household size and composition, to reflect the extent to which households of a different size require different levels of income to achieve the same standard of living. This adjusted figure is called 'equivalised income'.

Equivalised income allows households to be compared and ranked meaningfully. Without equivalisation any analysis of household incomes would tend to rank, for instance, one adult households below similar two adult households simply because of the number of adults rather than because of any difference in standard of living of the individuals in the household. Further comment on equivalence scales is contained in the Annex.

Finally, each individual in the household is assigned the same equivalised level of income. Since income is being used to indicate living standards, the income of the household (as opposed to individual or benefit unit - a benefit unit is a single adult or couple plus any dependent children) is the closest approximation to the living standards of the individuals in the household. It will be the case, in some instances, that this assumption of income being pooled across the household does not accurately reflect reality. However, the term 'household' implies that individuals share common housekeeping arrangements and eat meals together. It is therefore more likely that some sharing of resources between individuals takes place than none at all.

Income and living standards

As described above, the BHC and AHC income definitions are used together as an indicator of living standards. Although in most cases we consider income to be a good proxy for an individual's standard of living, it is by no means perfect. As the HBAI income series has developed, it has become clear that for certain groups of the population, particularly at the very bottom of the income distribution, income may relay an inaccurate message. This is a problem common to all analyses of income - not just HBAI.

In particular, the problem of accurately measuring the income of the self-employed is well known and has vexed researchers for some time. The large rise in the number of self-employed people during the 1980s has made this an issue of even greater importance. It is, though, only one way in which simply looking at income may not tell the whole story. Savings, built up by the household when in a healthier financial condition, can be used during periods of low income to maintain living standards; thereby complicating the relationship between current income and standard of living.

Clearly, the measurement of living standards is never going to be a simple matter. HBAI uses income as the most reliable single indicator of living standards; for some groups of the population their position in the income distribution may be misleading. For this reason it is essential to look at the related information available from the Family Expenditure Survey (FES): consumer durables, expenditure and savings are three possibilities. On their own these additional data are not as robust measures of living standards as income, but analysed in conjunction with income data they provide instructive insights into the circumstances of low income households, as the results discussed in this article will show.

Background to the 1990-1991 income distribution

Before attempting to describe the characteristics of the bottom 20 per cent of the income distribution, it is essential to put the analysis in context. This section briefly outlines the key economic factors which underpin the income distribution in 1990-1991. (Note that 1990-1991 as used in this article, and in HBAI, is the two calendar years 1990 and 1991 combined).

The years 1990-1991 marked a change in the economic performance of the United Kingdom. Following nine years of expansion - as measured by Gross National Product (GNP) - the economy contracted in 1991. This real terms fall in national income was accompanied by an upturn in the numbers of people unemployed. Unemployment had been falling until mid-1990, after which it began to rise rapidly. The number of recipients of income-related benefits (principally income support and housing benefit) also began to rise again in 1990 and 1991.

Inflation was rising at the start of 1990, it peaked at around 11 per cent in October 1990, thereafter it fell rapidly to around four per cent at the end of 1991. At the same time mortgage interest rates (an important factor in housing costs) had peaked at around 15.5 per cent in mid-1990, falling to around 11.5 per cent at the end of 1991.

The effect of these factors on the income distribution is mostly self-evident: for instance, unemployed people and people in receipt of income related benefits invariably figure in the lower part of the household income distribution. On the other hand, the effect of high interest rates on the income distribution is twofold: high interest rates reduce the AHC income measure of people paying off mortgages, but they increase the cash incomes of those individuals with savings.

THE RESULTS

Economic status

An individual's economic status is defined by the economic status of the benefit unit to which they belong. In this analysis a benefit unit is given the first economic status category that applies. This means that the 'other' category is simply people in those benefit units not already classified (for example non-working single parents, students in full-time further education and long-term sick or disabled people).

Chart A.1 highlights the predominance of the over 60s, unemployed and 'others' categories in the bottom quintile before housing costs. People in these not-in-work categories make up almost 70 per cent of the bottom quintile compared with just over 20 per cent of the rest of the population. A particularly interesting finding is that the full-time self-employed make up around ten per cent of the bottom quintile of incomes. This level is about the same as the proportion of self-employed in the remainder of the population. This contrasts markedly with the next three categories which all also contain a full-time worker - but are only a small proportion of the bottom quintile. Benefit units where all the adults are in full-time work make up only two per cent of those in the bottom quintile, but almost 30 per cent of the remainder of the population. In general, as one would expect, those in work appear higher up the income distribution than those not in work.

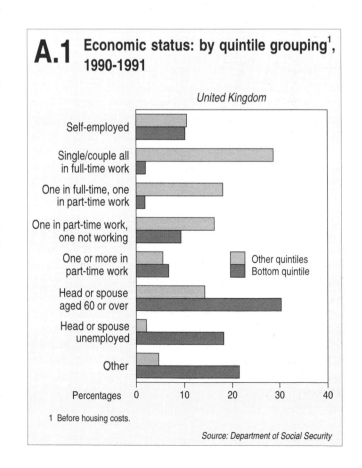

A.1 Economic status: by quintile grouping[1], 1990-1991

1 Before housing costs.

Source: Department of Social Security

Family type

In a similar fashion to the economic status analysis, an individual's family type is defined by the family type category into which their benefit unit falls **(Chart A.2)**.

The largest single group in the bottom quintile is couples with children, but they are not over-represented as can be seen by the proportion in the rest of the population. Couples without children make up just under ten per cent of the bottom quintile, but 25 per cent of the remaining population. The representation of pensioners in the bottom quintile is greater than in the rest of the population - this difference is more noticeable before than after housing costs. It is only the pensioner couples whose representation varies to any degree between the BHC and AHC analyses, where the proportion in the bottom quintile is a few percentage points lower.

The group which stands out is single parents. They make up around 15 per cent of the bottom quintile, but only four per cent of the rest of the population. The concentration of single parent families in the lower sections of the income distribution is related to the economic status of single parents. Of those single parents in the bottom quintile, only around 4 per cent were in full-time work.

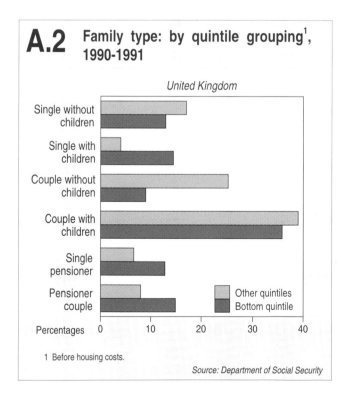

A.2 **Family type: by quintile grouping[1], 1990-1991**

United Kingdom

Percentages

1 Before housing costs.

Source: Department of Social Security

Children

In these analyses children are categorised initially into whether or not the benefit unit in which they live contains a full-time worker. These are then grouped by

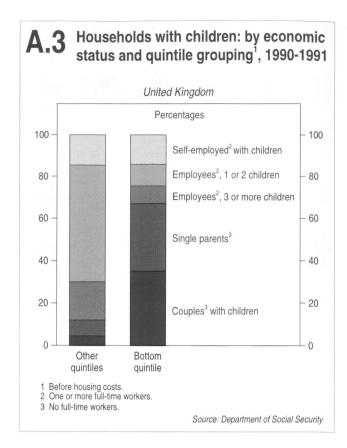

A.3 **Households with children: by economic status and quintile grouping[1], 1990-1991**

United Kingdom

Percentages

Self-employed[2] with children

Employees[2], 1 or 2 children

Employees[2], 3 or more children

Single parents[3]

Couples[3] with children

Other quintiles   Bottom quintile

1 Before housing costs.
2 One or more full-time workers.
3 No full-time workers.

Source: Department of Social Security

type of employment, for those in full-time work, and by family type in other cases.

Children made up 22 per cent of the United Kingdom population in 1990-1991 - some 12.5 million individuals. Just over 25 per cent of children were in the bottom quintile of the income distribution. Two thirds of those children in the bottom quintile lived in families without a full-time worker compared with only 11 per cent of children in the rest of the population **(Chart A.3)**. Children in families with a full-time employee made up only 18 per cent of the children in the bottom quintile, far below their representation in the rest of the population (nearly 75 per cent).

As has been observed of the self-employed group in the economic status analysis, children in full-time self-employed families are represented in the bottom quintile to the same degree as in the rest of the population. Again this is a very different pattern than that observed in other full-time working groups.

Income shares

Chart A.4 shows the share of total United Kingdom household income accruing to each quintile of the income distribution. The bottom quintile has the lowest share: seven per cent BHC and six per cent AHC. Income shares results for the lowest groups should be treated with some caution. In particular, results can be distorted where subtracting housing costs produces negative after housing costs income.

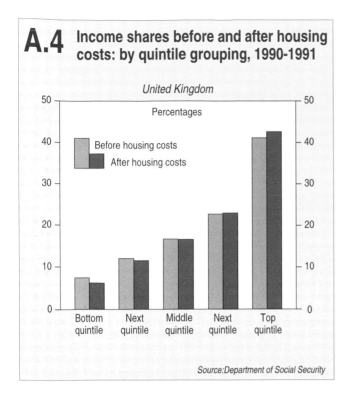

A.4 Income shares before and after housing costs: by quintile grouping, 1990-1991

United Kingdom

Percentages

- Before housing costs
- After housing costs

Source: Department of Social Security

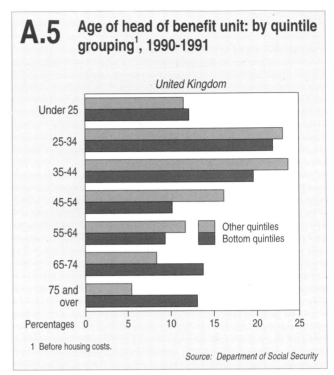

A.5 Age of head of benefit unit: by quintile grouping[1], 1990-1991

United Kingdom

Other quintiles
Bottom quintiles

Percentages

1 Before housing costs.

Source: Department of Social Security

Ages

In this analysis individuals are categorised by the age of the head of the benefit unit in which they live.

In general, the bottom quintile contains a higher proportion of older people in comparison with the rest of the population. Around 35 per cent of the bottom quintile live in benefit units headed by a person under 35 **(Chart A.5)**, which is around the same proportion as in the population as a whole. Those aged between 35 and 64 make up a further 39 per cent of the bottom quintile; much lower than in the rest of the population, where 52 per cent are in benefit units aged 35 to 64. This is in marked contrast to the over 65s, who make up 27 per cent of the BHC bottom quintile, but only 13 per cent of the remainder of the population.

The only noteworthy difference after housing costs is amongst over 65s, whose representation in the bottom quintile falls by four percentage points once housing costs are taken into account. This is a result of the high housing costs being paid by the younger groups (in particular the 24 to 34 age group).

Expenditure

The analysis in **Table A.6** shows the spending patterns of people in the bottom quintile BHC and AHC, and among the rest of the population. Note that the income measures BHC and AHC are simply used to rank the individuals in the table - after this ranking their spending patterns are examined.

In general a higher proportion of expenditure in the bottom quintile is spent on necessities - ie food, fuel and housing - and less on 'non-essentials' such as leisure activities. For those in the bottom quintile BHC, by far the largest proportion of their expenditure is on food (25 per cent). After that, housing (at 18 per cent) is by some way the next most important single item of expenditure.

For those in the bottom quintile AHC, housing expenditure is the largest item, making up 26 per cent of expenditure. For this group, food and housing together make up 50 per cent of their expenditure, as against only 32 per cent of the expenditure of the rest of the population.

A.6 Expenditure before and after housing costs: by quintile grouping, 1990-1991

United Kingdom			Percentages	
	Before housing costs[1]		After housing costs[1]	
	Bottom quintile	Other quintiles	Bottom quintile	Other quintiles
Food	25	18	23	18
Housing	18	15	26	14
Travel	12	17	11	17
Leisure	10	14	10	15
Fuel	8	4	8	4
Tobacco and alcohol	8	6	7	6
Clothes	6	7	6	7
Personal services	4	4	3	4
Other	9	14	9	14

1 Individuals are ranked by net equivalent household income.

Source: Department of Social Security

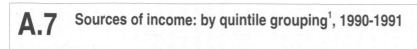

A.7 Sources of income: by quintile grouping[1], 1990-1991

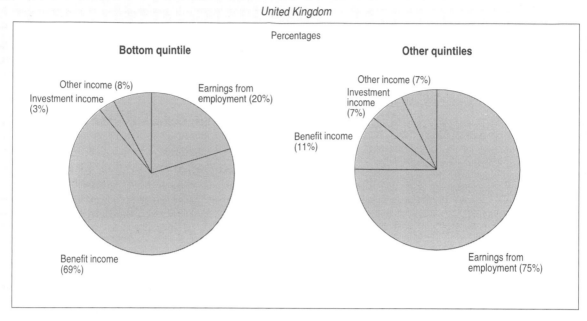

United Kingdom

Percentages

Bottom quintile

Other income (8%)
Investment income (3%)
Earnings from employment (20%)
Benefit income (69%)

Other quintiles

Other income (7%)
Investment income (7%)
Benefit income (11%)
Earnings from employment (75%)

1 Before housing costs.

Source: Department of Social Security

Sources of income

This analysis is only meaningful before housing costs. Other income includes occupational pensions, private benefits and child's income.

The profile of sources of income is very different in the bottom quintile **(Chart A.7)**. Only 20 per cent of the income of those in the bottom quintile comes from employment; the vast majority, 70 per cent, comes from social security benefits. By contrast, the income of the rest of the population is mostly from employment, 75 per cent, with only 11 per cent coming from benefit income.

Occupation

Individuals are categorised according to the occupation of the head of the benefit unit.

Over half the bottom quintile are in benefit units defined as retired or unoccupied employment **(Table A.8)**. Of those in work the largest single group are those in skilled manual work, who make up a fifth of the bottom decile. The three occupational groups, professionals, employers and managers and non-manual workers, represent only 11 per cent of individuals in the bottom quintile; but they make up 41 per cent of the remainder of the population.

A.8 Occupation of head of benefit unit: by quintile grouping[1], 1990-1991

United Kingdom		Percentages
	Bottom quintile	Other quintiles
Professional	1	7
Employers and managers	5	17
Non-manual	5	17
Skilled manual	20	24
Semi-skilled manual	9	9
Unskilled manual	4	2
Other employed	0	1
Retired	26	13
Unoccupied	30	9

1 Before housing costs.

Source: Department of Social Security

Consumer durables

An individual is defined as having access to a consumer durable if they live in a household which has that durable. **Chart A.9** covers those durables covered in the 1990 and 1991 FESs. Access in this sense therefore does not distinguish quality (eg old, new) of the durable or how it was obtained (eg rented, HP, bought outright).

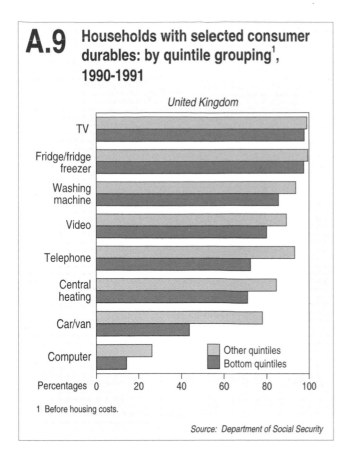

A.9 Households with selected consumer durables: by quintile grouping[1], 1990-1991

United Kingdom

TV
Fridge/fridge freezer
Washing machine
Video
Telephone
Central heating
Car/van
Computer

Other quintiles
Bottom quintiles

Percentages 0   20   40   60   80   100

1 Before housing costs.

Source: Department of Social Security

The level of access to all the consumer durables is lower for those individuals in the bottom quintile; though for TV and fridge/fridge freezer the difference is marginal. Less than half the bottom quintile have access to a car or van and just over 25 per cent live in a household without a telephone.

Capital

Data on the amount of savings held by individuals are notoriously badly reported by survey respondents. **Table A.10** is based on information derived from the FES which is known to substantially under-report the amount of capital held in the United Kingdom. These figures should therefore be treated with particular caution.

A.10 Capital held: by quintile grouping[1], 1990-1991

United Kingdom		Percentages
	Bottom quintile	Other quintiles
Under £3,000	88	66
£3,000-£6,000	3	7
£6,000-£9,000	1	4
£9,000-£12,000	1	2
Over £12,000	6	21

1 Before housing costs.

Source: Department of Social Security

The analysis shows the vast majority of people have savings below £3,000. Almost 90 per cent of those in the bottom quintile live in households with capital of under £3,000. Interestingly around 5 per cent of people in the bottom quintile of the income distribution are living in households with over £12,000 capital. This shows the difficulty of using current income as a measure of living standards.

Time in work in the last year

This analysis attempts to estimate the number of weeks worked in the last year by the head of benefit unit. Full information on individuals work patterns over the course of a year are not available, so some assumptions have been made to produce this analysis. For this reason these results ought to be treated with caution.

A.11 Time spent in work in the last year: by quintile grouping[1], 1990-1991

United Kingdom		Percentages
	Bottom quintile	Other quintiles
None	61	22
1-25 weeks	7	3
26-38 weeks	5	2
39-43 weeks	2	1
44-48 weeks	3	2
49-52 weeks	23	70

1 Before housing costs.

Source: Department of Social Security

As was apparent in the previous analyses of employment status, the majority of the bottom quintile are not currently in work and, as this analysis shows, have not worked at all in the last year **(Table A.11)**. Around a quarter have worked a full year compared with 70 per cent in the rest of the population.

Tenure type

In this analysis each person in the household is assigned the tenure type of the household.

People living in local authority or housing association property make up around half the bottom quintile **(Table A.12 overleaf)**. This percentage is about the same both before and after housing costs, this compares with around 17 per cent in the rest of the population. People in households paying mortgages make up 21 per cent of the bottom quintile BHC, but the relatively high housing costs in 1990-1991 mean that 27 per cent of the bottom quintile AHC are in households paying mortgages. By contrast individuals in households owned outright, who would typically have relatively low housing costs, make up 23 per cent of the BHC bottom quintile, but only 14 per cent of the AHC bottom quintile.

A.12 Tenure type, before and after housing costs: by quintile grouping, 1990-1991

United Kingdom	Before housing costs		After housing costs	
	Bottom quintile	Other quintiles	Bottom quintile	Other quintiles
Owner occupied				
Owned outright	23	20	14	23
Buying with a mortgage	21	58	27	56
Private rent	6	6	8	5
Local authority/housing association	50	17	51	16

(Percentages)

Source: Department of Social Security

Conclusion

Analysis of income is one way of looking at living standards. Tabulations of the characteristics of people in different parts of the income distribution, such as those presented here, give greater insights into those factors which might be causal (such as economic status); those which are largely outcomes of the individual's circumstances (such as expenditure); and those factors which provide useful supplementary information about living standards (such as access to consumer durables or level of savings).

The picture though is clouded by data difficulties. The income distribution is a useful but by no means complete indicator of living standards. Improvements in the quality of related information about savings, debt, personal choice and longitudinal data would help further in understanding the circumstances of families with relatively low living standards. As in all statistics the final cry is for better and more data.

To some extent the Department of Social Security is meeting the call for better data. The new Family Resources Survey (FRS) is a sample survey over three times as large as the FES which, it is hoped, will provide the DSS with information more attuned to meet its needs. The first full year's data will be for the financial year 1993/94. In due course the HBAI analysis will use the FRS: in the longer term this will go some way to providing clearer insights into the nature of low incomes and relative living standards.

ANNEX

Disposable income

In HBAI, and therefore this article, disposable income is usual net earnings after tax, national insurance and occupational pension contributions; profit or loss net of income tax and national insurance contributions; social security benefits (excluding Social Fund loans); occupational and private pension income; investment income; maintenance payments; education grants and scholarships (excluding student top-up loans); and the cash value of certain forms of non-cash payments such as luncheon vouchers and free school milk and meals. Income is also net of domestic rates (in Northern Ireland), community charge (in Great Britain) and repayment of Social Fund loans.

Housing costs

Housing costs in HBAI are rent, water rates, mortgage interest payments (net of tax relief), ground rent and service charges and owner occupiers' structural insurance premiums.

Equivalence scales

HBAI figures are equivalised using the McClements equivalence scales - there are different scales for BHC and AHC income. (Appendix 4 of HBAI contains detailed discussion of the scales.) There are many different equivalence scales in existence, derived by a wide range of methodologies. No one method or scale has gained general acceptance, but the McClements scale has been shown[3] to generate results which are in the middle of results from other suggested scales. In view of this, the principal scale on which HBAI analyses are carried out is the McClements scale.

Data problems

The main data source for HBAI is the Family Expenditure Survey (FES). It is the best continuous source of information on income and expenditure patterns available in the United Kingdom. The survey contains a wide range of questions which also provide information on topics such as whether the household has certain consumer durables (ie TVs, videos, cars etc), the amount of capital held and the type of housing in which the survey respondents live. Invariably though, this information is not perfect and additional areas of potential interest go uninvestigated due to constraints on the length of the survey. In particular, the income of the self-employed causes special difficulties for the FES.

For the self-employed, HBAI relies on FES profit or loss information for the last available set of account period (usually covering a year unless a new business). Therefore a self-employed household (ie where the head of the household is self-employed) may be reporting on the financial situation a significant length of time before the survey took place: the income recorded may not relate to their standard of living in the survey week or month. Furthermore, some of the self-employed will be making losses or very low profits which do not reflect the income from their self-employment on which they live (for instance, in the form of money drawn from their accounts for personal use, which is only available form the FES for people not making a profit). For these cases it may be difficult to relate to self-employment profit or loss with day-to-day income as an employee might receive.

REFERENCES

1. *Households Below Average Income - A Statistical Analysis 1979 to 1990/91*: produced by the Government Statistical Service for the Department of Social Security. Published by HMSO 1993.
2. *Households Below Average Income*: Adkin and Uglow, Statistical News, No 101, Summer 1993.
3. *Children and Household Living Standards*: Banks and Johnson, Institute for Fiscal Studies, 1993.

Chapter 1: Population

Population structure and changes

●   The population of Northern Ireland increased by 12 per cent between 1961 and 1991 while the population in Scotland was slightly lower in 1991 than 30 years earlier.   *(Table 1.2)*

●   The United Kingdom has an ageing population. The number of people over pensionable age is projected to exceed 16 million by 2031 - more than double the number in 1961.   *(Chart 1.5)*

●   Over half of the ethnic minority population, but only a third of the total population, lived in the South East in 1991.   *(Table 1.9)*

Births and deaths

●   The number of births each year in the United Kingdom is projected to exceed the number of deaths until the year 2028.   *(Chart 1.1)*

●   The mean age of mothers in England and Wales at childbirth within marriage rose in 1992 to 29.1 years for all births and, for the first birth, to 27.8 years - the highest age ever recorded.   *(Page 27)*

Migration

●   Nearly 800 thousand nationals from other EC states were living in the United Kingdom in 1991 - nearly double the number of UK nationals living elsewhere in the EC; two thirds of those living here were Irish nationals.   *(Table 1.15)*

●   There were nearly 25 thousand applications for asylum in the United Kingdom in 1992 - around a third were from Europe, mainly people from former Yugoslavia.   *(Table 1.18 and page 30)*

World population

●   The fastest rates of population growth are in the poorest countries. Annual growth between 1990 and 1995 is projected to be 2.9 per cent in Africa compared with only 0.3 per cent in Europe.   *(Table 1.19)*

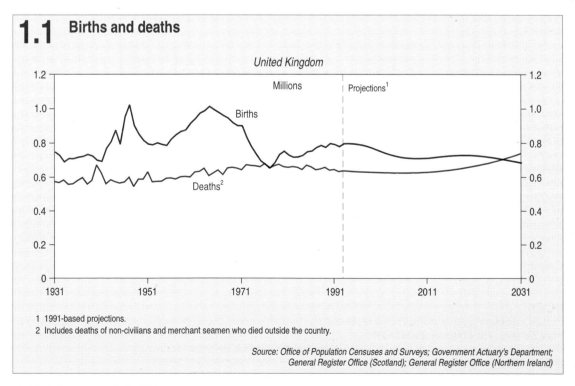

1.1 **Births and deaths**

United Kingdom

Millions

Projections[1]

Births

Deaths[2]

1 1991-based projections.
2 Includes deaths of non-civilians and merchant seamen who died outside the country.

Source: Office of Population Censuses and Surveys; Government Actuary's Department;
General Register Office (Scotland); General Register Office (Northern Ireland)

Population structure and changes

The first British Census was conducted in 1801, since when a census has been carried out every 10 years, with the exception of 1941 (during the Second World War). The most recent censuses of population for Great Britain and Northern Ireland were taken on 21 April 1991. As well as providing a count of the resident population, the answers to the 1991 Census provide information on housing, household characteristics, economic characteristics of the population (such as whether in employment or not and occupation) and, for the first time, the composition of the population by ethnic group. Some of the information provided by the Census is used in this chapter and throughout the rest of *Social Trends*.

The Census figures are used by the Registrars General as a major input to rebasing the annual series of resident population estimates. Between Censuses the figures are rolled forward using annual estimates of the components of population change - births, deaths and net migration.

Table 1.2 uses mid-1991 population estimates based on the 1991 Census figures. The population of the United Kingdom increased by just over nine per cent between 1961 and 1991. However, there were wide variations between the constituent countries: the highest increase, of nearly 12 per cent, was in Northern Ireland, while the population of Scotland was actually lower in 1991 than 30 years earlier. The population of the United Kingdom is projected to continue increasing for about 35 years, rising from 57.8 million in 1991 to 62.2 million in the year 2027, after which deaths are expected to

1.2 Population[1] of the United Kingdom

					Thousands
	1961	1971	1981	1991	2031
England	43,561	46,412	46,821	48,208	52,272
Wales	2,635	2,740	2,813	2,891	2,968
Scotland	5,184	5,236	5,180	5,107	4,995
Northern Ireland	1,427	1,540	1,538	1,594	1,861
United Kingdom	52,807	55,928	56,352	57,801	62,096

1 Data are mid-year estimates for 1961 to 1991 and 1991-based projections for 2031. These projections were based on a provisional estimate of the population of the United Kingdom of 57,649 thousand which was subsequently revised. See Appendix, Part 1: Population and population projections.

Source: Office of Population Censuses and Surveys; Government Actuary's Department; General Register Office (Scotland); General Register Office (Northern Ireland)

exceed births. The population of Scotland is projected to rise up to the turn of the century, when it will start falling as the loss through migration begins to exceed the small gain through natural increase. The population of Wales is projected to continue rising until the year 2015. The population of England is expected to begin falling in the year 2028 while Northern Ireland, with its higher fertility assumption, is expected to be still gaining population at the year 2031.

The population in the United Kingdom in mid-1991 was 57.8 million - an increase of 51 per cent since the beginning of the century **(Table 1.3)**. The highest annual growth, around 300 to 400 thousand per year, occurred during the first decade of the century and the 1960s, when births were high. The combination of a

1.3 Population change[1]

United Kingdom

Thousands

	Population at start of period	Average annual change				
		Live births	Deaths	Net natural change	Other[2]	Overall annual change
Census enumerated						
1901-1911	38,237	1,091	624	467	-82	385
1911-1921	42,082	975	689	286	-92	194
1921-1931	44,027	824	555	268	-67	201
1931-1951	46,038	785	598	188	25	213
Mid-year estimates						
1951-1961	50,290	839	593	246	6	252
1961-1971	52,807	963	639	324	-12	312
1971-1981	55,928	736	666	69	-27	42
1981-1991	56,352	757	655	103	42	145
Mid-year projections[3]						
1991-2001	57,801	786	633	154	53	207
2001-2011	59,719	721	626	95	44	139
2011-2021	61,110	725	644	81	6	87
2021-2031	61,980	710	698	12	0	12

1 See Appendix, Part 1: Population and population projections.
2 Net civilian migration and other adjustments.
3 1991-based projections based on a provisional estimate of the population of the United Kingdom of 57,649 thousand which was subsequently revised.

Source: Office of Population Censuses and Surveys; Government Actuary's Department; General Register Office (Scotland); General Register Office (Northern Ireland)

1.4 Age and sex structure of the population[1]

United Kingdom

Percentages and millions

	Under 16	16-39	40-64	65-79	80 and over	All ages (= 100%) (millions)
Mid-year estimates						
1961	24.9	31.4	32.0	9.8	1.9	52.8
1971	25.5	31.3	29.9	10.9	2.3	55.9
1981	22.3	34.9	27.8	12.2	2.8	56.4
1991	20.3	35.3	28.6	12.0	3.7	57.8
Males	21.4	36.7	29.0	10.6	2.3	28.2
Females	19.3	34.0	28.2	13.3	5.2	29.6
Mid-year projections[2]						
2001	21.0	32.8	30.5	11.4	4.2	59.7
2011	19.5	30.3	33.7	11.9	4.7	61.1
2021	18.5	30.0	32.3	14.0	5.2	62.0
2031	18.4	28.7	30.3	15.6	6.9	62.1
Males	19.0	29.7	30.9	14.9	5.5	30.7
Females	17.7	27.8	29.8	16.4	8.3	31.4

1 See Appendix, Part 1: Population and population projections.
2 1991-based projections based on a provisional estimate of the population of the United Kingdom of 57.6 million which was subsequently revised.

Source: Office of Population Censuses and Surveys; Government Actuary's Department; General Register Office (Scotland); General Register Office (Northern Ireland)

small number of births and a large number of deaths in the 1970s gave the smallest overall increase this century - 42 thousand per year. An even lower annual increase of 12 thousand per year is projected for the period 2021 to 2031.

In common with most of Western Europe the United Kingdom has an ageing population. In 1961 just under 12 per cent of the population were aged 65 or over **(Table 1.4)**. By 1991 nearly 16 per cent were in this age group and this proportion is projected to rise to just over 22 per cent in the year 2031. In contrast, the proportion of children under 16 fell from 25 per cent of the population in 1961 to 20 per cent in 1991; this is projected to fall further to 18 per cent in 2031.

Chart 1.5 shows the number people aged under 16 and those over pensionable age in the United Kingdom. The number of children fell steadily from 1974 to the late 1980s. Since then it has risen slowly again and is projected to reach 12.5 million at the turn of the century before falling back once more. The number of people over pensionable age is projected to continue to increase and to exceed 16 million by 2031.

These two age groups constitute the dependent population, ie a crude measure of that population which has to be supported by the people of working age. The number of people of working age increased from 32.6 million in 1975 to 35.5 million in 1991; it is projected to peak in the second decade of the new century before falling back to 34.6 million in 2031. Furthermore, whereas in 1951 there were 21 people of pensionable age for every 100 of working age, by 1991 there were 30 and in 2031 there are projected to be 46. In contrast the number of children under school-leaving age for every

100 people of working age fell from 36 in 1951 to 33 in 1991; it is also projected to be 33 in 2031. The combined number of children and pensioners for every 100 people of working age (the dependency ratio) was 57 in 1951 and rose slowly to 63 in 1991, but is projected to rise more rapidly to 79 by 2031.

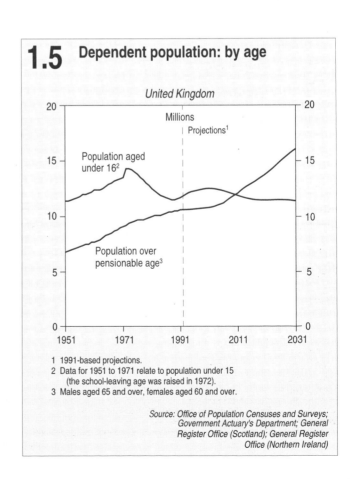

1.5 Dependent population: by age

United Kingdom

1 1991-based projections.
2 Data for 1951 to 1971 relate to population under 15 (the school-leaving age was raised in 1972).
3 Males aged 65 and over, females aged 60 and over.

Source: Office of Population Censuses and Surveys; Government Actuary's Department; General Register Office (Scotland); General Register Office (Northern Ireland)

1.6 Population: by sex and age, 1961 and 1991

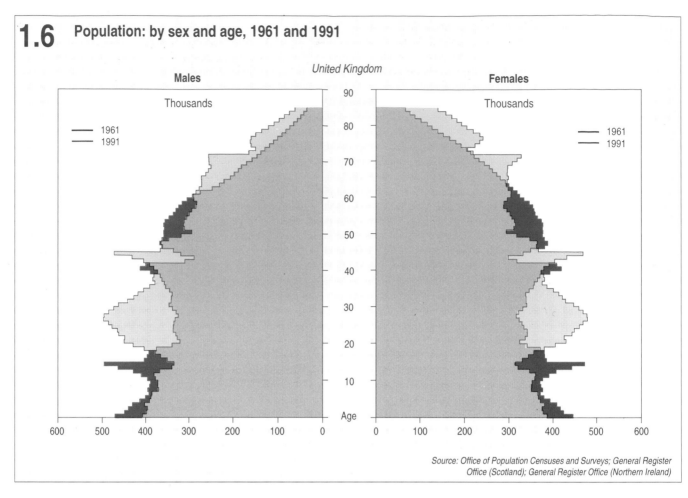

United Kingdom

Males

Thousands

— 1961
— 1991

Females

Thousands

— 1961
— 1991

Age

Source: Office of Population Censuses and Surveys; General Register
Office (Scotland); General Register Office (Northern Ireland)

The age structure of the population reflects the variation in the number of births in the past, together with subsequent changes arising from migration or death. **Chart 1.6** is a population pyramid which illustrates the number of people at each age in the United Kingdom in 1961 and 1991. The peak in the pyramid for people in their early teens in 1961 is a consequence of the baby boom which followed the Second World War, and this is again reflected in the peak for people in their mid 40s in 1991. A second peak in the 1991 figures amongst those in their late 20s is caused by the high birth rates of the 1960s. Conversely, the low number of births in the middle and late 1970s is reflected in the small number of teenagers in 1991.

Longer life expectancy (see **Chart 7.1**) partly explains the larger number of people aged 65 or over in 1991 compared with 1961, but the arrival of survivors from the post First World War baby boom at these ages around 1985 was of considerable importance. From the age of 70 the numbers in the population diminish quite sharply due to higher mortality at the older ages.

Chart 1.7 shows that there have been wide variations in population change between the different parts of the United Kingdom. The areas that are shaded red on the chart are those in which the population increased between 1981 and 1991, while those shaded grey had a fall in population. The counties with the fastest population increases were Cambridgeshire,

1.7 Population change: by area, mid 1981-1991

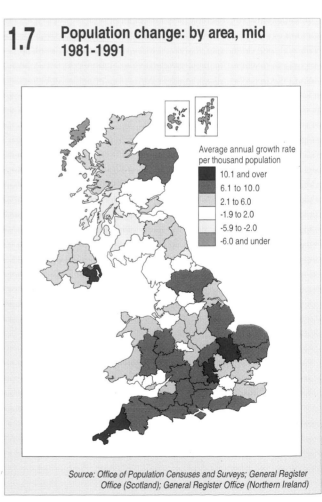

Average annual growth rate per thousand population

- 10.1 and over
- 6.1 to 10.0
- 2.1 to 6.0
- -1.9 to 2.0
- -5.9 to -2.0
- -6.0 and under

Source: Office of Population Censuses and Surveys; General Register
Office (Scotland); General Register Office (Northern Ireland)

Buckinghamshire and Cornwall - all with growth of more than one per cent per year on average between 1981 and 1991. Belfast and the Islands of Scotland experienced the largest decreases in population, at nine and seven per cent respectively.

From the 1991 Census results it is possible to produce a cross-analysis of the economically active by socio-economic group **(Chart 1.8)**. This shows that men are much more likely to be in the higher socio-economic groups than women. Around 3.7 million men were in the professional or employers and managers groups in 1991 - nearly three men for every woman. Women, on the other hand, were much more likely than men to be in the intermediate and junior non-manual group which includes most clerical workers; more than twice as many women were in this group than men.

The 1991 Census was the first in Great Britain to include a question on ethnic group. The results in **Table 1.9** show that slightly over three million people, 5.5 per cent of the population, described themselves as belonging to an ethnic minority group. The largest individual ethnic minority group was Indian, constituting 1.5 per cent of the population, or 28 per cent of the ethnic minority population as a whole, although the three Black categories (Black Caribbean, Black African and Black Other) together formed 1.6 per cent of the population and 30 per cent of the ethnic minority population.

The proportion of the people who are in ethnic minority groups varies considerably throughout the country. Over half of the ethnic minority population lived in the South East in 1991, compared with a third of the total population. Three in five of the Black population lived in

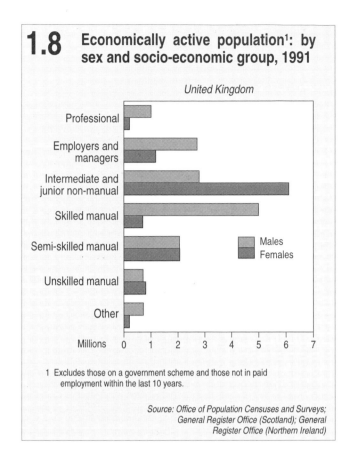

1.8 Economically active population[1]: by sex and socio-economic group, 1991

United Kingdom

Professional
Employers and managers
Intermediate and junior non-manual
Skilled manual
Semi-skilled manual
Unskilled manual
Other

Males
Females

Millions 0 1 2 3 4 5 6 7

1 Excludes those on a government scheme and those not in paid employment within the last 10 years.

Source: Office of Population Censuses and Surveys; General Register Office (Scotland); General Register Office (Northern Ireland)

Greater London compared with just over one in three people of Indian, Pakistani or Bangladeshi origin. In Greater London, 20 per cent of the population belonged to an ethnic minority group. Outside the South East the concentration was highest in the West Midlands, 8 per cent, while only 1 per cent of people living in each of Wales, Scotland, the North and the South West belonged to an ethnic minority group.

1.9 Population: by ethnic group and region, 1991

Thousands and percentages

	Black[1]	Indian, Pakistani or Bangladeshi	Other ethnic minority groups	All ethnic minority groups	White	All ethnic groups	Ethnic minority groups as a percentage of total population
Great Britain	891	1,480	645	3,015	51,874	54,889	5.5
North	5	21	13	39	2,988	3,027	1.3
Yorkshire & Humberside	37	144	33	214	4,623	4,837	4.4
East Midlands	39	120	29	188	3,765	3,953	4.8
East Anglia	14	14	15	43	1,984	2,027	2.1
South East	610	691	395	1,695	15,513	17,208	9.9
Greater London	535	521	290	1,346	5,334	6,680	20.2
Rest of South East	74	170	104	349	10,179	10,529	3.3
South West	22	17	24	63	4,547	4,609	1.4
West Midlands	102	277	45	424	4,726	5,150	8.2
North West	47	147	50	245	5,999	6,244	3.9
England	875	1,431	605	2,911	44,144	47,055	6.2
Wales	9	16	16	42	2,794	2,835	1.5
Scotland	6	32	24	63	4,936	4,999	1.3

1 Black Caribbean, Black African and Black other.

Source: Office of Population Censuses and Surveys; General Register Office (Scotland)

1.10

Population: by ethnic group and age, 1991

Great Britain   Percentages and thousands

	0-15	16-29	30-44	45-59	60 and over	All ages (= 100%) (thousands)
Ethnic group						
Ethnic minority group						
Black Caribbean	21.9	27.6	20.0	19.6	10.9	500
Black African	29.3	32.1	26.7	9.2	2.7	212
Black other	50.6	30.8	12.4	4.2	2.1	178
Indian	29.5	23.9	25.9	13.8	6.8	840
Pakistani	42.6	24.0	19.2	10.4	3.7	477
Bangladeshi	47.2	23.3	14.8	11.4	3.3	163
Chinese	23.3	29.7	29.4	12.0	5.7	157
Other Asian	24.4	25.2	33.0	13.3	4.1	198
Other	41.7	24.9	19.9	8.5	5.0	290
All ethnic minority groups	33.0	26.0	22.6	12.6	5.8	3,015
White	19.3	20.4	21.2	17.0	22.1	51,874
All ethnic groups	20.1	20.7	21.2	16.8	21.2	54,889

Source: Office of Population Censuses and Surveys; General Register Office (Scotland)

The concentration of ethnic minority groups also varies according to the type of area in which they live. In 1991 the proportion of the population from ethnic minorities in rural areas was below one per cent; whereas the proportions for most London boroughs and other metropolitan districts were over five per cent, and in a number of cases over ten per cent. More than a third of the population in Brent, Newham, Tower Hamlets and Hackney belonged to an ethnic minority group. Outside London the main concentrations were in Leicester, Slough, the West Midlands and the Pennine conurbations.

The age structure of the population varies between the different ethnic groups **(Table 1.10)**. In general ethnic minority groups tend to have a younger age distribution than the population as a whole. Three in five people from ethnic groups were under the age of 30, compared with two in five in the population as a whole. In the Bangladeshi and Black Other groups around half were under the age of 16.

Births and deaths

Chart 1.1, at the beginning of this chapter, shows that births in the United Kingdom have only exceeded one million per year twice since 1931 - in the post war baby boom of 1947 and again in 1964. The number of births each year has stayed at around 0.8 million since the mid 1980s. This is projected to begin gradually falling from 1994 as the large generation born in the 1960s pass their peak child-bearing ages. The number of deaths is generally projected to fall up to the beginning of the next century before gradually turning around to increase again to 740 thousand in 2031, again reflecting the high birth rate in the 1960s.

Over the next three and a half decades the number of births is projected to remain higher than the number of deaths, leading to a natural increase in the population. If the long term assumption holds that the same number of people leave the country as enter, then the population of the United Kingdom will start to fall once the number of deaths exceeds the number of births from the year 2028.

1.11

Total period fertility rate[1]

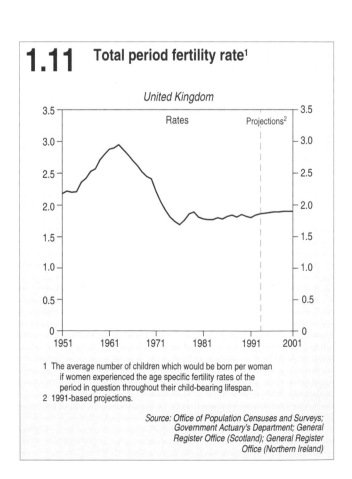

1 The average number of children which would be born per woman if women experienced the age specific fertility rates of the period in question throughout their child-bearing lifespan.
2 1991-based projections.

Source: Office of Population Censuses and Surveys; Government Actuary's Department; General Register Office (Scotland); General Register Office (Northern Ireland)

1.12 Mean age of mother at birth

England & Wales

Source: Office of Population Censuses and Surveys

In 1991 women aged 25 to 29 continued to show the highest fertility with an age-specific fertility rate of 120 births per thousand women in England and Wales. Over the decade 1981 to 1991 the pattern of child-bearing changed with a rise of 18 per cent in fertility of teenagers and decreases of 15 and 7 per cent in the fertility rates for the 20 to 24 and 25 to 29 age groups respectively. The older age groups have shown a consistent rise in fertility rates since the early 1980s; fertility rates amongst women aged 30 to 34 rose by 27 per cent over the period and those in the 35 to 39 age group by 48 per cent.

As a consequence of this trend towards older child-bearing the mean age of mothers at birth in England and Wales rose from 26.8 years in 1981 to 27.9 years in 1992 **(Chart 1.12)**. The mean age at childbirth within marriage rose to 29.1 years for all births and 27.8 years for the first birth, the highest ever recorded. The mean age of mothers at childbirth outside marriage was 25.2 years. Further information on births outside marriage is given in Chapter 2.

The total period fertility rate (TPFR) in **Chart 1.11** measures the average number of children a woman would be expected to have if she experienced the age-specific fertility rates of the year in question throughout her child-bearing life. It is a more reliable measure of fertility than the crude birth rate as it takes into account the number of women of child-bearing age. In 1992 the TPFR for the United Kingdom was 1.80, slightly lower than 1991 and still below the most recent peak of 1.89 seen in 1980 and the post-war peak of 2.95 in 1964. There is no sign of a trend towards a substantial rise in the TPFR; it is projected that by the year 2000 the TPFR will stabilise at 1.90 - well below the replacement level for the population of 2.1.

There were 634 thousand deaths in the United Kingdom in 1992, a decrease of two per cent on 1991 **(Table 1.13)**. The crude death rate, which takes no account of the age structure of the population, fell from 17.1 at the start of the century to 11.0 in 1992. In 1961 the male death rate was 12.6 compared with 11.4 for females. Since then the rates have been getting closer together and in 1991 and 1992 the crude death rate for females actually exceeded that for males. However, the rates for males continue to exceed those for females in every age group shown in the table. This apparent anomaly is due to the different age structures for men and women. The most dramatic falls have taken place in the under one age group. Further information on causes of death are given in Chapter 7.

1.13 Deaths: by sex and age

United Kingdom   Rates and thousands

	Death rates per 1,000 in each age group							Total deaths (thousands)
	Under 1[1]	1-15	16-39	40-64	65-79	80 and over	All ages	
Males								
1961	26.3	0.6	1.3	11.7	65.7	193.5	12.6	322.0
1971	20.2	0.5	1.1	11.4	59.9	174.0	12.1	328.5
1981	12.7	0.4	1.0	10.1	56.1	167.5	12.0	329.1
1991	8.3	0.3	1.0	7.3	48.2	148.2	11.1	314.4
1992	7.4	0.2	1.0	7.1	47.0	148.6	10.9	308.5
Females								
1961	18.2	0.7	0.8	6.5	41.0	156.8	11.4	309.8
1971	15.5	0.4	0.6	6.3	35.3	138.0	11.0	316.5
1981	9.6	0.3	0.5	5.8	32.1	126.2	11.4	328.8
1991	6.3	0.2	0.5	4.5	29.1	112.2	11.2	331.8
1992	5.7	0.2	0.5	4.4	28.4	111.1	11.0	325.7

1 Rate per 1,000 live births.

Source: Office of Population Censuses and Surveys; General Register Office (Scotland); General Register Office (Northern Ireland)

1.14 Migration[1] within the United Kingdom: inter-regional movements, 1992

Thousands

Region of destination	Region of origin										
	North	Yorkshire & Humberside	East Midlands	East Anglia	South East	South West	West Midlands	North West	Wales	Scotland	Northern Ireland
North	.	9	4	2	14	3	3	8	1	5	1
Yorkshire & Humberside	10	.	13	4	24	6	8	15	3	4	1
East Midlands	4	15	.	7	31	6	12	9	3	3	1
East Anglia	2	4	6	.	31	4	3	3	1	2	-
South East	13	22	26	23	.	50	27	28	15	17	4
South West	3	6	7	4	65	.	14	9	9	4	1
West Midlands	3	7	11	3	28	11	.	11	7	3	1
North West	7	14	8	3	27	7	11	.	7	6	1
Wales	1	3	3	1	16	8	8	10	.	2	-
Scotland	5	5	4	2	20	4	3	7	2	.	2
Northern Ireland	-	1	1	-	5	1	1	1	-	1	.

1 Data are based on patient movements recorded by the National Health Service Central Registers at Southport and Edinburgh and the Central Services Agency in Belfast.

Source: Office of Population Censuses and Surveys; General Register Office (Scotland); General Register Office (Northern Ireland)

Migration

Regional population changes within the United Kingdom are affected not just by births and deaths in the region but also by international migration and the movement of UK residents within the country. Registrations with doctors as indicated by the National Health Service Central Register are used as the basis for estimating internal migration in **Table 1.14**. Movements between the constituent countries in 1992 showed a net loss of ten thousand for England, with Scotland and Wales both gaining population, by seven and four thousand respectively.

The regions of England showed some change over the year with the South East still losing population by net migration; 36 thousand in 1992 compared with 42 thousand in 1991. The West Midlands and the North West were also net losers of population in 1992, while the South West gained the most population.

Migration between the United Kingdom and other European Community (EC) countries is increasing. Around 400 thousand UK nationals are living in other EC countries; around a quarter are living in Germany and a further 15 per cent in the Irish Republic **(Table 1.15)**. Conversely, 772 thousand other EC nationals were living in the United Kingdom in 1991, nearly double the number of UK nationals living in the EC; two thirds were Irish nationals.

Migration between the United Kingdom and other countries of the world is estimated from the International Passenger Survey. However the survey does not cover information about movements between the United Kingdom and the Irish Republic. Over the period 1988 to 1992 an average of 243 thousand people entered the country to stay for at least a year - a third more than in the same period ten years previously **(Table 1.16)**. The number of British citizens leaving the country to live abroad in 1988-1992 was, on average, 134 thousand a year - 11 per cent lower than ten years previously. The average net loss of 31 thousand British citizens in 1988-1992 was smaller than the net gain of 46 thousand non-British citizens. In 1988-1992, 58 per cent of

1.15 UK nationals living in other EC states and nationals of other EC states living in the United Kingdom, 1991

Thousands

	UK nationals living in other EC states[1]	EC nationals living in the United Kingdom
Belgium	24	9
Denmark	10	11
France	50	38
Germany[2]	103	42
Greece	19	16
Irish Republic	58	510
Italy	28	86
Luxembourg	4	..
Netherlands	42	20
Portugal	9	20
Spain	50	20

1 Data relate to 1992 with the exception of Greece and the Irish Republic, which relate to 1991, and France which relates to 1990.
2 Germany as constituted since 3 October 1990.

Source: Eurostat

1.16 Average annual international migration into, and out of, the United Kingdom[1]: by country of last or next residence[2]

United Kingdom   Thousands

	1978-1982			1983-1987			1988-1992		
	Inflow	Outflow	Balance	Inflow	Outflow	Balance	Inflow	Outflow	Balance
Country of last or next residence									
Commonwealth countries									
Australia	13.3	35.2	-21.9	15.3	27.4	-12.0	25.8	37.8	-12.0
Canada	5.8	18.9	-13.1	6.1	7.5	-1.4	5.9	9.9	-4.0
New Zealand	6.6	9.6	-3.0	8.8	7.4	1.3	12.6	6.9	5.7
African Commonwealth	13.6	10.5	3.1	13.8	7.0	6.8	12.8	6.5	6.3
Bangladesh, India, Sri Lanka	17.5	3.9	13.6	14.2	3.7	10.5	12.2	3.8	8.4
Pakistan	12.9	1.5	11.4	10.3	1.8	8.5	9.5	3.0	6.5
Caribbean	4.1	3.2	0.9	3.6	2.8	0.8	3.6	3.2	0.4
Other	15.6	12.9	2.7	16.6	14.9	1.7	17.9	16.3	1.6
Total Commonwealth	89.4	95.8	-6.4	88.6	72.6	16.1	100.4	87.4	13.0
Non-Commonwealth countries									
European Community	33.7	36.8	-3.0	51.9	44.6	7.3	62.5	58.3	4.2
Rest of Europe	13.1	11.8	1.3	8.4	8.0	0.4	14.2	12.0	2.2
United States of America	16.2	26.8	-10.6	25.3	30.3	-5.0	25.3	34.3	-9.0
Rest of America	3.6	4.8	-1.2	2.6	2.3	0.3	3.0	3.5	-0.5
Republic of South Africa	7.6	14.4	-6.8	11.6	5.4	6.1	8.0	6.2	1.8
Middle East	12.6	24.8	-12.2	15.6	17.4	-1.7	10.6	12.5	-1.9
Other	5.9	5.2	0.7	15.4	8.6	6.8	19.0	13.6	5.3
Total Non-Commonwealth	92.7	124.6	-31.9	130.9	116.6	14.3	142.6	140.4	2.1
All countries, of which	182.1	220.4	-38.3	219.6	189.2	30.4	243.0	227.9	15.1
British citizens	75.3	150.8	-75.6	103.8	119.0	-15.3	103.1	134.2	-31.0
Non-British citizens	106.8	69.6	37.3	115.8	70.2	45.7	139.9	93.7	46.1

1 Excludes the Channel Islands and the Isle of Man from 1988.
2 Data are from the International Passenger Survey and exclude migration with the Irish Republic and other categories. See Appendix, Part1: International Passenger Survey migration estimates.

Source: Office of Population Censuses and Surveys

immigrants were non-British citizens, much the same proportion as in 1978-1982; nearly half of these were from the EC compared with under a third in 1978-1988.

An alternative measure of longer term migration of non-British citizens is the number of people accepted for settlement, ie the number allowed to stay indefinitely in the United Kingdom under the *Immigration Act 1971*. These statistics do not cover those who are not subject to immigration control, such as those who have the right of abode in the United Kingdom.

In 1992, 52.6 thousand people were accepted for settlement **(Table 1.17)**, some 1.3 thousand fewer than in 1991 though 6.6 thousand more than the low figure in 1987. This somewhat lower number in 1992 mainly reflected a temporary slowdown in the rate of processing applications following the introduction of more detailed enquiries aimed at detecting bogus marriage cases. There were falls in the number of husbands, wives and children accepted for settlement, but an increase in acceptances of people recognised earlier as refugees or under exceptional leave arrangements. Acceptances on the basis of marriage comprised 56 per cent of the total in 1992, compared with 44 per cent in 1986. By nationality, 29 per cent of people accepted for settlement in 1992 were from the

Indian sub-continent, 19 per cent were from the rest of Asia, 17 per cent were from Africa and 14 per cent were from the Americas.

1.17 Acceptances for settlement: by category of acceptance

United Kingdom   Thousands

	1981	1986	1991	1992
New Commonwealth[1]				
Own right	4.1	2.4	1.7	1.6
Husbands	3.2	3.2	6.3	6.0
Wives	10.0	7.4	9.7	9.6
Children	10.7	6.4	4.5	4.5
Others	3.4	3.3	5.8	6.1
Total New Commonwealth	31.4	22.7	28.0	27.7
Rest of the world				
Own right	11.6	8.6	3.7	4.0
Husbands	3.4	3.6	5.4	4.9
Wives	6.8	6.8	9.3	9.0
Children	3.7	3.9	4.5	3.9
Others	2.3	2.4	3.1	3.2
Total rest of the world	27.7	25.2	25.9	24.9
Total acceptances	59.1	47.8	53.9	52.6

1 Includes Pakistan.

Source: Home Office

1.18 Applications for asylum (excluding dependants) and decisions[1]

United Kingdom				Numbers
	1986	1990	1991	1992
Applications received	4,270	26,200	44,840	24,600
Decisions taken[2,3]				
Recognised as refugee and granted asylum	350	920	510	1,120
Not recognised as refugee but granted exceptional leave	2,100	2,400	2,190	15,320
Refusals After full consideration or on safe third country grounds	530	710	2,600	3,270
Refused under paragraph 101 of the immigration rules[4]			790	15,200
Total refusals	530	710	3,380	18,460
Total decisions taken	2,980	4,020	6,080	34,900

1 See Appendix, Part 1: Asylum. Excludes South East Asian refugees.
2 Decision figures prior to 1992 may understate.
3 Decisions in a particular year do not necessarily relate to applications made in that year.
4 For failure to provide evidence to support the asylum claim within a reasonable period, including failure to respond to two invitations to establish identity. Separate figures available from 1 December 1991 only.

Source: Home Office

A significant factor in international migration in recent years has been the number of applicants seeking asylum in Western Europe. Asylum applications (excluding dependants) to the United Kingdom fell back noticeably in 1992 to 24.6 thousand **(Table 1.18)**, following measures introduced in November 1991 to deter multiple and other fraudulent applications, but remained over five times the number in 1986. Overall in 1992, 34 per cent of applications to the United Kingdom were from Europe (mainly people from former Yugoslavia), 31 per cent were from Africa and 25 per cent were from Asia (outside the Middle East). In addition to consideration of asylum applications from the former Yugoslavia, the Government announced that the United Kingdom was willing to receive one thousand particularly vulnerable cases (including ex-detainees) from Bosnia and other parts of former Yugoslavia, together with their dependants, perhaps totalling four thousand in all. These people are admitted on an exceptional basis, for a period of six months initially. As at 30 November 1993 a total of around 450 particularly vulnerable individuals and 650 dependants had arrived.

The total number of decisions taken in 1992 on asylum applications was substantially higher than in previous years reflecting an increase in staff resources and the introduction in November 1991 of the measures to deter fraudulent applications. A total of 34.9 thousand decisions were made in 1992, compared with the previous peak of seven thousand in 1989. Of the decisions taken, three per cent were to recognise as a refugee and grant asylum, 44 per cent were not recognised as refugees but were granted exceptional leave and over half were refused.

World population

Table 1.19 shows information that the United Nations has compiled on world population indicators. The worldwide rate of population growth has essentially been the same since 1975, at about 1.7 per cent per year. Fertility is actually falling slightly, from a total period fertility rate of 3.8 over the period 1975 to 1980 to 3.3 in 1990 to 1995. However, because of growth in the number of women of fertile age each year, and greater longevity, the world population is still rising. In 1975 the annual addition to world population was about 72 million, in 1992 it was 93 million and it is projected to peak between 1995 and 2000 at about 98 million. The 1993 global population of 5.57 billion is projected to increase to 6.25 billion in 2000, 8.5 billion in 2025 and 10 billion in 2050.

By and large the fastest rates of growth are in the poorest countries. Annual growth over the period 1990 to 1995 is projected at 3.0 per cent in Africa, 1.8 per cent in Asia and 1.8 per cent in Caribbean, Central and South America, compared with 0.3 per cent in Europe. Among developing countries the lowest growth rates are in east Asia and the Caribbean, both at 1.3 per cent. East Asia's growth rates reflect largely the situation in China, which has 85 per cent of the region's total population.

The world is steadily becoming more urban. In 1950, 83 per cent of the developing world's population lived in rural areas. By 1975 rural areas still accounted for nearly 75 per cent of the population but by the end of the present decade it is projected that this will be down to 60 per cent. By the early decades of the next century more than half of the world's population is expected to live in cities. Over the 1990s no less than 83 per cent of the world's population growth is expected to take place in towns and cities - 81 million people every year, the equivalent of around ten extra cities the size of Moscow, Delhi, Paris or Lagos.

1.19 World population indicators

	Population (millions)		Growth rate (percen- tages)	1990-1995				
	1992	2025	1990-1995	Birth rate[1]	Death rate[1]	Infant mortality[2]	Fertility rate per woman[3]	Life expectancy
Selected countries/areas								
Europe	512	541.8	0.3	13	11	10	1.7	75
European Community								
Belgium	10.0	9.9	0.1	12	11	8	1.7	76
Denmark	5.2	5.1	0.2	12	12	7	1.7	76
France	57.2	60.8	0.4	13	10	7	1.8	77
Ireland	3.5	3.6	-0.2	14	9	7	2.1	75
Germany	80.3	83.9	0.4	11	11	7	1.5	76
Greece	10.2	10.1	0.3	10	10	8	1.5	78
Italy	57.8	56.2	0.1	10	10	8	1.3	77
Netherlands	15.2	17.7	0.7	14	9	7	1.7	77
Portugal	9.9	10.1	0.0	12	10	12	1.5	75
Spain	39.1	40.6	0.2	11	9	7	1.4	78
United Kingdom	57.7	60.3	0.2	14	11	7	1.9	76
Other Western Europe								
Austria	7.8	8.3	0.4	12	11	8	1.5	76
Finland	5.0	5.2	0.3	13	10	6	1.8	76
Norway	4.3	4.9	0.5	15	11	8	2.0	77
Sweden	8.7	9.5	0.5	14	11	6	2.1	78
Switzerland	6.8	7.7	0.7	13	10	7	1.7	78
Other Southern Europe								
Albania	3.3	4.5	0.8	23	5	23	2.7	73
Yugoslavia (former)	23.9	26.1	0.3	14	10	23	1.9	72
Other Northern Europe								
Estonia	1.6	1.7	-0.2	14	12	14	2.0	71
Latvia	2.7	2.8	-0.3	14	12	10	2.0	71
Lithuania	3.8	4.1	0.2	15	10	10	2.0	73
Eastern Europe	96.9	107.2	0.2	14	11	16	2.0	71
Union of Soviet Socialist Republics (former)	284.5	344.5	0.5	16	10	21	2.3	70
North America	282.7	360.5	1.1	16	9	8	2.0	76
Canada	27.4	38.4	1.4	14	8	7	1.8	77
United States of America	255.2	322.0	1.0	16	9	8	2.1	76
Africa	681.7	1,582.5	2.9	43	14	95	6.0	53
Asia	3,233.0	4,900.3	1.8	26	8	62	3.2	65
Of which: Japan	124.5	127.0	0.4	11	7	5	1.7	79
Caribbean, Central and South America	457.7	701.6	1.8	26	7	47	3.1	68
Oceania	27.5	41.3	1.5	19	8	22	2.5	73
Of which: Australia	17.6	25.2	1.4	15	8	7	1.9	77
New Zealand	3.5	4.3	0.9	17	8	8	2.1	76
World	5,479.0	8,472.4	1.7	26	9	62	3.3	65
Developed regions[4]	1,224.7	1,403.3	0.5	14	10	12	1.9	75
Developing regions	4,254.3	7,069.2	2.0	29	9	69	3.6	62

1 Per thousand population.
2 Per thousand live births.
3 Total period fertility rate. The average number of children which would be born per woman if women experienced the age specific fertility rates of the period in question throughout their child-bearing span.
4 Europe, Northern America, Australia, New Zealand, Japan and the former Union of Soviet Socialist Republics.

Source: United Nations

REFERENCES AND FURTHER READING

The following list contains selected publications relevant to Chapter 1: Population. Those published by HMSO are available from the addresses shown on the back cover of *Social Trends*.

Annual Report of the Registrar General for Northern Ireland, HMSO

Annual Report of the Registrar General for Scotland, General Register Office (Scotland)

Asylum Statistics, Home Office

Birth Statistics (Series FM1), HMSO

Control of Immigration: Statistics - United Kingdom, HMSO

Demographic Statistics, Eurostat

Demographic Yearbook, United Nations

International Migration Statistics (Series MN), HMSO

Key Population and Vital Statistics (Series VS/PP1), HMSO

Labour Force Survey, HMSO

Mortality Statistics for England and Wales (Series DH1, 2, 3, 4, 5, 6), HMSO

OPCS Monitors, Office of Population Censuses and Surveys

Population Estimates, Scotland, HMSO

National Population Projections (Series PP2), HMSO

Population Projections for the Counties and District Health Authorities of Wales (1989 based), Welsh Office

Population Projections, Scotland (for Standard Areas), General Register Office (Scotland)

Subnational Population Projections - England (Series PP3), HMSO

The State of World Population, 1993, UNFPA

Population Trends, HMSO

Regional Trends, HMSO

Chapter 2: Households and Families

Households
● More than a quarter of households in 1991 consisted of one person living alone - almost double the proportion in 1961.
(Table 2.2)

● There were over five people, on average, living in each Bangladeshi household in 1991 - more than twice the average for all ethnic groups.
(Chart 2.3)

Families
● One parent families with dependent children nearly doubled as a proportion of all families with dependent children, from ten per cent in 1976 to 19 per cent in 1991.
(Chart 2.8)

● Of the seven million mothers with dependent children in Great Britain in 1991, just over one million were lone mothers.
(Page 36)

Marriage and divorce
● For every two marriages in the United Kingdom in 1991 there was one divorce.
(Tables 2.11 and 2.13)

● Nearly one in five unmarried men and women aged 16 to 59 were cohabiting in 1992.
(Chart 2.15)

Family building
● Over the last decade the proportion of births outside marriage has more than doubled to almost one in every three births in 1992, but three quarters were registered by both parents.
(Charts 2.19 and 2.21)

● On average, a woman in the United Kingdom can be expected to have 1.8 children - the second highest in the EC, after the Irish Republic.
(Table 2.16)

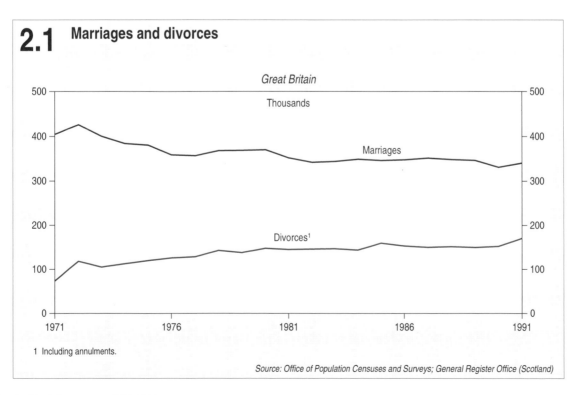

2.1 Marriages and divorces

Great Britain

Thousands

Marriages

Divorces[1]

1971   1976   1981   1986   1991

1 Including annulments.

Source: Office of Population Censuses and Surveys; General Register Office (Scotland)

2.2 Households[1]: by size

Great Britain

Household size	1961	1971	1981	1991
1 person	14	18	22	27
2 people	30	32	32	34
3 people	23	19	17	16
4 people	18	17	18	16
5 people	9	8	7	5
6 or more people	7	6	4	2
Number of households (= 100%)(millions)	16.2	18.2	19.5	21.9
Average household size (number of people)	3.1	2.9	2.7	2.5

1 See Appendix, Part 2: Households.

Source: Office of Population Censuses and Surveys;
General Register Office (Scotland);
General Register Office
(Northern Ireland)

Households

This chapter looks at the trends in the size and make up of households and families. The population living in institutions such as boarding schools, hospitals, old peoples homes, prisons and other communal establishments are generally excluded.

Since the Second World War, there has been a large increase in the number of people living alone. In 1991, more than a quarter of the households in Great Britain were one person households, almost double the proportion in 1961 **(Table 2.2)**. Over the same period, the proportion of households with five members or more halved to seven per cent. Overall, the average household size has fallen from just over three people in 1961 to 2.5 people in 1991.

2.3 Average household size: by ethnic group of head of household, 1991

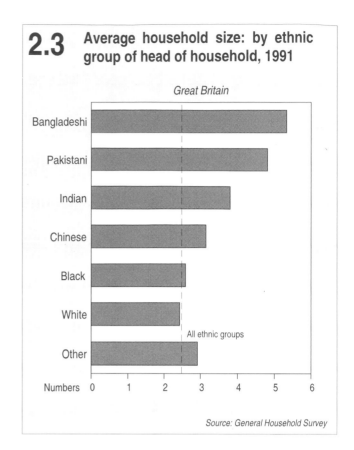

Great Britain

Source: General Household Survey

Average household size varies according to ethnic group. **Chart 2.3** shows that White households contain fewer people on average than ethnic minority households. Households headed by a Bangladeshi were the largest, with over five people on average per household in 1991.

The growth in the numbers of one person households is analysed in more detail in **Chart 2.4**. This shows that the biggest increase has been for men under

2.4 One person households as a percentage of all households: by age and sex

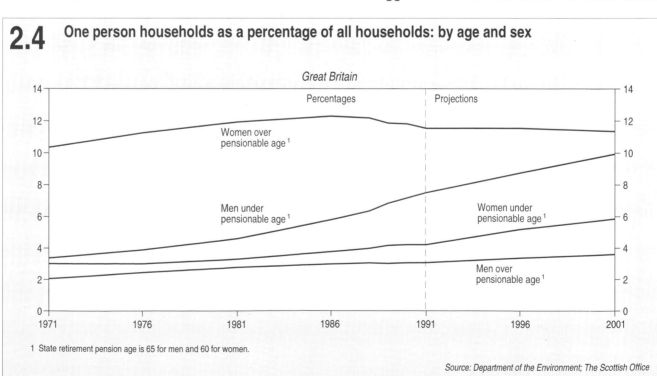

Great Britain

1 State retirement pension age is 65 for men and 60 for women.

Source: Department of the Environment; The Scottish Office

2.5 Households[1]: by country and type, 1992

	England	Scotland	Wales	Northern Ireland
				Percentages
One person households				
Under pensionable age	12	12	8	8
Over pensionable age	15	18	17	15
Two or more unrelated adults	3	2	3	3
One family households				
Married couple[2] with				
No children	28	26	28	21
1-2 dependent children[3]	20	17	22	22
3 or more dependent children[3]	4	5	3	11
Non-dependent children only	8	9	8	8
Lone parent[2] with				
Dependent children[3]	6	8	6	7
Non-dependent children only	3	3	3	4
Two or more families	1	1	1	1

1 See Appendix, Part 2: Households.
2 Other individuals who were not family members may also have been included.
3 These family types may also include non-dependent children.

Source: Office of Population Censuses and Surveys; Department of Finance and Personnel (Northern Ireland)

pensionable age. By the turn of the century, nearly one in ten households in Great Britain will comprise a man under pensionable age living alone. However, women over pensionable age are expected to continue to form the largest group of one person households, at around 11 per cent of all households in 2001.

Whilst the number of one person households has been growing, the number of 'traditional' households has been falling. **Table 2.5** illustrates the composition of households in the constituent countries of the United Kingdom in 1992. The most common household type in England, Scotland and Wales is a married couple without children. One family households with three or more dependent children are about three times more likely in Northern Ireland than in either England or Wales and twice as likely as in Scotland. One family households with between one or two children, or no children at all, comprise almost half the households in each country.

Families

Whereas a household is defined as a person living alone or a group of people living together, a family is a married, or cohabiting, couple with or without children, or a lone parent with children. People living alone are not considered a family. Between 1961 and 1992 there

2.6 People in households[1]: by type of household and family in which they live

Great Britain			Percentages and thousands[3]		
	1961	1971	1981	1991	1992
Living alone	3.9	6.3	8.0	10.7	11.1
Married couple, no children	17.8	19.3	19.5	23.0	23.4
Married couple with dependent children[2]	52.2	51.7	47.4	41.1	39.9
Married couple with non-dependent children only	11.6	10.0	10.3	10.8	10.9
Lone parent with dependent children[2]	2.5	3.5	5.8	10.0	10.1
Other households	12.0	9.2	9.0	4.3	4.6
All people in private households (= 100%)(thousands)	49,545	52,347	52,760	54,056	..

1 See Appendix, Part 2: Families.
2 These family types may also include non-dependent children.
3 1961, 1971, 1981 and 1991 Census data. 1992 General Household Survey.

Source: Office of Population Censuses and Surveys; General Register Office (Scotland)

was a threefold increase in the proportion of people living alone and a fourfold increase in the proportion of the population living in lone parent families **(Table 2.6)**. A declining proportion of people live in the 'traditional' family of a married couple with dependent children, though more people still live in this type of family than any other - 40 per cent of people in 1992.

2.7 Couples with dependent children as a percentage of all families: by ethnic group of family head, 1991

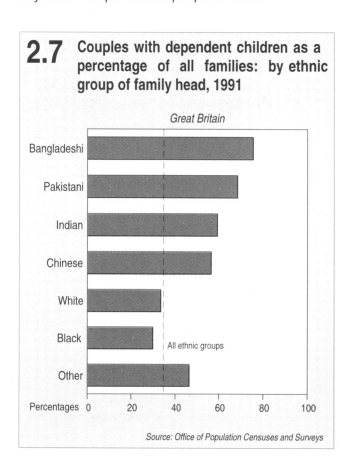

Great Britain

Source: Office of Population Censuses and Surveys

2.8 Families headed by lone mothers and lone fathers as a percentage[1] of all families with dependent children

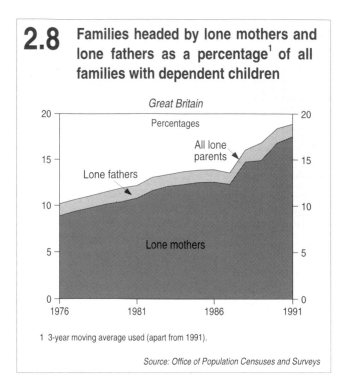

1 3-year moving average used (apart from 1991).

Source: Office of Population Censuses and Surveys

2.10 Proportion of families with children under five using facilities for childcare: by mother's economic activity status, 1991

Great Britain   Percentages

	Mother's economic activity status[1]				
	Working full-time	Working part-time	Unemp-loyed	Econom-ically inactive	All mothers[2]
School/nursery school	29	35	19	19	25
Unpaid family or friends	36	38	19	15	24
Private or voluntary scheme	11	20	16	17	17
Paid child minder/ nanny	38	15	3	2	11
Local authority scheme	3	7	5	8	7
Workplace facility	3	1	.	.	1
Any childcare facility[3]	81	82	53	51	64

1 Uses the International Labour Organisation definition of employment.
2 Includes women on government schemes and those whose working hours were not known.
3 Constituent items add to more than the total because some used more than one facility.

Source: General Household Survey

In 1991 around three quarters of families headed by a Bangladeshi comprised a married couple with dependent children; this compared with around a third amongst those families headed by a White or Black person **(Chart 2.7)**.

There were about 1.3 million one-parent families in Great Britain in 1991, containing approximately 2.2 million dependent children. Between 1971 and 1991, one-parent families with dependent children as a proportion of all families with dependent children more than doubled. The rate of increase has quickened in pace recently, mainly due to the increase in lone

2.9 Lone mothers as a percentage of all mothers: by ethnic group, 1989-1991

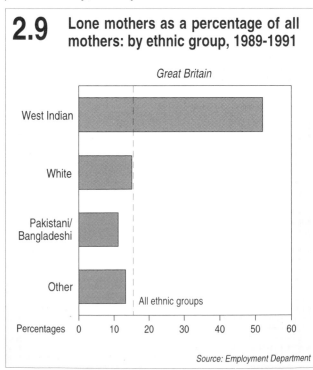

Source: Employment Department

mothers **(Chart 2.8)**. In the four years up to 1991 the number of single lone parents grew, increasing by 24 per cent, while the number of dependent children in one-parent families increased by half a million, from 1.7 million in 1987. In 1991 just over 17 per cent of families with dependent children were headed by a lone mother compared with just over 1 per cent headed by a lone father. The figures reflect the rise in both divorce and births outside marriage.

There were nearly 1.2 million lone mothers in Great Britain in 1991, out of a total of nearly 7.2 million mothers. **Chart 2.9** looks at the differing proportions of lone mothers in each ethnic group. Over half the mothers in the West Indian ethnic group were lone mothers in 1989-1991 compared with only just over one in ten of Pakistani/Bangladeshi mothers. Around a fifth of the lone parents in Great Britain were aged under 25.

As might be expected, families in which the mother worked are more likely than other families to use childcare facilities for the under fives. Whether the mother works full or part-time makes almost no overall difference to the likelihood of the family using child care. In 1991, almost two fifths of working mothers, whether working full-time or part-time, used unpaid family and friends to care for their children **(Table 2.10)**. However, women working full-time were more than twice as likely than women working part-time to use a paid childminder or nanny.

Marriage and divorce

In recent decades most European countries have experienced considerable social change. These changes have been reflected in various demographic indicators, such as marriage, divorce and cohabitation. Generally speaking, in most European countries the prevalence of divorce and cohabitation has risen, whilst marriage rates have declined. **Chart 2.1** which looks at marriage and divorce rates in Great Britain over the past two decades, shows that marriages have fallen by almost 16 per cent, whilst divorces have more than doubled over the same period.

There was a noticeable increase in the number of divorces between 1984 and 1985 following Section 1 of the *Matrimonial and Family Proceedings Act 1984,* which became law on 12 October 1984. The act had an immediate effect on divorce proceedings in England and Wales. This legislation allowed couples to petition for divorce after the first anniversary of their marriage, whereas under former legislation they could not usually petition for divorce unless their marriage had lasted at least three years. In 1991, the number of divorces was over 171 thousand - the highest on record. For every two marriages in Great Britain in 1991 there was one divorce.

In 1991 the numbers of people in the United Kingdom either marrying for the first time, or marrying for a second or subsequent time, fell to 350 thousand, nearly 50 thousand lower than in 1961**(Table 2.11).** Over a third of all marriages in 1991 were remarriages where either or both members of the couple had been divorced; thirty years ago this proportion was less than one in ten.

After the *Divorce Reform Act 1969* came into force in 1971 the marriage rate for divorced men and widowers overtook the rate for bachelors **(Chart 2.12).** It has fallen back since, and in 1991 was below the rate of 1961, though still above the rate for bachelors. This is

2.11 Marriages: by type

United Kingdom	Thousands and percentages			
	1961	1971	1981	1991
Marriages (thousands)				
First marriage for both partners	340	369	263	222
First marriage for one partner only				
Bachelor/divorced woman	11	21	32	32
Bachelor/widow	5	4	3	2
Spinster/divorced man	12	24	36	35
Spinster/widower	8	5	3	2
Second (or subsequent) marriage for both partners				
Both divorced	5	17	44	45
Both widowed	10	10	7	4
Divorced man/widow	3	4	5	4
Divorced woman/widower	3	5	5	4
Total marriages	397	459	398	350
Remarriages[1] as a percentage of all marriages	*14*	*20*	*34*	*36*
Remarriages[1] of the divorced as a percentage of all marriages	*9*	*15*	*31*	*34*

1 Remarriage for one or both partners.

Source: Office of Population Censuses and Surveys

2.12 Marriage and remarriage: by sex

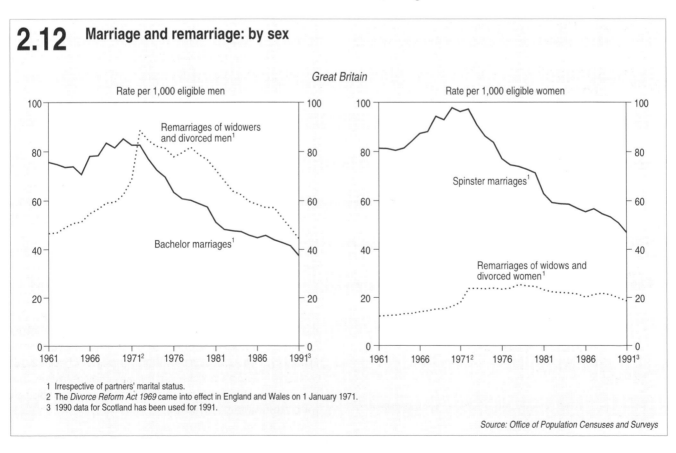

Great Britain

1 Irrespective of partners' marital status.
2 The *Divorce Reform Act 1969* came into effect in England and Wales on 1 January 1971.
3 1990 data for Scotland has been used for 1991.

Source: Office of Population Censuses and Surveys

2.13 Divorce: by duration of marriage

United Kingdom	Percentages and thousands			
	Year of divorce			
	1961	1971	1981	1991
Duration of marriage				
(percentages)				
0 - 2 years	1.2	1.2	1.5	9.3
3 - 4 years	10.1	12.2	19.0	14.0
5 - 9 years	30.6	30.5	29.1	27.0
10 - 14 years	22.9	19.4	19.6	18.3
15 - 19 years	}13.9	12.6	12.8	12.8
20 - 24 years		9.5	8.6	9.5
25 - 29 years	}21.2	5.8	4.9	5.0
30 years and over		8.9	4.5	4.1
All durations (= 100%)				
(thousands)	27.0	79.2	155.6	171.1

Source: Office of Population Censuses and Surveys;
General Register Office Scotland

in marked contrast to the rate for divorced women and widows, whose remarriage rate is very low in comparison.

In 1981, 1.5 per cent of divorces in Great Britain occurred within the first two years of marriage **(Table 2.13)**. The passing of the *Matrimonial and Family Proceedings Act 1984,* saw this proportion multiply sixfold to reach nearly ten per cent in 1991. Over a quarter of divorces in 1991 occurred after five to nine years of marriage, but a fifth occured after 20 or more years.

The increase in divorce rates has affected all age groups **(Table 2.14)**. The 25 to 29 age group shows the highest rate of divorce amongst both men and women in 1991.

2.14 Divorce: by sex and age

England & Wales				Rates[1]
	1961	1971	1981	1991
Males				
16 - 24	1.4	5.0	17.7	25.9
25 - 29	3.9	12.5	27.6	32.9
30 - 34	4.1	11.8	22.8	28.5
35 - 44	3.1	7.9	17.0	20.1
45 and over	1.1	3.1	4.8	5.6
All aged 16 and over	2.1	5.9	11.9	13.6
Females				
16 - 24	2.4	7.5	22.3	27.7
25 - 29	4.5	13.0	26.7	31.3
30 - 34	3.8	10.5	20.2	25.1
35 - 44	2.7	6.7	14.9	17.2
45 and over	0.9	2.8	3.9	4.5
All aged 16 and over	2.1	5.9	11.9	13.4

1 Per 1,000 married population.
Source: Office of Population Censuses and Surveys

2.15 People cohabiting as a percentage of the unmarried population: by sex and age, 1992

Source: General Household Survey

Results from the *General Household Survey* indicate that people are more likely to cohabit before second marriages than before first marriages, and that couples who cohabit before marriage have higher rates of divorce than those who do not. Of couples who married for the first time in the early 1980s, those who lived together before their wedding were 50 per cent more likely to have divorced after five years of marriage, and 60 per cent more likely to have divorced after eight years of marriage.

In 1992, women aged 16 to 29 were more likely to cohabit than their male counterparts **(Chart 2.15)**. However, over the age of 30 men were more likely to cohabit than women. Overall, 18 per cent of unmarried men and women aged 16 to 59 were living together.

Family building

Estimates of the number of children women will have and the size of families are an important part of the population projections discussed in Chapter 1. **Table 2.16** shows that the average number of children per woman fell in all European Community (EC) countries between 1970 and 1992. The Irish Republic had the highest fertility rate in both years; however Spain has gone from being one of the countries with the highest rate to one of the lowest over this period.

2.16 Average number of children per woman[1]: EC comparison, 1970 and 1992

Numbers

	1970	1992
Irish Republic	3.93	2.11
United Kingdom	2.43	1.80
Denmark	1.95	1.77
France	2.47	1.73
Luxembourg	1.98	1.65
Netherlands	2.57	1.59
Belgium	2.25	1.56
Portugal	2.83	1.48
Greece	2.39	1.41
Germany[2]	2.03	1.30
Italy	2.42	1.26
Spain	2.90	1.23
EUR 12	2.40	1.48

1 Estimated total period fertility rate.
2 As constituted since 3 October 1990.

Source: Eurostat

Approximately half of all conceptions ended in a birth within marriage in 1991 - down from nearly three in four in 1971. **(Table 2.17)**. In 1971, for eight per cent of all conceptions, marriage took place between conception and birth, compared with four per cent in 1991. The largest element in the fall in total conceptions between 1990 and 1991 was a decrease in conceptions within marriage.

An estimated 103 thousand conceptions occured in 1991 in England and Wales to women under 20, ten per cent fewer than in 1990. The rate per thousand for these women has also fallen for the first time in seven

2.17 Conceptions: by marital status and outcome

England & Wales	Percentages and thousands			
	1971	1981	1990	1991
Conceptions *(percentages)*				
Inside marriage				
Maternities	72.6	65.9	52.3	51.9
Legal abortions[1]	5.2	5.6	4.4	4.4
Outside marriage				
Maternities inside marriage	8.1	5.5	3.9	3.7
Maternities outside marriage[2]				
- joint registration	3.5	6.8	17.6	18.9
- sole registration	4.1	4.8	6.2	6.1
Legal abortions[1]	6.7	11.4	15.5	15.0
All conceptions (= 100%) (thousands)	835.5	752.3	871.5	853.7

1 Legal terminations under the *1967 Abortion Act*.
2 Births outside marriage can be registered by the mother only (sole registrations) or by both parents (joint registrations).
Source: Office of Population Censuses and Surveys

2.18 Teenage conceptions: by age

England & Wales			Rates[1]
	1981	1990	1991
Under 14	1.1	1.3	1.3
14	4.6	6.6	6.6
15	15.8	21.6	19.9
16	37.7	46.4	43.4
17	56.8	69.5	65.5
18	76.2	89.2	84.9
19	94.0	99.5	96.0
All aged under 20	57.1	69.0	65.3

1 Conceptions per 1,000 women. Rate for girls aged under 14 and under 20 are based on the population of girls aged 13 and 13-19 respectively.
Source: Office of Population Censuses and Surveys

years, from 69.0 in 1990 to 65.3 in 1991 **(Table 2.18)**. In 1991, 34 per cent of conceptions to women under 20 led to abortion.

The *Health of the Nation* target, set by the Department of Health, is to halve the rate of conceptions to girls under 16 in England by the year 2000. This implies a fall from 9.5 conceptions per thousand girls aged 13 to15 in 1989 to 4.8 per thousand by the year 2000.

The numbers of births outside wedlock has increased dramatically since 1960. Even over the last decade, the proportion of live births outside marriage more than doubled to almost one in every three births in 1992 **(Chart 2.19)**. This is in marked contrast to the first sixty

2.19 Live births outside marriage as a percentage of all births

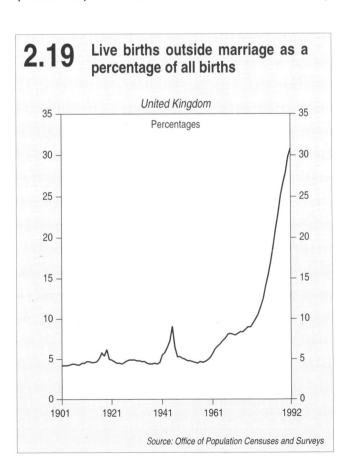

United Kingdom

Percentages

Source: Office of Population Censuses and Surveys

2.20 Live births outside marriage as a percentage of all births: by age of mother and region, 1992

Percentages

	Age of mother			
	Under 20	20-39	40 and over	All ages
United Kingdom	83.8	27.4	23.5	31.7
North	89.8	30.7	21.8	36.1
Yorkshire & Humberside	83.8	28.9	24.1	33.6
East Midlands	85.3	26.8	22.7	31.2
East Anglia	79.9	22.1	24.4	25.8
South East	80.2	25.7	22.7	28.4
South West	83.9	23.7	22.2	27.2
West Midlands	80.5	28.2	23.9	32.3
North West	87.4	32.5	22.8	37.3
England	83.5	27.3	22.9	31.1
Wales	87.0	28.9	23.4	34.0
Scotland	90.5	28.7	26.7	30.3
Northern Ireland	82.3	17.3	10.5	21.9

Source: Office of Population Censuses and Surveys;
General Register Office (Scotland);
General Register Office
(Northern Ireland)

years of this century when, apart from the period around the two World Wars, the percentage of live births outside marriage was around one in twenty.

2.21 Live births outside marriage as a percentage of all births: by registration

Source: Office of Population Censuses and Surveys

The younger the mother, the more likely that she will be unmarried **(Table 2.20)**. In Scotland and the North region of England nine out of ten mothers under the age of twenty were unmarried in 1992. Northern Ireland has the lowest proportion of births outside marriage at only 22 per cent, compared with 37 per cent in the North West region.

Despite there being an increase in the number of births outside marriage in England and Wales from eight per cent in 1971 to 31 per cent in 1992, there is evidence that many more of such births were occurring within stable relationships. Three quarters of births outside marriage in 1992 were registered by both parents, compared with 45 per cent in 1971 **(Chart 2.21)**.

The United Kingdom is not the only country where the numbers of births outside marriage are rising. All the countries in the EC have seen at least a doubling in the proportion of births outside marriage over the last 30 years **(Table 2.22)**. In 1991, almost half the births in Denmark were outside marriage. The largest proportionate increase was a tenfold rise in the Irish Republic. Greece has remained the country with the lowest proportion of births outside marriage throughout the last thirty years.

Statutory maternity rights of employees usually include the right to reinstatement after a period of maternity leave and the right to statutory maternity pay whilst on maternity leave. In the United Kingdom women must have a minimum of two years' continuous service with the same employer, working a minimum of 16 hours per week, to have the right to return to work, but in other EC countries all employed women have this right whatever their previous service.

2.22 Live births outside marriage as a percentage of all births: international comparison

Percentages

	1960	1970	1981	1991
United Kingdom	5.2	8.0	12.5	29.8
Belgium[1]	2.1	2.8	4.5	10.7
Denmark	7.8	11.0	35.7	46.5
France	6.1	6.9	12.7	31.8
Germany[2]	7.6	7.2	12.8	15.1
Greece	1.2	1.1	1.6	2.4
Irish Republic	1.6	2.7	5.4	16.6
Italy	2.4	2.2	4.4	6.6
Luxembourg	3.2	4.0	7.1	12.2
Netherlands	1.4	2.1	4.8	12.0
Portugal	9.5	7.3	9.5	15.6
Spain[3]	2.3	1.4	4.4	9.6
EUR 12	4.9	5.2	9.6	19.8

1 The 1991 column contains 1988 data.
2 As constituted since 3 October 1990.
3 The 1991 column contains 1990 data.

Source: Eurostat

2.23 Statutory maternity leave: international comparison, 1993

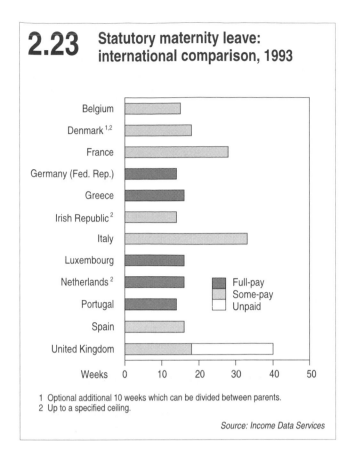

1 Optional additional 10 weeks which can be divided between parents.
2 Up to a specified ceiling.

Source: Income Data Services

In five EC countries - Germany, Greece, Luxembourg, Portugal and the Netherlands - women having a baby are eligible for full pay for between 13 and 16 weeks, but receive nothing after this period **(Chart 2.23)**. In the other EC countries, excluding the United Kingdom, they

2.24 Current use of contraception[1]: by age, 1991

Great Britain   Percentages

	16-19	20-34	35-49	All aged 16 to 49
Non-surgical				
Pill	31	37	6	23
IUD	0	5	6	5
Male condom	12	17	15	16
Cap	0	1	2	1
Withdrawal	1	3	3	3
Safe period	-	1	1	1
Spermicides	0	-	-	-
Injection	-	1	-	1
Surgical				
Female sterilisation	0	5	22	12
Male sterilisation	0	6	23	13
Total using at least one method	39	71	76	70

1 By women aged 16 to 49.

Source: General Household Survey

2.25 Abortions: by marital status and age

Great Britain   Percentages and thousands

	1971	1981	1986	1991	1992
Single women					
Under 16	4.3	4.3	3.9	2.8	2.8
16-19	36.1	38.7	34.0	27.3	25.5
20-34	55.9	54.6	59.9	67.1	68.5
35-44	1.9	2.0	2.2	2.7	3.1
45 and over	-	-	-	-	-
Age not known	1.6	0.4	-	-	-
Total (= 100%)					
(thousands)	63.4	96.4	115.2	127.6	121.8
Married women					
16-19	1.4	2.0	1.5	1.2	1.0
20-34	63.9	66.8	66.8	69.7	69.6
35-44	31.9	29.8	30.8	28.2	28.5
45 and over	0.9	1.0	0.9	0.9	0.8
Age not known	1.9	0.4	-	-	-
Total (= 100%)					
(thousands)	58.6	55.5	47.2	42.0	40.4
All women[1]					
Under 16	2.1	2.4	2.5	1.9	1.9
16-19	18.0	22.8	22.2	18.9	17.5
20-34	60.9	60.6	62.9	68.3	69.1
35-44	16.8	13.3	12.1	10.7	11.2
45 and over	0.5	0.4	0.3	0.3	0.3
Age not known	1.8	0.4	-	-	-
Total (= 100%)					
(thousands)	133.1	136.9	171.5	181.9	182.8

1 Includes women who are divorced, separated or whose marital status is not known.

Source: Office of Population Censuses and Surveys;
The Scottish Office Home and Health Department

receive at least 70 per cent of earnings for a minimum of 14 weeks. In the United Kingdom, maternity leave is exceptionally long - 40 weeks - but rates of maternity pay are 90 per cent of previous pay for the first six weeks, while for the next 12 weeks women receive a flat rate and then no maternity pay from weeks 19 to 40.

As in previous years, the most common form of non-surgical contraception used in 1991 was the pill. **(Table 2.24)**. Women aged between 20 and 34 were twice as likely to use at least one non-surgical method of contraception compared to the 35 to 49 age group, and are about one and a half times more likely to do so than 16 to 19 year olds. Sterilisation was most popular amongst the 35 to 49 year olds.

In 1992, nearly twice as many single women had abortions compared with 1971, and three times as many abortions were performed on single women as married women **(Table 2.25)**. Almost seven out of ten abortions amongst married women were carried out on those within the 20 to 34 age group, about the same proportion as amongst single women. The proportion of abortions performed on single women under the age of 16 has fallen by a third over the last 20 years.

REFERENCES AND FURTHER READING

The following list contains selected publications relevant to Chapter 2: Households and Families. Those published by HMSO are available from the addresses shown on the back cover of *Social Trends*.

Annual Report of the Registrar General for Northern Ireland, HMSO

Annual Report of the Registrar General for Scotland, General Register Office (Scotland)

Birth Statistics (Series FM1), HMSO

Demographic Statistics, Eurostat

Family Expenditure Survey Report, HMSO

General Household Survey, HMSO

Househould Projections, England, 1989-2011, HMSO

Key Population and Vital Statistics (Series VS/PP1), HMSO

Labour Force Survey, HMSO

Marriage and Divorce Statistics (Series FM2), HMSO

Population Trends, HMSO

Regional Trends, HMSO

Scottish Household Projections 1987 based (Statistical Bulletin HSG/1991/3), The Scottish Office

Welsh Social Trends, Welsh Office

1989 Based Household Projections for the Counties of Wales, Welsh Office

Chapter 3: Education

Education and childcare for children under five
- There was a threefold increase in the number of under fives in schools between 1965/66 and 1991/92. *(Table 3.2)*

Schools and their pupils
- An increasing proportion of secondary school children are over school leaving age - 13 per cent in 1991/92 compared with 9 per cent in 1980/81.

  (Table 3.3)

Further, higher and adult education
- Almost three fifths of further education students were female in 1991/92, compared with two fifths in 1970/71.

  (Chart 3.8)

- There were 1.3 million students in higher education in the United Kingdom in 1991/92 - more than double the number in 1970/71. *(Table 3.10)*

- In 1991/92, 30 thousand students from other EC countries were studying at publicly funded institutions in Great Britain; almost a threefold increase in just four years. *(Chart 3.11)*

Educational attainment
- Almost a sixth of those taking the pilot tests in mathematics for 14 year olds in 1992 reached at least the level expected of a 17 year old; a fifth only reached that expected of an 11 year old. *(Chart 3.17)*

- The proportion of school leavers in Great Britain without graded GCSEs or equivalent more than halved between 1975/76 and 1990/91. *(Chart 3.1)*

Resources
- Expenditure per pupil on education in secondary schools rose by two fifths in real terms between 1981-82 and 1991-92. *(Table 3.28)*

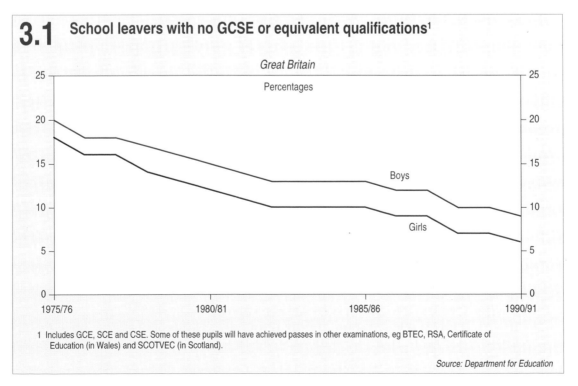

3.1 School leavers with no GCSE or equivalent qualifications[1]

Great Britain

Percentages

Boys

Girls

1975/76   1980/81   1985/86   1990/91

1 Includes GCE, SCE and CSE. Some of these pupils will have achieved passes in other examinations, eg BTEC, RSA, Certificate of Education (in Wales) and SCOTVEC (in Scotland).

Source: Department for Education

Education and childcare for children under five

In 1991/92, 53 per cent of all children aged three or four in the United Kingdom attended a school, compared with just 15 per cent in 1965/66 **(Table 3.2)**. This is mainly due to the increase in the number of under fives attending primary schools, both on a full-time and part-time basis. Over the same period, part-time attendance increased eightfold for nursery schools, to 69 thousand in 1991/92, and ten fold for non-maintained schools, to 20 thousand. Full-time places for the under fives are mainly occupied by four year olds whereas the majority of part-time places are taken by two and three year olds.

In addition to places in schools a growing number of under fives are catered for in day nurseries and playgroups and with child minders. Since 1965/66 there has been a sevenfold increase in such provision. Just over a half of these places were with registered playgroups in 1991/92.

Schools and their pupils

This section covers all pupils in public sector schools, assisted and independent schools and special schools for the handicapped.

The number of school children at any point in time is dependent upon birth rates in earlier years and the age at which pupils leave school. Increases in the birth rate in the United Kingdom in the mid-1960s led to an increase in the number of children starting school in the late 1960s. The number of pupils peaked at 11.3 million in 1977 and subsequently fell to 9.2 million in 1989/90, since when there has been a small increase. The number of secondary school pupils increased when the minimum school leaving age was raised from 15 to 16 in 1972/73. Between 1980/81 and 1990/91 the number of secondary school pupils dropped by a quarter **(Table 3.3)** but more stayed on past school leaving age.

The number of public sector primary schools remained broadly unchanged during the 1970s and then fell during the 1980s. The number of pupils, however, fell

3.2 Education and day care of children under five

United Kingdom   Thousands and percentages

		1965/66	1970/71	1975/76	1980/81	1985/86[1]	1989/90	1990/91	1991/92
Children under 5 in schools[2] (thousands)									
Public sector schools									
Nursery schools	- full-time	26	20	20	22	19	17	16	16
	- part-time	9	29	54	67	77	67	68	69
Primary schools	- full-time	209	263	350	281	306	346	357	359
	- part-time	-	38	117	167	228	286	303	318
Non-maintained schools	- full-time	21	19	19	19	20	27	28	29
	- part-time	2	14	12	12	15	19	20	20
Special schools	- full-time	2	2	4	4	4	4	4	4
	- part-time	-	-	1	1	2	2	2	3
Total		269	384	576	573	671	769	799	817
As a percentage of all children aged 3 or 4		*15.0*	*20.5*	*34.5*	*44.3*	*46.7*	*51.3*	*52.8*	*52.8*
Day care places[3] (thousands)									
Local authority day nurseries		21	23	35	32	33	33	33	30
Local authority playgroups					5	5	3	3	2
Registered day nurseries[4]		79	296	401	23	29	64	88	105
Registered playgroups					433	473	491	502	496
Registered child minders[5]		32	90	86	110	157	238	273	297
Total		128	409	522	603	698	830	899	929

1 Data for 1984/85 have been used for Scotland for children under 5 in schools.
2 Pupils aged under 5 at December/January of academic year.
3 Figures for 1965/66 and 1970/71 cover England and Wales at end-December 1966 and end-March 1972 respectively. From 1975/76 data are at end-March except for the Northern Ireland component which is at end-December of the preceding year up to 1987/88.
4 Figures are not available for registered nurseries in Scotland from 1987/88. Estimates have been made for the purpose of obtaining a United Kingdom total.
5 Because of a different method of collection of data relating to registered child minders between 1977/78 and 1980/81, these figures are less reliable. Includes child minders provided by local authorities. English and Welsh data include places for children under 8 in 1991/92.

Source: Department for Education; Department of Health; Welsh Office; The Scottish Office Education Department and Social Work Services Group; Department of Education, Northern Ireland; Department of Health and Social Services, Northern Ireland

3.3 School pupils[1]: by type of school[2]

United Kingdom   Thousands

	1970 /71	1980 /81	1990 /91	1991 /92
Public sector schools (full and part-time)				
Nursery	50	89	105	106
Primary	5,902	5,171	4,955	4,998
Secondary				
Under school-leaving age	..	4,202	3,044	3,083
Over school-leaving age	..	404	429	452
All secondary	3,555	4,606	3,473	3,535
Total public sector[3]	9,507	9,866	8,533	8,639
Non-maintained schools	621	619	613	614
Special schools[4] (full-time equivalent)	103	147	113	113
All schools	10,230	10,632	9,259	9,367

1 Part-time pupils are counted as one (except for special schools).
2 See Appendix, Part 3: Main categories of educational establishments and Stages of education.
3 Excludes public sector special schools.
4 Includes public and non-maintained sector.

Source: Department for Education; Welsh Office; The Scottish Office Education Department; Department of Education, Northern Ireland

3.5 Class sizes[1]: by type of school

England

	1980 /81	1985 /86	1990 /91	1991 /92
Primary schools *Percentage of classes with:*				
One teacher				
1 - 20 pupils	*20*	*17*	*12*	*11*
21 - 30 pupils	*55*	*58*	*62*	*63*
31 or more pupils	*22*	*19*	*19*	*19*
Two or more teachers	*3*	*6*	*7*	*7*
Number of classes (thousands)	161	142	147	148
Average number in class	26	26	27	27
Secondary schools *Percentage of classes with:*				
One teacher				
1 - 20 pupils	*44*	*46*	*44*	*42*
21 - 30 pupils	*45*	*45*	*47*	*49*
31 or more pupils	*8*	*6*	*4*	*4*
Two or more teachers	*2*	*3*	*5*	*5*
Number of classes (thousands)	174	155	130	131
Average number in class	22	21	21	21

1 Class size related to one selected period in each public sector school on the day of the count in January. Middle schools are included in either primary or secondary. See Appendix, Part 3: Stages of education.

Source: Department for Education

from a peak of 6.1 million in the early 1970s to 4.4 million in the mid-1980s, since when numbers have risen. In consequence, the average number of pupils per primary school fell from 226 in 1973/74 to just 176

3.4 Average register size of public sector schools

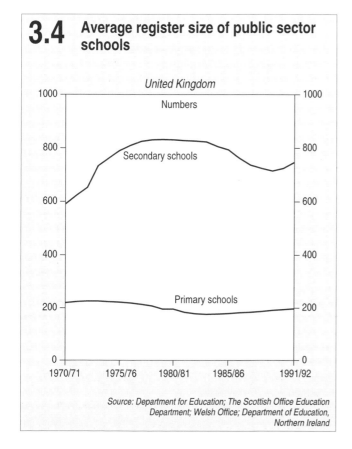

Source: Department for Education; The Scottish Office Education Department; Welsh Office; Department of Education, Northern Ireland

in 1983/84 and then rose again to 197 in 1991/92 **(Chart 3.4)**. The average number of pupils in public sector secondary schools rose from 591 in 1970/71 to 832 in 1979/80 and then fell to 715 in 1989/90. Since then it has risen again.

The average size of public sector primary and secondary school classes in England remained almost unchanged throughout the last decade **(Table 3.5)**. However, there has been a reduction in the percentage of small classes, most notably in primary schools, together with a reduction in the percentage of large classes. In both primary and secondary schools the proportion of classes with two or more teachers doubled during the period. These classes are normally large teaching groups assembled for special purposes such as physical education, religious instruction and choir practice.

The large increase between 1970/71 and 1980/81 in the number of pupils at special schools **(Table 3.6 overleaf)** was due mainly to the *Education (Handicapped Children) Act 1970* and the *Education (Mentally Handicapped Children) (Scotland) Act 1974*. Under these Acts the local education authorities, rather than the health authorities, assumed responsibility for all establishments catering for physically and mentally disabled children, including the provision of an assessment and statement of special needs. Since 1985/86 the number of children allocated a place in an ordinary public sector school rather than in a special school has more than doubled.

3.6 Pupils with special needs

England, Wales and Northern Ireland and United Kingdom   Numbers and thousands

	1970/71	1975/76	1980/81	1985/86	1990/91	1991/92
Hospital schools						
(England, Wales and Northern Ireland)						
Schools (numbers)	86	159	136	91	48	43
Full-time pupils (thousands)	3.6	9.5	7.1	4.4	0.9	0.7
Full-time teachers (thousands)	0.5	1.2	1.2	0.7	0.4	0.3
Other special schools or departments[1]						
(United Kingdom)						
Schools (numbers)	1,113	1,747	1,875	1,821	1,782	1,755
Full-time pupils (thousands)	99.5	139.5	139.2	126.0	110.8	111.0
Full-time (or equivalent)						
teachers (thousands)	9.3	15.8	18.4	18.5	19.1	19.1
Pupils with statements of special needs in						
public sector primary and secondary						
schools (United Kingdom) (thousands)	.	.	.	38.2	75.2	86.9

1 Includes all Scottish special schools. 1984/85 data for Scotland have been used for 1985/86. From 1987/88 includes schools and pupils previously the responsibility of the Northern Ireland Department of Health and Social Services.

Source: Department for Education; Welsh Office; The Scottish Office Education Department;
Department of Education, Northern Ireland

In 1991/92, seven per cent of all school children in Great Britain attended a non-maintained (independent) school - an increase from five per cent in 1975/76. The percentage increases with age: in 1991/92 only five per cent of under elevens attended non-maintained schools compared with 18 per cent of boys and 15 per cent of girls aged 16 and over **(Table 3.7)**.

Further, higher and adult education

'Further education' covers all non-advanced education after the period of compulsory education. It excludes those staying on at secondary school and those studying higher education at universities, polytechnics and some colleges. 'Higher education' includes all courses above GCE A level (and equivalent), including teacher training courses, at universities, polytechnics and some colleges.

3.7 Pupils in non-maintained schools as a percentage of all pupils[1]: by sex and age[2]

Great Britain   Percentages and thousands

	1975 /76	1980 /81	1985 /86[3]	1990 /91	1991 /92
Boys					
Under 11	4	4	5	5	5
11-15	7	6	7	8	8
16 and over	16	17	19	20	18
All boys	6	6	6	7	7
Girls					
Under 11	4	4	5	5	5
11-15	6	6	6	8	8
16 and over	13	12	14	15	15
All girls	5	5	6	7	7
All pupils					
(thousands)	573	568	569	619	619

1 At January.
2 Ages are as at December of the previous year for 1975/76 and 1980/81 and thereafter at previous August for England and Wales and December for Scotland.
3 Data for Scotland relate to 1984/85.

Source: Department for Education; Welsh Office;
The Scottish Office Education Department

3.8 Full and part-time students in further education: by sex

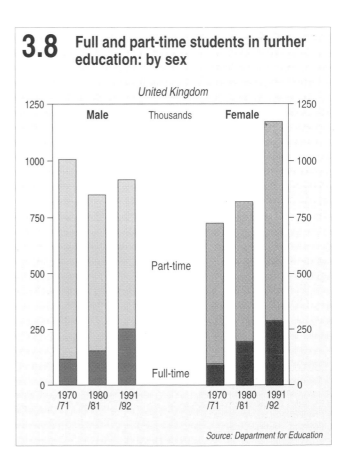

Source: Department for Education

In 1991/92 there were just over two million students on further education courses - a quarter more than in 1980/81 **(Chart 3.8)**. Female students accounted for 84 per cent of the increase. In 1990/91 just under a fifth of all students in further education were taking courses in business and financial studies. One in six were studying for GCSE, SCE or CSE qualifications.

The data in **Chart 3.9** are taken from 'Unfinished Business', a study by the Audit Commission and the Office for Standards in Education (OFSTED). Based on a sample of courses ending in summer 1991, around three in ten students in England and Wales taking two or more A levels or BTEC National or BTEC First courses either failed their examinations or left before the course had finished. On some courses in particular institutions fewer than one in five gained the qualification they set out to get. Non-completion and unsuccessful completion of courses is a significant waste of resources, costing about £500 million in England and Wales in 1992. The report identified a relationship between non-completion and prior GCSE results. It therefore suggested that intending students with modest GCSE results should be made aware of their low chances of success.

The number of students in higher education more than doubled between 1970/71 and 1991/92 **(Table 3.10)**. Part-time students accounted for only a third of the total

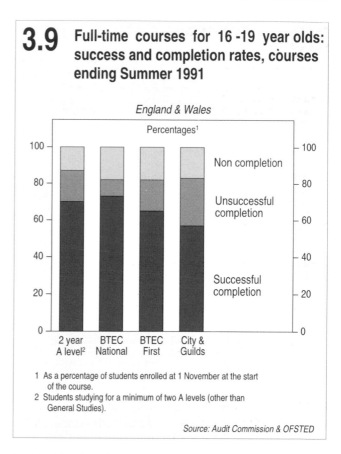

3.9 Full-time courses for 16-19 year olds: success and completion rates, courses ending Summer 1991

1 As a percentage of students enrolled at 1 November at the start of the course.
2 Students studying for a minimum of two A levels (other than General Studies).

Source: Audit Commission & OFSTED

in 1991/92 but their numbers have grown at a faster rate than those for full-time students, having almost

3.10 Full and part-time students in higher education[1,2]: by sex and type of establishment

United Kingdom   Thousands

	Males					Females				
	1970 /71	1975 /76	1980 /81	1985 /86	1991 /92[3]	1970 /71	1975 /76	1980 /81	1985 /86	1991 /92[3]
Full-time and sandwich students										
Universities										
Undergraduates	134	141	157	148	178	59	77	101	108	150
Postgraduates	33	37	34	37	46	10	13	15	17	28
Other[4]										
Undergraduates	} 107	123	{ 120	146	207	} 114	123	{ 95	129	211
Postgraduates			7	7	11			6	7	12
All full-time students	274	301	318	339	442	182	214	217	261	400
Part-time students										
Universities										
Undergraduates	3	2	2	5	6	2	2	2	5	8
Postgraduates	15	17	20	22	31	3	5	8	11	23
Open University[5]	14	34	38	43	51	5	22	29	36	48
Other[4]										
Undergraduates	} 110	115	{ 138	134	144	} 12	21	{ 42	65	107
Postgraduates			9	12	21			3	5	17
All part-time students	142	168	207	215	253	23	50	86	122	202
All students	416	470	524	553	695	205	264	303	384	602

1 See Appendix, Part 3: Stages of education.
2 Excludes students enrolled on nursing and paramedic courses at Department of Health establishments.
3 Excludes 2.5 thousand non-university students in Scotland recorded as sex unknown.
4 Polytechnics and other Higher Education establishments.
5 Calendar years beginning in second year shown. Excludes short course students up to 1982/83.

Source: Department for Education

3.11 Students from abroad: by origin

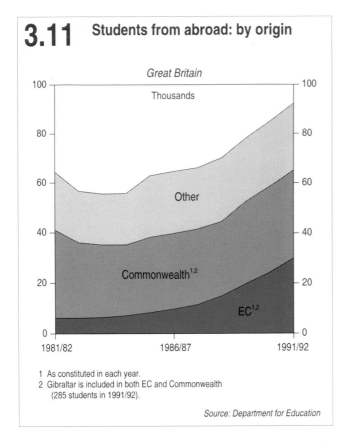

Great Britain

Thousands

Other

Commonwealth[1,2]

EC[1,2]

1981/82   1986/87   1991/92

1 As constituted in each year.
2 Gibraltar is included in both EC and Commonwealth
(285 students in 1991/92).

Source: Department for Education

3.13 Educational and economic activities of 16-18 year olds[1]

Great Britain		Percentages and thousands		
	1976	1981	1986	1990
In full-time education				
School	16	16	17	19
Further and higher education[2]	11	12	14	17
All in full-time education	27	28	31	36
YOP and YTS	.	5	10	15
In employment	65	53	43	} 49
Unemployed	8	13	15	
All 16-18 year olds (=100%)(thousands)	2,409	2,748	2,633	2,386

1 Age as at 31 August preceding year.
2 Includes sandwich students but excludes private education outside school and those on full-time YTS within colleges.

Source: Department for Education

92 thousand in 1991/92. Almost a third of all overseas students were from the Economic Community (EC) in 1991/92, more than three times the proportion in 1981/82 **(Chart 3.11)**. In 1991/92 almost a sixth of all overseas students came from Malaysia and Hong Kong. The most popular courses were in engineering and technology which accounted for almost a fifth of all enrolments. Two thirds of all foreign students were in universities.

Making international comparisons in education can be difficult due to the variety of educational systems and the way in which records are kept. In 1990 only 40 per cent of 16 to 18 year olds in the United Kingdom were

tripled over the previous 21 years. The number of female students also tripled over the same period - almost double the increase for male students.

The number of overseas students studying at publicly funded institutions in Great Britain fell from 64 thousand in 1981/82 to 55 thousand in 1983/84 and then rose to

3.12 Percentage of 16-18 year olds in education and training[1]: international comparison, 1990

Years and percentages

	Minimum leaving age (years)	16 years			16 to 18 years		
		Full-time	Part-time	All	Full-time	Part-time	All
Germany (Fed. Rep.)[2]	15	99	0	99	89	0	89
Netherlands[3]	16	93	5	98	77	10	87
Belgium[4]	14	92	4	96	82	4	87
France[5]	16	90	0	90	82	0	82
USA	16-18	96	0	96	81	1	82
Denmark[6]	16	92	0	92	79	0	79
Japan[7]	15	93	1	94	76	3	79
Canada[8]	16-17	100	0	100	78	0	78
Sweden[6]	16	83	0	83	73	0	73
United Kingdom[9]	16	57	37	94	40	31	71
Australia[4]	15-16	76	12	85	52	17	69
Italy[4]	14	54	15	69	47	18	65
Spain	16	71	0	71	61	0	61

1 Includes apprenticeships, YT and similar schemes.
2 Participants in the Dual System combining school education and on-the-job training are included in full-time education.
3 Includes compulsory part-time education for 16 and 17 year olds.
4 1983 for Italy, 1988 for Belgium and 1989 for Australia.
5 Apprenticeships are classified as full-time.
6 All regular formal education now classified as full-time.
7 Includes private sector higher education and an estimate for special training and miscellaneous schools providing vocational training.
8 Excludes certain part-time students, 16 per cent at 16-18 in 1989.
9 Includes estimates for public sector evening study and for private sector further and higher education.

Source: Department for Education

in full-time education or training **(Table 3.12)**. Although this rate rose from 33 per cent in 1986, it is still the lowest proportion amongst the countries shown in the table. However, almost a third of those in this age group in the United Kingdom were in part-time education - the highest rate for the countries shown.

In 1990, 36 per cent of 16 to 18 year olds were in full-time education - an increase of a nearly a third since 1981 **(Table 3.13)**. Over the same period the proportion 13on the Youth Opportunities Programme (and subsequent Youth Training Scheme and Youth Training) also increased by a third, to 15 per cent in 1990.

3.14 Destination of first degree graduates

Great Britain			Percentages and thousands	
			Year of graduation	
	1983	1986	1988	1991
United Kingdom employment[1]	48	53	55	44
Further education or training	21	19	18	20
Believed unemployed	10	7	5	10
Overseas graduates leaving United Kingdom	4	3	4	6
Not available for employment	2	2	3	4
Overseas employment[2]	2	2	2	3
Destination not known	13	14	12	13
All first degree graduates (= 100%)(thousands)	105	112	117	131

1 Permanent and temporary.
2 Home students.

Source: Department for Education

Of the 57 thousand first degree graduates who graduated in Great Britain in 1991, 44 per cent entered employment in the United Kingdom compared with a peak of 55 per cent in 1987 and 1988 **(Table 3.14)**. As would be expected, this percentage varies over time according to the general state of the labour market (see Chapter 4). In 1991, ten per cent of first degree graduates were

3.15 Adult literacy and numeracy

England & Wales				Thousands
	1986/87	1988/89	1990/91	1991/92
People seeking help				
Literacy	43	43	50	52
Numeracy	13	14	18	18
Both	23	23	32	34
Total	79	80	99	105
Students receiving tuition[1]				
Literacy	57	58	59	63
Numeracy	17	18	20	21
Both	34	35	41	43
Total	108	111	120	128

1 At first week in November.

Source: Adult Literacy & Basic Skills Unit

believed unemployed - double the proportion just three years earlier. A further fifth continued with their education.

Not only younger people can benefit from education. The latest report by The Adult Literacy and Basic Skills Unit (ALBSU) which promotes the teaching of basic numeracy and literacy skills shows that in November 1992, 128 thousand adults were receiving tuition **(Table 3.15)**. Over 23 thousand people were involved in providing the training, of which three fifths were volunteers. The remainder were employed by Local Education Authorities, voluntary groups, employment training schemes, colleges of further education, penal establishments and ALBSU itself.

Educational attainment

In 1992 some 600 thousand seven year olds were formally assessed in English, mathematics, science and technology; the results are shown in **Chart 3.16**. Pupils in Wales were also assessed in Welsh and Welsh as a second language. The tests were not statutory for independent schools but over two thousand children from such schools participated. The assessments were based on a combination of tests commissioned by the School Examinations and Assessment Council and on teachers' assessments of classroom work. In English, mathematics and technology, just over three quarters of all seven year olds reached the level expected of them: for science, it was 88 per cent. In English and science, a fifth of seven

3.16 Results of tests for 7 year olds: by sex and subject, 1992

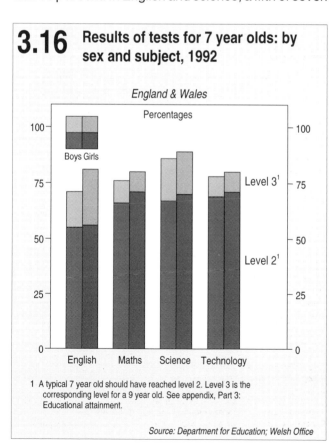

England & Wales

1 A typical 7 year old should have reached level 2. Level 3 is the corresponding level for a 9 year old. See appendix, Part 3: Educational attainment.

Source: Department for Education; Welsh Office

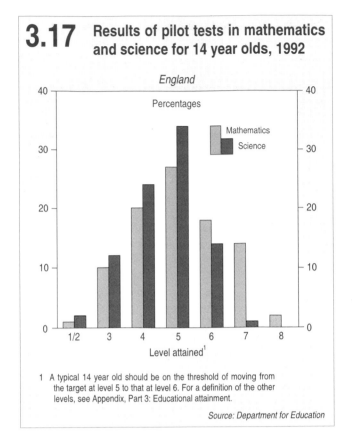

3.17 Results of pilot tests in mathematics and science for 14 year olds, 1992

England

Percentages

Mathematics
Science

Level attained[1]

1 A typical 14 year old should be on the threshold of moving from the target at level 5 to that at level 6. For a definition of the other levels, see Appendix, Part 3: Educational attainment.

Source: Department for Education

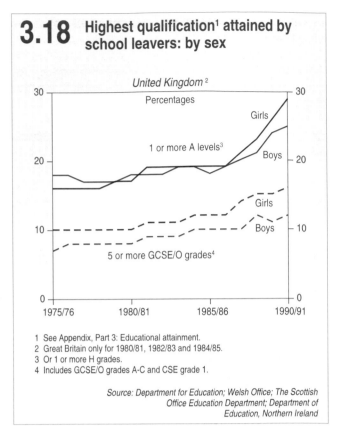

3.18 Highest qualification[1] attained by school leavers: by sex

United Kingdom[2]

Percentages

Girls
1 or more A levels[3]
Boys

Girls
Boys
5 or more GCSE/O grades[4]

1975/76   1980/81   1985/86   1990/91

1 See Appendix, Part 3: Educational attainment.
2 Great Britain only for 1980/81, 1982/83 and 1984/85.
3 Or 1 or more H grades.
4 Includes GCSE/O grades A-C and CSE grade 1.

Source: Department for Education; Welsh Office; The Scottish Office Education Department; Department of Education, Northern Ireland

year olds had reached the level expected of a nine year old. Girls did better in all subjects, especially in English where the proportion who attained at least level two was 11 percentage points higher than that for boys.

In 1992 all schools with 14 year olds were invited to participate in the pilot tests in mathematics and science set under the National Curriculum. The scale against which the results of the tests were measured is a continuation of that used for seven year olds. Hence, a 14 year old should be somewhere between level five (for a thirteen year old) and level six (for a fifteen year old). Three fifths of those who sat the tests in mathematics in England reached level five compared with just under a half of those who sat the tests in science **(Chart 3.17)**. Sixteen per cent of the mathematics candidates had reached the level expected of a 17 year old (level seven) but ten per cent had only attained that expected of a nine year old (level three).

In England, Wales and Northern Ireland the General Certificate of Secondary Education (GCSE) was introduced in 1988 to replace the General Certificate of Education (GCE) O levels and Certificate of Secondary Education (CSE). In Scotland the Scottish Certificate of Education (SCE) is approximately equivalent to the GCSE. Students wanting a greater breadth of curriculum than that offerred by A levels can take the Advanced Supplementary (AS) examination which was introduced in 1989. Some schools also offer awards issued by the Business and Technology Education Council (BTEC), the RSA Examination Board, the Scottish Vocational Education Council (SCOTVEC) or offer the Certificate of Education (Welsh Joint Education Committee).

Chart 3.1 shows that during the last 15 years there has been a significant fall in the proportion of school leavers with no graded results in GCSE, GCE, CSE or SCE. In 1975/76 around a fifth of all school leavers in Great Britain had no graded results compared with just nine per cent of boys and six per cent of girls in 1990/91.

In 1990/91, 25 per cent of boys and 29 per cent of girls had at least one A level pass or Scottish H grade (five H grades are regarded as roughly equal to three A levels) when they left school **(Chart 3.18)**. Fifteen years earlier only 18 per cent of boys and 16 per cent of girls had reached this level. A further 12 per cent of boys and 16 per cent of girls had at least five GCSEs (or Scottish equivalent) in 1990/91 compared with just seven and ten per cent respectively in 1975/76.

There are marked regional variations in school leavers' examination results **(Table 3.19)**. For example, 28 per cent of boys and 36 per cent of girls left school in Northern Ireland with one or more A level pass in 1990/91 compared with only 17 and 21 per cent respectively in the North of England. The Scottish figures are based on school leavers with one or more SCE Higher pass so are not directly comparable with figures for the rest of the United Kingdom. An analysis of school leavers with three or more A levels again shows Northern Ireland and the South East at the top of the league with around one in five reaching this level. In Scotland around one in seven obtained five or more SCE Highers - an approximate equivalent. At the other end of the scale, over one in six boys in Wales and Northern Ireland left school with no graded results compared with less than one in twenty in the South West.

3.19 School leavers' examination achievements[1]: by sex and region, 1990/91

Percentages and thousands

	1 or more A levels[2] (or SCE highers)		GCSEs[3] or SCE O/standard (no A levels or SCE highers)		No graded results[4]		All leavers (= 100%) (thousands)	
	Males	Females	Males	Females	Males	Females	Males	Females
United Kingdom	25.5	28.6	65.3	64.9	9.2	6.5	338.2	322.8
North	17.4	21.2	71.0	72.6	11.6	6.4	19.5	18.7
Yorkshire & Humberside	20.0	22.9	70.4	69.4	9.5	7.5	29.3	27.9
East Midlands	23.8	26.2	69.7	69.7	6.5	4.0	23.2	21.6
East Anglia	23.6	26.4	70.1	67.4	6.6	6.0	11.4	10.4
South East	29.0	31.1	62.7	63.5	8.3	5.4	93.9	89.8
South West	26.5	26.3	68.7	69.6	4.8	4.0	26.2	25.7
West Midlands	22.0	25.0	70.6	69.9	7.4	5.2	34.7	33.3
North West	22.9	23.4	67.2	68.5	9.9	8.1	39.1	37.2
England	24.6	26.6	67.2	67.5	8.2	5.8	277.3	264.6
Wales[5]	20.8	26.9	63.2	62.8	16.0	10.3	17.1	16.2
Scotland	35.1	44.1	53.2	47.0	11.7	8.9	31.7	30.4
Northern Ireland	27.9	35.6	55.9	54.7	16.1	9.8	12.1	11.6

1 Excludes results in further education.
2 Two AS levels are counted as equivalent to one A level.
3 And equivalent grades at GCE and CSE. Includes leavers with 1 AS level.
4 Some of these pupils will have achieved passes in other examinations. eg BTEC, RSA, Certificate of Education (in Wales) and SCOTVEC (in Scotland).
5 Includes leavers from independent schools.

Source: Department for Education; Welsh Office; The Scottish Office Education Department; Department of Education, Northern Ireland

Some GCSE subjects are obviously more popular than others. In 1990/91, 324 thousand children, just over half of all school leavers in Great Britain, obtained a GCSE grade A to C (or equivalent) in English while the other core subject - mathematics - was obtained by 37 per cent of leavers. **Chart 3.20** shows that girls outperformed boys in English, French, history and biology while boys outperformed girls in mathematics, geography, chemistry and physics.

In 1992 almost a quarter of men and a third of women aged 16 to 59 had no qualifications **(Table 3.21)**. Between 1984 and 1992 there was an increase in the proportion holding qualifications for all of the categories shown in the table.

3.20 School leavers with grades A - C at GCSE[1]: by subject and sex, 1990/91

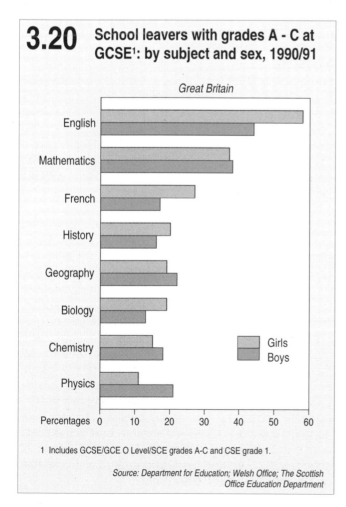

Great Britain

English
Mathematics
French
History
Geography
Biology
Chemistry
Physics

Girls
Boys

Percentages 0 10 20 30 40 50 60

1 Includes GCSE/GCE O Level/SCE grades A-C and CSE grade 1.

Source: Department for Education; Welsh Office; The Scottish Office Education Department

3.21 Highest qualification held[1]: by sex, 1984 and 1992

United Kingdom — Percentages and millions

	Males		Females	
	1984	1992	1984	1992
Degree or equivalent	9	12	4	7
Higher education below degree level	4	6	7	8
GCE A level or equivalent[2]	31	36	12	17
GCSE, grades A-C or equivalent	12	14	20	24
Other qualification[3]	7	9	11	12
No qualification	34	23	45	32
Not known	2	-	2	-
All aged 16-59 (=100%)(millions)	15.9	16.9	15.8	16.8

1 Persons aged 16 to 59.
2 Includes BTEC, City & Guilds and apprenticeships.
3 Includes CSE below grade 1, YT certificate (YTS for 1984), RSA other qualifications.

Source: Department for Education

3.22 Highest qualification held[1]: by socio-economic group of father, 1990-1991

Great Britain   Percentages

	Professional	Employers and managers	Intermediate and junior non-manual	Skilled manual and own account non-professional	Semi-skilled manual and personal service	Unskilled manual	All Persons
Degree	32	17	17	6	4	3	10
Higher education	19	15	18	10	7	5	11
GCE A level[2]	15	13	12	8	6	4	9
GCSE, grades A-C[2]	19	24	25	21	19	15	21
GCSE, grades D-G[2,3]	4	9	7	12	12	10	10
Foreign	4	4	4	3	2	2	3
No qualifications	7	19	18	40	50	60	35

1 Persons aged 25-59 not in full-time education. See appendix, Part 3: Education.
2 Or equivalent.
3 Includes commercial qualifications and apprenticeships.

Source: General Household Survey

There are also marked differences in educational attainment according to socio-economic group. **Table 3.22** shows the highest qualification level of those aged between 25 and 59 and not in full-time education by the socio-economic group of their father. As might be expected, academic achievement was greatest for those whose father was in the professional group (where almost a third had a degree) and lowest for those whose father was in the unskilled manual group (where three fifths were unqualified).

Almost a quarter of men and just under a third of women, of working age in Great Britain have no qualifications **(Chart 3.23)**. There are, however, marked variations by ethnic origin. For example, just over half of men and three fifths of women of Pakistani/ Bangladeshi origin have no qualifications. This is broadly

double the proportions of the white and black population. The black population is the only group in which women are better qualified than men.

Resources

For many students the standard maintenance grant is the major source of income. **Table 3.24** shows that the real value of this grant for students living outside London and away from home is now significantly lower than it was in 1981/82. However, in September 1990 student loans were introduced and in consequence the grant has not increased in cash terms since 1990/91.

3.23 Percentage of the working age[1] population without a qualification: by ethnic origin and sex, Spring 1993

1 Men aged 16-64 and women aged 16-59.
2 Includes Caribbean, African, and black people of non-mixed origin.
3 Includes Chinese, other ethnic groups of non-mixed origin and people of mixed origin.
4 Includes ethnic group not stated.

Source: Employment Department

3.24 Student awards

England & Wales

	Standard maint-enance grant[1] (£)	Real value (£) at 1992-93 prices deflated by		Average assessed contrib-ution[2] (percent -ages)	Student loans[3](£)
		Retail prices index	Average earnings index		
1981/82	1,535	2,805	3,756	14	.
1982/83	1,595	2,717	3,513	19	.
1983/84	1,660	2,690	3,359	20	.
1984/85	1,775	2,747	3,385	25	.
1985/86	1,830	2,674	3,245	30	.
1986/87	1,901	2,697	3,111	30	.
1987/88	1,972	2,685	3,010	31	.
1988/89	2,050	2,636	2,876	31	.
1989/90	2,155	2,576	2,766	31	.
1990/91	2,265	2,442	2,663	24	420
1991/92	2,265	2,346	2,441	21	580
1992/93	2,265	2,265	2,265	..	715

1 Excludes those studying in London and those studying elsewhere living in the parental home. Prior to 1982/83 Oxford and Cambridge were also excluded. Since 1984/85 the grant has included an additional travel allowance of £50.
2 By parents, spouses and students as a percentage of expenditure on fees, maintenance and assessed contributions assuming full payment of parental and other contributions including a notional assessment in respect of students for whom fees only were paid by LEAs.
3 Maximum loan at current prices for students studying outside London and living away from home. Different amounts are payable in the final year.

Source: Department for Education

3.25 Employment in education: by type of establishment

United Kingdom			Thousands
	1970/71	1980/81	1990/91
Full-time teachers and lecturers			
Schools			
Public sector			
Primary schools[1]	203	222	210
Secondary schools[2]	199	281	234
Non-maintained schools[2,3]	36	43	45
Special schools	10	19	19
All schools	448	565	508
Establishments of further and higher education[4]	69	89	91
Universities[5]	29	34	32
All establishments[6]	546	693	637

1 Includes nursery schools.
2 From 1989/90 Voluntary Grammar Schools in Northern Ireland are recorded in the maintained sector.
3 Excludes independent schools in Scotland.
4 Includes former colleges of education.
5 Excludes the Open University and the independent University College of Buckingham.
6 Includes teachers classified as miscellaneous in England and Wales (over 6.5 thousand in 1990/91) not included elsewhere.
Source: Department for Education

The number of school teachers rose significantly during the 1970s and then fell again during the 1980s **(Table 3.25)**. This reflected the increase in the school population during the 1970s (the result of the increased birth rate in the 1960s) and smaller classes. A notable feature over the two decades has been the sharp increase in the proportion of teaching staff in schools who are graduates. In 1970/71 only a quarter of school teachers had a degree compared with over half in 1990/91. In 1990/91, 63 per cent of all school teachers were female.

3.26 Pupil/teacher ratios[1]: by type of school

United Kingdom				Ratios[1]
	1970/71	1980/81	1990/91	1991/92
Public sector schools				
Nursery	26.6	21.5	21.5	21.6
Primary	27.1	22.3	21.8	21.8
Secondary[2]	17.8	16.4	15.0	15.2
All public sector schools	22.6	19.0	18.3	18.4
Non-maintained schools[3]	14.0	13.1	10.7	10.6
Special schools	10.5	7.4	5.7	5.7
All schools	22.0	18.2	17.0	17.1

1 See Appendix, Part 3: Pupil/teacher ratios.
2 Includes voluntary grammar schools in Northern Ireland from 1989/90 (formerly allocated to the non-maintained sector).
3 Excludes independent schools in Scotland in 1970/71 and in Northern Ireland in all years.
Source: Department for Education

Table 3.26 shows that there was a fall in pupil/teacher ratios for all types of schools between 1970/71 and 1980/81. Since then, the fall in the number of pupils in public sector primary schools has been almost matched by a corresponding fall in the number of teachers, hence pupil/teachers ratios in these schools have remained almost unchanged. Ratios for non-maintained and special schools, however, continued to fall and in the latter there are now fewer than six pupils to each teacher.

Table 3.27 shows that between 1970-71 and 1991-92 government expenditure on education rose by about half in real terms. Spending on special schools increased almost threefold although in 1991-92 it still only accounted for four per cent of total spending on education.

3.27 Government expenditure on education in real terms: by type

United Kingdom		£ million at 1991-92 prices[1] and percentages	
	1970-71	1980-81	1991-92
Schools			
Nursery	58	114	} 7,621
Primary	4,713	5,886	
Secondary	5,523	7,754	8,287
Special	442	917	1,280
Higher, further and adult education[2]	2,884	3,517	3,734
Polytechnics and Colleges Funding Council	.	.	993
Universities	2,325	2,698	2,668
Other education expenditure	706	1,027	1,394
Total	16,651	21,913	25,976
Related education expenditure	2,727	2,995	2,974
VAT on above expenditure	674	369	532
Total expenditure	20,051	25,277	29,482
Total expenditure as a percentage of GDP	5.2	5.5	5.1

1 Adjusted to real terms using the GDP market prices deflator.
2 Includes fees for polytechnics and colleges transferred to the Polytechnics and Colleges Funding Council in April 1989.
Source: Department for Education

While expenditure on education rose between 1981-82 and 1991-92, there was a significant fall in the number of pupils in public sector schools. Hence, between these years, expenditure in real terms per pupil in nursery and primary schools increased by a third and in secondary schools by almost two fifths **(Table 3.28 overleaf)**. Real expenditure per pupil on administrative and clerical staff, though not a significant part of overall expenditure, rose eightfold.

3.28 Expenditure per pupil[1]: by type of school, 1981-82 and 1991-92

England	Nursery and primary schools		Secondary schools	
£ per pupil at 1991-92 prices	1981-82	1991-92	1981-82	1991-92
Expenditure on:				
Staff				
Teaching	776	986	1,091	1,501
Educational support	62	120	69	124
Premises-related	70	44	79	45
Administrative, clerical and other	11	89	14	116
Premises	60	179	71	284
Books and equipment	32	54	57	93
Other supplies[2]	4	0	19	26
Other expenditure[2]	99	46	157	76
Net unit cost[3]	1,106	1,469	1,540	2,145

1 Recurrent institutional expenditure per full-time equivalent pupil. This includes costs of providing tuition but excludes certain costs such as central administration and school meals.
2 Includes unspent balances held by schools for future use under Local Management Schemes in 1991-92.
3 The sum of expenditure on items shown in the table less certain charges.

Source: Department for Education

Chart 3.29 compares public expenditure on education as a percentage of Gross National Product (GNP) for selected countries in 1989. For the countries listed, Denmark spent the highest proportion while Germany and Japan spent the lowest proportions. Expenditure per head of the population is another way in which an

3.29 Public expenditure[1] on education as a percentage of GNP: international comparison, 1989

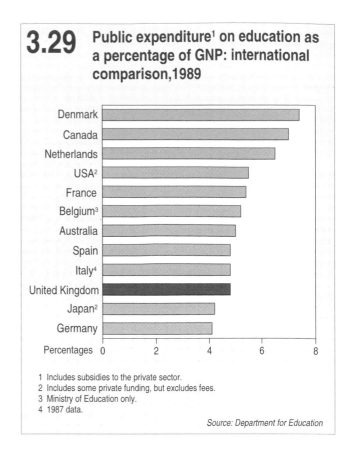

1 Includes subsidies to the private sector.
2 Includes some private funding, but excludes fees.
3 Ministry of Education only.
4 1987 data.

Source: Department for Education

international comparison may be made. This placed Canada, Denmark and the USA at the upper end of the range in 1989. The United Kingdom occupied an intermediate position on both measures.

REFERENCES AND FURTHER READING

The following list contains selected publications relevant to Chapter 3: Education. Those published by HMSO are available from the addresses shown on the back cover of *Social Trends*.

Committee of Directors of Polytechnics: First Destination of Students, A Statistical Report
Education Statistics Actual, CIPFA
Education Statistics Estimates, CIPFA
Education Statistics for the United Kingdom, HMSO
Employment Gazette, HMSO
Northern Ireland Education Department Statistical Bulletins, HMSO
Regional Trends, HMSO
Statistical Bulletins, Department for Education
Statistics of Education, Finance and Awards England and Wales, HMSO
Statistics of Education, Further Education, Department for Education
Statistics of Education, Schools, Department for Education
Statistics of Education, Schools Examination Survey, HMSO

Statistics of Education, Teachers in Service, HMSO
Statistics of Education in Wales, Welsh Office
Statistics of Finance and Awards, Department for Education
The Handbook of Education Unit Costs, CIPFA
The Scottish Office Education Department Statistical Bulletins, The Scottish Office
The Scottish Office Social Work Services Group Statistical Bulletins, HMSO
Training Statistics, Employment Department
Unfinished Business, Full-time Educational Courses for 16-19 Year Olds, Audit Commission and OFSTED
United Kingdom National Accounts (CSO Blue Book), HMSO
Universities Statistics Series, Universities' Statistical Record
Youth Cohort Study, Social and Community Planning Research

Chapter 4: Employment

The labour force

● A third of single women of working age were economically inactive in 1993 - more than twice the proportion for men.
(Chart 4.3)

● Nearly three out of four White women of working age were economically active in Spring 1993, compared with only one in four of Pakistani/Bangladeshi origin.
(Table 4.6)

● Three out of four men aged 16 and over in the United Kingdom were economically active in 1991 - the highest rate in the EC.
(Table 4.7)

Type of employment

● People from the Pakistani or Bangladeshi ethnic groups have the highest rate of self-employment - one in five workers from these ethnic groups were self-employed in Spring 1993.
(Chart 4.9)

● Nine in every ten women and more than seven in ten men working in part-time jobs in Spring 1993 were doing so out of choice.
(Table 4.13)

Time at work

● Only half a million working days were lost through labour disputes in 1992, the lowest figure since records began more than a hundred years ago.
(Chart 4.16)

Unemployment

● More than one in five economically active men aged 19 and under, and nearly one in six women, were unemployed (on the internationally standard measure) in Spring 1993.
(Table 4.20)

Employment and training measures

● Just under half of Youth Training leavers in 1991-92 were in full-time work six months later, while a quarter were unemployed.
(Table 4.28)

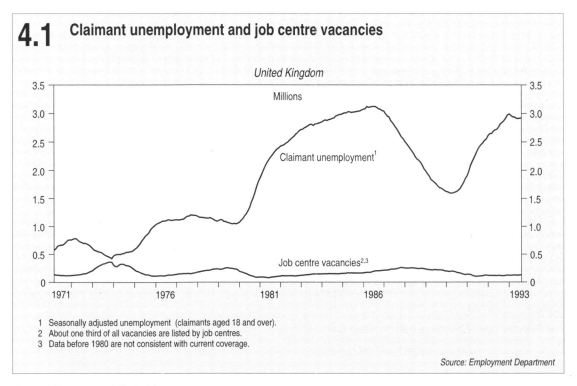

4.1 **Claimant unemployment and job centre vacancies**

United Kingdom

Millions

Claimant unemployment[1]

Job centre vacancies[2,3]

1 Seasonally adjusted unemployment (claimants aged 18 and over).
2 About one third of all vacancies are listed by job centres.
3 Data before 1980 are not consistent with current coverage.

Source: Employment Department

4.2 Workforce and workforce in employment[1]

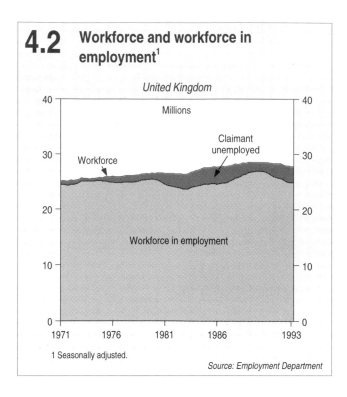

United Kingdom

Millions

1 Seasonally adjusted.

Source: Employment Department

4.3 Population of working age[1]: by sex and economic status[2], 1993

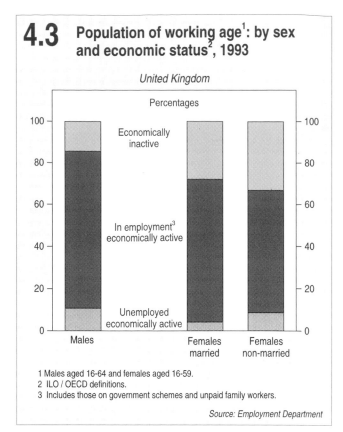

United Kingdom

Percentages

1 Males aged 16-64 and females aged 16-59.
2 ILO / OECD definitions.
3 Includes those on government schemes and unpaid family workers.

Source: Employment Department

The labour force

Chart 4.2 gives data on the workforce, which includes the claimant unemployed as well as all those in employment and distinguishes between these groups. Since 1971 the numbers of claimant unemployed in the United Kingdom peaked at more than three million during 1986 and came close to three million again at the beginning of 1993. Conversely, the workforce in employment fell to below 24 million in 1982 and 1983; it then rose to just under 27 million in early 1990 but has fallen steadily since. The total size of the workforce depends both on demographic factors and economic activity rates.

Chart 4.3 shows an economic activity breakdown of the population of working age in the United Kingdom. In 1993, three out of four men of working age were in employment compared with only two in three married women. A third of non-married women were economically inactive - more than twice the proportion for all men.

The United Kingdom has an ageing population and an ageing workforce. **Table 4.4** shows the age structure of the civilian labour force. In 1986, almost one in four of the labour force was under 25 - by 2001 this number will have fallen to less than one in six before increasing

4.4 Civilian labour force: by age

Great Britain   Millions

	16-19	22-24	25-34	35-44	45-54	55-59	60-64	65 and over	All aged 16 and over
Estimates									
1984	2.6	3.5	5.9	6.0	4.9	2.0	1.2	0.4	26.6
1986	2.5	3.7	6.1	6.3	4.9	2.0	1.1	0.4	26.9
1990	2.3	3.6	7.0	6.6	5.2	1.9	1.1	0.5	28.2
1991	2.1	3.5	7.2	6.6	5.3	1.9	1.1	0.5	28.1
1992	1.9	3.3	7.2	6.5	5.6	1.9	1.1	0.5	28.0
Projections									
1996	1.8	2.8	7.5	6.7	6.1	1.9	1.0	0.5	28.2
2001	1.9	2.6	6.9	7.7	6.3	2.2	1.0	0.5	29.0
2006	2.1	2.8	6.2	8.0	6.3	2.6	1.1	0.5	29.6

Source: Employment Department

4.5 Civilian labour force economic activity rates[1]: by sex and age

Great Britain   Percentages

	16-19	20-24	25-34	35-44	45-54	55-59	60-64	All aged 16 and over[2]
Males								
Estimates								
1984	73.5	85.0	93.7	95.4	93.0	82.5	57.3	74.5
1986	73.2	86.2	93.7	94.8	91.8	81.1	53.8	73.8
1990	75.6	86.8	94.3	94.7	91.5	81.0	54.4	74.3
1991	73.4	85.6	93.9	94.7	91.0	80.3	54.1	73.7
1992	70.6	84.4	93.2	94.0	91.0	78.0	52.9	73.0
Projections								
1996	67.5	80.5	92.9	93.9	90.2	77.6	48.6	71.9
2001	67.9	77.0	92.9	94.0	89.8	77.7	46.6	71.2
2006	69.5	77.0	92.8	94.0	89.5	77.7	45.9	70.4
Females								
Estimates								
1984	69.4	70.2	61.1	70.9	69.5	51.8	21.8	49.0
1986	70.3	70.7	63.5	72.1	70.5	51.8	19.1	49.6
1990	71.5	75.1	70.0	76.5	72.8	54.9	22.7	52.9
1991	70.7	72.7	69.7	76.7	72.7	54.5	24.1	52.6
1992	67.3	71.8	69.4	77.0	74.5	54.7	23.4	52.6
Projections								
1996	64.4	71.4	72.3	79.0	75.4	55.2	22.6	53.6
2001	65.4	72.0	76.0	82.0	76.2	55.9	24.0	55.3
2006	67.4	74.2	79.5	85.0	76.5	56.6	25.9	56.5

1 The percentage of the resident population, or any sub-group of the population, who are in the civilian labour force.
2 Includes those aged 65 and over.

Source: Employment Department

slightly by 2006. The proportion aged 45 and over in the labour force is projected to increase slightly from 31 per cent in 1986 to 35 per cent in 2006.

The age structure of the labour force depends partly on the age structure of the general population, and so, for example, the relatively high birth rates of the 1960s increased the number of 16 year old entrants to the civilian labour force in the second half of the 1970s. However, this effect reached its peak in 1981 after which the number of 16 year old entrants began to fall.

The proportion of the resident population above the minimum school leaving age, who are in the civilian labour force is usually referred to as the economic activity rate. We can see from **Table 4.5** that there has

been a general trend towards women becoming increasingly economically active. Over half of all women over 16 are now economically active, with the rate amongst 35 to 44 year olds exceeding three out of every four. These trends are projected to continue through to the turn of the century.

The increase in female activity rates between 1986 and 1990 has been partly due to an increase in the availability of part-time jobs and other social and economic changes encouraging women into the labour force. Certain population factors also affect female economic activity rates. For example, a rise in the average age at which women have children has contributed to increased activity rates for younger women. However, between 1990 and 1991 the economic activity rate for women

4.6 Population of working age economic activity rates: by age, sex and ethnic group, Spring 1993

Great Britain   Percentages

	16-19	20-29	30-39	40-49	50-59/64	Males aged 16-64	Females aged 16-59
Ethnic group							
White	62.0	82.1	84.5	86.7	69.0	86.1	71.9
Black [1]	41.7	75.2	75.2	87.3	70.3	80.4	66.0
Indian	25.1	72.5	77.6	86.3	61.3	80.8	61.4
Pakistani/Bangladeshi	35.4	52.8	52.1	50.2	41.1	72.3	24.8
Other [2]	47.0	60.0	68.7	84.3	75.5	76.0	58.6
All ethnic groups [3]	60.1	81.0	83.5	86.4	68.7	85.6	70.8

1 Includes Caribbean, African and other black people of non-mixed origin.
2 Includes Chinese, other ethnic minority groups of non-mixed origin and people of mixed origin.
3 Includes ethnic group not stated.

Source: Employment Department

4.7 Economic activity rates[1]: by sex, EC comparison, 1991

Percentages

	Males	Females	All
Denmark	74.8	62.0	68.3
United Kingdom	75.0	53.0	63.6
Portugal	73.7	50.5	61.3
Germany	72.8	48.6	60.1
Netherlands	71.7	45.1	58.2
France	65.9	47.6	56.3
Irish Republic	72.6	37.0	54.6
Luxembourg	69.5	36.3	52.4
Italy	67.8	36.5	51.5
Belgium	62.4	38.5	50.0
Spain	66.9	33.3	49.3
Greece	65.8	33.7	49.1

1 The civilian labour force aged 16 years and over as a percentage of the population aged 16 and over.

Source: Eurostat

aged 16 to 24 fell slightly. This is probably linked with an increase in the numbers entering further and higher education (see **Table 3.10**).

The changing age and sex structure of the population, and hence the labour force, can present recruitment problems for employers. Those employers who rely on young labour market entrants as a significant source of their recruits face declining numbers over future years. However, if employers make use of alternative recruits, such as those made redundant, women returning to the labour market and older workers, this may affect whether the activity rates in future are as projected in **Table 4.5**. If employers are particularly successful in attracting women back to work through measures such as flexible hours or subsidised child care, then activity rates for women may rise even faster.

Economic activity rates, especially those for women and for the young, vary amongst the different ethnic groups. In Spring 1993 nearly three in four White

women of working age were economically active, compared with only one in four of Pakistani/Bangladeshi origin **(Table 4.6)**. Amongst 16 to 19 year olds, Indians had the lowest economic activity rate at 25 per cent compared with over 60 per cent for the population as a whole but this may be linked to a higher proportion of Indians studying full-time at this age.

The United Kingdom had the highest economic activity rate amongst men in the European Community (EC) in 1991, at about 75 per cent **(Table 4.7)**, closely followed by Denmark. However, Denmark had the highest proportion of economically active women which, at 62 per cent, was nearly twice the rate in both Spain and Greece.

Type of employment

Table 4.8 shows the number of employees in employment and also those who are self-employed. Women have been accounting for an increasing proportion of employees in Great Britain. By June 1993 there were nearly equal proportions of male and female employees. However, only a quarter of the self-employed were female - the same proportion as in 1986. Over the last few years there has been a switch between employment in manufacturing and service industries. In 1986, one in four employees were employed in manufacturing industries which fell to one in five in 1993. This compares with two in three employees working in the service industries in 1986 which increased to almost three in four in 1993.

Amongst those in employment, people from the Pakistani or Bangladeshi ethnic groups are three to four times more likely to be self-employed than those from the Black ethnic groups **(Chart 4.9)**. In Spring

4.8 Employees in employment and the self-employed[1]: by sex and by industry

Great Britain

Thousands and percentages

	SIC[2] (1980)	Employees			Self-employed		
		1986	1991	1993	1986	1991	1993
All industries (thousands)	0-9	20,886	21,719	20,795	2,566	3,066	2,902
of which:							
Males		55	52	51	75	76	75
Females		45	48	49	25	24	25
Manufacturing	2-4	25	21	20	8	9	10
Services	6-9	67	71	73	63	61	62
Other	0,1,5	9	8	7	29	29	28

1 As at June each year.
2 Standard Industrial Classification.

Source: Employment Department

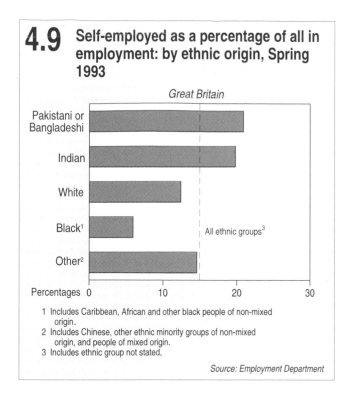

4.9 Self-employed as a percentage of all in employment: by ethnic origin, Spring 1993

Great Britain

Percentages

1 Includes Caribbean, African and other black people of non-mixed origin.
2 Includes Chinese, other ethnic minority groups of non-mixed origin, and people of mixed origin.
3 Includes ethnic group not stated.

Source: Employment Department

4.11 People with a second job[1]: by sex

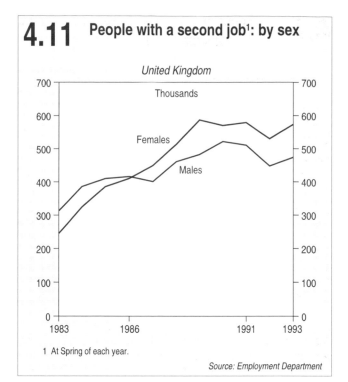

United Kingdom

Thousands

1 At Spring of each year.

Source: Employment Department

1993, one in five of employed people in the Pakistani or Bangladeshi ethnic groups was self-employed, though this had fallen from one in four at Spring 1992.

Chart 4.10 shows that around two fifths of the people in employment worked in manual occupations in Spring 1993. However, amongst those in employment from the Indian ethnic group, nearly twice as many were in non-manual occupations as were in manual

occupations. In the Pakistani/Bangladeshi group the number in manual occupations marginally exceeded that in non-manual occupations.

More women than men have second jobs **(Chart 4.11)**. However, in the first half of the 1980s the reverse was true. In 1986, the levels were virtually the same, but by the Spring of 1987 more women than men had second jobs. The largest gap between the sexes occurred in 1989 with almost 590 thousand women having two jobs - over 100 thousand more than men at that time.

Table 4.12 shows those in employment in the United Kingdom by sex and whether working full or part-time. Since 1990 the number of women in full-time employment has fallen by nearly five per cent while the number in part-time employment has risen by two per

4.10 People in employment: by ethnic group and manual/non-manual[1], Spring 1993

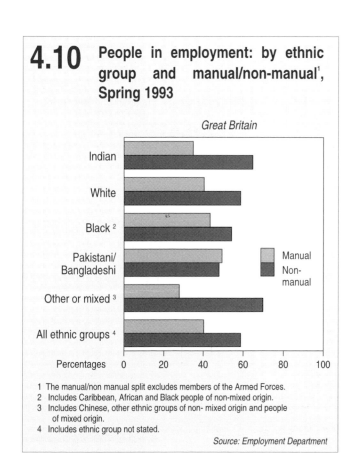

Great Britain

Percentages

1 The manual/non manual split excludes members of the Armed Forces.
2 Includes Caribbean, African and Black people of non-mixed origin.
3 Includes Chinese, other ethnic groups of non- mixed origin and people of mixed origin.
4 Includes ethnic group not stated.

Source: Employment Department

4.12 Full and part-time[1] employment[2] : by sex

United Kingdom				Thousands
	Males		Females	
	Full-time	Part-time	Full-time	Part-time
1984	13,240	570	5,422	4,343
1985	13,336	575	5,503	4,457
1986	13,430	647	5,662	4,566
1987	13,472	750	5,795	4,696
1988	13,881	801	6,069	4,808
1989	14,071	734	6,336	4,907
1990	14,109	789	6,479	4,928
1991	13,686	799	6,350	4,933
1992	13,141	885	6,244	5,081
1993	12,769	886	6,165	5,045

1 Full/part-time is based on respondents self-assessment. Excludes those who did not state whether they were full or part-time.
2 At Spring each year. Includes employees, self-employed, those on government training schemes and unpaid family workers.

Source: Employment Department

4.13 Reasons for taking a part-time[1] job: by sex and marital status, Spring 1993

United Kingdom   Percentages and thousands

| | | Females | | |
	Males	Married	Non-married	All females
Student/still at school	29.4	0.6	33.4	6.9
Ill or disabled	3.3	1.0	1.3	1.1
Could not find a full-time job	29.0	8.4	18.3	10.3
Did not want a full-time job	36.2	88.0	45.4	79.9
Part-time workers[2] (=100%) (thousands)	886	4,078	967	5,045

1 Part-time is based on respondent's self assessment.
2 Includes those who did not state the reason for taking a part-time job.

Source: Employment Department

cent. Part-time employment has generally been on an upward trend over the last decade; between 1984 and 1993 the number of women in part-time employment increased by 16 per cent and the number of men increased by 55 per cent. Despite these increases in the numbers of men employed part-time, they still make up less than one in every fifteen men in any form of employment, whereas the corresponding proportion for women has remained a little under one in two.

Most people work part-time out of choice **(Table 4.13)**. However, in 1993 nearly 15 per cent accepted part-time work because they could not find a full-time job, compared with just over ten per cent a year earlier. Amongst men and non-married women around three in ten took a part-time job because they were a student or still at school.

Time at work

4.14 Average hours usually worked[1] per week[2]: by sex, EC comparison, 1991

  Hours

	Males	Females	All
Portugal	42.5	38.5	40.8
Greece	40.7	37.8	39.7
Spain	40.7	37.3	39.6
Irish Republic	41.0	34.9	38.5
Luxembourg	40.3	34.9	38.4
Italy	39.6	35.3	38.0
France	39.9	34.8	37.6
United Kingdom	43.5	30.3	37.3
Germany	39.5	32.6	36.6
Belgium	38.1	31.8	35.6
Denmark	36.4	31.6	34.1
Netherlands	35.7	25.9	31.9

1 Employees only.
2 Excludes meal breaks but includes paid and unpaid overtime.

Source: Eurostat

4.15 People usually engaged in weekend working, shift work and night work, Spring 1993

United Kingdom   Thousands and percentages

	Total (thousands)[1]	As a percentage of all in employment
Saturday working only	6,054	23.9
Working both Saturday and Sunday	2,543	10.0
Sunday working only	2,990	11.8
Shift work[2]	3,954	15.6
Night work	1,544	6.1

1 It is possible for respondents to appear in more than one category.
2 Includes both weekend and night shifts.

Source: Employment Department

Portugal was the only country in the EC where employees worked, on average, more than 40 hours per week in 1991 **(Table 4.14)**. Although the United Kingdom, overall, was around the EC average, men worked the longest hours of all the countries in the EC - an average of 43.5 per week in 1991. Conversely, the average hours worked by women in the United Kingdom, at 30.3, was the second lowest after the Netherlands.

Table 4.15 shows the number of people who worked so-called 'unsocial' hours in 1992 and 1993, that is people working weekends, at night and on shift work. As the same person may work more than one of these types of work, it is not possible to calculate how many people work 'unsocial' hours by adding together figures from the table. In 1993, around a quarter of those in employment worked on Saturdays, and a further fifth worked either on Sunday only or both Saturday and Sunday.

4.16 Labour disputes: working days lost

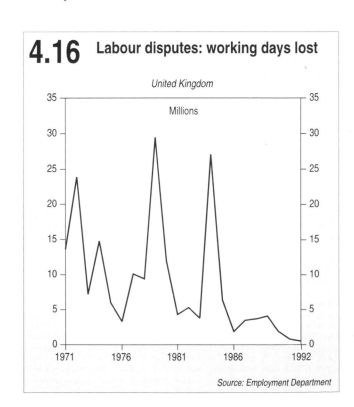

Source: Employment Department

4.17 Percentage of working week lost due to illness: EC comparison, 1991

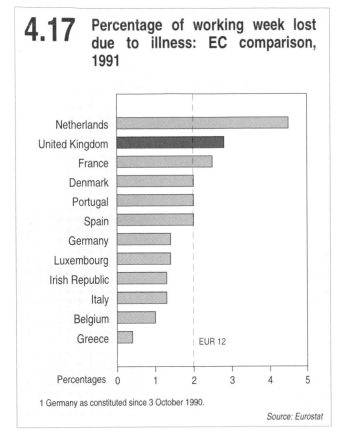

Percentages

1 Germany as constituted since 3 October 1990.

Source: Eurostat

The prevalence of working days lost through labour disputes is declining. **Chart 4.16** shows that in 1992, half a million working days were lost through labour disputes, the lowest figure since records began more than a hundred years ago. The number of days lost to strike action has fluctuated widely over the past twenty years, although the peaks can be attributed to major disputes in very large industries such as coal and steel.

A lot of work has been put into harmonising labour force surveys across the EC and it is now possible to compare sickness absence in different countries. **Chart 4.17** shows the latest available comparison. In the Netherlands, 4.5 per cent of the working week was lost to illness or injury in 1991. The United Kingdom has the next highest rate at 2.8 per cent.

Unemployment

Unemployment is used as both an economic and a social indicator and can be defined in a number of different ways. In the United Kingdom there are two basic methods. The first, the claimant count, uses administrative systems to count those people recorded as unemployed at government offices. Rules for unemployment and other benefits change from time to time, and this affects the claimant count. However, in order to provide a series free from distortions caused by changes in the coverage of the administrative systems, the Employment Department publishes a seasonally adjusted series which is consistent with the current coverage of the count. This is recalculated back

to 1971 each time there is a significant change in coverage and this is the series given most prominence in the media.

Chart 4.1 shows the number of claimant unemployed consistent with the current coverage of the claimant count and the number of vacancies remaining unfilled at job centres. Job centres receive notification of only about a third of all vacancies. At August 1993 vacancies stood at 128 thousand, the highest since March 1991. The number of claimant unemployed rose above one million in December 1975 and it then took just over five years to rise above two million, but only four years to pass three million. The number of unemployed peaked in July 1986 at 3.1 million, before falling sharply to 1.6 million in early 1990. There has been an equally dramatic rise back to nearly three million in January 1993, since when the number has fallen.

The second measure of unemployment is obtained by surveying individuals, who are asked whether they have a job and, if not, whether they would like work and what steps they have taken to find it. The Labour Force Survey is the main source of survey data on the unemployed and uses the International Labour Organisation (ILO) definition (see the glossary of terms at the end of this chapter). Collecting, verifying and analysing the information takes time, and estimates are not available as quickly or as frequently as claimant count estimates, but they have the advantage of not being affected to the same extent by benefit rule changes.The Employment Department uses both methods by publishing the monthly claimant count and by sponsoring the Labour Force Survey.

4.18 Comparisons of alternative measures of unemployment

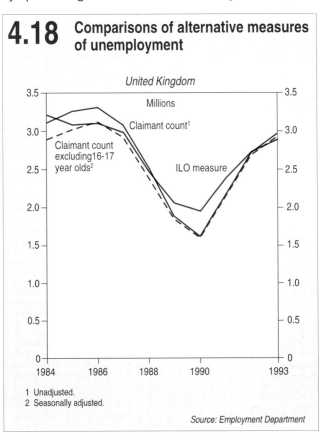

1 Unadjusted.
2 Seasonally adjusted.

Source: Employment Department

4.19 Unemployment rates adjusted to OECD concepts[1]: international comparison

Percentages

	1976	1981	1983	1984	1985	1986	1987	1988	1989	1990	1991	1992
United Kingdom	5.6	9.8	12.4	11.7	11.2	11.2	10.2	8.5	7.1	6.8	8.7	9.9
Belgium	6.4	10.8	12.1	12.1	11.3	11.2	11.0	9.7	8.0	7.2	7.2	7.9
France	4.4	7.4	8.3	9.7	10.2	10.4	10.5	10.0	9.4	8.9	9.4	10.3
Germany [2]	3.7	4.4	8.0	7.1	7.2	6.4	6.2	6.2	5.6	4.8	4.2	4.6
Italy	6.6	7.8	8.8	9.4	9.6	10.5	10.9	11.0	10.9	10.3	9.9	10.5
Netherlands	5.5	8.5	12.0	11.8	10.6	9.9	9.6	9.2	8.3	7.5	7.0	6.8
Portugal	..	..	7.9	8.4	8.5	8.4	7.0	5.7	5.0	4.6	4.1	4.1
Spain	4.6	13.9	17.2	20.0	21.4	21.0	20.1	19.1	16.9	15.9	16.0	18.1
Australia	4.7	5.7	9.9	8.9	8.2	8.0	8.1	7.2	6.1	6.9	9.5	10.7
Canada	7.1	7.5	11.8	11.2	10.4	9.5	8.8	7.7	7.5	8.1	10.2	11.2
Finland	3.8	4.8	5.4	5.2	5.0	5.3	5.0	4.5	3.4	3.4	7.5	13.0
Japan	2.0	2.2	2.6	2.7	2.6	2.8	2.8	2.5	2.3	2.1	2.1	2.2
Sweden	1.6	2.5	3.5	3.1	2.8	2.7	1.9	1.6	1.4	1.5	2.7	4.8
United States	7.6	7.5	9.5	7.4	7.1	6.9	6.1	5.4	5.2	5.4	6.6	7.3

1 See Appendix, Part 4: Definitions of unemployment-OECD concepts.
2 As constituted since 3 October 1990.

Source: OECD

Chart 4.18 compares the two measures: the ILO measure (from the Labour Force Survey estimates) and the claimant count (both the seasonally adjusted and unadjusted series). The ILO measure is used consistently throughout this section. The three measures show broadly similar trends - a general decline in the number of unemployed between 1986 and 1990 followed by a rise more recently.

A more common way of expressing unemployment figures is as a rate. Unemployment is measured differently in different countries and so the Organisation for Economic Co-operation and Development (OECD) uses a standard set of concepts to compare unemployment between countries. These rates are estimated by OECD to conform, as far as possible, to ILO guidelines and they are calculated as percentages of the total labour force.

There is some evidence of common international trends in unemployment. Many of the countries shown in **Table 4.19** had falling unemployment between the mid 1980s and 1990, but most, including the United Kingdom, then returned to rising unemployment.

Unemployment in the United Kingdom is highest amongst the young **(Table 4.20)**. In Spring 1993 more than one in five economically active males and nearly one in six economically active females aged 19 and under were unemployed, higher than in 1992 but lower than in 1986. Since 1986 the rate of unemployment amongst men aged 65 and over in the labour market has halved.

4.20 Unemployment rates[1]: by sex and age

United Kingdom   Percentages

	1986	1991	1992	1993
Males				
16-19	21.8	16.5	18.7	22.0
20-29	15.7	12.3	15.3	16.4
30-39	9.4	7.8	10.4	10.3
40-49	7.8	5.8	7.8	8.8
50-64	9.3	8.4	10.4	11.9
65 and over	9.3	5.9	4.9	4.6
All males aged 16 and over	11.7	9.2	11.5	12.4
Females				
16-19	19.8	13.2	13.8	16.0
20-29	14.4	9.4	9.4	10.2
30-39	10.1	6.9	7.2	7.0
40-49	6.7	4.9	5.0	4.7
50-59	6.1	5.1	5.0	5.6
60 and over	5.1	4.4	3.1	3.9
All females aged 16 and over	10.7	7.2	7.2	7.5

1 Unemployment based on the ILO definition as a percentage of all economically active. At Spring each year.

Source: Employment Department

4.21 Unemployment rates[1]: by region

United Kingdom   Percentages

	1989	1990	1991	1992	1993
North	10.7	8.6	10.6	11.2	11.2
Yorkshire & Humberside	8.0	6.8	9.1	9.9	9.8
East Midlands	6.0	5.1	7.8	8.7	9.0
East Anglia	3.8	3.8	6.2	7.1	8.3
South East	3.1	3.9	7.4	9.4	10.3
South West	4.8	4.5	7.7	9.1	9.2
West Midlands	6.9	5.9	9.0	10.7	11.6
North West	8.8	7.5	9.9	10.1	10.9
Wales	7.9	6.6	9.2	8.9	9.5
Scotland	9.8	8.0	9.2	9.5	10.1
Northern Ireland	15.4	13.7	14.1	12.1	12.5

1 Unemployment based on the ILO definition as a percentage of all economically active. At Spring each year.

Source: Employment Department

4.22 Unemployment[1]: by sex, age and duration, Spring 1993

United Kingdom   Percentages and thousands

	Duration of unemployment (percentages)						
	Up to 13 weeks	Over 13 up to 26 weeks	Over 26 weeks up to one year	Over one year up to two years	Over two years up to three years	Over three years	Total[2] (= 100%) (thousands)
Males							
16-19	26.8	19.9	26.6	20.2	5.6	-	192
20-29	18.5	17.0	20.0	22.3	11.6	10.3	666
30-39	15.2	14.9	18.5	22.7	11.8	16.8	404
40-49	17.3	14.5	15.5	23.1	11.3	18.1	317
50-64	13.5	14.1	18.9	20.4	10.0	23.1	377
All aged 16 and over [3]	17.6	15.8	19.4	21.9	10.7	14.5	1,967
Females							
16-19	32.9	19.4	24.6	18.4	-	-	126
20-29	29.9	18.1	23.5	16.1	6.5	5.9	321
30-39	24.9	20.0	22.4	17.2	7.7	7.7	207
40-49	27.0	13.7	21.3	19.2	8.4	10.5	142
50-59	20.3	10.8	21.6	20.6	10.5	16.1	106
All aged 16 and over [3]	27.6	17.0	22.7	17.8	7.5	7.4	924
Total persons (thousands)	600	468	591	595	280	354	2,891

1 Unemployment is based on the ILO definition.
2 Includes those who did not state their duration.
3 Includes men aged 65 and over and women aged 60 and over who were unemployed.

Source: Employment Dempartment

Unemployment rates differ between the regions in Great Britain. With the exception of the North and Yorkshire and Humberside, the unemployment rate increased in all the regions between 1992 and 1993 **(Table 4.21)**. East Anglia had the lowest rate of unemployment in 1993, but one of the biggest percentage point increases in the rate since 1989. In 1993, unemployment was highest in Northern Ireland, the West Midlands and the North.

Table 4.22 shows the duration of unemployment for those people who were unemployed in the United Kingdom in Spring 1993. The proportions of both men and women who are long-term unemployed increases with age. For example, over 53 per cent of men aged 50 to 64 were unemployed for more than a year, compared with only 26 per cent of those aged 16 to 19. Long term unemployment is defined as being out of work for more than 52 weeks. Men are more likely to be long-term unemployed than women. In Spring 1993 nearly one in two men who were unemployed had been unemployed for over a year at the time of the survey, compared with only one in three women.

Unemployment varies considerably according to the person's ethnic group **(Chart 4.23)**. About 30 per cent of the Pakistani/Bangladeshi and 28 per cent of the Black economically active were unemployed in Spring 1993. Amongst both these groups, about 15 per cent

of the economically active had been unemployed for over a year, compared with the British average of four per cent.

4.23 Unemployment rates[1]: by ethnic group, Spring 1993

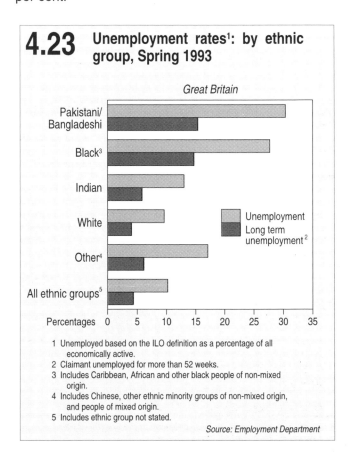

Great Britain

1 Unemployed based on the ILO definition as a percentage of all economically active.
2 Claimant unemployed for more than 52 weeks.
3 Includes Caribbean, African and other black people of non-mixed origin.
4 Includes Chinese, other ethnic minority groups of non-mixed origin, and people of mixed origin.
5 Includes ethnic group not stated.

Source: Employment Department

4.24 Main method of job search of the unemployed[1]: by socio-economic group, Spring 1993

United Kingdom   Percentages

	Professional	Employers and managers	Intermediate non-manual	Junior non-manual	Skilled manual	Semi-skilled manual	Unskilled manual	Economically inactive
Percentage[2] of each group using the following:								
Visiting a jobcentre/careers office[3]	9.4	17.4	26.0	27.8	27.3	40.3	35.8	18.6
Study situations vacant	34.5	35.6	33.8	39.7	25.7	29.6	29.7	55.5
Answering advertisements [4]	17.6	17.5	15.1	14.2	11.1	8.5	7.9	20.2
Personal contacts	11.4	11.7	7.4	5.8	17.8	11.9	13.1	25.3
Direct approach to firms/ employers	15.3	7.4	8.5	6.5	10.4	7.0	10.9	31.9
Name on private agency books	8.3	5.5	4.4	4.0	1.2	1.1	0.6	4.2
Other [5]	5.2	6.4	6.8	2.7	7.2	2.6	2.8	17.4

1 Unemployment is based on the ILO definition.
2 Percentages are based on data excluding those who did not know or preferred not to state their job search methods and those temporarily not looking for work because they were either waiting to start a new job, temporarily sick.
3 Includes Jobclubs, Jobcentres and Training/Employment Agency offices.
4 Includes notices outside factories or in shop windows.
5 Includes advertising in newspapers/journals and awaiting job application results.

Source: Employment Department

Table 4.24 shows how the methods of job searching vary by socio-economic group. Visiting a jobcentre or careers office is the favoured method of manual workers, whilst professionals are the most likely to have their names on private agency books or make a direct approach to an employer. Job search methods also vary by age. The younger unemployed tend to use job centres to look for work, while those of more mature years rely more on situations vacant and advertisements. The frequency with which people search for jobs is related to the duration of their unemployment. A study of people attending Restart interviews found that those who had short spells of unemployment were more likely to search actively for work. Overall, in 1992 only half of the people interviewed had applied for a job in the previous four weeks. Of those who had, half had made only one application.

Table 4.25 shows redundancy rates in the different regions of the Great Britain. Redundancy rates were lower in 1993 than in 1991 in all regions. The most marked decrease was in Wales where the rate more than halved over the two year period. In 1993, the North had the highest redundancy rate of all the regions, with about one in every 60 employees being made redundant.

Employment and training measures

4.25 Redundancy rates: by region, Spring 1991 and 1993

Great Britain   Rates[1]

	1991	1993
Great Britain	17.8	12.4
North	18.4	16.5
Yorkshire & Humberside	15.5	13.0
East Midlands	19.4	13.9
East Anglia	14.1	..
South East	17.8	11.3
South West	14.7	12.5
West Midlands	21.2	13.9
North West	17.7	12.3
Wales	26.3	11.4
Scotland	14.4	11.5

1 Redundancy rate per 1,000 employees. The table reflects redundancies in the three months prior to interview.

Source: Employment Department

4.26 Proportion of employees[1] receiving job related training[2]: by socio-economic group, Spring 1993

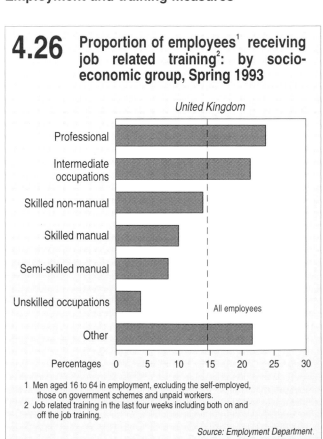

1 Men aged 16 to 64 in employment, excluding the self-employed, those on government schemes and unpaid workers.
2 Job related training in the last four weeks including both on and off the job training.

Source: Employment Department.

4.27 Employment position of young people: by activity, 1989 and 1991[1]

England & Wales   Percentages

	1989 activity				
	Full-time education	Full-time employment	YTS or government scheme	Out of work	Other
1991 activity					
Full-time education	51	2	3	4	9
Full-time employment	35	82	72	32	41
YT[2] or government scheme	2	2	5	6	7
Out of work	6	10	15	40	13
Other	7	3	6	18	31
Total	100	100	100	100	100

1 Young people in their first post-compulsory education year in 1989 (ie aged 16 or 17 in 1989 and aged 18 or 19 in 1991).
2 Youth Training Scheme became Youth Training from May 1990.

Source: Employment Department

In Spring 1993, people in professional and intermediate occupations were more than twice as likely to have received job related training in the previous four weeks than their counterparts in manual occupations **(Chart 4.26)**. Over a fifth of those in professional and intermediate occupations had received such training, compared with around ten per cent of those in skilled and partly skilled occupations. Overall nearly 15 per cent of employees had received job related training in the previous four weeks.

The Youth Cohort Study (YCS) follows groups of 16 to 19 year olds from full-time education into the labour market. It samples young people at three points, and some 20 thousand people are contacted. Each sample is unique in allowing a 'before and after' analysis as young people enter the labour market. The YCS figures are used in **Table 4.27** to look at how the labour market activities of the cohort of young people changed between 1989 and 1991. Nearly three quarters of those on a Youth Training Scheme (YTS) or other government

scheme in 1989 were in full time employment two years later. However four in every ten of those out of work in 1989 were still out of work in 1991.

The likelihood of young people getting a full-time job after youth training has fallen over recent years **(Table 4.28)**. In 1992, 44 per cent of YT leavers were in full-time work six months after leaving; in 1990-91 it was 52 per cent.

In July 1991 the Confederation of British Industry (CBI) launched 'World Class Targets'. This lists eight specific targets designed to improve the skills base in the economy. The targets were developed by the CBI in consultation with organisations representing employers, education and training establishments and with Training and Enterprise Councils and Local Enterprise Companies. One of the targets is that by 1997, 80 per cent of all young people attain NVQ/SVQ level II or its academic equivalent in their foundation education and training. The target centrally underpins the future of government training policy and is a key indicator of success. This is supported by education, government

4.28 Destination[1] of Youth Training leavers

Great Britain   Percentages and thousands

	1984-85	1985-86	1986-87[2]	1987-88	1988-89	1989-90	1990-91	1991-92[3]
Full-time work								
Same employer	23	28	28	23	32	34	29	28
Different employer	} 32	25	29	{ 33	29	28	23	16
Self-employed				1	1	2	1	1
Part-time work	1	4	4	4	4	3	4	4
Full-time course	3	3	3	4	3	4	6	6
Different YT Scheme	6	7	11	12	12	11	10	9
Other	2	4	3	3	3	4	5	7
Unemployed	32	28	23	21	14	14	20	25
All leavers[4](=100%)(thousands)	368	418	428	326	414	379	328	278

1 Six months after leaving.
2 The information on leavers in 1986-87 is not representative of two year YTS, as there are very few two year completers before April 1988.
3 Includes leavers from Youth Credits.
4 The figures for 1989-90, 1990-91 and 1991-92 leavers are not all leavers but the number of leavers for whom leaving certificates were returned: it is estimated that leaving certificates are returned for around 85 per cent of leavers.

Source: Employment Department

4.29 Proportion of 16-24 year olds at or above NVQII[1] or its academic equivalent

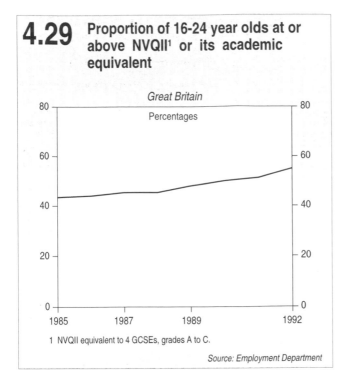

Great Britain

Percentages

1 NVQII equivalent to 4 GCSEs, grades A to C.

Source: Employment Department

and business and is rapidly growing in importance as an indicator of the progress we need to make to be competitive in our workforce skills. The proportion of 16 to 24 year olds at or above NVQ level II or equivalent has gradually increased from 44 per cent in 1985 to 55 per cent in 1992 **(Chart 4.29)**.

REFERENCES AND FURTHER READING

The following list contains selected publications relevant to Chapter 4: Employment. Those published by HMSO are available from the addresses shown on the back cover of *Social Trends*.

British Social Attitudes, Gower
CBI Quarterly Industrial Trends Survey, CBI
Employment Gazette, Harrington Kilbride
General Household Survey, HMSO
Labour Force Survey, HMSO
Labour Force Survey Quarterly Bulletin, Employment Department
Labour Market Quarterly Report, Employment Department
Main Economic Indicators, OECD
Northern Ireland Labour Force Survey Statistics Notice, HMSO
Regional Trends, HMSO
Scottish Economic Bulletin, HMSO
Skills Bulletin, Employment Department
Time Rates and Hours of Work, Employment Department
Training Statistics, HMSO
Youth Cohort Study, Employment Department

Glossary of terms

Employees (Labour Force Survey measure) - a count, obtained from household surveys, of persons aged 16 and over who regard themselves as paid employees. People with two or more jobs are counted only once.

Employees in employment (employer survey based measure) - a count, obtained from surveys of employers, of jobs held by civilians who are paid by an employer who runs a PAYE tax scheme. People with more than one job are therefore counted more than once.

The self-employed - a count mainly obtained from household surveys, of persons aged 16 and over who regard themselves as self-employed, ie who in their main employment work on their own account, whether or not they have any employees.

Government employment and training programmes - a count, obtained from household surveys, of those who said they were participants on Youth Training, Employment Training, Employment Action or Community Industry or a programme organised by a TEC/ LEC.

Work-related government training programmes - a count, obtained from administrative returns, of all participants who receive some form of work experience in the course of their placement but who do not have a contract of employment and are not self-employed.

The labour force in employment - a count, obtained from household surveys and censuses, of employees in employment, self-employed persons, participants in government employment and training programmes, and persons doing unpaid family work

The workforce in employment - a count of employees in employment (from employer survey based measure), self-employed persons all HM forces and participants in government employment and training programmes.

The claimant unemployed - a measure, known as the claimant count, and derived from administrative sources, which counts as unemployed those people who are claiming unemployment related benefits at Employment Service local offices (formerly Unemployment Benefit Offices).

The ILO unemployed - an International Labour Organisation (ILO) recommended measure, used in household surveys such as the Labour Force Survey, which counts as unemployed those aged 16 and over who are without a job, are available to start work in the next two weeks and who have been seeking a job in the last four weeks or are waiting to start a job already obtained.

The workforce - the **workforce in employment** plus the **claimant unemployed**.

The economically active - the **labour force in employment** plus the **ILO unemployed**.

The civilian labour force - the **labour force in employment** plus the **ILO unemployed** less **HM forces**.

Claimant unemployment rate - the percentage of the **workforce** who are **claimant unemployed**.

ILO unemployment rate - the percentage of the **economically active** who are **ILO unemployed**.

The economically inactive - people who are neither part of the labour force in employment nor ILO unemployed. For example, all people under 16 and full-time students, those looking after a home or retired, or those permanently unable to work.

The population of working age - males aged 16 to 64 years and females aged 16 to 59 years.

Civilian economic activity rate - the percentage of the population in a given age group which is in the civilian labour force.

Some of these terms are covered in more detail in the appendix.

Chapter 5: Income and Wealth

Household income

● Real disposable income per head increased between 1991 and 1992 to reach a record high, reversing the previous year's fall. *(Chart 5.2)*

● The rate of increase of average earnings in Great Britain fell to 3.3 per cent in March 1993, the lowest recorded since 1967. *(Chart 5.1)*

● Pensioners' income, averaged over 1990 and 1991, was 35 per cent higher in real terms than in 1981. *(Chart 5.6)*

Taxes

● It is estimated that there will be 25 million income taxpayers in 1993-94, with total income tax liabilities of about £65 billion. *(Table 5.11)*

Income distribution

● The share of income of the bottom fifth of households has fallen between 1981 and 1990-1991. Only the top fifth had a larger share of total income in 1990-1991 than they had in 1981. *(Table 5.20)*

Wealth

● The richest one per cent of people owned 18 per cent of total marketable wealth in 1991, a slightly lower proportion than in 1976. *(Table 5.23)*

● The higher their social class the more likely a person is to own shares. Those in social classes A and B make up less than a fifth of the population but owned a third of shares held by individuals in 1992. *(Chart 5.24)*

National income

● After taking into account the different price levels in each country, gross domestic product per head in the United Kingdom in 1991 was lower than in the United States and most EC countries. *(Chart 5.27)*

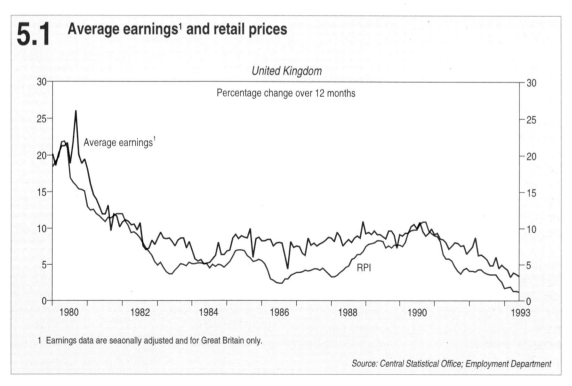

5.1 Average earnings[1] and retail prices

United Kingdom

Percentage change over 12 months

1 Earnings data are seaonally adjusted and for Great Britain only.

Source: Central Statistical Office; Employment Department

This chapter looks at the distribution of income and wealth in the United Kingdom today. It also describes how income has changed in recent years including examining the effects of changes in taxes and benefits.

Household income

Disposable income is the amount of money people actually have available to them to spend or invest. It is what is left after taking account of taxes on income, national insurance (NI) contributions and contributions to pension schemes. **Chart 5.2**, which is expressed in real terms, shows how income has changed after allowing for inflation. Real disposable income per head increased between 1991 and 1992, reversing the previous year's fall. It is now at its highest level ever, nearly 80 per cent higher than in 1971.

Households receive income from a number of sources and these are listed in **Table 5.3**. Wages and salaries are still by far the most important source of household income (57 per cent in 1992) although their importance is decreasing gradually. Just over a tenth of household income now comes from private pensions and annuities, more than double the proportion in 1971. This is explained by the growing numbers of elderly people in the United Kingdom, and that increasingly more people are entitled to occupational pensions. The share of income coming from self-employment has remained fairly constant despite the growth in the numbers of self-employed (see **Table 4.8**).

The proportion of household income paid in income tax has remained steady over recent years but fell slightly between 1991 and 1992 to stand at 13 per cent.

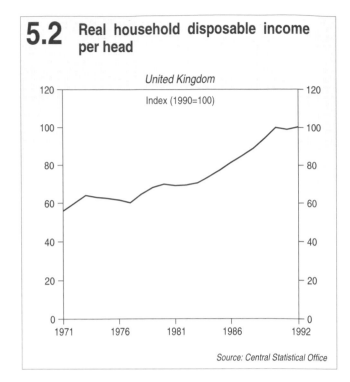

5.2 **Real household disposable income per head**

United Kingdom

Index (1990=100)

Source: Central Statistical Office

On a regional basis, the most recent household income figures available are for 1991 **(Chart 5.4)**. At that time the lowest average weekly disposable income was in Northern Ireland (£116) whilst the highest was in Greater London (£156) and the rest of the South East (£141). Since the mid 1980s disposable income in the South East, East Anglia and the South West has remained consistently above the United Kingdom average. In 1991 disposable income in Scotland rose above the average for the United Kingdom for the first time. As well as differences in levels, there are also differences in the sources of income. The higher proportions of

5.3 Household income[1]

United Kingdom | | | | | | | | | Percentages and £ billion

	1971	1976	1981	1986	1987	1988	1989	1990	1991	1992
Source of income (percentages)										
Wages and salaries[2]	68	67	63	59	59	59	59	58	58	57
Income from self-employment[3]	9	9	8	10	10	11	11	11	10	9
Rent, dividends, interest	6	6	7	8	8	8	9	10	9	8
Private pensions, annuities, etc	5	5	6	8	9	8	8	8	10	11
Social security benefits	10	11	13	13	12	11	11	10	11	12
Other current transfers[4]	2	2	2	3	3	3	2	2	2	3
Total household income (= 100%) (£ billion)	44.7	100.4	202.1	313.9	341.4	376.3	422.0	472.7	500.9	529.5
Direct taxes etc (percentages of total household income)										
Taxes on income	14	17	14	14	14	14	14	14	14	13
National insurance contributions[5]	3	3	3	4	4	4	4	3	3	3
Contributions to pension schemes	1	2	2	2	2	2	2	2	2	2
Total household disposable income (£ billion)	36.4	78.3	162.4	251.9	275.0	302.8	340.6	382.5	408.3	435.2

1 See Appendix, Part 5: The household sector.
2 Includes Forces' pay and income in kind.
3 After deducting interest payments, depreciation and stock appreciation.
4 Mostly other government grants, but including transfers from abroad and from non-profit-making bodies.
5 By employees and the self-employed.

Source: Central Statistical Office

5.4 Average weekly household disposable income per head: by region, 1991

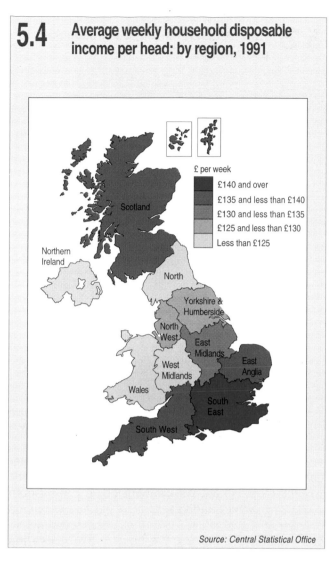

£ per week
- £140 and over
- £135 and less than £140
- £130 and less than £135
- £125 and less than £130
- Less than £125

Source: Central Statistical Office

income from state and occupational pensions in the South West are because of the large number of retired people in the region. Self-employment income is more important in East Anglia and Northern Ireland, partly due to the importance of agriculture to the regional economies.

Earnings from employment are the main source of household income. Earnings change from year to year, according to the amount of overtime, bonuses, shift allowances, grade increments and other productivity and incentive payments. In addition, many workers also have an annual pay settlement or review. One measure of changes in earnings is the average earnings index and **Chart 5.1** (at the beginning of the chapter) shows the annual percentage change in this index and compares it with the change in retail prices. For the majority of the period covered by the chart it can be seen that increases in earnings have outpaced changes in retail prices; annual increases in average earnings peaked at nearly 26 per cent in September 1980, dropped rapidly, and then fluctuated between 5 and 11 per cent for the next decade. It then fell to 3.3 per cent in March 1993, the lowest level recorded since 1967.

Another, more detailed, source of earnings data is provided by the New Earnings Survey. This is an annual survey of employers and collects information on full-time adult employees whose earnings during the survey period were unaffected by absence. This survey allows us to look at how the spread or distribution of earnings has changed over time. **Chart 5.5** shows, for men and women separately, the growth in real weekly earnings over time. The lowest decile is the maximum

5.5 Real[1] weekly earnings: by sex

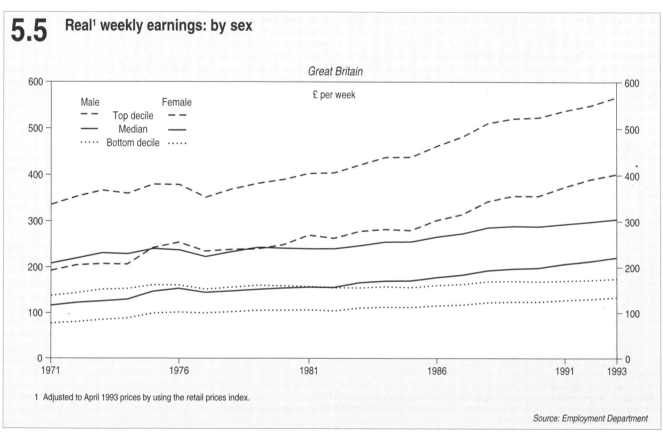

Great Britain

£ per week

Male — Female
- Top decile
- Median
- Bottom decile

1 Adjusted to April 1993 prices by using the retail prices index.

Source: Employment Department

5.6 Real income of pensioners[1,2]: by source

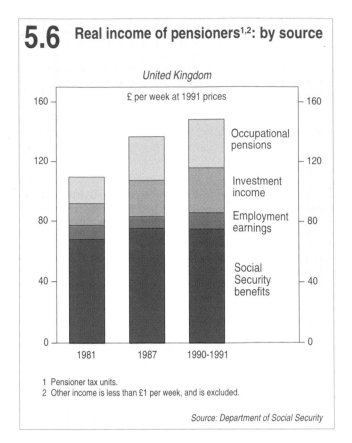

United Kingdom

£ per week at 1991 prices

Occupational pensions
Investment income
Employment earnings
Social Security benefits

1981 · 1987 · 1990-1991

1 Pensioner tax units.
2 Other income is less than £1 per week, and is excluded.

Source: Department of Social Security

5.7 Benefit expenditure: by recipient group[1], 1992-93

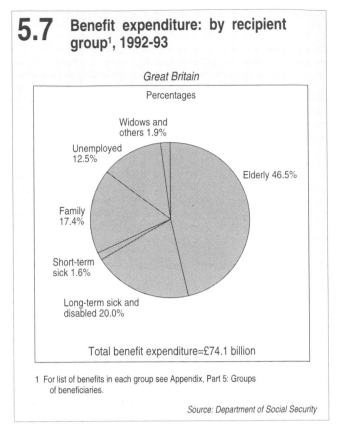

Great Britain

Percentages

Widows and others 1.9%
Unemployed 12.5%
Family 17.4%
Short-term sick 1.6%
Long-term sick and disabled 20.0%
Elderly 46.5%

Total benefit expenditure=£74.1 billion

1 For list of benefits in each group see Appendix, Part 5: Groups of beneficiaries.

Source: Department of Social Security

amount earned by the bottom ten per cent of employees, the median is the maximum amount earned by the bottom 50 per cent and the highest decile is the minimum amount earned by the top ten per cent of employees. The chart clearly shows that the earnings gap between the highest and lowest earners has increased over time. For men the lowest decile has increased by 27 per cent since 1971 to reach £175 in April 1993, whilst the highest decile has increased by 69 per cent to £567 in the same period. For women there is a similar trend although the earnings levels are lower. When considering these data it should be remembered that it is not necessarily the same people who are in the top and bottom decile groups in each

year. For example it is possible for someone who is below the bottom decile point in one year to receive a pay increase which moves them above the bottom decile by the following year.

The numbers of pensioners in the United Kingdom has continued to increase but there have been changes in the make-up of their incomes. **Chart 5.6** shows that pensioners' income in the combined years of 1990 and 1991 was 35 per cent higher in real terms than in 1981. The main reasons for this are increases in investment income, which has doubled in value, and in occupational pensions whose value has nearly doubled.

5.8 Social security benefits[1] for unemployed claimants[2]: by sex

Great Britain — Percentages and thousands

	1961	1971	1981	1991	1992
Unemployed male claimants receiving					
Unemployment benefit only	47.2	40.9	28.2	20.0	17.8
Unemployment and income support/supplementary benefit	9.4	13.6	11.4	6.1	5.2
Income support/supplementary benefit only	21.9	27.1	46.0	62.5	64.8
Neither unemployment benefit nor income support	21.6	18.4	14.4	11.4	12.2
Total unemployed male claimants (= 100%)(thousands)	283	721	1,994	1,773	2,073
Unemployed female claimants receiving					
Unemployment benefit only	39.7	41.0	38.9	28.4	26.7
Unemployment and income support/supplementary benefit	2.5	6.7	3.8	2.1	2.1
Income support/supplementary benefit only	12.2	20.5	37.4	51.3	52.3
Neither unemployment benefit nor income support	45.5	31.8	20.0	18.2	18.9
Total unemployed female claimants (= 100%)(thousands)	101	138	710	540	614

1 At November each year except for 1981 when figures for February 1982 are used. From April 1988 supplementary benefit was replaced by income support.
2 Prior to 1981 count of registered unemployed; for 1981 count of registered unemployed claimants; after 1981 count of unemployed claimants.

Source: Department of Social Security

Social security benefits are the second most important source of income after wages and salaries. **Chart 5.7** shows total benefit expenditure broken down by recipient group. It can be seen that nearly half of all benefit expenditure in 1992-93 was accounted for by payments to the elderly. Benefit payments to the sick and disabled amounted to around a fifth of the total and these were closely followed by payments to families.

Table 5.8 looks at the main benefits received by unemployment claimants. Since 1961 the main change has been a decrease in the percentage of unemployed claimants who receive only unemployment benefit but an increase in those who only receive income support/supplementary benefit.

The table shows that there are differences between male and female claimants: 12 per cent of men received neither of the two benefits in 1992, while the figure for women was 19 per cent. The vast majority of

unemployment claimants will however receive national insurance credits which can count towards future benefit entitlement.

Expenditure on individual non-contributory benefits together with the number of recipients is given in **Table 5.9**. Of these, income support expenditure was the highest in 1992-93 at nearly £14.5 billion, a real terms increase of 20 per cent on the previous year .

The benefit system has changed over time, with new benefits introduced and others withdrawn. In 1992 two new benefits, the disability living allowance and disability working allowance were introduced. Disability living allowance (DLA) has replaced attendance allowance for people disabled before the age of 65 and mobility allowance, and extends the help which these benefits formerly provided. In 1992-93 there was an average of over 900 thousand people receiving DLA at any one time.

5.9 Non-contributory benefits-expenditure in real terms[1] and recipients[2]: by type of benefit

Great Britain   £ million at 1992-93 prices[1] and thousands

	Expenditure (£ million at 1992-93 prices[1])				Recipients[2] (thousands)			
	1976-77	1981-82	1991-92	1992-93	1976-77	1981-82	1991-92	1992-93
Non-income-related benefits								
Child benefit[3]	1,914	6,217	5,371	5,767	6,915	13,145	12,205	12,485
One-parent benefit	.	140	258	277	.	470	835	895
Non-contributory retirement pension	127	72	37	36	80	50	30	30
Industrial disablement benefit	588	581	608	596	.	.	295	295
Industrial death benefit	91	87	66	63	.	.	25	25
War pension	996	883	871	968	415	345	280	310
Attendance allowance	401	608	1,766	1,458	230	350	975	765
Invalid care allowance[4]	7	11	295	366	5	5	170	195
Severe disablement allowance[4]	120	240	617	652	105	180	305	320
Mobility allowance	28	319	1,099	125	30	210	665	.
Disability living allowance	.	.	.	1,095	.	.	.	935
Disability working allowance	.	.	.	4	.	.	.	5
Lump sum payment to non-contributory pensioners	.	11	11	12	.	600	1,100	1,200
Income-related benefits								
Supplementary pension	2,016	2,614	.	.	1,675	1,740	.	.
Supplementary allowance	4,011	6,309	.	.	1,305	1,985	.	.
Income support	.	.	12,054	14,461	.	.	4,660	5,320
Family income supplement	63	122	.	.	70	125	.	.
Family credit	.	.	648	864	.	.	355	420
Maternity grant	53	29	.	.	..	..	.	.
Housing benefit - rent rebates and allowances[4]	707	1,036	2,672	3,520	..	1,840	4,110	4,315
Rate rebates/ community charge benefit	.	.	1,112	1,451	.	.	6,335	6,655
Social Fund[5]	.	.	217	231	.	.	..	..
Administration and miscellaneous service[6]	2,009	918	2,148	2,462	.	.	.	.

1 Expressed in real terms using the GDP deflator.

2 Estimated average number receiving benefit at any one time, except for lump sum payments, maternity grant and social fund payments which, because they are single payments, are the total number paid in each year.

3 Child benefit recipients relate to the number of qualifying children except for 1976-77 which relates to the number of qualifying families. In 1976-77 tax allowances were the main comparable form of child support.

4 There have been a number of changes to the system of assistance with housing costs. In particular, from 1990-91 most rent rebate expenditure is accounted for by the Department of the Environment and the Welsh Office, and is therefore not included.

5 Net expenditure after repayment of loans.

6 1976-77 figure represents administration cost of both contributory and non-contributory benefits.

Source: Department of Social Security

5.10 Contributory benefits-expenditure in real terms[1] and recipients[2]: by type of benefit

Great Britain

£ million at 1992-93 prices[1] and thousands

	Expenditure (£ million at 1992-93 prices[1])				Recipients[2] (thousands)			
	1976-77	1981-82	1991-92	1992-93	1976-77	1981-82	1991-92	1992-93
Retirement pensions	19,782	22,356	26,485	26,856	8,250	9,015	9,920	9,910
Widows benefit	1,548	1,274	1,047	1,468	490	460	345	340
Invalidity benefit	2,058	2,526	5,534	6,100	510	660	1,365	1,490
Lump sum payments to contributory pensioners	.	186	118	115	.	10,100	11,400	11,500
Unemployment benefit	1,967	3,138	1,660	1,838	625	1,220	675	715
Sickness benefit	1,942	1,254	283	315	520	445	120	135
Statutory sick pay	.	.	725	710	.	.	330	330
Maternity allowance	211	291	32	32	80	125	15	15
Statutory maternity pay	.	.	357	366	.	.	85	85
Death grant	53	31	.	.	..	..	.	.
Industrial disablement benefit	588	581	608	596	200	260	295	295
Industrial death benefit	91	87	66	63	30	30	25	25
Administration and miscellaneous services[3]	2,009	1,351	1,273	1,307	.	.	.	.

1 Expressed in real terms using the GDP deflator.
2 Estimated average number receiving benefit at any one time, except for lump sum payments and death grants, which because they are single payments are the total number paid in each year.
3 Figure for 1976-77 represents administration cost of both contributory and non-contributory benefits.

Source: Department of Social Security

Disability working allowance supplements the incomes of disabled people who work but have limited earning power.

By far the largest expenditure on contributory benefits is on retirement pensions **(Table 5.10)**. These were received by 9.9 million people in 1992-93 and cost £26.9 billion, an increase of around 35 per cent in real terms since 1976-77.

When interpreting the recipient figures in **Tables 5.9** and **5.10** it should be remembered that some people receive more than one benefit.

Taxes

During 1993-94 it is estimated that there will just over 25 million taxpayers with a total income tax bill of about £65 billion **(Table 5.11)**. The average rate of tax payable ranges from just three per cent at the lower end of the income scale (less than £5,000 per year) to 30 per cent at the higher end (over £40,000 per year). Around 1.9 million people now pay tax at the higher rate. Income tax rates have been reduced markedly since 1978-79, particularly for those with higher incomes. The basic rate has been cut from 33 per cent to 25 per cent and in 1992-93 a new lower rate of tax was

5.11 Income tax payable: by income[1] range, 1993-94[2]

United Kingdom

	Total annual income (£ million)	Tax payable at lower rate		Tax payable at basic rate		Tax payable at excess over basic rate		Total tax payable (£ million)	Average rate of tax payable (percentages)	Average amount of tax payable (£)
		Number of taxpayers (millions)	Amount (£ million)	Number of taxpayers (millions)	Amount[3] (£ million)	Number of taxpayers (millions)	Amount (£ million)			
Annual income										
£3,445-£4,999	9,400	2.2	290	0.0	0	0.0	0	290	3	130
£5,000-£7,499	24,700	3.9	1,390	1.6	250	0.0	0	1,640	7	420
£7,500-£9,999	34,900	4.0	1,880	3.6	1,710	0.0	0	3,590	10	900
£10,000-£14,999	75,900	6.1	3,060	6.1	7,040	0.0	0	10,100	13	1,640
£15,000-£19,999	68,000	3.9	1,970	3.9	8,540	0.0	0	10,500	15	2,670
£20,000-£29,999	77,400	3.2	1,610	3.2	11,700	0.1	20	13,400	17	4,140
£30,000-£39,999	33,600	1.0	490	1.0	5,930	0.9	640	7,060	21	7,180
£40,000 and over	61,500	0.8	420	0.8	12,700	0.8	5,180	18,300	30	21,950
All ranges	385,000	25.1	11,100	20.3	47,900	1.9	5,840	64,900	17	2,580

1 Total income of the individual for income tax purposes including earned and investment income. All figures in the table relate to taxpayers only.
2 Based on a projection from the 1991-92 Survey of Personal Incomes.
3 Including the basic rate component of tax payable at higher rate.

Source: Inland Revenue

5.12 Percentage of income paid in income tax and national insurance contributions[1]: by marital status and level of earnings[2]

United Kingdom				Percentages
	1971-72	1981-82	1991-92	1993-94[3]
Single person				
Half average earnings				
Tax	14.3	17.5	12.8	11.5
NIC	7.7	7.7	6.2	6.2
Average earnings				
Tax	22.2	23.7	18.9	18.3
NIC	5.8	7.7	7.6	7.6
Twice average earnings				
Tax	26.2	27.3	22.0	22.7
NIC	3.3	6.1	6.0	6.0
Married man[4]				
Half average earnings				
Tax	7.5	10.5	6.5	5.9
NIC	7.7	7.7	6.2	6.2
Average earnings				
Tax	18.8	20.2	15.7	15.3
NIC	5.8	7.7	7.6	7.6
Twice average earnings				
Tax	26.8	25.1	20.4	20.4
NIC	3.3	6.1	6.0	6.0

1 Employees' contributions. Assumes contributions at Class 1, contracted in, standard rate.
2 Average earnings for full-time adult male manual employees working a full week on adult rates.
3 1992-93 based projections.
4 Assuming wife not in paid employment.

Source: Inland Revenue

introduced. All taxpayers now pay a rate of 20 per cent on the first £2,500 of taxable income; almost five million people only pay tax at this rate. The higher tax rates which rose to a maximum of 83 per cent on earned income have been replaced by one 40 per cent rate, and the surcharge of up to 15 per cent on investment income has been abolished.

The percentage of income paid in income tax in 1993-94 is lower than in any other year shown in **Table 5.12**, but it increased slightly in the year to 1993-94. Employee's national insurance contributions are now lower as a proportion of earnings than in 1971 for those on half average earnings, but higher for those on average and twice average earnings.

So far, this chapter has looked at how earnings, income tax, NI contributions and benefits have all changed over time. **Table 5.13** shows the combined effect of these changes, and of inflation. Of the categories shown single women have experienced the greatest real increase since 1971, at over 80 per cent for someone on median earnings. Over the same period real income for a single man on median earnings has increased by 49 per cent whilst that for a married man with two children has gone up by 42 per cent.

Although there have been real terms increases in earnings at all levels, these increases have been much less at the lower end of the distribution. Real net

earnings have increased by just over 35 per cent since 1971 for a single man with no children earning at the lowest decile point, but at the top decile point real weekly net earnings have increased by nearly 70 per cent.

It should be noted that changes in the distribution of earnings do not necessarily indicate the movements in earnings of individuals or groups of individuals. They are caused by several factors including the change in the structure of employment. Over time, individuals move within the distribution.

Chart 5.14 shows the proportion of personal income taken by direct taxes and social security contributions for various countries. In 1990 the proportion varied from 14 per cent in Japan to 26 per cent in Sweden, with the United Kingdom at the lower end of the tax burden scale. When making international comparisons, it is often necessary to make adjustments to definition and coverage. This means that the United Kingdom figures used here will not be strictly comparable with figures used elsewhere in this chapter. Also, a number of other factors must be taken into account, particularly the differing balance between direct and indirect taxation used by different countries. There is also considerable

5.13 Real[1] weekly earnings[2] after income tax, national insurance contributions, child benefit and family credit: by selected family type

Great Britain				£ per week[1]
	1971	1981	1991	1992
Single man, no children				
Lowest decile point	98.9	108.0	130.9	134.6
Median	146.3	160.3	211.3	217.6
Highest decile point	231.4	261.0	380.9	390.6
Single woman, no children				
Lowest decile point	63.4	80.6	103.5	107.5
Median	88.5	111.4	155.0	161.7
Highest decile point	138.1	180.7	263.5	277.8
Married man[3], no children				
Lowest decile point	106.1	116.3	139.5	142.9
Median	153.5	168.6	219.9	225.8
Highest decile point	238.6	269.4	389.5	402.2
Married man[3], 2 children[4]				
Lowest decile point[5]				
Family credit claimed	124.3	134.8	164.3	168.7
Family credit not claimed[6]	124.3	134.8	156.4	160.3
Median	171.6	187.1	236.8	243.3
Highest decile point	256.7	287.8	406.3	419.6

1 At April 1992 prices.
2 Figures relate to April each year and to full-time employees on adult rates whose pay for the survey pay-period was not affected by absence.
3 Assuming no wife's earnings.
4 Aged under 11.
5 In years up to 1987, there was no entitlement to Family Income Supplement for this category.
6 Families with capital of more than £3,000 would only be eligible to receive reduced amounts of family credit, or may not be eligible at all.

Source: Inland Revenue; Department of Social Security

5.14 Percentage of personal income taken by direct taxes and social security contributions[1]: international comparison, 1990

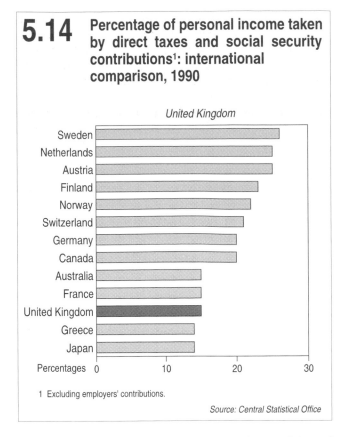

United Kingdom

Sweden
Netherlands
Austria
Finland
Norway
Switzerland
Germany
Canada
Australia
France
United Kingdom
Greece
Japan

Percentages 0   10   20   30

1 Excluding employers' contributions.

Source: Central Statistical Office

is indirect taxation - Value Added Tax (VAT), customs duties, car tax, and so on. The Central Statistical Office's work on the effects of taxes and benefits on income, measures both direct and indirect taxation based on income and expenditure data from the Family Expenditure Survey. **Chart 5.15** shows the percentage of gross household income taken in direct and indirect taxation in the United Kingdom. The overall tax burden has only changed slightly since 1979 and in 1991 stood at 35 per cent, two percentage points lower than in 1979.

Chart 5.16 shows what proportion of the disposable income of households headed by someone under retirement age is taken by indirect taxes. It can be seen clearly that the lower the disposable income, the more indirect taxation bites. For households in the top fifth of the income distribution, 14 per cent of their disposable income was accounted for by indirect taxes compared with 29 per cent for the bottom fifth, though in value terms the payments by the top fifth of households were much greater.

difference in government involvement in provision of services and financial support (eg medical care, pensions, etc) which are free at the point of use.

So far, this section on taxes has concentrated on the effect direct tax (ie income tax) has on earnings and income. A major factor in the tax burden facing people

Income distribution

Directly or indirectly most government income is raised from households, and its spending benefits households. Clearly some households will be taxed more than they benefit, and others will benefit more than they are taxed - this is often called the redistribution of income. Initially, households receive income from various sources: from their employment; from occupational pensions; from

5.15 Percentage of gross household income taken by direct and indirect taxation

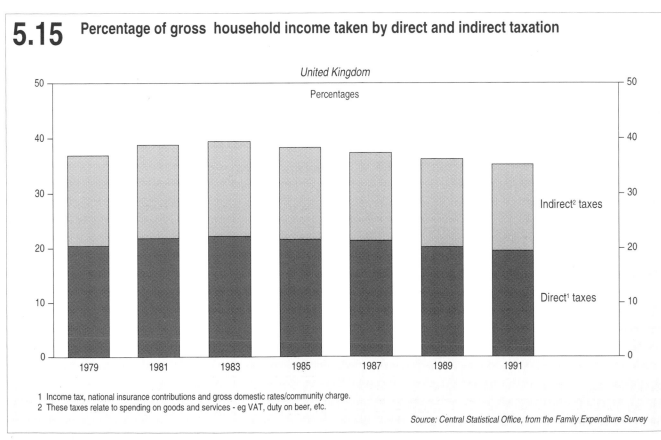

United Kingdom

Percentages

Indirect[2] taxes

Direct[1] taxes

1979 1981 1983 1985 1987 1989 1991

1 Income tax, national insurance contributions and gross domestic rates/community charge.
2 These taxes relate to spending on goods and services - eg VAT, duty on beer, etc.

Source: Central Statistical Office, from the Family Expenditure Survey

5.16 Indirect taxes as a percentage of disposable income: by income grouping[1] of non-retired households, 1991

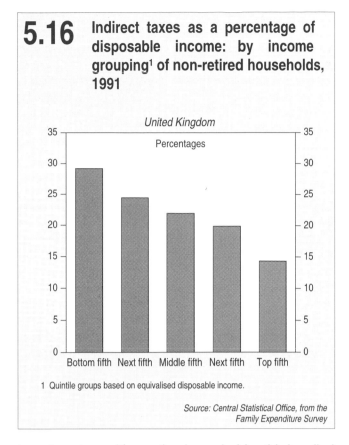

United Kingdom

Percentages

1 Quintile groups based on equivalised disposable income.

Source: Central Statistical Office, from the Family Expenditure Survey

investments; and from other households - this is called original income. Cash benefits from the state (eg retirement pensions and income support) are added to original income to give gross income. Household income is then reduced by income tax payments, NI contributions and community charge payments (or more recently the council tax), to leave disposable income. Some household spending is accounted for by indirect taxes such as VAT leaving them with post-tax income. Lastly, households benefit from government expenditure on services such as education and health.

Adding in the value of these gives a household's final income. Where a household gets more money and services from the government than it pays for in taxes and other contributions, the tax-benefit system has redistributed income in the household's favour.

The redistribution statistics are presented by quintile group of household income. Before considering these analyses it is important to consider which type of households are in which quintile group. Households headed by someone who is retired or unoccupied tend to have lower incomes and are concentrated in the lower quintile groups **(Table 5.17)**; this group made up three quarters of households in the bottom quintile group in 1991. At the other end of the scale, nearly half of all households in the top group are headed by a professional, an employer or a manager. The effect of government intervention on household income is greatest for retired households and those non-retired households with no economically active people, on whom the bulk of state benefits are targeted.

In 1991, original income ranged from an average of £1,570 per household for the bottom fifth of households to £37,220 for the top fifth **(Table 5.18 overleaf)**. After adding in cash benefits, deducting taxation and other contributions, and adding in benefits in kind, final income ranged from £6,230 to £26,910 - narrowing the gap between the two groups. The bottom two fifths of the income distribution have gained from the income redistribution, ie their final income is more than their original income. It is, not surprisingly, those households at the top of the income distribution who pay the most taxes, both direct and indirect.

Chart 5.19 shows the relative importance of different sources of income for each quintile group. Cash benefits are very important for the lowest quintile group (71 per

5.17 Composition of quintile groups of household income: by occupational group of head of household, 1991

United Kingdom

Percentages

	Quintile groups of households ranked by equivalised disposable income[1]					
	Bottom fifth	Next fifth	Middle fifth	Next fifth	Top fifth	All households
Occupational group of head of household						
Professional	-	1	4	7	14	5
Employers and managers	3	4	9	17	34	13
Intermediate and junior non-manual	3	7	14	21	22	13
Skilled manual	10	17	27	26	15	19
Semi-skilled manual	6	10	12	9	2	8
Unskilled manual	3	3	3	2	-	2
Retired	49	44	22	12	7	27
Unoccupied	25	15	9	6	4	12
Other[2]	-	-	1	1	1	1
All occupational groups	100	100	100	100	100	100

1 Equivalised disposable income has been used for ranking the households into quintile groups; see Appendix, Part 5: Equivalisation scales.
2 Mainly armed forces.

Source: Central Statistical Office, from the Family Expenditure Survey

5.18 Redistribution of income through taxes and benefits[1], 1991

United Kingdom   £ per year

| | Quintile groups of households ranked by equivalised disposable income[2] | | | | | |
	Bottom fifth	Next fifth	Middle fifth	Next fifth	Top fifth	All households
Average per household (£ per year[2])						
Earnings of main earner	1,000	3,870	8,880	13,400	23,990	10,230
Earnings of others in the household	90	610	2,440	5,060	7,640	3,170
Occupational pensions, annuities	200	570	990	1,190	1,550	900
Investment income	180	420	740	1,170	3,630	1,230
Other income	100	180	250	290	400	240
Total original income	1,570	5,650	13,310	21,100	37,220	15,770
plus Benefits in cash						
Contributory	1,920	1,990	1,350	840	560	1,330
Non-contributory	1,970	1,530	970	530	330	1,060
Gross income	5,460	9,170	15,630	22,470	38,110	18,170
less Income tax[3] and NIC[4]	200	780	2,140	3,830	7,660	2,920
less Community charge[5] (gross)	540	580	660	680	660	620
Disposable income	4,730	7,820	12,830	17,960	29,790	14,620
less Indirect taxes	1,320	1,870	2,920	3,690	4,470	2,860
Post-tax income	3,410	5,940	9,900	14,270	25,320	11,770
plus Benefits in kind						
Education	1,090	900	1,190	890	560	920
National Health Service	1,480	1,410	1,280	1,120	940	1,250
Housing subsidy	140	120	50	30	10	70
Travel subsidies	50	50	50	60	90	60
School meals and welfare milk	70	30	20	10	10	30
Final income	6,230	8,450	12,500	16,380	26,910	14,090

1 See Appendix, Part 5: Redistribution of income for definitions of the income measures.
2 Equivalised disposable income has been used for ranking the households into quintile groups; see Appendix, Part 5: Equivalisation scales.
3 After tax relief at source on mortgage interest and life assurance premiums.
4 Employees' national insurance contributions.
5 Rates in Northern Ireland.

Source: Central Statistical Office, from the Family Expenditure Survey

5.19 Sources of gross household income: by income grouping[1], 1991

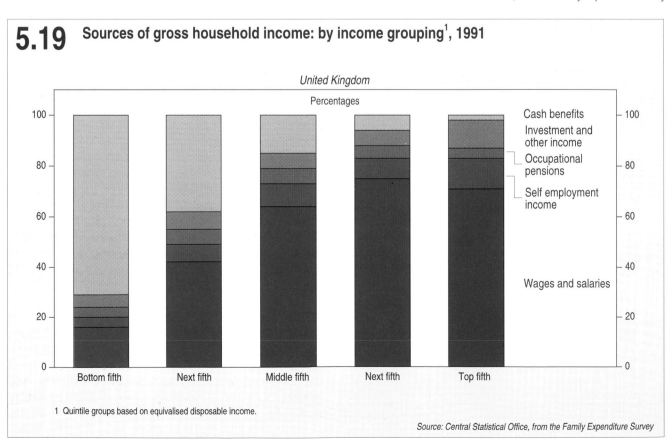

United Kingdom

1 Quintile groups based on equivalised disposable income.

Source: Central Statistical Office, from the Family Expenditure Survey

cent of income in 1991) but decrease in importance as you move up the income scale. The converse is true for wages and salaries, and self-employment income; together these make up 83 per cent of household income for the top quintile group.

The Department of Social Security also analyses the Family Expenditure Survey data, focusing on households below average income. This analysis is described in detail in the article at the beginning of this book. The methodology used is different in several respects from that used in previous items, including that it is based on quintiles of individuals instead of quintiles of households. **Table 5.20** shows that the share of income of the bottom quintile group has fallen between 1979 and the combined years of 1990 and 1991. Only the top quintile group had a larger share of total income in 1990-1991 than it had in 1979. When housing costs are taken into account, the gap between the top and bottom group widens.

Some care should be exercised when interpreting these figures. The table does not monitor how the real income of individual households has changed over time, it compares the income share in 1990-1991 of certain groups of households with the position of corresponding groups in earlier years. It should be borne in mind that the composition of any quintile group is different from year to year as some households and individuals move from one quintile group to another.

Table 5.21 is on the same basis as Table 5.18, and shows how real median incomes have changed over time. The table is expressed in indices with the median income of the bottom group set at 100 in 1979. This

5.21 Real median income[1]: by quintile group

United Kingdom Indices (1979 bottom fifth=100)

	Bottom fifth	Next fifth	Middle fifth	Next fifth	Top fifth	Average of all indivi- duals
		Quintile groups of individuals				
Net income before housing costs						
1979	100	137	173	220	300	192
1981	98	133	171	218	310	192
1987	104	147	197	258	392	231
1988-1989	104	153	210	278	417	247
1990-1991	103	156	216	293	446	260
Net income after housing costs						
1979	100	138	177	226	312	197
1981	96	135	174	225	323	196
1987	99	143	200	267	406	236
1988-1989	100	153	217	289	438	255
1990-1991	97	155	222	304	467	267

1 The unit of analysis is the individual and the income measure is net equivalent household income. See Appendix, Part5: Households Below Average Income and Equivalisation scales.

Source: Department of Social Security

enables comparisons to be made more easily, both between quintile groups, and over time. For example, before housing costs, the real median income of the bottom fifth increased by just three per cent between 1979 and 1990-1991, while the corresponding figure for the top fifth is 49 per cent. After housing costs the real median income of the bottom fifth actually fell between 1979 and 1990-1991, but increased for all other groups.

5.20 Distribution of disposable household income[1]

United Kingdom Percentages

	Bottom fifth	Next fifth	Middle fifth	Next fifth	Top fifth	Total
		Quintile groups of individuals				
Net income before housing costs						
1979	10	14	18	23	35	100
1981	10	14	18	23	36	100
1987	9	13	17	23	39	100
1988-1989	8	12	17	23	40	100
1990-1991	7	12	17	23	41	100
Net income after housing costs						
1979	10	14	18	23	35	100
1981	9	14	18	23	36	100
1987	8	12	17	23	40	100
1988-1989	7	12	17	23	41	100
1990-1991	6	12	17	23	43	100

1 The unit of analysis is the individual and the income measure is net equivalent household income. See Appendix, Part 5: Households Below Average Income and Equivalisation scales.

Source: Department of Social Security

Wealth

The value of net wealth held by the personal sector was £2,300 billion in 1992, virtually unchanged from the previous year **(Table 5.22 overleaf)**. A third of all personal sector wealth is now in dwellings, up from a quarter in 1971 but lower than in recent years because of the fall in house values. The largest increase is for life assurance and pension funds; this proportion has doubled since 1971 and currently stands at 31 per cent. The proportion of wealth invested in stocks and shares fell from 23 per cent in 1971 to only eight per cent in 1981, although there has been little change since then. This was due to a substantial fall in share prices during the early 1970s.

Table 5.23 (overleaf) shows the distribution of marketable wealth amongst the top half of the wealth distribution. For all marketable wealth there has been little change in the distribution since 1976. The share of the richest one per cent has however fallen slightly and in 1991 this group owned 18 per cent of total marketable wealth.

5.22 Composition of the net wealth[1] of the personal sector

United Kingdom		Percentages and £ billion		
	1971	1981[2]	1991[2]	1992[2]
Net wealth (percentages)				
Dwellings (net of mortgage debt)	26	36	37	33
Other fixed assets	10	10	6	5
Non-marketable tenancy rights	12	12	8	8
Shares and deposits with building societies	7	8	8	8
National Savings, notes and coin and bank deposits	13	10	10	10
Stocks, shares and unit trusts	23	8	8	9
Life assurance and pension funds	15	16	27	31
Other financial assets net of liabilities	-6	0	-4	-4
Total (= 100%) (£ billion)	172	740	2,270	2,300

1 See Appendix, Part 5: Net wealth of the personal sector.
2 Data have been revised from 1976 onwards to include certain public sector pensions.

Source: Central Statistical Office

The table also shows the distribution of marketable wealth after the value of dwellings (net of mortgage debt) has been removed. This series is more volatile over time but wealth defined in this way is much more concentrated in the upper part of the distribution. For example the richest ten per cent own half of total marketable wealth, but just the richest five per cent own half of marketable wealth excluding dwellings.

5.23 Distribution of wealth[1]

United Kingdom		Percentages and £ billion		
	1976	1981	1986	1991
Marketable wealth				
Percentage of wealth owned by[2]				
Most wealthy 1%	21	18	18	18
Most wealthy 5%	38	36	36	37
Most wealthy 10%	50	50	50	50
Most wealthy 25%	71	73	73	71
Most wealthy 50%	92	92	90	92
Total marketable wealth (£ billion)	280	565	955	1694
Marketable wealth less value of dwellings				
Percentage of wealth owned by[2]				
Most wealthy 1%	29	26	25	28
Most wealthy 5%	47	45	46	50
Most wealthy 10%	57	56	58	63
Most wealthy 25%	73	74	75	79
Most wealthy 50%	88	87	89	92

1 Estimates for 1976, 1981 and 1986 are based on the estates of persons dying in those years. Estimates for 1991 are based on estates notified for probate in 1991-92. Estimates are not strictly comparable between 1991 and earlier years.
2 Percentages and total marketable wealth are of population aged 18 and over.

Source: Inland Revenue

During the 1980s, wider share ownership was an important government objective. In 1980 there were between two and a half and three million shareholders in Great Britain, but by mid 1992 there were nine and a quarter million. It is thought that shareholding peaked at around 11 million in 1990 following the privatisation of the electricity companies.

Chart 5.24 looks at share ownership by social class in 1992 and shows that the higher the social class the more likely people are to own shares. Those in social classes A and B (intermediate and higher management or professional) make up only 18 per cent of the population but own 33 per cent of shares held by individuals. Conversely 31 per cent of the population is in social classes D and E but they own only 15 per cent of shares.

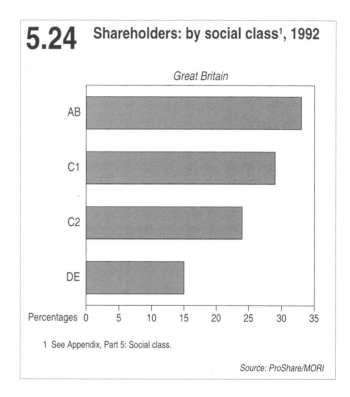

5.24 Shareholders: by social class[1], 1992

Great Britain

1 See Appendix, Part 5: Social class.

Source: ProShare/MORI

National income

Gross Domestic Product (GDP) is one measure of the income of the nation. **Chart 5.25** shows the real changes in GDP since 1951, by expressing GDP as an index based on 1990 prices. GDP at factor cost fell between 1990 and 1992, but for the vast majority of the period there has been continued growth. The only other falls were in the mid 1970s (the oil price shock) and the early1980s (the worldwide recession). Quarterly information (not shown on the chart) shows that GDP has increased in each quarter from the first quarter of 1992 to the third quarter of 1993.

Each year the Central Statistical Office produces a regional breakdown of GDP. **Table 5.26** is one way of presenting these data, using indices based on GDP per head with the United Kingdom average equal to 100. This means that, in any year, a region with a value greater than 100 has a GDP per head higher than the United Kingdom average. The pattern, not surprisingly, is the same as for household income (see **Chart 5.4**): the highest GDP per head is in Greater London and the rest of the South East, the lowest is in Northern Ireland.

Chart 5.27 shows an international comparison of GDP per head. These data although presented in sterling have been calculated using purchasing power parities. This is to make the data more comparable by taking into account the different price levels in each country. For example if a particular commodity, such as bread, is more expensive in one country than another then incomes would need to need to be higher in that country just to reach the same standard of living. The chart shows that, at nearly £14,100, the United States has the highest GDP per head of the countries shown. The United Kingdom, at £9,900 per head, is well down the list although still nearly twice that of Greece.

The final table in this chapter **(Table 5.28 overleaf)** shows how general government (central government plus local authorities) income is financed. The largest source of income continues to be from taxes on expenditure; these accounted for 35 per cent of government income in 1992. Taxes on income were the second largest source of income in 1992, although at 29 per cent they were at their lowest proportion since 1980 when they were also 29 per cent.

5.26 Gross domestic product in current prices at factor cost : by region

Index per head (UK = 100)

	1981	1986	1991	1992
United Kingdom[1]	100	100	100	100
North	94	90	90	91
Yorkshire & Humberside	92	94	92	93
East Midlands	97	97	97	95
East Anglia	97	101	100	102
South East	117	116	117	116
Greater London	128	125	126	123
Rest of South East	109	111	112	111
South West	93	95	94	94
West Midlands	91	92	92	93
North West	95	93	90	90
England	102	102	102	102
Wales	84	84	85	86
Scotland	97	94	96	99
Northern Ireland	79	80	81	81

1 United Kingdom less continental shelf.

Source: Central Statistical Office

The general government borrowing requirement, the gap between revenue and expenditure, was over nine per cent of income in 1981. This became a debt repayment for the years 1987 to 1990 but returned to borrowing in 1991. The general government borrowing requirement was nearly 12 per cent of general government income in 1992.

5.25 Gross Domestic Product[1]

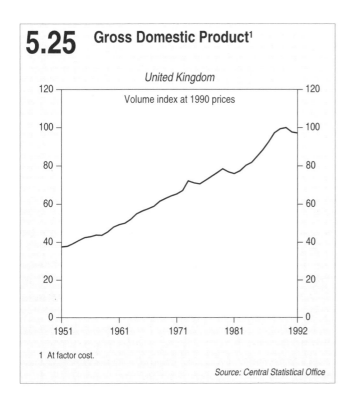

Source: Central Statistical Office

1 At factor cost.

5.27 Gross domestic product per head: international comparison, 1991

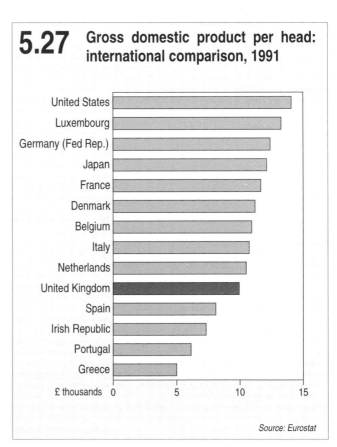

Source: Eurostat

5.28 General government income: by source

United Kingdom   Percentages and £ million

	1981	1986	1990	1991	1992	1992 (£ million)
Taxes on income	29.9	32.2	35.4	32.4	29.1	73,452
of which						
Personal sector	23.9	25.3	28.4	27.4	25.8	64,975
less tax credits ·	-1.1	-1.9	-2.7	-2.6	-2.8	-7,069
Companies[1]	4.5	5.9	6.9	5.7	4.7	11,849
Public corporations	0.1	0.2	0.1	0.2	0.1	199
Non-residents	2.4	2.7	2.8	1.7	1.4	3,498
Taxes on expenditure	35.1	38.9	36.2	36.7	34.8	87,679
of which						
Customs and excise revenue[2]	21.3	26.3	26.6	27.9	26.7	67,382
Non-domestic rates[3]	.	.	4.3	5.9	5.5	13,839
Local authorities rates[3]	8.4	9.4	2.4	0.1	.	124
Community charge	.	.	4.0	3.5	3.1	7,859
Social security contributions	13.2	16.2	16.0	15.7	14.8	37,464
of which						
Employers	7.3	8.4	9.3	9.2	8.7	21,996
Employees	5.6	7.4	6.2	6.0	5.6	14,219
Self-employed and non-employed persons	0.3	0.4	0.5	0.5	0.5	1,249
Gross trading surplus, rent and royalties	4.1	2.6	1.9	1.9	1.8	4,580
Interest, dividends and miscellaneous current transfers	3.8	3.7	3.1	2.7	2.3	5,696
Imputed charge for non-trading capital consumption	1.6	1.6	1.8	1.6	1.4	3,603
Taxes on capital[4]	1.2	1.8	2.0	1.5	1.2	2,913
Other capital receipts	-	0.1	0.1	0.1	0.1	205
Transactions in financial liabilities (net)	11.1	2.7	-0.6	3.8	11.4	28,857
of which						
Borrowing requirement	9.4	2.0	-0.7	3.6	11.7	29,554
Total (= 100%) (£ million)	120,994	161,429	216,435	230,965	252,308	252,308

1 Includes financial institutions.
2 Includes VAT.
3 National non-domestic rates (a central government tax) replaced local authority non-domestic rates in Great Britain from April 1990.
4 Death duties, capital transfer tax, capital gains tax and development land tax.

Source: Central Statistical Office

REFERENCES AND FURTHER READING

The following list contains selected publications relevant to Chapter 5: Income and Wealth. Those published by HMSO are available from the addresses shown on the back cover of *Social Trends.*

Economic Trends, HMSO
Employment Gazette, Harrington Kilbride
Family Spending, HMSO
Fiscal Studies, Institute for Fiscal Studies
General Household Survey, HMSO
Households Below Average Income, A Statistical Analysis, HMSO
Inland Revenue Statistics, HMSO

New Earnings Survey, HMSO
Regional Trends, HMSO
Social Security, Departmental Report, HMSO
Social Security Statistics, HMSO
Statistical Supplement to the Autumn Statement, HMSO
Tax/Benefit Model Tables, Department of Social Security
The Personal Income Tax Base: A Comparative Study, OECD
The Tax/benefit Position of Production Workers, OECD
United Kingdom National Accounts (The CSO Blue Book), HMSO

Chapter 6: Expenditure

Personal and household expenditure

- Expenditure on tobacco fell by a third in real terms between 1971 and 1992, while expenditure on post and telecommunications tripled.
  (Table 6.2)

- Average weekly household expenditure per week in 1992 was highest in the South East at £320 and lowest in the North at £236.
  (Table 6.6)

Prices

- A 1951 pound was worth just 7 pence in 1992 - a fourteenth of its original value.
  (Chart 6.1)

- In 1992 average inflation in Greece was nearly four times that in the United Kingdom.
  (Chart 6.12)

Consumer credit and household saving

- In 1992, 4.8 per cent of household income was saved - the biggest proportion since these records began in 1970.
  (Chart 6.17)

- One in six consumer payments in 1992 were made by either plastic payment cards or cheques, compared with only one in twenty in 1976.
  (Table 6.18)

Public expenditure

- Nearly three fifths of the EC budget is spent on agriculture and fisheries.
  (Table 6.22)

- Social security accounted for around a third of general government expenditure in 1992.
  (Table 6.21)

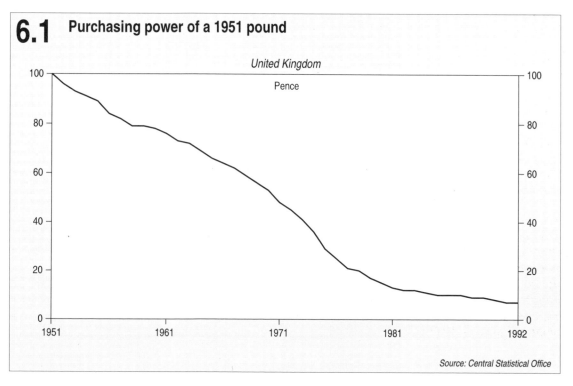

6.1 Purchasing power of a 1951 pound

United Kingdom

Pence

Source: Central Statistical Office

6: EXPENDITURE

Whereas Chapter 5 looks at people's income, this chapter reveals how they spend it and how much of it they manage to save. The chapter also includes statistics on retail prices, consumer credit and public expenditure.

Personal and household expenditure

Table 6.2 gives a detailed breakdown of household expenditure at 1990 constant prices. Total household expenditure increased by 66 per cent in real terms

6.2 Household expenditure[1]

United Kingdom

	1971	1981	1986	1990	1991	1992 Indices/ percentages	1992 £ million (current prices)
Indices at constant 1990 prices							
Food	87	91	95	100	100	101	45,367
Alcoholic drink	72	91	96	100	97	95	24,612
Tobacco	138	122	102	100	97	93	10,124
Clothing and footwear	52	67	92	100	98	99	21,246
Housing	68	81	93	100	100	101	57,561
Fuel and power	86	94	102	100	108	106	14,407
Household goods and services							
Household durables	53	69	86	100	97	100	11,711
Other	66	68	84	100	99	100	12,555
Transport and communication							
Purchase of vehicles	51	59	81	100	79	77	16,132
Running of vehicles	47	65	84	100	98	97	27,784
Other travel	56	70	83	100	97	102	13,284
Post and telecommunications	33	63	80	100	100	101	7,117
Recreation, entertainment and education							
TV, video, etc	19	46	77	100	100	101	8,132
Books, newspapers, etc	101	97	92	100	96	96	5,174
Other	36	62	76	100	99	100	24,295
Other goods and services							
Catering (meals, etc)	55	58	72	100	94	92	32,530
Other goods	44	60	75	100	99	99	14,216
Other services	31	45	71	100	98	95	26,549
Less expenditure by foreign tourists, etc	48	72	94	100	86	87	-8,801
Household expenditure abroad	34	66	78	100	96	100	10,225
Total household expenditure	59	72	85	100	98	98	374,220
Percentage of total household expenditure at current prices							
Food	*20.1*	*16.4*	*13.8*	*12.3*	*12.3*	*12.1*	45,367
Alcoholic drink	*7.3*	*7.3*	*6.9*	*6.4*	*6.6*	*6.6*	24,612
Tobacco	*4.8*	*3.6*	*3.1*	*2.5*	*2.7*	*2.7*	10,124
Clothing and footwear	*8.5*	*6.7*	*7.0*	*6.1*	*5.9*	*5.7*	21,246
Housing	*12.4*	*14.9*	*15.3*	*14.2*	*14.6*	*15.4*	57,561
Fuel and power	*4.5*	*5.1*	*4.6*	*3.6*	*4.0*	*3.8*	14,407
Household goods and services	*7.8*	*6.9*	*6.7*	*6.5*	*6.5*	*6.5*	24,266
Transport and communication	*14.3*	*17.2*	*17.5*	*18.3*	*17.3*	*17.2*	64,317
Recreation, entertainment and education	*8.8*	*9.4*	*9.4*	*10.0*	*10.0*	*10.0*	37,601
Other goods, services and adjustments	*11.4*	*12.5*	*15.6*	*20.0*	*20.0*	*20.0*	74,719
Total	*100.0*	*100.0*	*100.0*	*100.0*	*100.0*	*100.0*	374,220

1 See Appendix, Part 6: Household expenditure.

Source: Central Statistical Office

6.3 Consumers' expenditure at constant prices: by selected item

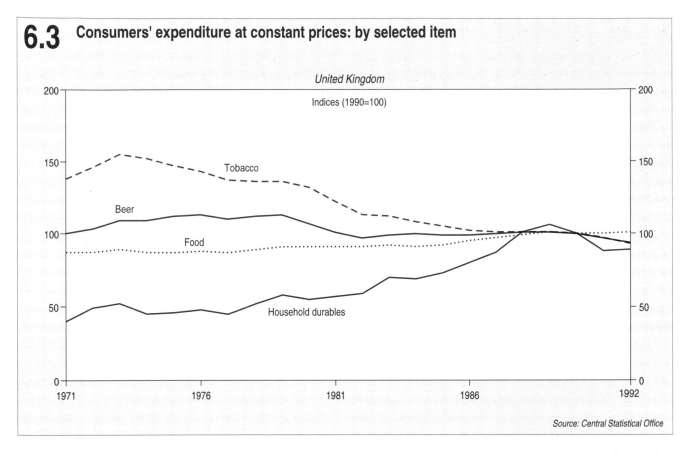

United Kingdom

Indices (1990=100)

Source: Central Statistical Office

between 1971 and 1992. The various components within household expenditure have grown at differing rates over this time period and some of these are illustrated in **Chart 6.3**. Expenditure on tobacco has declined steadily since 1971 so that, in 1992, 33 per cent less was spent on it after allowing for inflation.

6.4 Average weekly expenditure per person: by selected household type, 1992

United Kingdom

One adult:
- Retired[1]
- Retired[2]
- Not retired

One man, one woman:
- Retired[1]
- Retired[2]
- Not retired

One adult, one child

One adult, two children

Two adults, one child

Two adults, two children

£ per person per week   0   50   100   150   200

1 Mainly dependent on state pensions.
2 Not mainly dependent on state pensions.

Source: Central Statistical Office

Spending on services, on the other hand, nearly doubled in constant prices between 1971 and 1990 but then fell by one per cent between 1990 and 1992.

The bottom half of **Table 6.2** shows the changes in the pattern of household spending in current price terms. While expenditure on food increased in real terms between 1971 and 1992, its proportion of total household spending declined by eight percentage points. There was a general trend of spending switching from food to other goods and services.

The average weekly expenditure per person in **Chart 6.4** is shown by selected household type. In 1992, a single working person under retirement age was spending around £190 a week, whereas a single pensioner who was mainly dependant on a state pension was only spending around £70 a week. As far as families were concerned, two adults with two children spent an average of nearly £93 a week per person while two adults with one child spent just over £115 a week per person.

The income of the household affects its pattern of expenditure **(Table 6.5 overleaf)**. Households with less than £100 of disposable income per week spent nearly a quarter of their expenditure on food and a further quarter on housing, fuel, light and power. Those with over £400 of weekly disposable income, on the other hand, spent only 15 per cent of their expenditure on food and only a further 20 per cent on housing, fuel, light and power. People earning between £200 and £400 spent proportionately more than twice the amount on motoring and fares than people below £100.

6.5 Household expenditure: by level of disposable income, 1992

United Kingdom Percentages and £ per week

	Housing	Fuel, light and power	Food	Alcohol and tobacco	Clothing and footwear	Household goods and services	Motoring and fares	Leisure goods and services	Other goods and services	Average expend- iture (= 100%) (£ per week)
Normal weekly disposable income										
Under £100	16.0	10.7	23.6	6.8	5.8	14.9	7.7	10.4	4.1	95.21
£100 -£200	16.7	6.9	21.4	7.2	5.6	12.8	12.8	12.2	4.3	173.18
£200 - £400	18.0	4.6	18.1	6.4	6.2	12.7	16.0	13.5	4.5	287.40
Over £400	17.3	3.2	14.5	5.2	6.1	13.0	18.0	18.4	4.3	509.91
All households	17.4	4.8	17.5	6.0	6.0	13.0	15.8	15.0	4.4	271.83

Source: Central Statistical Office

Household spending varies between the different parts of the United Kingdom **(Table 6.6)**. The South East had the highest average total household expenditure per week in 1992 at £320 while the North had the lowest, at just under £236. In the East Midlands, the South East and the South West, a higher proportion of spending went on housing than on food in 1992; in all other regions, a higher proportion was spent on food than on any other category shown in the table. It is not possible to compare these figures for household expenditure with those published in previous editions of *Social Trends* as mortgage interest payments have replaced imputed rents in housing expenditure. This has particularly affected Northern Ireland.

Households headed by people in the professional and employers and managerial groups have the highest ownership of the consumer durables shown in **Table 6.7**, with the exception of TVs and videos. At 98 to 99 per cent, TVs have reached saturation point for all groups. However, only a third of households had a CD player in 1992, while a quarter had a home computer.

Chart 6.8 uses data from Walls' (food manufacturers) Survey for 1993 which asked parents how their children were spending their pocket money. Children were nearly five times more likely to spend money on crisps, sweets and ice cream than on clothes and twice as likely to buy comics and magazines as books and stationery.

6.6 Household expenditure: by region, 1992

United Kingdom Percentages and £ per week

	Housing	Fuel, light and power	Food	Alcohol and tobacco	Clothing and footwear	Household goods and services	Motoring and fares	Leisure goods and services	Other goods and services	Average expend- iture (= 100%) (£ per week)
United Kingdom	17.4	4.8	17.5	6.0	6.0	13.0	15.8	15.0	4.4	271.83
North	14.0	5.6	19.0	8.4	6.8	12.9	15.9	13.0	4.5	235.53
Yorkshire & Humberside	17.0	5.4	18.6	7.5	6.6	11.5	13.5	15.3	4.7	241.22
East Midlands	17.3	4.8	16.9	6.0	6.3	13.3	16.7	13.8	4.8	272.81
East Anglia	16.8	4.5	18.0	5.5	5.9	16.0	16.1	12.9	4.5	277.43
South East	19.1	4.1	16.1	4.9	5.2	12.7	16.6	17.0	4.3	320.10
South West	19.1	4.5	17.0	5.6	5.1	13.8	15.0	15.8	4.1	270.41
West Midlands	17.4	5.4	19.2	6.5	6.3	12.1	16.5	12.1	4.5	236.64
North West	16.1	5.2	18.0	6.8	6.8	12.9	15.0	14.6	4.5	253.12
England	17.8	4.7	17.3	5.9	5.8	12.9	15.9	15.3	4.4	276.93
Wales	16.8	5.6	18.5	6.2	6.5	14.6	14.5	13.2	4.2	251.22
Scotland	15.1	5.4	19.3	7.6	7.2	13.0	13.7	14.2	4.4	237.67
Northern Ireland	9.8	5.6	20.4	5.8	8.5	14.4	20.7	10.8	3.9	256.55

Source: Central Statistical Office

6.7 Households with durable goods: by socio-economic group of head, 1992

Great Britain   Percentages

	Economically active							
	Professional	Employers and managers	Other non-manual	Skilled manual[1]	Unskilled manual	All economically active	Economically inactive	All heads of households
Television	99	99	98	99	98	99	99	99
Colour	97	98	97	97	93	97	94	96
Black and white only	1	1	2	2	5	2	5	3
Telephone	98	98	93	87	73	91	86	89
Washing machine	96	96	93	93	88	94	79	88
Deep-freezer[2]	94	94	87	91	87	91	76	85
Video	87	91	84	88	73	87	48	72
Microwave oven	68	77	67	71	55	70	41	59
Tumble drier	66	71	56	57	44	60	32	49
CD player	54	53	45	40	29	44	15	33
Home computer	52	41	33	27	21	33	7	23
Dishwasher	41	38	19	12	4	21	7	16

1 Includes semi-skilled manual.
2 Includes fridge-freezer.

Source: General Household Survey

6.8 Percentage of children spending pocket money on selected items, 1993

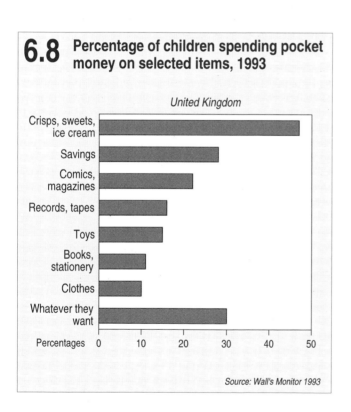

Source: Wall's Monitor 1993

Prices

The growth rate of retail prices in the United Kingdom, usually referred to as the rate of inflation, is measured by changes in the retail prices index (RPI). This index monitors the month to month change in a representative 'basket' of goods and services bought by a typical household and is regarded as an important barometer of the economy of the United Kingdom showing the impact of inflation on family budgets. The index affects us all since it can affect tax allowances, salaries, savings, state benefits and pensions, as these and many other payments are often uprated using the index.

The index is compiled using a representative selection of more than 600 separate goods and services for which price movements are regularly measured in about 180 towns around the country. Around 150 thousand separate price quotations are used each month in compiling the index, one recent addition being the introduction of a foreign holiday component with effect from February 1993.

The 12 monthly change in the RPI fell from its high level in the early 1980s to stay around or below five per cent for most of the period from January 1983 to July 1988. The rate then generally increased to reach a peak of 10.9 per cent in September and October of 1990 **(Chart 6.9)**. It then fell steadily and has been below two per cent since January 1993. In June 1993, the rate fell to 1.2 per cent - the lowest 12 month rate since February 1964.

In the 'basket' of goods and services that is used to compile the RPI, a relative importance or 'weight' is attached to each constituent item. This 'weight' is revised each year using the latest information available from the Family Expenditure Survey. For example, out of a total weight of 1,000, clothing and footwear accounted for 106 in 1961 but for only 58 in 1993, reflecting the fall in the proportion of spending on clothing and footwear.

6.9 Retail prices index

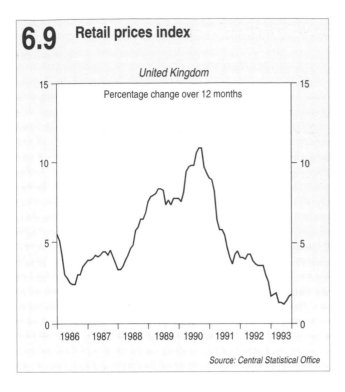

United Kingdom

Percentage change over 12 months

Source: Central Statistical Office

Table 6.10 does not show all the items covered by the RPI but it does illustrate how prices for the more important goods and services in the 'basket' have changed. Between 1991 and 1992, the average annual percentage change in the RPI fell from 5.9 per cent to 3.7 per cent. However, while the overall index increased by 3.7 per cent, tobacco rose by 11 per cent while housing costs fell by 0.7 per cent.

The RPI does not cover households with very high incomes (the top four per cent) or those households with retired people mainly dependent on state pensions and benefits. These households are excluded to make the RPI more representative of typical households. Special price indices for one and two person pensioner households have been calculated separately although for technical reasons they exclude housing costs. In 1992, both pensioner price indices increased at a slower rate than the general RPI excluding housing.

An obvious consequence of rising prices is that the amount of goods and services that can be purchased with a given sum of money, the purchasing power, decreases. **Chart 6.1** illustrates the erosion of the purchasing power of a pound since 1951. Between 1951 and 1971 its purchasing power had halved and by 1976 it had halved again. High inflation in the late 1970s and early 1980s meant that the value continued to drop so that by 1992 the 1951 pound was worth just seven pence - a fourteenth of its original value.

6.10 Index of retail prices: rates of change

United Kingdom

Percentages and weights

	Average annual percentage change							Weights
	1981	1986	1988	1989	1990	1991	1992	1992
General index								
All items	11.9	3.4	4.9	7.8	9.5	5.9	3.7	1,000
All items except housing	10.9	3.0	4.1	5.4	6.9	7.6	4.7	828
All items except mortgage interest payments	12.2	3.6	4.6	5.9	8.1	6.7	4.7	936
Food	8.4	3.4	3.5	5.6	8.1	5.2	2.1	152
Catering	9.6	6.3	6.6	6.3	8.5	10.0	6.3	47
Alcoholic drink	16.9	4.5	5.1	5.6	9.7	12.4	6.4	80
Tobacco	23.5	9.9	3.3	2.9	6.8	14.3	11.0	36
Housing	18.1	5.7	8.9	20.3	21.0	-1.8	-0.7	172
Fuel and light	21.3	1.3	2.5	5.6	8.0	7.9	2.2	47
Clothing and footwear	1.4	2.8	3.3	5.3	4.6	3.0	0.3	59
Household goods	6.1	2.7	3.7	4.0	4.8	6.2	3.3	77
Household services	17.0	4.8	4.8	5.3	6.3	8.3	5.8	48
Personal goods and services	9.0	5.2	4.8	6.8	7.5	8.7	6.6	40
Leisure goods	7.7	1.8	2.5	3.2	4.7	4.7	2.6	47
Leisure services[1]	12.4	4.8	6.4	6.5	8.2	11.5	8.1	32
Motoring expenditure	11.9	-1.4	4.5	5.5	6.1	7.4	6.8	143
Fares and other travel costs	10.7	6.6	5.9	7.2	7.1	9.8	6.2	20
Pensioner indices[2]								
All items except housing								
One-person households	11.4	3.2	3.7	5.5	7.5	7.1	3.5	1,000
Two-person households	11.6	3.2	3.8	5.4	7.5	7.2	3.9	1,000

1 Foreign holidays were introduced into the retail prices index, within the leisure services component, with effect from February 1993.
2 Pensioner indices relate to households in which at least 75 per cent of total income is derived from state pensions and benefits.

Source: Central Statistical Office

6.11 Purchasing power of the pound in the European Community[1], 1981 and 1992

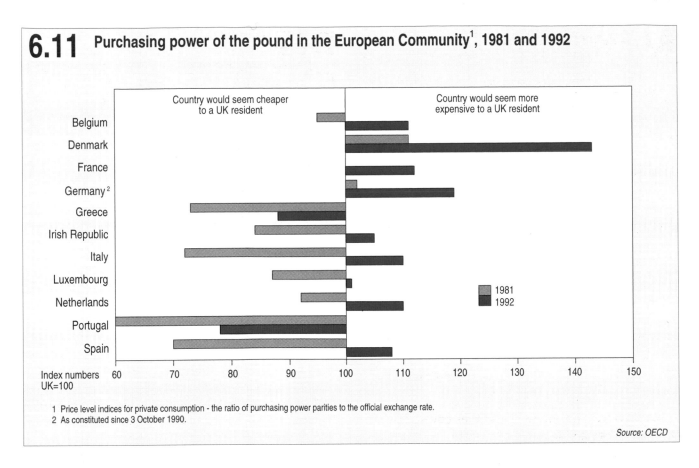

Country would seem cheaper to a UK resident

Country would seem more expensive to a UK resident

1981
1992

Index numbers UK=100

1 Price level indices for private consumption - the ratio of purchasing power parities to the official exchange rate.
2 As constituted since 3 October 1990.

Source: OECD

Purchasing power also varies between countries. **Chart 6.11** shows the purchasing power of the pound in the European Community (EC). The purchasing power parity between the United Kingdom and another country is the amount of that country's currency needed to buy goods and services costing one pound in the United Kingdom. If this is greater than the official exchange rate the country would seem more expensive to a United Kingdom resident. This allows a quick and simple comparison of those countries which would appear more expensive to a United Kingdom resident and those which would appear cheaper. In 1981, only Germany and Denmark would have seemed expensive to someone from the United Kingdom, but by 1992, these had been joined by seven other countries and only Greece and Portugal were cheaper.

As the member states of the EC develop closer ties, it is useful to draw some comparisons between them. Greece had the highest average annual inflation rate of all the EC member states between 1991 and 1992 **(Chart 6.12)**. At nearly 16 per cent it was more than four times the rate of the United Kingdom. Denmark had the lowest rate at 2.1 per cent, closely followed by Belgium and France.

Most goods and services are purchased from people's earnings. **Table 6.13** illustrates how price levels and price changes vary over time by showing how long it would take someone to earn enough to pay for certain goods. The table is based on the net income of a married man on average earnings with two children under 11 whose wife was not earning and a single woman on average earnings with a child. Between 1971 and 1993, the length of time necessary to work for all items fell for both the married man and the single woman. There is also now a greater earnings parity between the two categories in terms of the table definition. Whereas in 1971 a single woman had to

6.12 Change in consumer prices: EC comparison, 1991-1992

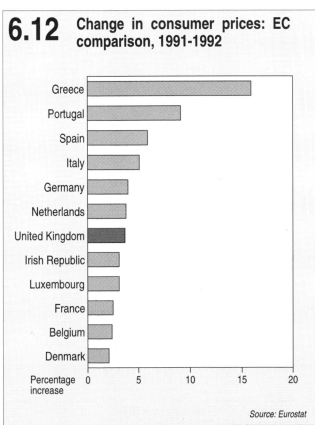

Percentage increase

Source: Eurostat

6.13 Length of time necessary to work to pay for selected commodities and services[1]

Great Britain	Married couple with husband only working[2]		Single female parent with child	
	1971	1993	1971	1993
Hours and minutes				
1 large loaf (white sliced)	9	5	13	6
1lb of rump steak	56	35	83	42
500g of butter (home produced)	19	12	29	14
1lb tomatoes	20	6	30	7
1lb apples	12	3	17	4
1 pint of fresh milk	5	3	7	4
1 dozen eggs (55-60g)	22	9	33	11
100g of coffee (instant)	22	11	33	14
1 pint of beer (draught bitter)	14	12	20	14
20 cigarettes (king size filter)	22	20	33	24
Motor car licence	40:20	18:16	59:54	21:51
Colour television licence	19:21	11:42	28:45	13:59
1 litre of petrol (4 star)	8	5	12	6

1 Length of time necessary for a person on average hourly adult earnings for all industries and services to work so that his/her net income pays for the various goods. At April.
2 Married man with non-earning wife and two children under 11.

Source: Central Statistical Office

work ten minutes longer than a married man to earn enough to buy a pound of tomatoes, in 1993 she had to work only one minute more. One of the more noticeable differences is the time taken to pay for a motor car licence. A married man has seen the time taken approximately halved, from 40 hours 20 minutes in 1971 to 18 hours 16 minutes in 1993, but a single woman has seen the time cut by almost two thirds, from 59 hours 54 minutes to 21 hours 51 minutes.

Consumer credit and household saving

6.15 Composition of consumer credit

United Kingdom			Percentages and £ billion	
	1982	1987	1991	1992
Bank credit card lending	12.7	16.7	18.2	18.7
Bank loans[1]	66.5	62.7	62.8	62.6
Finance houses[2]	8.3	11.9	10.2	9.5
Insurance companies	2.0	2.5	2.8	2.9
Retailers	10.5	6.0	4.7	4.9
Building Society loans[3]	0.0	0.2	1.3	1.4
Credit outstanding at end of year (= 100%)(£ billion)	15.9	36.2	53.8	52.9

1 Banks and all other institutions authorised to take deposits under the *Banking Act 1987.*
2 Finance houses and other credit companies (excluding institutions authorised to take deposits under the *Banking Act 1987*).
3 Building Society unsecured loans to individuals or companies (i.e. Class 3 loans as defined in the *Building Societies Act 1986*).

Source: Central Statistical Office

Consumer credit in the United Kingdom has increased substantially since 1976 **(Chart 6.14)**. In cash terms, it rose from £5.5 billion in 1976 to £53.8 billion in 1991, but then fell slightly to £52.9 billion in 1992. In real terms, the amount outstanding more than trebled between 1976 and 1989, but then fell by nine per cent to just over £15.2 billion in 1992 (at 1976 prices). These figures exclude borrowing for house purchase. Information on mortgage debt can be found in Chapter 8.

Bank loans still remain the main source of consumer credit in the United Kingdom, although their overall share continues to decline to stand at just under 63 per cent in 1992 **(Table 6.15)**. Bank credit card lending, on the other hand, continues to rise steadily accounting for 13 per cent of outstanding credit in 1982 and 19 per

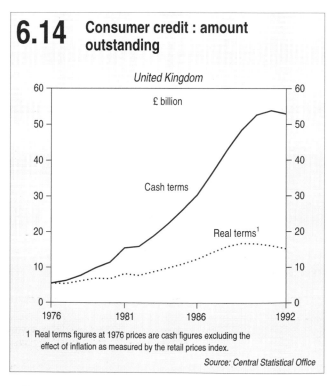

6.14 Consumer credit : amount outstanding

United Kingdom

£ billion

Cash terms

Real terms[1]

1 Real terms figures at 1976 prices are cash figures excluding the effect of inflation as measured by the retail prices index.

Source: Central Statistical Office

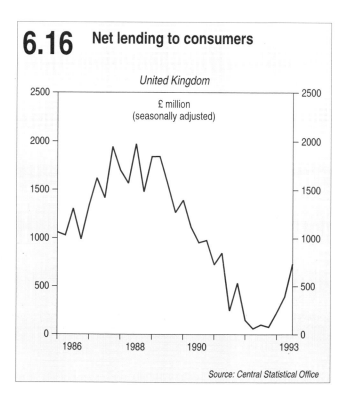

6.16 Net lending to consumers

United Kingdom

£ million (seasonally adjusted)

Source: Central Statistical Office

6.17 Household saving as a percentage of household disposable income

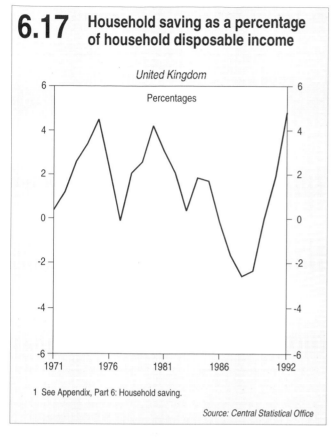

United Kingdom

Percentages

1 See Appendix, Part 6: Household saving.

Source: Central Statistical Office

cent in 1992. Retailers accounted for only five per cent of consumer credit in 1992, half the proportion of ten years earlier.

The recent path of consumer credit is best measured by figures on net lending to consumers **(Chart 6.16)**. These show that net lending peaked at nearly £2 billion in the third quarter of 1988 and then fell sharply to a low of £60 million in the second quarter of 1992. It has been recovering since then, and was £0.7 billion in the third quarter of 1993 - still only a third of the level experienced during the peak years of the 1980s credit boom.

If people are spending less, as the country has experienced in recent times, then one alternative is for them to save instead. During the period from 1986 to 1989, household saving as a percentage of household disposable income was negative **(Chart 6.17)** that is, the total of all households' current expenditure exceeded their disposable income (sometimes referred to as dissaving). After 1990 the figure became positive and in 1992 it reached 4.8 per cent. Since household savings are measured as the difference between two much larger figures (disposable income and current expenditure), the estimates are subject to a wide margin of error.

Consumers can choose to pay for goods and services by a variety of methods of payment. **Table 6.18** looks at how the methods have changed since 1976; it combines regular payments, such as those for gas, electricity and telephone bills, and spontaneous payments which are made face to face at retail outlets, to other individuals and for such items as entertainment and mail order goods.

Between 1976 and 1992, there was a swing of 17 percentage points from cash payments to non-cash payments. Of the non-cash payments, cheques accounted for the largest proportion throughout the period, although the number of payments by this method fell by a third. Conversely, over the same period, the proportion of payments by credit and charge cards more than doubled. Those by debit cards increased more than fivefold in the three years from 1989 to 1992. There has also been a more modest rise in the number of standing orders and direct debits from 21 per cent in 1976 to 25 per cent in 1992.

6.18 Consumer payment: by method

Great Britain

Percentages

	1976	1981	1984	1989	1990	1991	1992
All payments							
Cash[1]	93	88	86	80	78	78	76
Non-cash	7	12	14	20	22	22	24
Non-cash payments							
Cheque	68	68	64	55	52	50	46
Standing Order/Direct Debit	21	20	22	23	23	24	25
All plastic payment cards	7	9	13	18	20	23	25
of which:-							
Credit/charge card	6	8	12	15	15	14	14
Retailer card	-	1	-	1	1	1	1
Debit card	0	0	0	2	4	8	11
Other[2]	2	2	1	4	4	3	4

1 Cash payments under fifty pence in 1976, and £1 from 1981 onwards, are excluded.
2 Includes deductions made directly from wages and salaries, and payments made by Postal Order.

Source: Research Surveys of Great Britain Ltd for
Association for Payment Clearing Services

6.19 Type of savings: by social class[1], age and sex, 1993[2]

Great Britain   Percentages

| | Social class | | | | Age | | | | | All |
	AB	C1	C2	DE	16-34	34-64	65 and over	Males	Females	adults
Percentage of adults holding:										
Building society account	78	70	68	49	62	68	62	63	65	65
Bank account	94	87	83	66	77	85	77	83	79	81
Premium Bonds	45	34	25	15	16	35	34	28	28	28
Unit trusts or investment trusts	19	13	6	2	4	13	7	11	7	9
Shares[3]	27	14	8	4	8	16	9	14	9	12
Government privatisation shares	23	13	7	3	5	14	12	13	8	10
National Savings Bank Investment/										
Ordinary account	11	13	10	7	10	10	10	10	10	10
National Savings certificates/bonds	14	12	3	4	5	7	13	8	7	7

1 See Appendix, Part 6: Social class.
2 Fieldwork took place in February and March 1993.
3 Excluding government privatisations.

Source: Council of Mortgage Lenders

Table 6.19 looks at the sort of ways people saved their money in 1993. Over four fifths of the adults have bank accounts - the most popular form of saving at 81 per cent. Building society accounts are held by 65 per cent of adults, a rise of 50 percentage points since 1968. There are large differences between the social classes shown in the table. Nearly all people in class AB have a bank account compared with only two thirds of those in class DE. The difference is even more marked for unit and investment trusts; people in class AB are nearly ten times more likely to hold them than people in class DE.

Public expenditure

All the items discussed so far have concentrated on spending by individuals and households. This next section examines spending by general government (central government and local authorities) and the EC.

Like individuals, government spends money on goods, services and interest payments but it also has transfer payments to make, such as pensions, grants and loans. The wider measure including these payments is known as general government expenditure (GGE) and

6.20 General government expenditure as a percentage of GDP[1]

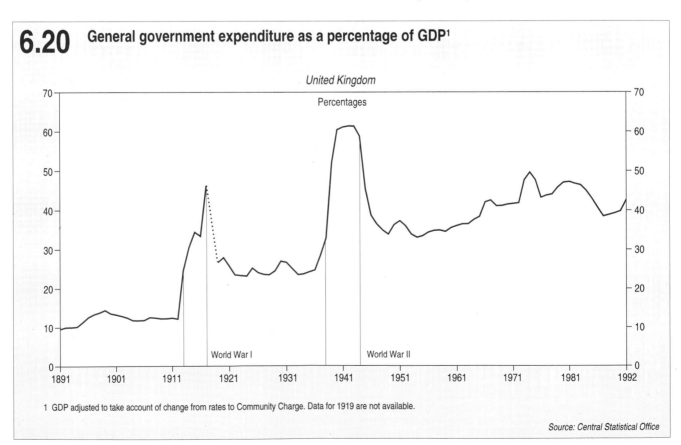

United Kingdom

Percentages

1 GDP adjusted to take account of change from rates to Community Charge. Data for 1919 are not available.

Source: Central Statistical Office

is used for analysing overall trends in public spending. Growth in GGE may be compared to growth in the economy as a whole by expressing it as a percentage of gross domestic product (GDP).

Chart 6.20 shows that two of the peaks in this percentage coincided with the periods of the First and Second World Wars, at nearly 50 and 60 per cent respectively. Although GGE as a percentage of GDP fell back at the end of each war, it never dropped as far as its pre-war level. During the Korean War, the percentage again rose slightly (1951 and 1952) and in 1975 the percentage reached a post-war high at nearly 50 per cent. It then fell away again before rising as the United Kingdom entered the recession of the early 1980s, reaching just over 47 per cent in 1982. Ten years after this, it is showing a slight rise once more, again mainly due to the effects of the recession.

6.21 General government expenditure: by function

United Kingdom	Percentages and £ billion			
	1981	1986	1991	1992
Defence[1]	10.8	11.8	9.2	9.7
Public order and safety	3.7	4.2	5.6	5.5
Education	12.2	11.9	12.9	12.7
Health	11.4	11.8	13.7	13.8
Social security	26.6	30.8	32.3	33.1
Housing and community amenities	6.1	5.0	4.0	4.3
Recreational and cultural affairs	1.4	1.5	1.7	1.6
Fuel and energy	0.3	-0.7	-1.5	-0.6
Agriculture, forestry and fishing	1.4	1.3	1.2	1.1
Mining, mineral resources, manufacturing and construction	3.0	1.2	0.7	0.5
Transport and communication	3.6	2.3	3.0	2.5
General public services	3.9	3.9	4.9	4.8
Other economic affairs and services	2.5	2.5	2.0	2.0
Other expenditure	13.1	12.7	9.4	9.1
Total expenditure (= 100%)(£ billion)	117.1	162.3	228.3	254.1

1 Includes contributions by other countries towards the United Kingdom's cost of the gulf conflict - £2.1 billion in 1991.

Source: Central Statistical Office

6.22 European Community expenditure: by sector

	Percentages and £ billion			
	1981	1986	1991	1993
Agriculture and fisheries	65.5	66.0	61.6	58.8
Regional policy	13.6	7.1	11.8	13.6
Social policy	3.5	7.0	7.5	8.3
Cooperation with developing countries	4.2	3.0	4.1	4.6
Research, energy, industry and transport	1.8	2.2	3.2	3.4
Administration	5.3	4.4	5.0	5.2
Other	6.2	10.2	4.0	1.8
Total expenditure (£ billion)(= 100%)	9.8	23.2	37.6	49.4

Source: Commission of the European Communities

A more detailed breakdown of general government expenditure by function is given in **Table 6.21**. Expenditure totalled £254 billion in 1992, a rise of just over 11 per cent since 1991. The table is compiled on the same basis as the *CSO National Accounts 'Blue Book'* and treats privatisation proceeds as an offset to expenditure on each function. It is possible therefore, as in the case of fuel and energy in 1991, to have a net expenditure figure which is negative.

Social security accounted for about a third of total government expenditure in 1992, rising by more than ten billion pounds between 1991 and 1992. The next highest area of government expenditure was health which remained at nearly 14 per cent of total expenditure.

A different look at expenditure is taken in **Table 6.22** with a breakdown of EC expenditure by sector. Agriculture and fisheries has accounted for the largest percentage over the years shown, taking nearly three fifths of the budget in 1993, although its importance has lessened. Social policy, research, energy, industry and transport have risen over the period shown, the proportion on the latter nearly doubling while regional policy is expected to recover its position in 1993 to the same proportions as in 1981. In the ten years between 1981 and 1991, the total expenditure of the EC increased fivefold.

REFERENCES AND FURTHER READING

The following list contains selected publications relevant to Chapter 6: Expenditure. Those published by HMSO are available from the addresses shown on the back cover of *Social Trends*.

British Tourism Survey, Monthly, British Tourist Authority
Business Monitor MM23 (Retail Prices Index), HMSO
Credit Business First Release, CSO
Economic Trends, HMSO
Employment Gazette, HMSO
Family Spending - A Report on the 1992 Family Expenditure Survey, HMSO
Financial Statistics, HMSO
Financial Statement and Budget Report, HMSO

General Household Survey, HMSO
International Passenger Survey, HMSO
Local Government Financial Statistics England, HMSO
Regional Trends, HMSO
Scottish Economic Bulletin, HMSO
The Government's Expenditure Plans, HMSO
United Kingdom National Accounts (The CSO Blue Book), HMSO
Welsh Economic Trends, HMSO

Social Trends 24, © Crown copyright 1994

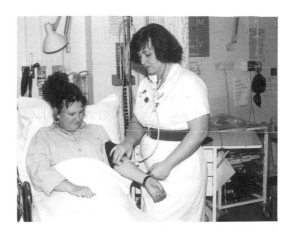

Chapter 7: Health and Personal Social Services

The nation's health

- On the mortality rates of 1994 a baby boy can expect to reach almost his 74th birthday, whilst a girl can expect to reach her 79th. *(Chart 7.1)*

- The number of cot deaths halved between 1991 and 1992. *(Chart 7.4)*

- In 1992 death rates from lung cancer for women were less than half those for men. *(Chart 7.5)*

Diet

- We drank 1.7 pints of skimmed and semi-skimmed milk per person per week in 1992, virtually the same amount as whole milk. *(Chart 7.15)*

Social habits and health

- The percentage of men who smoked cigarettes fell by over 20 percentage points between 1972 and 1990, whilst that for women fell by 12 percentage points. *(Chart 7.17)*

- Around a third of men in both the North and North West drank more than the recommended maximum sensible limits of alcohol in 1990 - double the proportion in East Anglia. *(Chart 7.18)*

Health services

- The number of day cases dealt with in NHS hospitals increased by 20 per cent between 1990-91 and 1991-92. *(Table 7.24)*

- Around 7.4 million people in the United Kingdom were covered by private health insurance in 1991, slightly less than in 1990. *(Chart 7.32)*

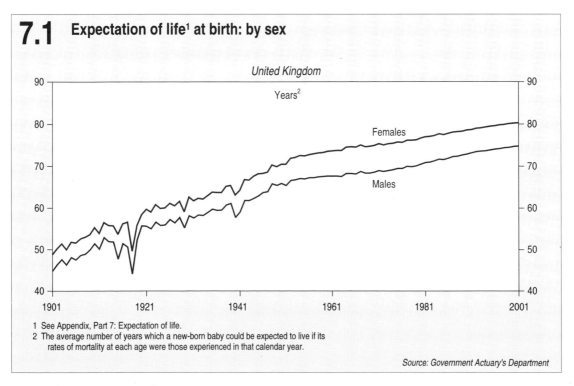

7.1 **Expectation of life¹ at birth: by sex**

United Kingdom

Years²

1 See Appendix, Part 7: Expectation of life.
2 The average number of years which a new-born baby could be expected to live if its rates of mortality at each age were those experienced in that calendar year.

Source: Government Actuary's Department

The nation's health

All three countries in Great Britain, together with Northern Ireland, have produced health strategies designed to address the major causes of premature death and preventable illness. The latest are the English *Health of the Nation* and the Scottish *Scotland's Health: A Challenge to us all* published in July 1992. All have set specific targets for priority areas. Priorities and targets vary between the four strategies although common to all are circulatory diseases, certain cancers and accidents and their associated risk factors, such as smoking.

The number of years we can expect to live is a good indicator of the health of the nation. The improvements that have occurred in health care, education, housing and nutrition throughout this century are reflected in the longevity shown in **Chart 7.1**. On the mortality rates expected in 1994, a baby boy can be expected to live until nearly his 74th birthday and a baby girl until her 79th. In comparison on the mortality rates of 50 years ago they would only reach their 62nd and 67th birthdays respectively. The expectation of life is currently increasing by about two years every decade.

Increases in the number of years we can expect to live have been accompanied by a large reduction in levels of infant mortality over the last 70 years **(Chart 7.2)**. Recently, as very low levels of infant mortality have been reached, improvements have been less pronounced. In 1992 the rate stood at 6.6 per thousand live births, which is about a quarter less than the rate five years ago. Differences in infant mortality between the social classes remain - rates are higher for babies whose fathers are in the unskilled and semi-skilled manual groups (see Social Trends 23, Chart 7.2).

In 1992 about five per cent of male, and about four per cent of female, infant deaths were due to infectious diseases **(Table 7.3)**. As children grow up they become more exposed to infection and build up resistance either naturally, as a result of exposure to disease, or artificially as a result of immunisation **(see Table 7.21)**.

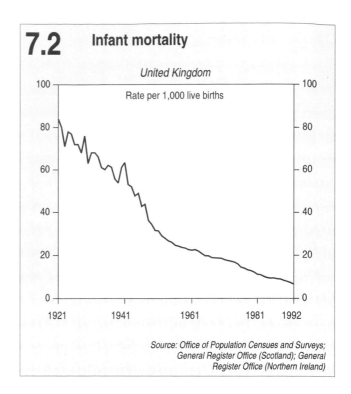

7.2 Infant mortality

United Kingdom

Rate per 1,000 live births

Source: Office of Population Censuses and Surveys; General Register Office (Scotland); General Register Office (Northern Ireland)

7.3   Selected causes of death[1]: by sex and age, 1992

United Kingdom   Percentages and thousands

	Under 1	1-14	15-39	40-64	65-79	80 and over	All ages
Males							
Infectious diseases	4.8	5.1	1.7	0.7	0.4	0.3	0.5
Cancer	1.0	17.3	13.5	34.3	31.6	20.9	28.0
Circulatory diseases[2]	4.0	4.0	10.7	43.8	48.2	47.3	45.5
Respiratory diseases	11.9	5.1	3.4	5.3	10.3	16.7	11.1
Injury and poisoning	17.6	34.2	52.7	6.6	1.3	1.2	4.2
All other causes	60.8	34.2	18.0	9.3	8.3	13.5	10.7
All males (= 100%)(thousands)	1.1	1.3	10.2	58.4	140.9	94.9	306.6
Females							
Infectious diseases	4.3	4.8	1.9	0.6	0.4	0.3	0.4
Cancer	1.5	18.0	33.3	51.8	30.6	14.2	24.3
Circulatory diseases[2]	5.6	4.4	10.7	26.7	46.6	52.3	46.6
Respiratory diseases	10.6	5.6	3.4	5.8	9.2	13.7	11.1
Injury and poisoning	16.8	25.8	28.9	4.0	1.4	1.4	2.2
All other causes	61.3	41.4	21.8	11.1	11.8	18.0	15.3
All females (= 100%)(thousands)	0.7	0.9	4.8	36.4	111.5	169.9	324.2

1 See Appendix, Part 7: Death certificates.
2 Includes heart attacks and strokes.

Source: Office of Population Censuses and Surveys; General Register Office (Scotland); General Register Office (Northern Ireland)

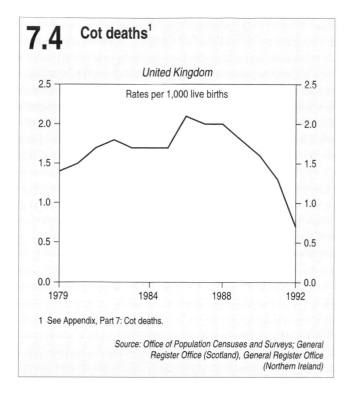

7.4 Cot deaths[1]

United Kingdom

Rates per 1,000 live births

1 See Appendix, Part 7: Cot deaths.

Source: Office of Population Censuses and Surveys; General Register Office (Scotland), General Register Office (Northern Ireland)

aged 65 and over. Conversely the proportion of deaths due to circulatory diseases increased tenfold from age under one to age 80 plus.

Some infant deaths occur without warning where the child appears otherwise perfectly healthy. The death rate from these so-called cot deaths, or more correctly, Sudden Infant Death Syndrome, halved between 1991 and 1992, to 0.7 per thousand live births - about a third of the number five years ago **(Chart 7.4)**. However, a certain amount of confusion has existed in the use of this classification of infant death, simply because it contains unexplained deaths. Recent recommendations by experts to avoid cot deaths include placing the baby to sleep on its back, keeping the room temperature between 16 and 20 degrees Centigrade, and not over-wrapping the baby with clothes. Parents have also been advised to avoid exposing the baby to cigarette smoke during the period before birth and afterwards.

The death rate from stomach cancer has declined over the past 20 years amongst both men and women; it halved in women between 1972 and 1992 **(Chart 7.5)**. Lung cancer is one of the most preventable carcinomas; at least 80 per cent of cases are due to tobacco smoke, inhaled either passively or actively. In 1992 the rates for lung cancer deaths in women were around half those for men. However, male death rates from lung cancer fell by a quarter in the 20 years to 1992, whilst female rates actually increased by over three quarters over the

In other age groups different causes of death are more prevalent. For example, more than half of deaths amongst males aged 15 to 39 were as a result of injury or poisoning, nearly double the female proportion for the same age group. However, for both sexes, these proportions declined to just over one per cent for people

7.5 Standardised mortality rates[1] from cancers: by sex and selected sites

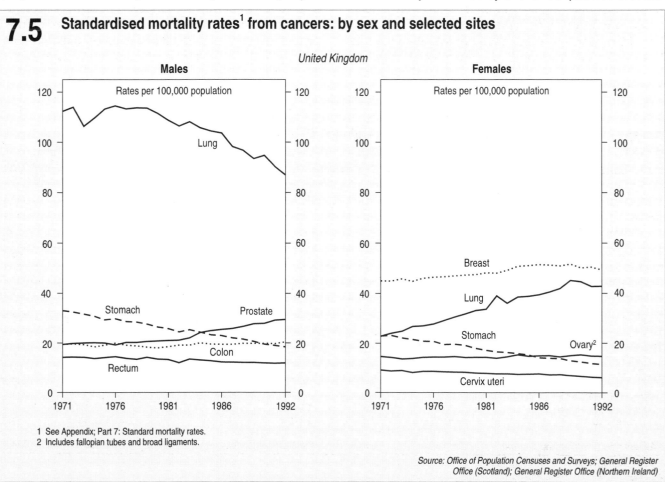

United Kingdom

Males

Rates per 100,000 population

Lung

Stomach

Prostate

Colon

Rectum

Females

Rates per 100,000 population

Breast

Lung

Stomach

Ovary[2]

Cervix uteri

1 See Appendix; Part 7: Standard mortality rates.
2 Includes fallopian tubes and broad ligaments.

Source: Office of Population Censuses and Surveys; General Register Office (Scotland); General Register Office (Northern Ireland)

same period. Overall the number of deaths from lung cancer per head of population in the United Kingdom is amongst the highest in Europe **(Chart 7.6)**.

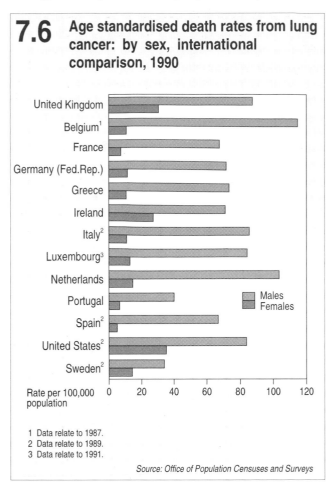

7.6 **Age standardised death rates from lung cancer: by sex, international comparison, 1990**

United Kingdom
Belgium[1]
France
Germany (Fed.Rep.)
Greece
Ireland
Italy[2]
Luxembourg[3]
Netherlands
Portugal
Spain[2]
United States[2]
Sweden[2]

Males
Females

Rate per 100,000 population

1 Data relate to 1987.
2 Data relate to 1989.
3 Data relate to 1991.

Source: Office of Population Censuses and Surveys

Some infectious diseases occur in epidemics and are liable to large annual fluctuations. For example, an upsurge of whooping cough generally occurs every four years, though the peaks of just over 70 thousand cases in 1978 and 1982 were notable because of the fall in the numbers being immunised against the disease in the mid-1970s. (Further information on vaccination and immunisation can be found in Table 7.23.) Tuberculosis, the notifications of which had been declining, has increased since 1988 **(Chart 7.7)** although deaths from tuberculosis have continued to decline.

The Human Immunodeficiency Virus (HIV) is the virus which causes Acquired Immune Deficiency Syndrome (AIDS). A characteristic of the virus is the long period between infection and the onset of AIDS. For example, ten years after infection only approximately half of those infected will have developed AIDS, though a substantial number will have symptoms associated with immunodeficiency. In the 12 months to the end of June 1993 nearly 1.6 thousand new AIDS cases were reported in England and Wales. The 1991 based projections shown in **Chart 7.8** estimate that by 1997 heterosexual sex will account for about one third of new AIDS diagnoses, with the numbers still increasing, although infection transmitted through sex between men will still dominate the picture.

Table 7.9 shows that up to the end of June 1993 there had been nearly 7.7 thousand cases and nearly 4.8 thousand deaths in the United Kingdom from AIDS since the first case was reported in 1982. The majority of men dying from AIDS were probably infected as a

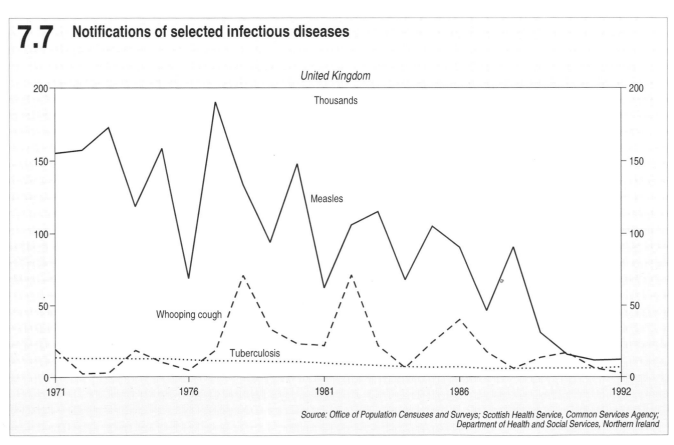

7.7 **Notifications of selected infectious diseases**

United Kingdom

Thousands

Measles

Whooping cough

Tuberculosis

Source: Office of Population Censuses and Surveys; Scottish Health Service, Common Services Agency; Department of Health and Social Services, Northern Ireland

7.8 AIDS: actual and projected new cases per year

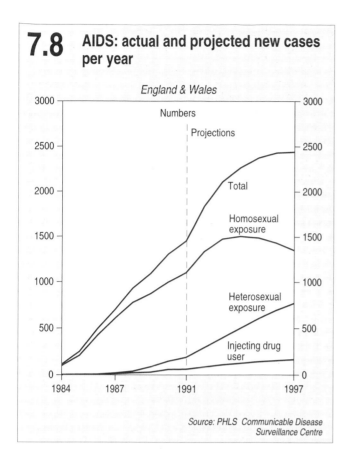

Source: PHLS Communicable Disease Surveillance Centre

result of intercourse with a homosexual partner, whilst most women reported were probably infected abroad through intercourse with a man. Until a cure is found for the disease the only ways to limit its spread are public health measures, such as health education to change peoples' sexual and drug use behaviour and screening donated blood.

7.9 AIDS - total cases and deaths: by exposure category, to 30 June 1993[1]

United Kingdom			Numbers
	Cases		
	Males	Females	Deaths
Sexual intercourse			
Between men	5,899	.	3,746
Between men and women	451	329	371
Injecting drug use	263	112	223
Blood			
Blood factor (eg haemophilia)	361	6	291
Blood/tissue transfer	13	31	27
Mother to child	43	47	43
Other/undetermined	91	14	61
Total	7,140	559	4,794

1 Cumulative reported cases and deaths up to the end of June 1993.

Source: PHLS Communicable Disease Surveillance Centre; Communicable Diseases (Scotland) Unit

7.10 Selected sexually transmitted diseases: by sex

United Kingdom			Thousands
	1981	1986	1991[1]
New cases seen			
Male			
Syphilis	3	2	1
Gonorrhoea	37	28	12
Herpes simplex	7	11	11
Non-specific genital infection	99	118	77
Female			
Syphilis	1	1	-
Gonorrhoea	21	18	8
Herpes simplex	5	9	12
Non-specific genital infection	33	56	46

1 Data refer to 1991-92 for Wales.

Source: Department of Health; Welsh Office; Scottish Health Service, Common Services Agency; Department of Health and Social Services, Northern Ireland

There were around 168 thousand new cases of sexually transmitted diseases (excluding HIV) seen at NHS genito-urinary medicine clinics in the United Kingdom in 1991 **(Table 7.10)**. With the exception of herpes simplex, the number of new cases for each of the conditions shown in the table was lower in 1991 than five years earlier. These figures do not give a complete picture of the incidence of these diseases as patients may also receive treatment elsewhere. They do however give a useful indication of the trends as it is estimated that about 90 per cent of patients are treated by NHS genito-urinary medicine clinics.

Amongst those who had some natural teeth, nearly two thirds of professional, compared with just over a third of unskilled manual workers, attended the dentist for a regular check-up in 1991 **(Table 7.11)**. The percentage of adults visiting the dentist for a regular check-up was lower in 1991 than in 1985 in all socio-economic groups, except in the unskilled manual group.

7.11 Percentage of adults[1] who went to the dentist for a regular check-up: by socio-economic group, 1985 and 1991

Great Britain		Percentages
	1985	1991
Professional	68	63
Employers and managers	62	59
Intermediate and junior non-manual	58	54
Skilled manual	41	41
Semi-skilled manual	39	37
Unskilled manual	30	36
All adults[1]	50	48

1 Aged 16 and over with some natural teeth.

Source: General Household Survey

7.12 Percentage of adults[1] with no natural teeth: by age and socio-economic group, 1991

Great Britain   Percentages

	16-24	25-34	35-44	45-54	55-64	65-74	75 and over	All aged 16 and over
Professional	0	-	2	2	7	23	32	5
Employers and managers	0	-	2	5	15	33	51	10
Intermediate and junior								
* non-manual*	-	1	2	7	23	42	56	14
Skilled manual	1	1	5	13	33	55	75	20
Semi-skilled manual	0	-	4	18	44	59	77	25
Unskilled manual	0	4	8	26	49	75	81	34
All socio-economic groups	-	1	3	10	29	49	67	17

1 Aged 16 and over.

Source: General Household Survey

In 1991 more than a quarter of people aged 45 to 54 in the unskilled manual group had lost all their natural teeth, compared with only two per cent of those in the professional group **(Table 7.12)**.

7.13 Percentage of adults[1] wearing glasses or contact lenses: by sex and socio-economic group, 1992

Great Britain   Percentages

	Males	Females	All adults[1]
Professional	70	61	68
Employers and managers	59	65	61
Intermediate and junior			
* non-manual*	54	60	58
Skilled manual	44	59	47
Semi-skilled manual	43	54	49
Unskilled manual	42	66	57
All socio-economic groups[1]	51	60	55

1 Aged 16 and over who are economically active.

Source: General Household Survey

7.14 Formally notified cases of food poisoning

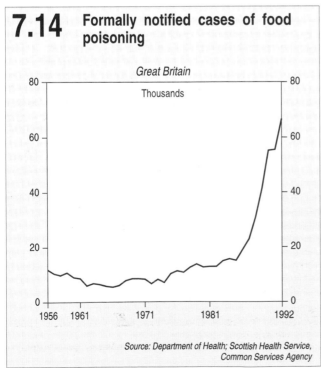

Great Britain

Thousands

Source: Department of Health; Scottish Health Service, Common Services Agency

Amongst the economically active, with the exception of those in professional occupations, females are more likely than males to wear glasses or contact lenses **(Table 7.13)**. Men in the higher social classes are more likely to wear glasses or contact lenses than those in manual occupations. The same is not true for women where the highest proportion of glasses/contact lens wearing is in the unskilled manual group

Formally notified cases of food poisoning in Great Britain have increased nearly sixfold in the last 35 years, and have doubled in only the last four years **(Chart 7.14)**. However increased awareness of food poisoning by the public and the medical profession towards the end of 1988 may have contributed to this increase.

Diet

There have been marked changes in the type of food households eat over the past 30 years **(Chart 7.15)**. Doctors advise eating less fats containing saturated fatty acids, to avoid high levels of cholesterol in the blood and the risk of heart disease. As a result there has been a switch in household consumption from butter, firstly towards margarine and, more recently, to low and reduced fat spreads. The average person drinks less milk today than in 1961. In 1992 we drank virtually the same amount of whole milk as skimmed and semi-skimmed milks, at 1.7 pints per person per week.

Similarly the amount of carcase beef and lamb (ie excluding meat products) we eat has generally fallen over the last 30 years. In 1992 each person ate, on average, under five ounces of beef and veal per week, only about half of the amount consumed in 1961. Lamb and mutton consumption has fallen more sharply; the average amount consumed in 1992 had dropped to almost a third of the figure 30 years ago. Conversely the consumption of poultry has increased to over eight ounces per week, more than twice the figure 25 years ago.

7.15 Changing patterns in the consumption of food at home

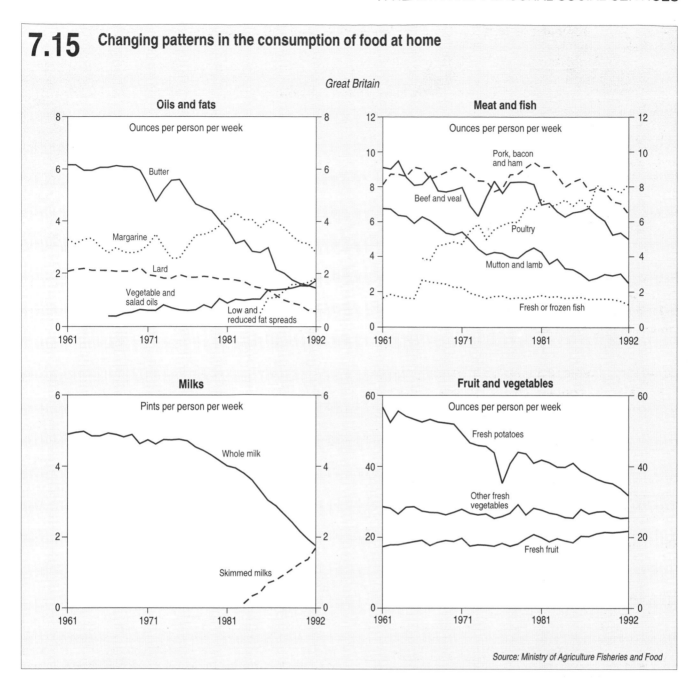

Great Britain

Source: Ministry of Agriculture Fisheries and Food

Social habits and health

Smoking is the greatest cause of preventable death in this country and can lead to, among other diseases, lung cancer, respiratory disease or heart disease. The definition of heavy smoking used in **Table 7.16** is 20 or more cigarettes per day. The proportion of men and women smoking heavily is greatest in unskilled and manual occupations, whereas the proportion with excessive alcohol consumption is highest amongst those in the employers and managers socio-economic group.

The proportion of men who smoked cigarettes fell by over 20 percentage points between 1972 and 1990, from 52 to 31 per cent, while the proportion of women has also fallen but at a slower pace, from 41 to 29 per cent **(Chart 7.17)**. The number of men who have never,

7.16 Heavy cigarette smoking[1] and consumption of alcohol above sensible limits[2]: by socio-economic group[3], 1990

Great Britain				Percentages
	Males		Females	
	Smoking	Alcohol	Smoking	Alcohol
Professional	5	26	6	14
Employers and managers	12	30	7	14
Intermediate and junior				
non-manual	8	26	7	11
Skilled manual	17	28	11	9
Semi-skilled manual	18	26	12	9
Unskilled manual	22	26	13	6
All socio-economic groups[3]	14	27	9	11

1 20 or more per day.
2 22 units or more for males, and 15 units or more for females, per week.
3 Adults aged 16 and over.

Source: General Household Survey

7.17 Smoking habits of adults[1]: by sex

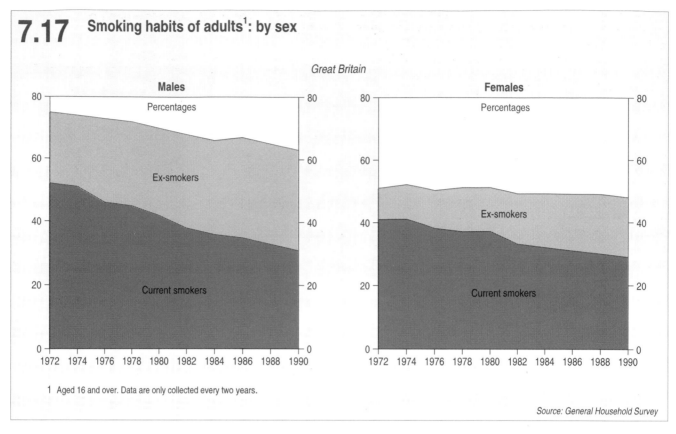

1 Aged 16 and over. Data are only collected every two years.

Source: General Household Survey

or only occasionally, smoked has increased from one in four, to over one in three over the same period. Amongst women there has been little change, with over a half of women in 1990 having never, or only occasionally, smoked.

Alcohol consumption above sensible limits is thought to be associated with increased likelihood of social problems and ill health. The recommended maximum sensible amounts are 21 units per week for men and 14 units per week for women. The percentage of men

7.18 Consumption of alcohol above sensible limits[1]: by sex and region, 1990

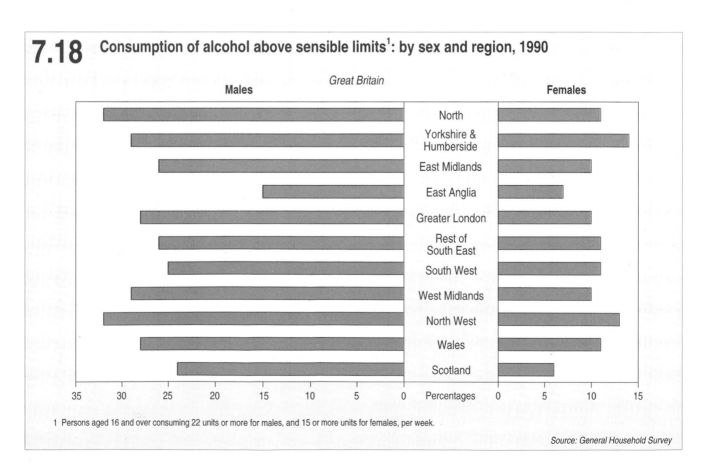

1 Persons aged 16 and over consuming 22 units or more for males, and 15 or more units for females, per week.

Source: General Household Survey

exceeding these guidelines is much higher than that for women, though the percentages vary from region to region. In 1990 a higher proportion of men in the North and North West regions exceeded these limits than in any other region, whilst the largest percentage amongst women was recorded in Yorkshire and Humberside **(Chart 7.18)**.

The number of new drug addicts who have been formally notified as being addicted to any of 14 drugs has increased twelvefold in just under 20 years **(Table 7.19)**. The table shows that most new addicts are addicted to heroin. There has also been a large increase in new addicts dependant on methadone. This is probably due to the use made of methadone in the treatment of heroin addiction. The table probably reflects only a small proportion of those people using drugs, since many will not have sought medical help and so will not have been notified. The figures also exclude the large numbers of misusers of other controlled drugs such as cannabis, LSD, amphetamines, barbiturates or benzodiazepines where doctors are not required to report addiction.

7.19 New addicts notified: by type of drug

United Kingdom					Numbers
	1973	1981	1986	1991	1992
Heroin	508	1,660	4,855	6,328	7,658
Methadone	328	431	659	2,180	2,493
Cocaine	132	174	520	882	1,131
Morphine	226	355	343	185	161
Dipipanone	28	473	116	155	158
Dextromoramide	28	59	97	89	76
Pethidine	27	45	33	37	49
Opium	0	0	23	12	5
Others	2	4	4	1	0
Total addicts notified[1]	806	2,248	5,325	8,007	9,663

1 As an addict can be reported as addicted to more than one notifiable drug, the figures for individual drugs cannot be added together to produce totals.

Source: Home Office

Prevention

Cervical cancer is commonly preceded by pre-cancerous stages which persist for a long time and which can be treated easily. For women screened every five years the incidence of cancer can be reduced by over 80%. In 1990-91 more than one smear was taken for every five women in Great Britain **(Chart 7.20)**. By 1991-92, 80 per cent of all women aged 20 to 64 (the target population) in England had undergone a test in the last five and a half years. This percentage had increased from just over 60 per cent two years before.

A national scheme for breast screening in women was announced in 1987, to combat a disease which kills over 15 thousand women a year nationally. Nine out of ten women who die from breast cancer are aged over

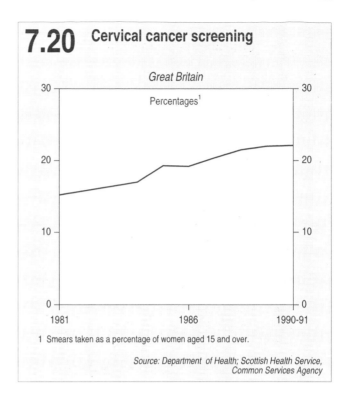

7.20 Cervical cancer screening

Great Britain

Percentages[1]

1 Smears taken as a percentage of women aged 15 and over.

Source: Department of Health; Scottish Health Service, Common Services Agency

50. Invitations for screening are sent out to women aged 50 to 64. It is estimated that early detection could cut the number of deaths in this age group by 25 per cent. In 1991-92 more than a million women in the United Kingdom, over 70 per cent of those invited, were screened. The best results were achieved in East Anglia where more than eight out of ten women in the target age group were screened. The highest incidence of the disease was reported in Wales where the disease was detected in nine in every thousand women screened.

In 1991-92 almost nine out of ten children in the United Kingdom were immunised against the diseases shown in **Table 7.21** before their second birthday. The percentage of children immunised against whooping cough in 1991-92 was more than double the 1976 proportion, which was low due to scares about the safety of the earlier vaccine. In their teens children may

7.21 Immunisation of children[1]

United Kingdom				Percentages
	1971[2]	1976	1981	1986 1991-92[3]
Diphtheria	80	73	82	85	96
Whooping cough	78	39	46	66	88
Poliomyelitis	80	73	82	85	94
Tetanus	80	73	82	85	94
Measles, mumps and rubella[4]	46	45	54	71	91

1 Children born two years earlier and immunised by the end of the specified year, except for measles only in Scotland, where it is in respect of children born three years earlier.
2 England & Wales only.
3 Scotland figures are for 1992.
4 Includes measles only vaccine. Combined vaccine was not available prior to 1988.

Source: Department of Health; Welsh Office; Scottish Health Service, Common Services Agency; Department of Health and Social Services, Northern Ireland

be immunised against tuberculosis and girls may be vaccinated with rubella to prevent contracting the disease in pregnancy. Latest data for Scotland indicate that in 1992 nearly 99 per cent of eligible children had been immunised against tuberculosis and over 80 per cent of eligible girls had been vaccinated with rubella.

Accidents

The overall number of accidental deaths in 1992, at under 12 thousand, was a third lower than in 1971 **(Table 7.22)**. This excludes those deaths where it is not known if the death was accidental or on purpose. Road accidents remain the most common cause of accidental death in Great Britain; they accounted for nearly 40 per cent of all accidental deaths in 1992 and are discussed in detail in Chapter 13.

7.22 Accidental deaths: by cause

Great Britain				Numbers
	1971	1981	1991[1]	1992[1]
Railway accident	212	95	90	70
Road accident[2]	8,009	4,902	5,078	4,668
Other transport accident	222	144	111	126
Other accident				
At home or in communal establishments	7,045	..	4,717	4,521
Elsewhere	3,807	..	2,427	2,307
Total other accidents[3]	10,905	10,039	7,203	6,887
Total accidental deaths[3]	19,348	15,180	12,482	11,900

1 See Appendix, Part 7: Death certificates.
2 These figures are not comparable with those issued by the Department of Transport. See Appendix, Part 13: Road deaths.
3 Late effects of accidental injury are not available by place of occurrence for England and Wales but are included in the totals for other accidents and total accidental deaths.

Source: Office of Population Censuses and Surveys; General Register Office (Scotland)

Health services

The Patient's Charter came into force on 1 April 1992 and is part of the wider strategy based on the Government's Citizen's Charter initiative to improve standards in the delivery of public services. The Patient's Charter makes clear to patients what their rights are and what standards of service they can expect. It sets national and local standards which focus attention on those areas of service requiring greatest attention.

From April 1991 major changes were made to the National Health Service (NHS) and the health authorities became responsible for purchasing health services for their residents from hospitals and other units. At the same time the concept of NHS Trusts was established. Hospitals can apply to become an NHS Trust and if successful they become operationally independent from district or regional management and are free to raise their own funds, advertise their services and to bid for contracts to treat patients.

The first trusts were established in April 1991 in England, and numbered 57 units; they had grown to 296 units at 1 April 1993 but four have since dissolved. Trust numbers are subject to the effects of mergers, reconfiguration and dissolution. Outside England, at 1 April 1993, six trusts existed in Northern Ireland, a total of 14 in Wales and a total of 17 in Scotland.

More hospital patients are being treated in fewer beds. Between 1981 and 1991-92 the number of in-patient cases in England increased by a third to almost eight million. Over the same period the average number of beds available fell by just under a third, with the largest reduction in mental illness wards **(Table 7.23)**. Outside England, over the same period, the number of beds fell by 26 per cent in Northern Ireland, 19 per cent in Wales and 16 per cent in Scotland, while the number of patients treated increased by 8, 33 and 17 per cent respectively.

7.23 National Health Service in-patient[1] summary: by ward type, 1981 and 1991-92

England	Acute[2]	General patients elderly	Maternity	Mental illness	Mental handicap[3]	Thousands and rates Total
1981						
Finished consultant episodes (thousands)	4,469	280	796	188	28	5,760
Average daily available beds (thousands)	145	56	18	85	47	351
In-patients episodes per available bed (rate)	31	5	44	2	1	16
1991-92						
Finished consultant episodes (thousands)	5,966	508	1,010	221	54	7,759
Average daily available beds (thousands)	115	42	14	50	21	242
In-patients episodes per available bed (rate)	52	12	72	4	3	32

1 See Appendix, Part 7: In-patient activity.
2 Wards for general patients, excluding elderly, younger physically disabled, neonate cots not in maternity units.
3 Excluding mental handicap community units.

Source: Department of Health

7.24 National Health Service hospital activity: day cases and out-patients, all specialties

United Kingdom   Thousands and numbers

	1971[1]	1976[2]	1981	1986	1989-90	1990-91	1991-92
Day case attendances (thousands)	..	558	859	1,840	1,480	1,616	1,954
New out-patient attendances (thousands)							
Accidents and emergency	9,500	10,463	11,321	12,663	13,570	13,563	13,400
Other out-patients	9,319	9,178	9,810	10,713	10,593	10,586	11,082
Average attendances per new out-patient (numbers)							
Accidents and emergency	1.6	1.5	1.4	1.3	1.3	1.2	1.2
Other out-patients	4.1	4.2	4.4	4.3	4.2	4.2	4.1

1 Great Britain only.
2 Day case attendances data are for Great Britain only.

Source: Department of Health; Welsh Office; Scottish Health Service, Common Services Agency; Department of Health and Social Services, Northern Ireland

In 1991-92 NHS hospitals in the United Kingdom dealt with almost two million day cases, an increase of 20 per cent on a year earlier, and more than double the amount ten years before **(Table 7.24)**.

The number of patients experiencing long waiting times has fallen in the last five years. By March 1993, 57 thousand patients in England had been waiting more than 12 months for hospital treatment, compared with 208 thousand in March 1988 **(Chart 7.25)**. However the number of patients waiting under 12 months increased by over a third over the same period.

At March 1993, 995 thousand people were on a NHS waiting list in England. Of the people on the waiting list in Northern Ireland in March 1993, 18 per cent had been waiting over 12 months, twice the percentage in North West Thames, the English Regional Health Authority with the longest waiting list **(Chart 7.26)**. The lowest percentage of people waiting for this length of time was recorded by the Mersey region.

People with mental illness or learning disabilities have always been cared for in the community but with improvements in health and social services, more use is being made of community care and day patient treatment.

Chart 7.27 shows the general increase in the number of discharges after a stay of five or more years in NHS hospitals. In consequence the number of beds available in NHS hospitals for people with mental illness and

7.25 Distribution of waiting time[1]: National Health Service hospital day cases and in-patients

England

Thousands

(Bar chart showing waiting times for years 1988, 1991, 1992, 1993 with categories: Under 1 year, 1-2 years, Over 2 years)

1 At 31 March.

Source: Department of Health

7.26 Percentage of National Health Service patients waiting over 12 months: by region, 1993[1]

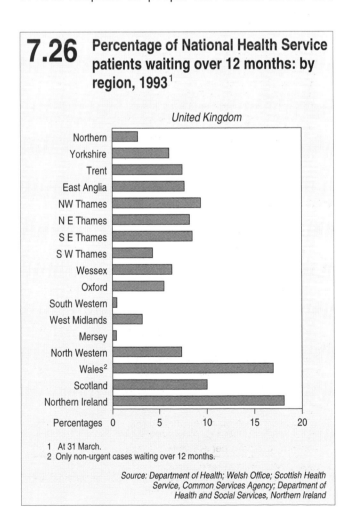

United Kingdom

1 At 31 March.
2 Only non-urgent cases waiting over 12 months.

Source: Department of Health; Welsh Office; Scottish Health Service, Common Services Agency; Department of Health and Social Services, Northern Ireland

7.27 Discharges from mental illness and learning disability hospitals and units: stays of five or more years

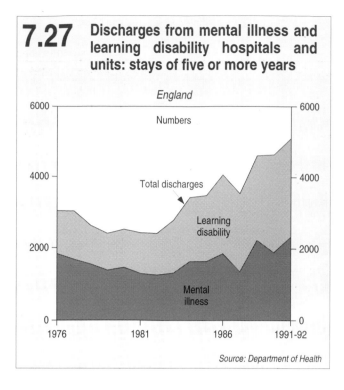

Source: Department of Health

7.29 Organ transplants: by type

	Heart and lung	Heart	Kidney	Liver	Cornea[1]
United Kingdom					Numbers
1972	0	0	421	0	..
1976	0	0	670	0	..
1981	0	24	905	11	..
1986	51	176	1,493	127	..
1987	72	243	1,485	172	..
1988	101	274	1,575	241	..
1989	94	295	1,732	295	1,758
1990	95	329	1,730	359	2,132
1991	79	281	1,628	420	2,237
1992	53	325	1,640	506	2,423

1 Includes only those transplants reported to the United Kingdom Transplant Support Service Authority.

Source: Department of Health

learning disabilities has fallen. In 1991-92 the number of beds available for mental illness patients in England was less than two thirds the number in 1982, whilst the number of beds available for people with learning disabilities was less than half the 1982 number **(Chart 7.28)**. The number of voluntary and private sector places for people with mental illness or learning disabilities has risen significantly, as has the number of day hospital places; this is supported by an increase in the number of community nurses and community psychiatric nurses.

In 1988 over five million organ donor cards had been distributed and by 1992 the number had almost doubled to ten and a half million. With modern medical care transplant patients can enjoy a near normal life following their transplant. In the United Kingdom 2.4 thousand cornea transplants were known to have been performed in 1992, compared with 1.6 thousand kidney transplants **(Table 7.29)**.

The general practitioner (GP) fundholding initiative is a voluntary scheme which gives participating practices control of the prescribing and staff resources and enables them to purchase specified Health and Community Health Service (HCHS) services and procedures. From April 1991, practices with a patient list size of nine thousand or more could apply to become GP fundholders in their own right. Smaller practices could group together to join the scheme if they wish. The GP fundholding scheme gives GPs the chance to make decisions about how the NHS money can best be used in order to meet the needs of their patients in the most effective way. In April 1991 there were 305 practices. This has grown to over 1.2 thousand practices at April 1993 covering 25 per cent of the population of England.

There were 32 thousand doctors in general practice in 1992 - more than ever before **(Table 7.30)**. The number of patients per doctor has been declining over recent years to 1.87 thousand in 1992. The number of dentists, however, has remained much the same for the past three years, and the number of persons per dentist has also remained constant. Nearly 490 million prescriptions were dispensed in 1992, more than double the number in 1961 and over four per cent more than in the previous year.

7.28 Mental illness and learning disability hospitals and units: average daily available beds

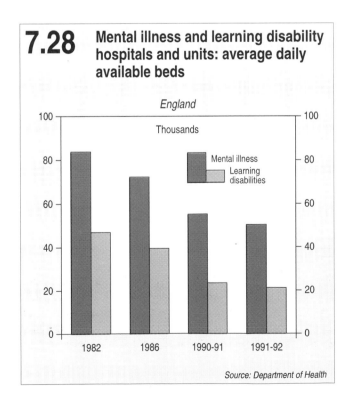

Source: Department of Health

7.30 Family practitioner and dental services

United Kingdom

	General medical and pharmaceutical services						General dental services	
	Number of doctors[1] in practice (thousands)	Average number of patients per doctor (thousands)	Prescriptions dispensed[2] (millions)	Average total cost[3] per prescription (£)	Average number of prescriptions per person	Average prescription cost[3] per person[4] (£)	Number of dentists[5] in practice (thousands)	Average number of persons per dentist (thousands)
1961	23.6	2.25	233.2	0.41	4.7	1.9	11.9	4.4
1971	24.0	2.39	304.5	0.77	5.6	4.3	12.5	4.5
1981	27.5	2.15	370.0	3.46	6.6	23.0	15.2	3.7
1986	30.2	1.99	397.5	5.11	7.0	36.0	17.3	3.3
1987	30.7	1.97	413.6	5.47	7.3	40.0	17.6	3.2
1988	31.2	1.94	427.7	5.91	7.5	44.1	18.0	3.2
1989	31.5	1.91	435.8	6.26	7.5	47.2	18.4	3.1
1990	31.6	1.90	446.6	6.68	7.8	52.1	18.6	3.1
1991	31.7	1.90	467.8	7.14	8.2	58.5	18.6	3.1
1992	32.0	1.87	488.2	7.64	8.6	65.5	18.6	3.1

1 Unrestricted principals only. See Appendix, Part 7: Unrestricted principals.
2 Includes items dispensed by community pharmacists and appliance contractors only.
3 Net ingredient cost (basic cost) less discount, and includes dispensing fees, container allowances etc.
4 Based on the number of people on the NHS prescribing list.
5 Principals plus assistants.

Source: Department of Health

While Table 7.23 shows that the number of beds in NHS hospitals has declined in recent years, **Table 7.31** shows that the number of beds in private hospitals, nursing homes and clinics has increased. In England the number of beds more than doubled in the last five years, whilst there was almost a three and a half times increase in the number of beds in Wales.

7.31 Private health services: number of beds

England			Thousands and percentages	
	1971	1981	1986	1991-92
NHS hospitals authorised beds for private in-patient care (thousands)	4.5	2.7	3.0	..
Registered private nursing homes, hospitals and clinics				
Total available beds (thousands)	25.3	31.9	62.1	147.2
Percentage of available beds in premises with an operating theatre	*..*	*..*	*14.5*	*6.5*

Source: Department of Health

7.32 Private medical insurance[1]: persons insured

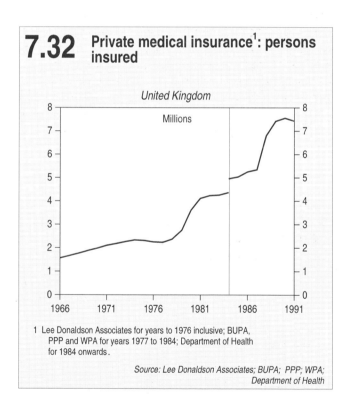

United Kingdom

Millions

1 Lee Donaldson Associates for years to 1976 inclusive; BUPA, PPP and WPA for years 1977 to 1984; Department of Health for 1984 onwards.

Source: Lee Donaldson Associates; BUPA; PPP; WPA; Department of Health

The number of persons insured with private health insurance increased by around 50 per cent between 1985 and 1990, but fell by 1.7 per cent in 1991 according to Department of Health figures **(Chart 7.32)**.

A survey carried out by MORI in 1989 found that about a third of people would consider using alternative medical treatments acupuncture, homeopathy or osteopathy, whilst less than a quarter opposed any form of alternative medicine **(Table 7.33)**. Around one

7.33 Use of alternative medicine, 1989

Great Britain   Percentages

	Seriously consider	Personally used
Homeopathy	37	11
Osteopathy	32	10
Faith or spiritual healing	12	5
Acupuncture	33	4
Hypnosis	19	3
Chiropractic	13	3

Source: MORI

in ten people had personally used homeopathy or osteopathy. The number of Registered Osteopaths increased tenfold in the last 50 years, to 1,606 in 1992.

A hospice is a medical unit for patients with diseases which no longer respond to curative treatment. They provide palliative care, which means, they focus on controlling a patient's pain and other symptoms, ease suffering and enhance the remaining life a patient has. The majority of hospice in-patients are cancer sufferers, though 42 per cent of units accept patients with other diseases. Almost all hospices now receive funds from the Department of Health, but they are managed by a number of organisations. The number of in-patient hospice beds in the United Kingdom has increased nearly threefold in the last 15 years **(Chart 7.34)**; in January 1993 more than 60 per cent were being managed by voluntary organisations, which are in turn registered charities.

7.34 Hospice beds[1]

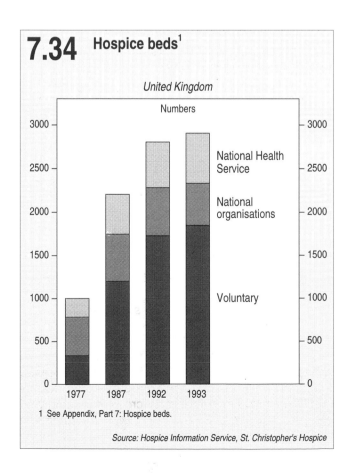

United Kingdom

1 See Appendix, Part 7: Hospice beds.

Source: Hospice Information Service, St. Christopher's Hospice

Personal social services

7.35 Children in care: admissions to care and children removed to a place of safety

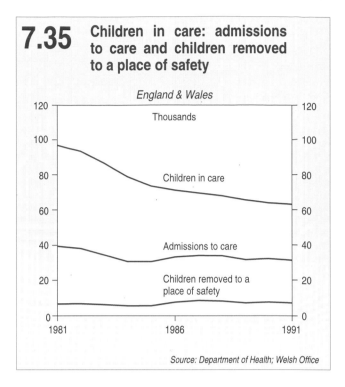

England & Wales

Source: Department of Health; Welsh Office

The *Children Act 1989 (England and Wales)* was implemented in October 1991 and changed the law on the care of children. **Chart 7.35** illustrates the trends before the Act was introduced. The number of admissions to care each year in England and Wales fell by a fifth between 1981 and 1991 and the total number of children in care fell by a third, to about 60 thousand in March 1991. One aim of the *Children Act 1989* was for authorities to work with families to provide help to

7.36 Children and young persons on the Child Protection Registers: by sex and age, 1992[1]

England & Wales   Thousands and rates

	Boys	Girls
Children aged (thousands)		
Under 1	1.4	1.2
1-4	6.5	6.1
5-9	6.7	6.3
10-15	4.9	6.1
16 and over	0.5	1.0
All children	19.9	20.7
Children aged (rates[2])		
Under 1	3.8	3.6
1-4	4.7	4.6
5-9	4.0	4.0
10-15	2.6	3.4
16 and over	0.7	1.7
All children	3.4	3.7

1 At 31 March.
2 Rates per 1,000 population in each age group.

Source: Department of Health; Welsh Office

7.37 Elderly and disabled residents supported by local authorities: by type of home

England				Thousands
	1982	1986	1991	1992
Elderly and younger physically disabled				
Local authority	108.7	106.2	84.1	73.0
Voluntary and private[1]	17.3	7.8	7.3	9.5
Total	126.0	114.0	91.4	82.5
Mentally ill				
Local authority	2.9	2.5	2.2	1.9
Voluntary and private[1]	2.2	1.3	1.6	1.7
Total	5.1	3.8	3.8	3.6
People with learning disabilities				
Local authority	11.5	12.3	11.6	11.5
Voluntary and private[1]	5.1	4.8	7.8	8.7
Total	16.6	17.2	19.4	20.1
All persons				
Local authority	123.1	121.1	97.9	86.4
Voluntary and private[1]	24.7	14.0	16.7	19.8
Total	147.8	135.0	114.7	106.2

1 Includes supported residents in other accommodation.

Source: Department of Health

keep the family together, and the number of children being looked after by local authorities in March 1992 was 55 thousand, 5 thousand less than a year earlier.

At 31 March 1992 there were 20 thousand boys and 21 thousand girls on Child Protection Registers in England and Wales. **Table 7.36** shows that amongst those aged 16 and over, girls were more than twice as likely than boys to be on the register, largely reflecting the incidence of sexual abuse.

The total number of elderly, younger physically disabled, mentally ill and people with learning disabilities supported by local authorities in all types of homes has fallen each year for the past decade **(Table 7.37)**. However, the number of people with learning disabilities supported by local authorities in voluntary and private homes increased, by 70 per cent between 1982 and 1992. From April 1993, as part of the Government's community care reforms, new arrangements have applied to the funding of voluntary and private homes which will mean that in future many more residents in these homes will be supported by local authorities.

Resources

In 1992 households in the United Kingdom spent 1.4 per cent of their total expenditure on the health goods and services listed in **Table 7.38**. This was almost double the proportion of a decade earlier. The largest

7.38 Household expenditure on health in real terms[1]

United Kingdom	£ per week at 1992 prices[1] and percentages			
	1981	1986	1991	1992
National Health Service				
Prescription charges and medical appliances	0.17	0.18	0.19	0.18
Payments for dentist, amenity hospital bed	0.19	0.16	0.35	0.39
Non-National Health Service				
Medicines, lotions, dressings, appliances	0.80	1.09	1.40	1.43
Medical, dental, nursing and optical fees (except spectacles)	0.56	0.64	0.86	0.55
Spectacles	0.28	0.55	0.63	0.80
Medical insurance premiums	0.19	0.37	0.58	0.56
Total weekly expenditure on above	2.17	2.99	4.01	3.91
Expenditure on above items as a percentage of total household expenditure	*0.9*	*1.2*	*1.5*	*1.4*

1 Adjusted to real terms using the retail prices index.

Source: Central Statistical Office

item in 1992 was expenditure on non-NHS medicines, lotions, dressings, appliances, etc which accounted for over 35 per cent of household expenditure on health goods and services.

In real terms English Health Authorities' capital expenditure increased by over a half between 1981-82 and 1992-93. Their current expenditure accounted for two thirds of total NHS expenditure in 1992-93, with departmental administration representing only one per cent of the total **(Table 7.39)**.

7.39 National Health Service expenditure: by sector

England	£ million at 1992-93 prices[1]			
	1981-82	1986-87	1991-92	1992-93
Health authorities - current	14,388	15,561	18,821	19,878
Health authorities - capital	1,228	1,497	1,695	1,908
Family health services	4,616	5,222	6,223	6,640
Other health services	..	..	683	703
Departmental administration	..	..	270	316
Total cost of NHS services	20,861	23,050	27,694	29,445

1 Adjusted to real terms using the GDP deflator.

Source: Department of Health

Total numbers employed in the health service have not changed significantly since 1981 **(Table 7.40)**. However, total numbers of medical and dental staff in the Regional and District Health Authorities increased by nearly 20 per cent between 1981 and 1992 while the number of ancillary workers fell by more than half.

7.40 Persons employed in the health and personal social services[1]

United Kingdom
Thousands

	1981	1986	1988	1989	1990	1991	1992
Regional and District Health Authorities and NHS Trusts							
Medical and dental (excluding locums)	49.7	52.4	53.7	55.1	56.6	57.8	58.8
Nursing and midwifery (excluding agency staff)	492.8	505.4	507.6	508.5	505.2	501.3	484.5
Professional and technical	80.2	93.4	98.0	99.6	103.0	106.5	110.8
Administrative and clerical	133.3	137.2	142.9	149.6	159.2	172.7	187.0
Ancillary	220.1	167.4	146.4	136.6	127.6	115.1	106.1
Other non-medical	56.2	55.3	52.4	50.8	48.4	53.2	53.4
Total health service staff	1,032.2	1,011.0	1,001.0	1,000.0	1,000.0	1,006.6	1,000.6
Family health services[2]	54.3	57.3	59.3	59.8	59.7	54.0	54.3
Personal social services							
Social work staff	28.4	32.2	34.6	35.0	36.5	37.6	39.6
Managerial, administrative and ancillary	27.7	30.4	32.9	34.6	39.3	41.1	42.9
Other[3]	194.8	217.7	226.3	239.7	234.8	228.9	224.3
Total personal social services staff	250.9	280.3	293.9	309.2	310.6	307.6	306.8

1 Figures for family health services are numbers, all other figures are whole-time equivalents, see Appendix, Part 7: Persons employed in heal;th and personal social services.
2 Includes Great Britain data in respect of ophthalmic practitioners.
3 Includes home help service and other community support staff, day care, residential day care and other staff.

Source: Department of Health; Welsh Office; Scottish Health Service, Common Services Agency; Scottish Education Department, Social Work Services Group; Department of Health and Social Services, Northern Ireland

REFERENCES AND FURTHER READING

The following list contains selected publications relevant to Chapter 7: Health and Personal Social Services. Those published by HMSO are available from the addresses shown on the back cover of *Social Trends*.

Activities of Social Service Departments, Welsh Office
Annual Report of the Registrar General for Northern Ireland, HMSO
Annual Report of the Registrar General for Scotland, General Register Office (Scotland)
Cancer Statistics Registrations (Series MB1), HMSO
Children in Care in England and Wales, Department of Health
Communicable Disease Statistics (Series MB2), HMSO
Family Spending - A Report on the 1992 Family Expenditure Survey, HMSO
Fifty Years of the National Food Survey 1940-1990, HMSO
General Household Survey, HMSO
Health and Personal Social Services Statistics for England, HMSO
Health and Personal Social Services Statistics for Northern Ireland, DHSS Northern Ireland
Health and Personal Social Services Statistics for Wales, Welsh Office
Health and Safety Statistics, HMSO
Health Survey for England 1991, HMSO
Hospital and Health Service Yearbook, Health and Safety Executive

Hospital Waiting List Statistics: England, Department of Health
Mortality Statistics for England and Wales (Series DH1, 2, 3, 4), HMSO
National Food Survey, HMSO
NHS Hospital Activity Statistics for England 1974-1989/90, Department of Health
Personal Social Services Statistics, CIPFA
Population Trends, HMSO
Regional Trends, HMSO
Residential Accommodation for the Elderly and for Younger Physically Handicapped People, HMSO
Scotland's Health: A Challenge to us all, HMSO
Scottish Health Service Costs, The Scottish Office
Scottish Health Statistics, Common Services Agency, Scottish Health Service
Smoking among Secondary School Children, HMSO
Social Work Services group of The Scottish Office, Statistical Bulletins
Statistical Publications on aspects of Health and Personal Social Services activity in England (Various), Department of Health
Statistics of Drug Addicts Notified to the Home Office, United Kingdom, Home Office
Statistics of Elective Admissions and Patients Waiting, Department of Health
Survey of Children and Young Persons on Child Protection Registers, Department of Health

Chapter 8: Housing

Housing supply

- A quarter of a century ago more than twice as many new dwellings were being completed per year as in 1992.
  (Chart 8.1)

- More than twice as many dwellings were owner occupied in 1992 compared with 1961. *(Chart 8.2)*

Housing standards

- The worst dwellings were more likely to be found in urban or isolated rural areas than in suburban or rural residential areas in 1991. *(Chart 8.9)*

- By 1991 the number of dwellings lacking a basic amenity had fallen to one per cent of the housing stock, compared with two and a half per cent in 1986. *(Page 112)*

Homelessness

- There has been a decrease of more than a third in the numbers of households temporarily housed in bed and breakfast accommodation in 1992 from 12.2 thousand at the start of 1992 to 7.7 thousand. *(Table 8.15)*

Housing costs and expenditure

- Building society mortgage interest rates in June 1993 were the lowest for over 20 years. *(Chart 8.19)*

- Around 350 thousand mortgage loans were in arrears by more than six months at the end of June 1993. *(Table 8.20)*

Characteristics of occupants

- Four out of five households from the Indian ethnic group owned their own homes in 1990-1992 - the average for all households in Great Britain was two out of three. *(Table 8.25)*

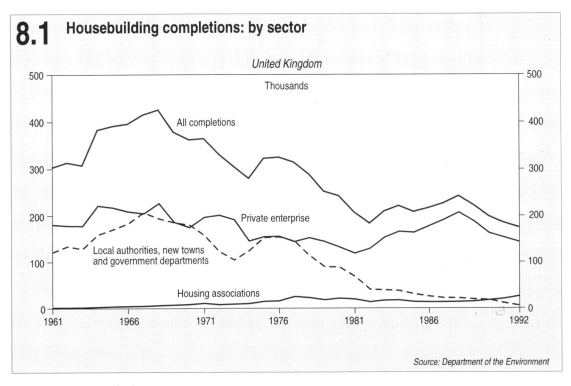

8.1 Housebuilding completions: by sector

United Kingdom
Thousands

Source: Department of the Environment

Housing supply

There were almost 24 million dwellings in the United Kingdom at December 1992, and more than twice as many dwellings were owner occupied compared with 1961 **(Chart 8.2)**. Over the same period the number of dwellings rented from local authorities or new towns increased up to the late 1970s before falling back to the level of the mid 1960s. Other rented dwellings halved between 1961 and 1992. Half the total dwelling stock in England is over 50 years old, with a quarter built before 1919.

In 1991 there were over 500 thousand vacant private sector dwellings in England, just over three per cent of the total stock. Over half had been built before 1919 and over three quarters were in urban areas. The greatest number of vacant private sector properties were in the South East while the North West had the largest number of vacant local authority dwellings.

Table 8.3 shows average annual changes in the stock of dwellings. The annual change fell from a net gain of 243 thousand per year during the 1970s to an average of 183 thousand between 1990 and 1992.

The Housing Act 1980 and its Scottish equivalent gave local authority tenants and tenants of other public bodies the right to buy their own homes, with discounts, if they had been a tenant for more than three years. This was subsequently reduced to two years by the *Housing and Building Control Act 1984*, which also increased the maximum available discount from 50 to 60 per cent. The maximum available discount for flats was further increased in January 1987 to 70 per cent.

8.3 Average annual change in dwelling stock

United Kingdom				Thousands
	1961 -1969	1970 -1979	1980 -1989	1990 -1992
New construction				
Private enterprise	200	166	163	156
Housing associations	4	14	16	21
Local authorities		120	36	11
New towns	} 164 {	13	3	1
Government departments		2	0	0
Total new construction	368	315	218	189
Other changes				
Slum clearance[1]	..	-67	-16	-9
Other[2]	..	-5	5	3
Total other changes	..	-72	-11	-6
Total net gain	..	243	207	183

1 Figures for Northern Ireland are for demolitions only.
2 Comprises net gains from conversions and other causes, and losses other than by slum clearance. Excludes figures for Wales and Northern Ireland. Figures for Scotland are not avaliable between 1981 and 1985.
Source: Department of the Environment; Welsh Office; The Scottish Office; Department of the Environment, Northern Ireland

By the end of 1992 more than two million public sector tenants in Great Britain had made applications to buy their homes, with nearly seven in ten actually making a purchase. Annual sales peaked at 200 thousand in 1982 with a smaller peak in 1989. Only 65 thousand were sold during 1992 **(Chart 8.4)**.

8.4 Right to buy applications for, and sales of, dwellings owned by local authorities and new towns

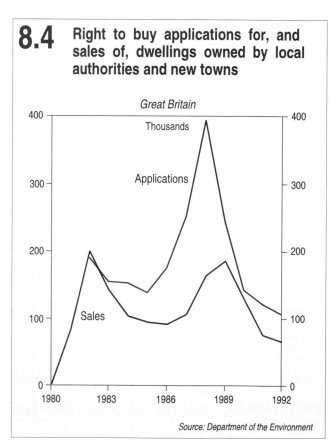

Source: Department of the Environment

8.2 Stock of dwellings: by tenure[1]

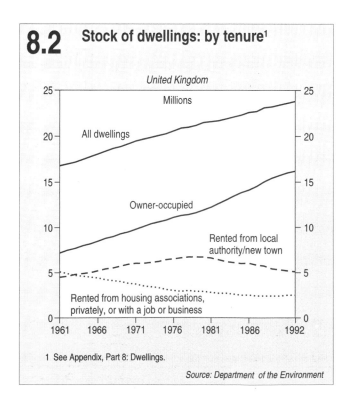

1 See Appendix, Part 8: Dwellings.

Source: Department of the Environment

Chart 8.1, at the beginning of this chapter, shows the number of new dwellings completed in the United Kingdom by the various sectors. A quarter of a century ago twice as many dwellings per year were completed as in 1992. Completions by the public sector have declined since 1967, with 206 thousand dwellings completed in 1967 compared with five thousand in 1992. Private enterprise dominates housebuilding at present, accounting for over 80 per cent of completions in 1992, although housing associations have almost doubled their output in the last five years.

The number of bedrooms in a house is an indication of its size. Between 1976 and 1992 the trend was away from the construction of three bedroom dwellings towards two bedroom dwellings and larger dwellings (Table 8.5).

In the United Kingdom around two thirds of the housing stock was owner occupied in 1991, with one in five properties owned by local authorities or new towns and one in ten by housing associations. Table 8.6 shows that the provision of local authority homes to new tenants is made for a number of reasons. The largest

8.5 Housebuilding completions: by sector and number of bedrooms

England & Wales		Percentages and thousands			
	1976	1981	1986	1991	1992
Private enterprise					
1 bedroom	4	7	12	14	13
2 bedrooms	23	23	28	30	30
3 bedrooms	58	50	40	32	34
4 or more bedrooms	15	21	20	24	23
All houses and flats (= 100%)(thousands)	138	104	156	136	125
Housing associations					
1 bedroom	44	58	60	43	34
2 bedrooms	34	28	29	37	40
3 bedrooms	21	12	10	18	23
4 or more bedrooms	1	2	1	2	3
All houses and flats (= 100%)(thousands)	15	17	11	18	24
Local authorities and new towns					
1 bedroom	32	39	46	42	35
2 bedrooms	26	28	30	34	38
3 bedrooms	38	28	21	20	26
4 or more bedrooms	4	5	2	4	1
All houses and flats (= 100%)(thousands)	124	58	21	9	4
All housebuilding completions					
1 bedroom	18	22	18	19	17
2 bedrooms	25	25	28	31	32
3 bedrooms	47	39	36	30	32
4 or more bedrooms	9	14	17	20	19
All houses and flats (= 100%)(thousands)	277	180	187	162	153

Source: Department of the Environment; Welsh Office

8.6 Allocation of local authority housing

England & Wales	Percentages and thousands			
	1981 -82	1986 -87	1990 -91	1991 -92
New tenants (percentages)				
Displaced through slum clearance, etc	5	2	1	1
Homeless[1]	16	24	31	33
Key workers and other priorities	9	7	5	5
Ordinary waiting list	67	62	54	48
On non-secure tenancies[2]	3	4	10	13
All new tenants (= 100%)(thousands)	264.8	257.0	251.1	250.6
Tenants transferring or exchanging (thousands)	172.1	194.4	170.8	177.4
All tenants (thousands)	436.9	451.3	421.9	428.0

1 Households housed under the homelessness provisions of the *Housing (Homeless Persons) Act 1977* and the *Housing Act 1985*.
2 As defined in Schedule 1, *Housing Act 1985*. Non-secure tenancies in Wales are included under the other categories listed.

Source: Department of the Environment; Welsh Office

single category of new tenants is those who have had their names on the waiting list, although this proportion is declining. In England and Wales in 1991-92, a third of those to whom new lettings were made were households declared as homeless. This proportion has more than doubled compared with a decade earlier, although the number of newly housed households has remained roughly constant over the same period.

Since 1981, the number of new specialised dwellings for the elderly built by the private sector in England has increased significantly to 1.7 thousand in 1992 (Table 8.7). However, building activity by local authorities and new towns, once the largest providers of specialised dwellings for the elderly, has fallen substantially over the same period. Overall, the number of specialised dwellings for the elderly completed in 1992 was slightly more than a third the number of a decade earlier.

8.7 Completions of new specialised dwellings for the elderly: by sector

England			Numbers
	1981	1991	1992
Sheltered housing			
Private enterprise	130	1,622	1,339
Housing associations	1,929	1,240	1,442
Local authorities/new towns	5,558	1,536	751
Other housing			
Private enterprise	62	277	404
Housing associations	261	611	564
Local authorities/new towns	4,636	290	94
Total dwellings for the elderly	12,576	5,576	4,594

Source: Department of the Environment

8.8 Percentage of housing stock which is owner-occupied: EC comparison, 1990

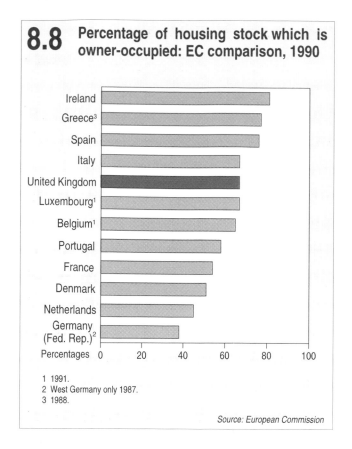

1 1991.
2 West Germany only 1987.
3 1988.

Source: European Commission

8.9 Worst housing[1] as a percentage of all dwellings: by area, 1991

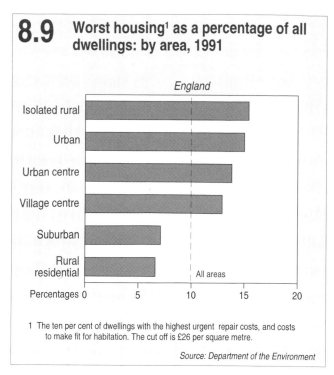

1 The ten per cent of dwellings with the highest urgent repair costs, and costs to make fit for habitation. The cut off is £26 per square metre.

Source: Department of the Environment

The percentage of housing stock that is owner occupied varies throughout the European Community. **Chart 8.8** shows that households in the Irish Republic are more than twice as likely to be owner occupiers than those in Germany. In around half of the other countries, including the United Kingdom, at least two out of three households own their own homes, either outright or with a mortgage.

Housing standards

The next three items present some of the results from the 1991 English House Condition Survey undertaken by the Department of the Environment. For this survey the 'worst' housing is defined as the ten per cent of dwellings with the highest repair costs, the cut-off being £26 per square metre, to make the dwelling fit for habitation. This roughly equates to just over £2,000 for the average 80 square metre dwelling. The likelihood of worst, or best, housing conditions in any area is determined by the age, type and tenure of the housing stock, with age being the main determinant.

Chart 8.9 shows that the proportion of worst dwellings is greater in urban areas, village centres and isolated rural areas than in suburban or rural residential areas. Regionally, Inner London has the highest proportion of dwellings in the worst condition, at 16 per cent, largely because half its stock was built before 1919.

Occupancy of the worst housing varies according to ethnic group. **Chart 8.10** highlights which ethnic groups were experiencing worst housing in 1991. White and

West Indian households were less likely than average to be living in the worst housing. However one in five households headed by a Pakistani or Bangladeshi were in unsatisfactory housing, more than twice the average for all ethnic groups.

By 1991 the number of dwellings lacking a basic amenity (eg a wash hand basin, hot and cold water, indoor WC, kitchen sink, shower or bath) had fallen to one per cent of the housing stock in England, compared with two and a half per cent in 1986. Virtually all dwellings had an electricity suppy, with 90 per cent having a modern system; 87 per cent of dwellings are on mains gas and 96 per cent are on mains drainage.

8.10 Households in worst housing[1]: by ethnic group of head of household, 1991

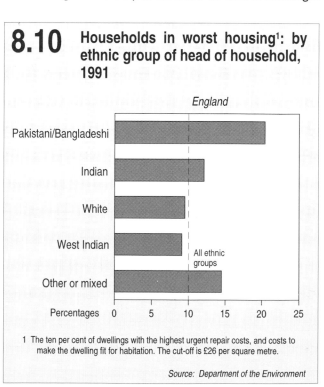

1 The ten per cent of dwellings with the highest urgent repair costs, and costs to make the dwelling fit for habitation. The cut-off is £26 per square metre.

Source: Department of the Environment

8.11 Rooms per person: by ethnic group of head of household, 1981 and 1991

England   Percentages and thousands

| | 1981 | | | | 1991 | | | |
	Under 1	1 to 2	Over 2	All households (= 100%) (thousands)	Under 1	1 to 2	Over 2	All households (= 100%) (thousands)
Ethnic group								
Indian	16	70	14	177	7	64	28	228
Pakistani/Bangladeshi	30	60	10	70	33	52	15	128
West Indian	8	71	21	182	2	58	41	209
Other or mixed	8	70	22	157	5	63	32	274
All ethnic minority groups	13	69	18	586	9	61	31	839
White	2	55	43	16,507	1	45	54	18,405
Not stated	4	57	39	132	2	47	51	64
All ethnic groups	2	56	42	17,225	1	46	53	19,309

Source: Department of the Environment

Room occupancy provides a measure of overcrowding. **Table 8.11** shows some striking differences in room occupancy by ethnic group of head of household in England. Households headed by a Pakistani or Bangladeshi experienced an increase in overcrowding in terms of rooms per person between 1981 and 1991, when one in three households had less than one room per person. At the other end of the scale, the proportions of households headed by West Indians or Indians with two or more rooms per person doubled over the decade from 1981. In the main, the extent of overcrowding in the local authority sector in England is twice that for owner occupiers.

Homelessness

Local authorities have the primary responsibility for dealing with homeless people. Under legislation (*Part III of the Housing Act 1985* and the Scottish equivalent) they are required to help homeless people in defined categories of 'priority need'. Essentially these are families with young children, women expecting babies, and those vulnerable through old age, physical disability, mental handicap or illness. They may also help others not in one of these priority need categories, either by securing accommodation or by providing advice and assistance to help them find accommodation themselves.

A council's first responsibility is to satisfy itself that the applicant is homeless or threatened with homelessness. Once satisfied the council must determine whether the applicant has a priority need. If this is the case, then the council has some responsibility to provide accommodation. The legislation does not require councils to provide local authority homes in all cases,

as it also allows them to make arrangements for the homeless to be housed by a housing association or to help them find a private sector tenancy.

In 1992 local authorities in Great Britain accepted responsibility under the housing legislation to secure permanent accommodation for 167 thousand households, slightly fewer than in the previous year **(Table 8.12)**. Nearly two thirds of those receiving assistance in 1992 had dependent children; this has

8.12 Homeless households found accommodation by local authorities: by priority need category[1]

Great Britain   Percentages and thousands

	1986	1989	1991	1992
Priority need category				
Household with dependent children	65	68	65	62
Household member pregnant	14	13	13	13
Household member vunerable because of:				
Old age	7	6	4	4
Physical handicap	3	3	3	4
Mental illness	2	2	3	4
Other reasons	6	6	10	12
Homeless in emergency	3	2	1	1
All in priority need[2] (= 100%)(thousands)	107.7	128.7	159.4	161.2
Not in priority need (thousands)	10.2	14.1	9.4	6.1
All homeless households found accommodation	117.9	142.9	168.8	167.3

1 Households for whom local authorities accepted responsibility to secure permanent accommodation under the *Housing Act 1985* which defines 'priority need'. Data for Wales include some households given advice and assistance only.
2 Includes actions where priority need category is not known.

Source: Department of the Environment; Welsh Office; The Scottish Office

been the case for a number of years, though this proportion has fallen slightly. The proportion of households with a member who is vunerable due to mental illness has doubled since 1989 although still only accounts for four per cent of those in priority need. The number not in priority need who received accommodation in 1992 was less than half that in 1989.

Households may become homeless for varying reasons, as shown in **Chart 8.13.** In both 1981 and 1992 the most frequent reason was that parents, relatives or friends were no longer willing or able to accommodate. The largest increase, by almost two and a half percentage points between 1981 and 1992, was in the proportion of homeless households found accommodation due to the breakdown of a relationship with a partner, followed by court orders due to mortgage default or rent arrears. Information on county court possession orders and warrants is given in Table 8.21 and Chart 8.22.

In addition to the 167 thousand households accepted as homeless in 1992, 90 thousand households applied to a local authority but were found not to be homeless, an increase of almost a third since 1986 **(Table 8.14)**. Altogether there has been a 40 per cent increase in enquiries made to local authorities under the housing legislation over the same period. England is the only country to include the intentionally homeless as a

8.14 Local authority enquiries under the homelessness legislation: by outcome

Great Britain				Thousands
	1986	1990	1991	1992
Households applying as homeless				
Accepted[1]				
- in priority need	108	149	159	161
- not in priority need[2]	10	14	9	6
Intentionally homeless[3]	3	5	6	6
Given advice and assistance only[4]	59	86	81	85
Found not to be homeless[4]	69	85	88	90
Total enquiries[4]	249	340	344	348

1 Households for whom local authorities accepted responsibility to secure permanent accommodation under the homelessness provisions of the *Housing Act 1985*.
2 Figures for England for April-December 1991 include only households where the applicant has been initially assessed as possibly eligible for re-housing and about whom a final decision was issued during the year.
3 England only.
4 Figures for England probably include some households only given temporary accommodation.

Source: Department of the Environment; Welsh Office; The Scottish Office

category in their homeless statistics. The number of households being classified as intentionally homeless in England has doubled since 1986, to six thousand.

There was a large increase in the number of households housed by local authorities in temporary accommodation between 1982 and 1992 **(Table 8.15)**. The total number of families in temporary accommodation was almost 63 thousand in 1992 compared with under ten thousand in 1982. Short life leasing was the most common type of accommodation used by local authorities in 1992, with a tenfold increase during the last decade. This includes mobile homes and other licensing agreements with local authorities which generally are cheaper forms of accommodation than bed and breakfast and hostels.

8.13 Homeless households[1] found accommodation by local authorities: by reason[2] for homelessness, 1981 and 1992

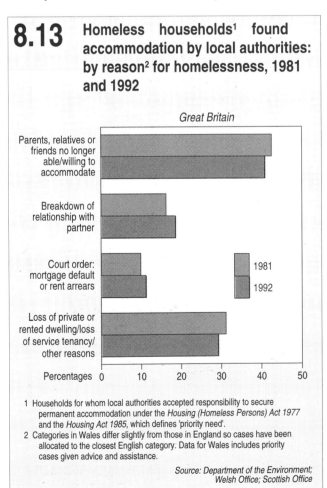

Great Britain

1 Households for whom local authorities accepted responsibility to secure permanent accommodation under the *Housing (Homeless Persons) Act 1977* and the *Housing Act 1985*, which defines 'priority need'.
2 Categories in Wales differ slightly from those in England so cases have been allocated to the closest English category. Data for Wales includes priority cases given advice and assistance.

Source: Department of the Environment; Welsh Office; Scottish Office

8.15 Households living in temporary accomodation[1]

England				Thousands
	Bed and breakfast	Hostels	Short life leasing	Total
1982	1.6	3.5	4.2	9.3
1983	2.7	3.4	3.7	9.8
1984	3.7	4.0	4.6	12.3
1985	5.4	4.7	5.8	15.9
1986	9.0	4.6	7.2	20.8
1987	10.4	5.2	9.2	24.8
1988	11.0	6.2	12.9	30.1
1989	11.5	8.0	18.4	37.9
1990	11.1	9.0	25.1	45.3
1991	12.2	10.0	37.8	59.9
1992	7.7	10.7	44.5	62.9

1 Includes homeless households awaiting outcome of homeless enquiries. Data are at end of year.

Source: Department of the Environment

The number of households in bed and breakfast accommodation increased more than sevenfold between 1982 and 1991 but then fell by nearly 40 per cent in 1992.

Housing costs and expenditure

As the result of falling house prices, declining mortgage interest rates and an increase in real earnings, there was a marked improvement in affordability in 1992. Initial repayment levels for first time buyers were, on average, £3,200 per year in 1992, representing approximately 18 per cent of their total income **(Chart 8.16)**. The latest information shows that this proportion fell to just under 14 per cent in mid 1993 - the lowest level since 1983.

8.16 Average mortgage repayment as a percentage of average income

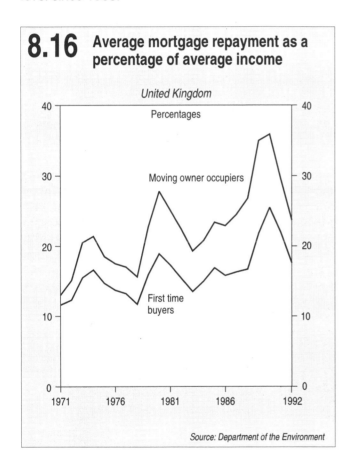

Source: Department of the Environment

After four years of recession in the housing market, house prices began stabilising in 1993. In the first nine months of 1993 average dwelling prices in the United Kingdom were slightly higher than in 1992 and more than two and a half times higher than 1982, both for new and existing properties **(Table 8.17)**.

Between Spring 1992 and Spring 1993 average house prices in Scotland, Wales and Northern Ireland rose while in all the English regions they fell. The fall was most marked in the South West and the West Midlands, where prices fell by seven per cent **(Chart 8.18)**.

8.17 Dwelling prices

	Average price (£)			Mix-adjusted[1] dwellings price index (1990=100)
	New dwellings	Other dwellings	All dwellings	
1982	28,205	23,083	23,644	37.7
1983	30,817	25,901	26,471	42.1
1984	33,080	28,557	29,106	46.1
1985	36,103	30,476	31,103	50.2
1986	43,562	35,464	36,276	57.0
1987	49,692	39,336	40,391	66.7
1988	61,873	47,961	49,355	83.8
1989	73,544	52,568	54,846	101.3
1990	75,037	57,760	59,785	100.0
1991	73,507	60,986	62,455	98.6
1992	73,190	59,226	60,821	94.9
1993[2]	73,315	61,423	62,709	94.3

United Kingdom   £ and indices

1 See Appendix, Part 8: Dwellings.
2 Third quarter.

Source: Department of the Environment

8.18 Percentage changes in average house prices [1]: by region, 1991-1992[2]

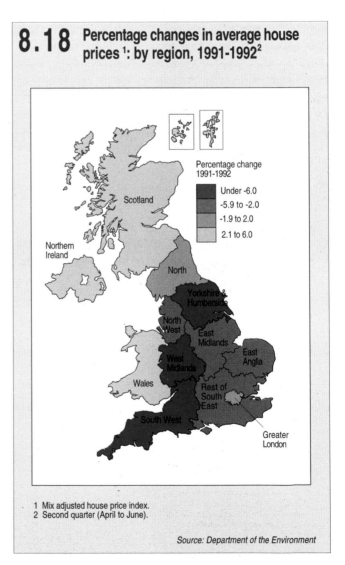

1 Mix adjusted house price index.
2 Second quarter (April to June).

Source: Department of the Environment

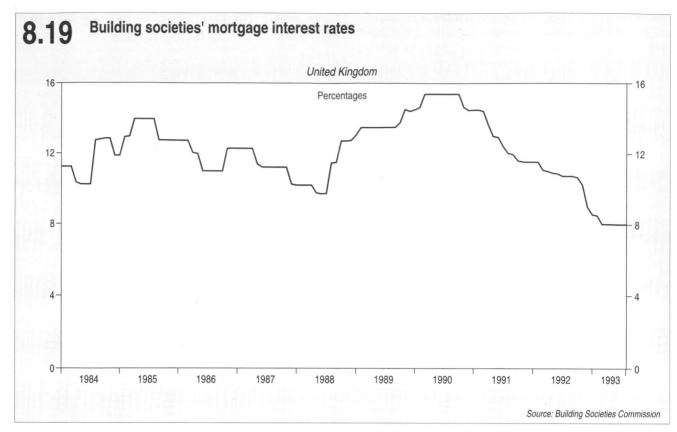

8.19 Building societies' mortgage interest rates

United Kingdom

Percentages

Source: Building Societies Commission

Mortgage costs are affected by a number of factors, including the size of mortgage advances and the level of interest rates. **Chart 8.19** looks at how building society mortgage interest rates changed between January 1984 and August 1993. The highest rate during the last decade was 15.4 per cent between March and October 1990. Since then, the rate has fallen progressively.

If people are unable to maintain their mortgage repayments, due for example to high interest rates or a drop in their income, their properties may be taken into possession by mortgage lenders. Between 1989 and 1990 the number of properties taken into possession in the United Kingdom due to mortgage difficulties almost trebled. In 1991 it reached 75 thousand before falling to 68 thousand in 1992 **(Table 8.20)**. In the middle of 1993, 350 thousand mortgage loans were in arrears by more than six months.

8.20 Mortgage lenders[1]: number of mortgages, arrears and possessions

United Kingdom   Thousands

		Loans in arrears at end-period		Properties taken into possession in period
	Number of mortgages	By 6-12 months	By over 12 months	
1971	4,506	17.6	..	2.8
1976	5,322	16.0	..	5.0
1981	6,336	21.5	..	4.9
1986	8,138	52.1	13.0	24.1
1987	8,283	55.5	15.0	26.4
1988	8,564	42.8	10.3	18.5
1989	9,125	66.8	13.8	15.8
1990	9,415	123.1	36.1	43.9
1991	9,815	183.6	91.7	75.5
1992	9,922	205.0	147.0	68.5
1993	9,998	191.6	158.0	31.8

1 Council of Mortgage Lenders' estimates as at 31 December in each year except 1993, 30 June. Estimates only cover members of the Council, these account for 95 per cent of all mortgages outstanding.
Source: Council of Mortgage Lenders

8.21 County Court possession orders[1] made: by region and tenure, 1992

England & Wales   Percentages and thousands

	Mortgaged	Rented	All dwellings (= 100%) (thousands)
North	46	54	13.8
Yorkshire & Humberside	60	40	14.8
East Midlands	62	38	15.0
East Anglia	66	34	6.2
Greater London	40	60	59.6
Rest of South East	69	31	44.8
South West	73	27	14.0
West Midlands	59	41	19.8
North West	58	42	24.9
England	56	44	212.8
Wales	64	36	11.0

1 Not all possession orders lead to repossessions.
Source: Lord Chancellor's Department

A county court possession summons is the means by which a lender begins the process of obtaining a court order for recovery of a property. In most regions in 1992, county court mortgage possession orders formed a higher proportion of total orders than those made on rented property **(Table 8.21)**. Only in Greater London and the North was the reverse true.

Not all possession orders will result in eviction. Possession orders can be suspended on condition that arrears are repaid, settled in full, or other arrangements are agreed between the relevant parties. **Chart 8.22** shows the numbers of warrants issued and executed by the county courts in England and Wales for repossession. The coverage of this item differs from that in Table 8.21 in that although it only covers England and Wales, it includes not just properties taken into possession by mortgage lenders, but all repossessions of residential premises and land whether rented or mortgaged. In 1992 the number of warrants issued dropped for the first time since 1984 to 124 thousand, a seven per cent decrease on 1991. Despite this, the number of warrants executed increased to just over 62 thousand, including some which will have been issued in previous years. Between 1984 and 1992 warrants issued and executed both increased two and a half times.

Tax relief is available on a loan to purchase a property in the United Kingdom, providing that the house is used as the borrower's main residence. In 1992-93 tax relief, at 25 per cent, was available on the interest paid on the first £30,000 of a mortgage loan. This tax relief will be restricted to 15 per cent from April 1995. **Chart 8.23** shows the cost in real terms to the government of this tax relief. Between 1961-62 and 1990-91 it increased tenfold to reach £8.3 billion at 1992-93 prices. The substantial drop in 1991-92 was due to a fall in interest

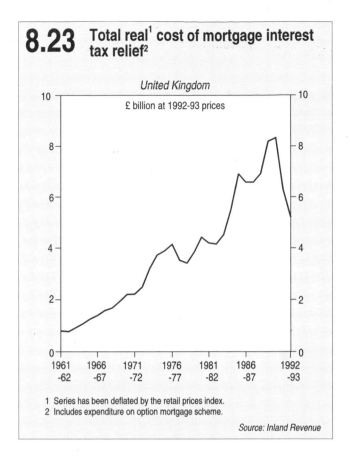

8.23 Total real[1] cost of mortgage interest tax relief[2]

United Kingdom

£ billion at 1992-93 prices

1 Series has been deflated by the retail prices index.
2 Includes expenditure on option mortgage scheme.

Source: Inland Revenue

rates and the ending of the higher rate relief, whereas that in 1992-93 was due to the continuing fall in interest rates.

Characteristics of occupants

Table 8.24 shows that households headed by professionals and employers and managers are the most likely to own a home with a mortgage. The highest percentage owning their homes outright are the economically inactive, most of whom are retired. Amongst those of working age, unskilled manual workers are five times more likely to be in rented accommodation than employers and managers.

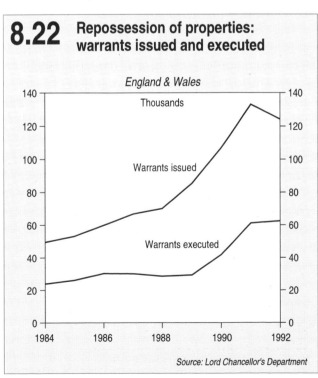

8.22 Repossession of properties: warrants issued and executed

England & Wales

Thousands

Warrants issued

Warrants executed

Source: Lord Chancellor's Department

8.24 Tenure: by socio-economic group, 1992

Great Britain			Percentages
	Owned with mort-gage	Owned outright	Rented[1]
Professional	72	15	13
Employers and managers	77	13	11
Intermediate non-manual	69	11	20
Junior non-manual	58	15	27
Skilled manual	61	14	25
Semi-skilled manual	42	13	46
Unskilled manual	29	17	54
Economically inactive	10	43	47

1 Includes those renting from a housing association and those renting with a job or business.

Source: General Household Survey

Four out of five heads of household from the Indian ethnic group are owner occupiers **(Table 8.25)**. This far exceeds the average of around two out of three for Great Britain as a whole. Over half of households headed by someone of Black Caribbean origin were in rented accommodation - a higher proportion than for any other ethnic group.

8.25 Tenure: by ethnic group of head of household, 1990-1992[1]

Great Britain		Percentages
	Owner occupied	Rented
Ethnic group		
Indian	*80*	*20*
Pakistani/Bangladeshi	*66*	*34*
Black Caribbean	*46*	*54*
Other	*50*	*50*
All ethnic minority groups	*60*	*40*
White	*67*	*33*
All ethnic groups[2]	*66*	*34*

1 Combined data for 1990, 1991 and 1992.
2 Includes those who gave no answer to the ethnic group question.

Source: General Household Survey

REFERENCES AND FURTHER READING

The following list contains selected publications relevant to Chapter 8: Housing. Those published by HMSO are available from the addresses shown on the back cover of *Social Trends*.

English House Condition Survey, 1991, HMSO
General Household Survey, HMSO
Housebuilding in England by Local Authority Areas, HMSO
Housing and Construction Statistics (Great Britain), annual and quarterly, HMSO
Housing Finance, Council of Mortgage Lenders
Inland Revenue Statistics, HMSO
Labour Force Survey Housing Trailer, HMSO
Local Housing Statistics: England and Wales, HMSO

Northern Ireland Housing Statistics, HMSO
Regional Trends, HMSO
Rent Officer Statistics, Department of the Environment
Scottish Development Department Statistical Bulletins on Housing, The Scottish Office
Social Security Statistics, HMSO
Welsh House Condition Survey, 1986, Welsh Office
Welsh Housing and Dwelling Survey, Welsh Office
Welsh Housing Statistics, Welsh Office
1988 Private Renters Survey, HMSO

Chapter 9: Environment

Attitudes to the environment
- At almost 2.2 million in 1992, the membership of the National Trust (excluding the National Trust for Scotland) has increased nearly eightfold since 1971. *(Table 9.2)*

- In 1992 almost half of all motorists used unleaded petrol, compared with only 5 per cent four years before. *(Chart 9.3)*

Greenhouse effect and ozone depletion
- Power stations were responsible for a third of carbon dioxide emissions in the United Kingdom in 1991. *(Chart 9.4)*

Air quality and pollution
- Road transport accounts for 90 per cent of carbon monoxide emissions, half of nitrogen oxide emissions and two fifths of black smoke emissions. *(Page 122)*

Water quality
- Four out of five bathing waters tested in the United Kingdom complied with EC standards in 1993. *(Table 9.11)*

Waste
- The number of local authority bottle bank sites in the United Kingdom trebled between 1984 and 1991 to just over seven thousand. *(Page 124)*

Land use
- The area of broadleaved trees planted in 1992-93 was three times that planted in 1988-89. *(Chart 9.16)*

Landscape and nature conservation
- The breeding population of the tree sparrow in 1992 was only 15 per cent of what it was in 1971. *(Table 9.19)*

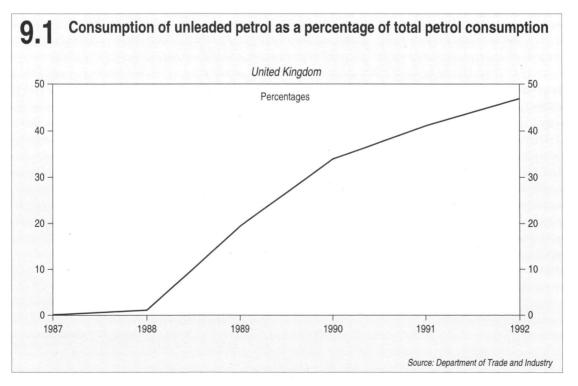

9.1 **Consumption of unleaded petrol as a percentage of total petrol consumption**

United Kingdom

Percentages

Source: Department of Trade and Industry

9: ENVIRONMENT

This chapter focuses on the environment, from the public's interest in environmental issues, to the effect in general that human activity is having on it.

Attitudes to the environment

The growth in the membership of the voluntary environmental organisations reflects our growing awareness of environmental issues. The National Trust, excluding the National Trust for Scotland, had the largest membership of all the organisations shown in **Table 9.2** at almost 2.2 million in 1992 - nearly an eightfold increase since 1971. Other organisations have also shown remarkable growth, for example membership of Greenpeace was nearly 14 times larger in 1992 than in 1981.

The use of unleaded petrol is increasing. A survey carried out by MORI in 1992 found that more than eight out of ten motorists in Great Britain either already used unleaded petrol, or would use it if they could **(Chart 9.3)**. Just over half of all motorists were able to use unleaded petrol, though seven per cent chose not to. However, in 1988 less than 15 per cent were able to and, of these people, nearly two out of three decided not to. The use of leaded petrol by motor vehicles is the major source of lead in the air and it is discussed in the section on air quality and pollution later in the chapter.

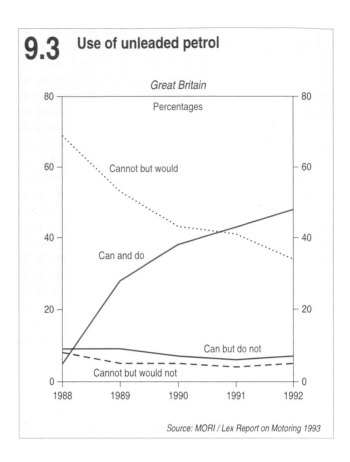

9.3 Use of unleaded petrol

Great Britain

Percentages

Cannot but would

Can and do

Can but do not

Cannot but would not

Source: MORI / Lex Report on Motoring 1993

9.2 Membership of selected voluntary environmental organisations

United Kingdom				Thousands
	1971	1981	1991	1992
British Trust for Conservation Volunteers[1]	1	..	9	10
British Trust for Ornithology	5	7	9	9
Campaign for the Protection of Rural Wales	..	2	4	4
Civic Trust[2]	214	..	222	222
Council for the Protection of Rural England	21	29	45	46
Friends of the Earth[3]	1	18	111	116
Greenpeace	..	30	408	411
National Trust	278	1,046	2,152	2,186
National Trust for Scotland	37	110	234	237
Ramblers Association	22	37	87	94
Royal Society for Nature Conservation	64	143	250	250
Royal Society for the Protection of Birds	98	441	852	850
Woodland Trust	..	20	150	150
World Wide Fund for Nature	12	60	227	209

1 Data for 1971 and 1991 relate to two years earlier. Data for 1992 relates to 1993.
2 Members of local amenity societies registered with the Civic Trust.
3 England, Wales and Northern Ireland only.
Source: Organisations concerned

Greenhouse effect and ozone depletion

The increase of carbon dioxide in the atmosphere since the beginning of the Industrial Revolution is due to man's activity - largely in burning fossil fuels and

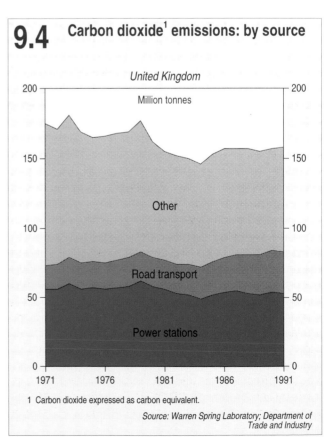

9.4 Carbon dioxide[1] emissions: by source

United Kingdom

Million tonnes

Other

Road transport

Power stations

1 Carbon dioxide expressed as carbon equivalent.

Source: Warren Spring Laboratory; Department of Trade and Industry

9.5 Carbon dioxide and methane emissions: by source, 1991

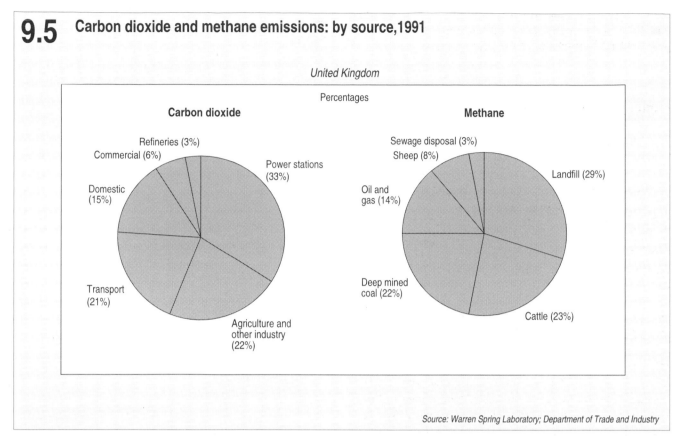

United Kingdom

Percentages

Carbon dioxide

- Refineries (3%)
- Commercial (6%)
- Domestic (15%)
- Power stations (33%)
- Transport (21%)
- Agriculture and other industry (22%)

Methane

- Sewage disposal (3%)
- Sheep (8%)
- Oil and gas (14%)
- Landfill (29%)
- Deep mined coal (22%)
- Cattle (23%)

Source: Warren Spring Laboratory; Department of Trade and Industry

destroying the forests. It is a major contributor to the greenhouse effect, as it is one of the gases which allows sunlight to pass through and strike the earth, but it then behaves rather like a blanket preventing the heat escaping. Assessments by the Intergovernmental Panel on Climate Change indicate that the concentrations of carbon dioxide in the atmosphere have increased by around 25 per cent since 1750. The largest source of carbon dioxide emissions in 1991 was power stations, which burn fossil fuels. They produced over 50 million tonnes of carbon dioxide, a third of all emissions **(Chart 9.4)**. Overall emissions of carbon dioxide were ten per cent lower in 1991 than 20 years ago, though they have shown little change since the mid 1980s. However, emissions from motor vehicles have nearly doubled to 30 million tonnes in the last 20 years.

Methane is another gas which contributes to the greenhouse effect. It is more effective than carbon dioxide in trapping the heat of the sun but it is present in much smaller quantities. The largest source of methane is landfill gas **(Chart 9.5)**, that is gas produced by decaying household and commercial refuse which has been buried in the ground. Current estimates imply that 500 million tonnes of methane per year are released globally from human activity, of which the United Kingdom's share is more than three million tonnes. However estimates of methane emissions are currently under review and this may revise the estimates of emissions to around five million tonnes. While the biggest direct contribution to the global warming is made by carbon dioxide, 72 per cent, methane accounts for ten per cent and chloroflurocarbons (CFCs) just under 13 per cent.

There has been a dramatic fall in sales in the European Community (EC) of CFCs used in aerosols since 1987. In 1992 the amount of CFCs sold in aerosols was less than a tenth of the amount sold five years ago **(Chart 9.6)**. It is also worth noting that the EC expanded in size during the period covered by the chart, making the fall

9.6 EC sales of CFCs[1]: by use

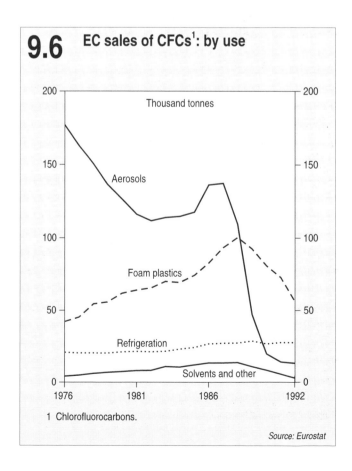

Thousand tonnes

- Aerosols
- Foam plastics
- Refrigeration
- Solvents and other

1976   1981   1986   1992

1 Chlorofluorocarbons.

Source: Eurostat

in sales more notable. There was some growth in sales of CFCs in foam plastics in the EC up to 1988, but since then there has been a drop of almost 45 per cent.

In addition to global warming CFCs also give rise to products which damage the ozone layer. This layer protects the earth from harmful ultraviolet-B radiation, by reducing the amount which reaches the earth's surface. Ultraviolet-B may cause skin cancer in people and have harmful effects on plant and animal life. The effects of ozone-depleting substances since the 1970s has led to a significant depletion of the layer, such that in Spring 1993 the depth of the layer was the thinnest ever recorded over the United Kingdom.

Air quality and pollution

The majority of air pollutants are caused by industry or transport. For example, nearly three quarters of sulphur dioxide emissions are produced by power stations and half of volatile organic compounds are produced by industry. Road transport, on the other hand, accounts for about 90 per cent of carbon monoxide emissions, 50 per cent of nitrogen oxides and 42 per cent of black smoke emissions. In 1991 emissions of black smoke and sulphur dioxide were both about half of the level they were 20 years ago, while emissions of carbon monoxide increased by almost half over the same period **(Table 9.7)**.

Acid deposition is the term used to describe the process by which acidic gases are deposited on land or water, sometimes at great distance from the source of the pollution. Sulphur dioxide, nitrogen oxides and hydrogen chloride are the gases which are the main contributors to acid rain. Acid deposition can inhibit plant nutrition and restrict the range of plant and animal life. In addition, it also damages buildings, by attacking stone, concrete and metal.

9.7 Air pollution: emissions of selected pollutants

		United Kingdom			Million tonnes
	Black smoke	Carbon monoxide	Nitrogen oxides[1]	Sulphur dioxide	Volatile organic compounds
1971	0.92	4.64	2.26	6.06	2.22
1976	0.65	4.68	2.28	5.18	2.31
1981	0.53	5.10	2.30	4.44	2.52
1986	0.57	5.80	2.48	3.90	2.67
1987	0.53	6.07	2.60	3.90	2.69
1988	0.52	6.42	2.68	3.81	2.71
1989	0.50	6.81	2.76	3.72	2.72
1990	0.47	6.70	2.78	3.78	2.68
1991	0.50	6.74	2.75	3.57	2.68

1 Nitrogen oxides expressed as nitrogen dioxide equivalent.

Source: Warren Spring Laboratory, Department of Trade and Industry

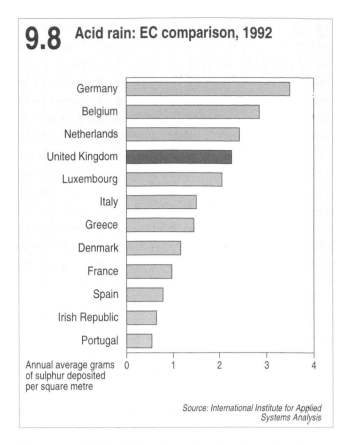

9.8 Acid rain: EC comparison, 1992

Annual average grams of sulphur deposited per square metre

Source: International Institute for Applied Systems Analysis

The amount of sulphur deposited is dependent upon the level of rainfall and the concentration of sulphur in the rain. **Chart 9.8** shows the extent of sulphur deposition in the EC in 1992. The amount deposited in Germany was the highest in the EC; it was more than six times the amount deposited in Portugal, the EC country with the lowest level of deposition. The amount deposited in the United Kingdom was around two thirds of the German level. However the extent of environmental damage caused by this deposition is dependent not only upon the level of sulphur deposition but also on the susceptibility of the soil to acid attack - the most susceptible soils are those with a low clay or organic content.

Lead is absorbed by people via food, air, water and soil or dust. Once inhaled or ingested it can accumulate in the body and can lead eventually to health problems, particularly in children. Lead gets into the atmosphere from burning leaded petrol and coal, or as a result of industrial processes, such as metal smelting. The largest single source of lead in the air originates from burning leaded petrol. Directives by the EC have progressively reduced the amount of lead in petrol, and since 1986 unleaded petrol has been available in the United Kingdom. The relative reduction of fuel duty on unleaded, compared with leaded, petrol since 1987 has boosted sales and in February 1993 the amount of unleaded petrol delivered to petrol stations in the United Kingdom exceeded leaded petrol for the first time. **Chart 9.1**, at the beginning of the chapter, shows growth in sales of unleaded petrol in the United Kingdom as a percentage of total petrol sales.

9.9 Unleaded petrol sales as a percentage of all petrol sales: EC comparison, 1992

Percentages

	1988	1991	1992
Germany[1]	43.7	77.0	84.0
Denmark	32.1	63.4	69.6
Netherlands	25.9	59.8	69.5
Luxembourg	8.5	44.7	57.8
Belgium	0.3	37.4	47.0
United Kingdom	1.1	40.8	46.8
France	0.2	25.0	34.1
Irish Republic	..	23.9	30.2
Greece	..	7.3	16.4
Italy	0.7	6.7	13.1
Portugal	..	8.2	13.1
Spain	0.1	3.1	6.1
EUR12	13.3	40.7	47.1

1 German Federal Republic for 1988 and Germany as constituted since 3 October 1990 for 1991 and 1992.

Source: Eurostat

The highest percentage of unleaded petrol sold in the EC in 1992 was recorded by Germany, where 84 per cent of petrol sold was unleaded **(Table 9.9)**. Denmark, the Netherlands and Luxembourg were the only other countries to sell more unleaded petrol than leaded. Motorists attitudes to the use of unleaded petrol are shown in **Chart 9.2**.

Water quality

Although there was an overall improvement in water quality between 1958 and 1980, since then the quality of water in the rivers and canals of England and Wales has fallen slightly. In Scotland the improving trend has continued. In England and Wales around 15 per cent of total river length was downgraded to a lower quality

9.10 River and canal quality: by region, 1990

United Kingdom — Percentages

	Good	Fair	Poor	Bad
North West	55	26	15	4
Northumbria	86	11	3	-
Severn-Trent	52	37	10	1
Yorkshire	70	15	12	3
Anglian	57	36	8	-
Thames	61	32	7	-
Southern	69	23	7	1
Wessex	60	34	5	1
South West	51	30	17	2
Welsh[1]	84	9	6	1
Scotland	97	2	-	-
Northern Ireland[2]	82	15	3	-

1 Regional boundaries are based on river catchment areas and not county borders.
2 Data are for 1991.

Source: National Rivers Authority; The Scottish Office; Department of the Environment, Northern Ireland

class between 1985 and 1990, while around 11 per cent was upgraded. However, this net overall downgrading was due, in part, to changes in the surveying methods and the effects of two dry summers. In Scotland different classifications are used, although the categories broadly correspond with those used in the rest of the United Kingdom.

Table 9.10 shows that Scotland was the region with highest proportion, 97 per cent, of river length in the best quality category in 1990, whilst the South West had the lowest proportion at 51 per cent. The North West region had the longest length of rivers in the poorest quality category.

Much of the sewerage system in the United Kingdom was built in Victorian times. The homes of 96 per cent of the population are connected to mains sewers and 85 per cent are served by sewage treatment works. Sewage which is not treated by treatment works is either disposed of by septic tanks or by direct outfalls to rivers and the sea. The sewerage system is being upgraded to meet the requirements of the *EC Urban Waste Water Treatment Directive* which requires that all significant discharges of sewage are treated.

The quality of Britain's bathing waters has improved in recent years and in 1993, 80 per cent of bathing waters complied with the standards of the *EC Bathing Water Directive*. The compliance rate varies from 39 per cent in the North West to 95 per cent in Yorkshire, excluding Thames which only has three bathing waters **(Table 9.11)**. Details of the EC directive are given in Part 9 of the Appendix.

9.11 Compliance with EC Bathing Water Directive[1] coliform standards: by coastal region, 1988 and 1993

United Kingdom — Numbers and percentages

	Identified bathing waters (numbers)		Percentage complying	
	1988	1993	1988	1993
United Kingdom	403	457	66	80
North West	33	33	18	39
Northumbrian	19	34	47	74
Yorkshire	22	22	95	95
Anglian	28	33	68	85
Thames	2	3	0	100
Southern	65	67	42	87
Wessex	38	42	79	83
South West	109	133	84	80
Welsh	48	51	77	82
England & Wales	364	418	66	79
Scotland	23	23	52	78
Northern Ireland	16	16	88	94

1 See Appendix, Part 9: Quality of bathing water.

Source: National Rivers Authority; The Scottish Office; Department of the Environment, Northern Ireland

Waste

Around 400 million tonnes of waste are produced annually in the United Kingdom. The sectors with the largest waste generation are agriculture with 80 million tonnes and mining and quarrying with 110 million tonnes. We also import a small amount of hazardous waste for treatment and disposal and some scrap materials for use in recycling and recovery processes. In 1991-92 almost 47 thousand tonnes of hazardous wastes were imported under the *Transfrontier Shipment Regulation of 1988*. This was 50 per cent more than was imported in 1989-90, which is the first year for which complete records under this regulation are available. Around 30 per cent of the waste imported in 1991-92 came from Switzerland, which was the largest single exporter of hazardous wastes to the United Kingdom **(Chart 9.12)**.

Of the national waste arisings, approximately 15 million tonnes is estimated to come from weekly household collections. It is thought that half of this waste could be recycled and the Government has set a target of recycling half of this recyclable fraction of 'dustbin' waste by the year 2000. Currently only five per cent of household waste is recycled. **Chart 9.13** shows what proportion of various materials consumed in the United Kingdom is made of recycled material. These figures include scrap from industrial and commercial, as well as domestic, sources. The amount of cullet (scrap glass) reused has doubled since 1984 due to a threefold increase in the amount of cullet collected in bottle banks. The number of bottle bank sites also trebled between 1984 and 1991 to nearly 7.2 thousand.

9.12 Imports of hazardous waste: by country of origin, 1991-92

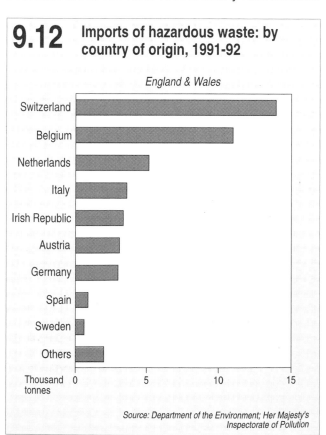

England & Wales

Source: Department of the Environment; Her Majesty's Inspectorate of Pollution

9.13 Recycled scrap as a proportion of total consumption for selected materials

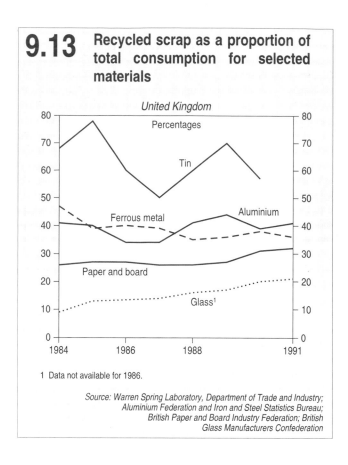

United Kingdom

1 Data not available for 1986.

Source: Warren Spring Laboratory, Department of Trade and Industry; Aluminium Federation and Iron and Steel Statistics Bureau; British Paper and Board Industry Federation; British Glass Manufacturers Confederation

Land use

More than three quarters of the land area in the United Kingdom is still used for agriculture; a further 10 per cent is covered by forest and woodland **(Chart 9.14)**.

9.14 Land use, 1991

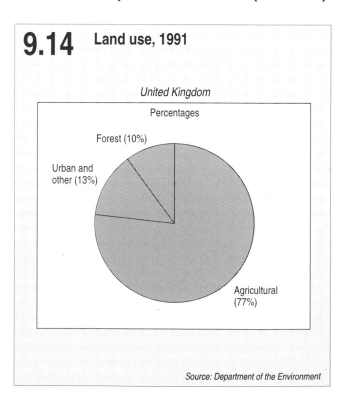

United Kingdom

Source: Department of the Environment

9.15 Agricultural land use[1]

United Kingdom   Thousand hectares

	1961	1971	1981	1986	1990	1991	1992	1993
Crop areas, of which:	4,276	4,838	4,995	5,239	5,013	4,955	4,980	4,508
Wheat	739	1,097	1,491	1,997	2,013	1,980	2,067	1,762
Barley	1,549	2,288	2,327	1,916	1,516	1,393	1,297	1,163
Other cereals (excluding maize)	768	424	161	111	128	126	123	105
Rape grown for oilseed[2]	..	5	125	299	390	440	421	374
Sugar beet not for stockfeeding	173	190	210	205	194	196	197	197
Potatoes (early and maincrop)	285	256	191	178	177	176	180	167
Other crops	761	577	490	533	595	644	696	740
Bare fallow	123	74	76	48	64	64	53	49
Grasses	7,999	7,240	7,013	6,801	6,843	6,835	6,764	6,732
Sole right rough grazing	..	5,550	5,021	4,829	4,713	4,679	4,674	4,618
All other land on agricultural holdings[3]	..	285	488	543	680	712	791	1,372
Common rough grazing	..	1,128	1,214	1,216	1,236	1,233	1,230	1,230
Total agricultural land	..	19,115	18,808	18,676	18,549	18,479	18,493	18,509

1 Figures include estimates for minor holdings in England and Wales but not for Scotland and Northern Ireland.
2 England and Wales only for 1971 and 1981.
3 Includes woodland and set-aside land.

Source: Ministry of Agriculture, Fisheries and Food; Welsh Office; The Scottish Office Agriculture and Fisheries Department; Department of Agriculture, Northern Ireland

Although there has been little change in the amount of land used for agriculture, there have been major changes in the crops grown. Most recently the amount of land under cereals and other arable crops declined between June 1992 and June 1993 **(Table 9.15)**. The area under wheat, for example, fell by 15 per cent, while that for rape grown for oilseed fell by 11 per cent. This has resulted from the radical overhaul of payments to the arable sector under the 1992 reform of the *EC Common Agricultural Policy.*

Direct aids are now being given to farmers in place of high guaranteed support prices. Farmers are eligible for this aid if they set aside a proportion of their land, subject to certain conditions, thus removing it from arable production. This explains most of the 73 per cent increase in the category 'Other land on agricultural holdings' between 1992 and 1993.

Since 1947 the area of forest and woodland cover in Great Britain has increased by nearly 70 per cent. By far the majority of trees planted twenty years ago were conifers **(Chart 9.16)**. However in 1992 only 9.0 thousand hectares of conifers were planted, a third of the area planted in 1988-89, while the area of broadleaves planted in 1992, at 8.6 thousand hectares, was nearly three times that of 1988-89.

Landscape features such as hedgerows, walls and fences are important for land management and often provide important wildlife habitats. In recent years agricultural intensification has led to a loss of such boundaries. According to the 1990 Countryside Survey the lenght of headrows in Great Britain fell by 23 per

cent between 1984 and 1990. Most of this loss was a result of a change in the form of hedges, for example, from a managed hedge to a line of trees. About 20 thousand kilometres (ten per cent) of walls were also lost over this period, whilst boundary fences showed a net increase of 75 thousand kilometres - 11 per cent.

9.16 New tree planting

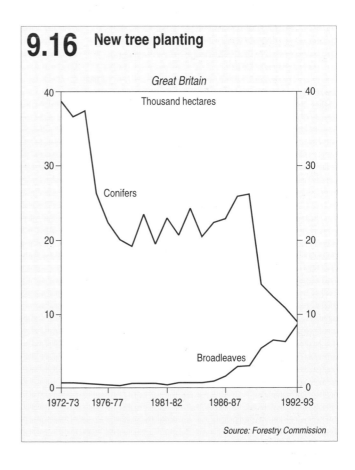

Source: Forestry Commission

Radioactivity

Everyone is exposed to radiation; the majority of the exposure, or the 'dose', we receive comes from naturally occurring radiation such as radon gas from the ground and buildings around us, the food we eat or from cosmic radiation reaching the earth's surface **(Chart 9.17)**. The main source of natural radiation is radon gas which contributes half the dose received by people in the United Kingdom each year.

Radon gas is produced by the decay of the trace amounts of uranium that occur in virtually all rocks. In open air radon disperses quickly and levels outdoors are low. However, elevated levels can accumulate in enclosed spaces such as buildings, and in areas of porous rocks containing above average levels of uranium these levels can be appreciable. Radon Affected Areas have been declared in the English counties of Cornwall, Derbyshire, Devon, Northamptonshire and Somerset, in the Scottish regions of Grampian and Highland and in the south east corner of Northern Ireland.

Around 15 per cent of the radiation we receive comes from artificial sources and the majority of this we receive in the form of X-rays or from other medical treatment. Less than 0.5 per cent can be attributed to fallout from nuclear weapons and incidents such as Chernobyl; discharges from power stations contribute less than 0.1 per cent to the average annual dose.

Landscape and nature conservation

National Parks in England and Wales, Areas of Outstanding National Beauty in England, Wales and Northern Ireland, and National Scenic Areas in Scotland are the major designations to protect areas of the finest landscape in the United Kingdom; together they account for nearly 20 per cent of the total land area of the United Kingdom. Within these designated areas developments may be carried out, but the rules are more restricted than elsewhere. Nearly two thirds of East Sussex was designated in this way - the largest proportion for any English county.

Green Belts are areas of designated land in which strict control over development restricts the sprawl of built-up areas, preserves the special character of historic towns and assists in urban regeneration. Green Belts in England cover 1.5 million hectares, almost 12 per cent of the country and more than double the total in 1979. There are five Green Belts in Scotland covering over 155 thousand hectares, about two per cent of the country, and in Northern Ireland Green Belts cover 200 thousand hectares, 17 per cent of the land area. There are no Green Belts in Wales. In England the county with the highest percentage of land designated in this category is Surrey, where just over three quarters is Green Belt. **Chart 9.18** gives an overall picture by illustrating the total area of each county designated as

9.18 Land designated as Green Belt, National Parks or areas of Outstanding Natural Beauty,[1] 1992

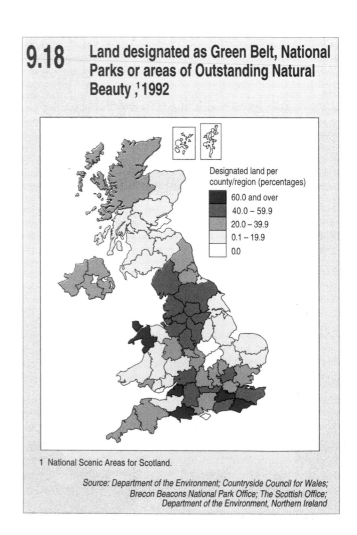

Designated land per county/region (percentages)
- 60.0 and over
- 40.0 – 59.9
- 20.0 – 39.9
- 0.1 – 19.9
- 0.0

1 National Scenic Areas for Scotland.

Source: Department of the Environment; Countryside Council for Wales; Brecon Beacons National Park Office; The Scottish Office; Department of the Environment, Northern Ireland

9.17 Radiation exposure of the population: by source, 1991

United Kingdom

Percentages

- Medical (14.0%)
- Other (0.5%)
- Cosmic (10.0%)
- Radon in air (50.0%)
- Food and drink (11.5%)
- Ground and Buildings (14.0%)

Natural (85.5%) — Artificial (14.5%)

Source: National Radiological Protection Board

9.19 The breeding populations[1] of farmland birds

Great Britain					Indices
	1971	1976	1980	1986	1991
Corn Bunting	137	130	100	48	42
Goldfinch	69	110	100	43	97
Greenfinch	95	112	100	85	91
Grey Partridge	158	133	100	60	48
Jackdaw	73	81	100	153	127
Kestrel	93	107	100	79	109
Lapwing	83	102	100	71	54
Linnet	126	126	100	52	66
Little Owl	55	78	100	72	42
Reed Bunting	132	182	100	70	83
Skylark	95	108	100	56	50
Starling	82	102	100	81	66
Stock Dove	55	76	100	138	143
Tree Sparrow	170	161	100	37	27
Turtle Dove	109	144	100	62	32
Whitethroat	126	109	100	83	91
Yellow Wagtail	71	109	100	83	83
Yellowhammer	89	94	100	92	67

1 See Appendix, Part 9: Farmland birds.

Source: British Trust for Ornithology

Green Belt, National Park or Area of Outstanding Natural Beauty. On this basis the county with the highest proportion of designated land is also Surrey.

Changing agricultural practices may have affected the populations of some of our species of birds. The Common Birds Census carried out by the British Trust for Ornithology measures changes in the breeding bird population in Great Britain between years. It has shown that those species whose habitats include lowland farms have been particularly affected. For example, the area occupied by the barn owl fell by nearly 40 per cent between 1970 and 1990. This is because modern farming methods have considerably reduced the number of old trees and barns, the birds' usual habitat. Other species have also declined in numbers. The fall was greatest amongst the seed eating species such as the tree sparrow, the numbers of which fell in 1991 to only 15 per cent of their level 20 years ago **(Table 9.19)**. Only two species, jackdaws and stock doves, recorded large increases.

Natural resources

Fish stocks in the seas around the United Kingdom are determined primarily by the intensity with which they are fished and natural factors. They are not generally affected by the relatively low level of pollution found in the sea. **Table 9.20** illustrates the stocks of fish in the seas around the United Kingdom in terms of spawning stock biomass, which is the weight of fish capable of reproducing. The table shows that the North Sea herring population was seriously affected by over-fishing in the 1970s. Stocks have now virtually recovered

9.20 Fish stocks: by sea area and selected species

United Kingdom				Thousand tonnes
	1970-1979[1]	1980-1989[1]	1990	1991	1992
North Sea					
Cod	195	122	62	56	51
Haddock	314	201	71	55	105
Sole	47	38	94	80	74
Herring[2]	169	692	1,247	1,277	1,320
West of Scotland					
Cod	29	24	18	17	19
Haddock	71	63	22	19	23
Western English Channel					
Sole	3	4	1	1	1

1 Annual averages.
2 Includes Eastern English Channel.

Source: Ministry of Agriculture, Fisheries and Food

to the 1960s levels, following the suspension of herring fishing in the North Sea between 1978 and 1982. In contrast stocks of North Sea cod continue to decrease and amounted to only 51 thousand tonnes in 1992 - a third of the level of 150 thousand tonnes, which is considered by the Advisory Committee on Fish Management to be the lowest desirable biological level.

Around 70 per cent of the proven reserves of oil and nearly 60 per cent of the proven reserves of gas have been recovered from the United Kingdom continental shelf **(Table 9.21)**. However the exploration and appraisal of new oilfields has increased the reserves by more than production since 1988; the continuation of this may result in the quantities so far produced representing less than a quarter of the final amount eventually extracted.

9.21 Oil and gas reserves, 1992

United Kingdom continental shelf	Million tonnes and billion cubic metres	
	Oil (million tonnes)	Gas (billion cubic metres)
Fields already discovered		
Proven reserves	2,170	1,465
Probable reserves	755	740
Possible reserves	710	515
Total initial reserves in present discoveries of which:	2,170-3,635	1,465-2,720
Already recovered	1,560	855
Estimates in potential future discoveries	530-3,370	270-1,277
Total recoverable reserves	2,700-7,005	1,735-3,997
Potential additional reserves	160-500	140-325

Source: Department of Trade and Industry

9.22 Production of primary fuels

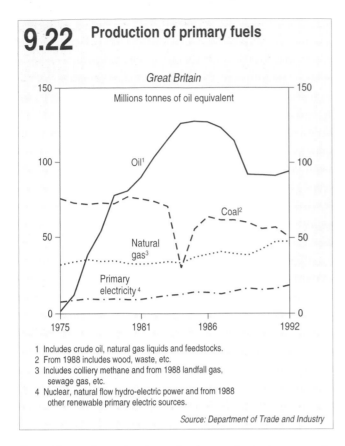

Great Britain

1 Includes crude oil, natural gas liquids and feedstocks.
2 From 1988 includes wood, waste, etc.
3 Includes colliery methane and from 1988 landfall gas, sewage gas, etc.
4 Nuclear, natural flow hydro-electric power and from 1988 other renewable primary electric sources.

Source: Department of Trade and Industry

9.23 Electricity generation: by fuel used, EC comparison, 1991

Percentages

	Oil	Coal[1]	Other fossil fuel[2]	Nuclear	Other[3]
United Kingdom	9.5	65.2	2.6	20.8	2.0
Belgium	2.5	22.9	13.5	59.7	1.4
Denmark	3.7	90.9	3.1	.	2.3
France	3.1	8.6	1.6	72.7	14.0
Germany (Fed. Rep.)	2.7	56.6	9.3	27.9	3.6
Greece	24.5	65.7	0.3	.	9.6
Irish Republic	16.0	52.6	24.7	.	6.7
Luxembourg	1.8	.	41.5	.	56.8
Netherlands	4.6	30.6	60.4	4.4	0.2
Italy	46.5	12.7	18.1	.	22.8
Portugal	33.3	32.3	2.9	.	31.5
Spain	6.4	37.1	1.9	35.9	18.8
EUR12	10.2	38.4	9.4	33.6	8.4

1 Includes coal derivatives, and peat for Irish Republic.
2 Includes natural gas, derived gas, steam, wood, peat and industrial residues.
3 Hydro-electric and geothermal.

Source: Eurostat

Overall, total production of primary fuels has nearly doubled since 1975 **(Chart 9.22)**. Oil production in the United Kingdom peaked in 1985 and then fell until 1991. A small rise was recorded in 1992 and further increases are expected in succeeding years as new fields come on stream, reaching a secondary peak in the mid to late 1990s. Coal production has been declining since the miners strike in the 1980s, as the demand for coal by industry, particularly for electricity generation, has been declining. On the other hand since 1975 the production of primary electricity (ie nuclear and hydro-electric power and other renewable primary electricity sources such as wind power) has been generally increasing and the amount produced in 1992 was more than double the amount in 1975.

Natural gas production has increased by more than 40 per cent since 1984; in 1992 it stood at nearly 48 million tonnes of oil equivalent.

Coal was by far the most important fuel for electricity generation in the United Kingdom in 1991, with over three times more electricity generated by coal than nuclear power, the next most important source **(Table 9.23)**. France generates nearly three quarters of its electricity using nuclear power, more than three times the proportion in the United Kingdom. In recent years there has been an increase in the amount of electricity generated by gas, household rubbish and even wind power. Electricity produced by nuclear power stations results in the emission of far less greenhouse gases, but potential risks such as routine emissions of radioactivity, the problem of waste disposal and radioactive contamination accidents persist.

REFERENCES AND FURTHER READING

The following list contains selected publications relevant to Chapter 9: Environment. Those published by HMSO are available from the addresses shown on the back cover of *Social Trends*.

Development of the Oil and Gas Resources of the United Kingdom, Department of Trade & Industry
Digest of Agricultural Census Statistics, HMSO
Digest of the United Kingdom Energy Statistics, HMSO
Digest of Environmental Protection and Water Statistics, HMSO
Environment 1991, Eurostat

Environmental Digest for Wales, Welsh Office
Eurostat Environment Statistics, HMSO
Forestry Facts and Figures, Forestry Commission
National Radiological Protection Board Statement on Radon in Homes, HMSO
OECD Environmental Data Compendium, EUROSTAT
Radon Affected Areas, HMSO
Scottish Environmental Statistics, Scottish Office
The Householder's Guide to Radon, Department of the Environment
The UK Environment, HMSO
This Common Inheritance, HMSO

Chapter 10: Leisure

Availability of leisure time

●   Men in full-time employment enjoyed on average nearly 46 hours of free time per week in 1992-93, 14 more than women.

(Chart 10.1)

Home-based leisure activities

●   People in the United Kingdom watched nearly 27 hours of television a week in 1992.   *(Table 10.4)*

●   In 1992 the number of CDs sold in the United Kingdom exceeded the number of cassettes sold for the first time.

(Chart 10.8)

Social and cultural activities

●   Fewer than two visits to the cinema were made on average in 1992 by people in the United Kingdom, less than half the number made in the USA.   *(Chart 10.14)*

Sporting activities

●   Average attendances in the Football Association Premier League were 2 per cent lower than in the former Football League Division One in the previous season.   *(Table 10.22)*

●   Over the whole of the United Kingdom in 1993 the North West of England had the best provision of swimming pools.

(Chart 10.23)

Holidays

●   About a quarter of adults took two or more holidays in 1992, more than three times the proportion 25 years ago.

(Chart 10.24)

Resources

●   Expenditure on leisure accounted for about 17 per cent of the household budget in the United Kingdom in 1992.

(Table 10.29)

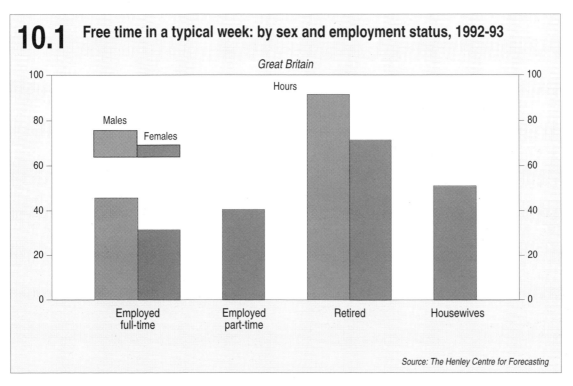

10.1   **Free time in a typical week: by sex and employment status, 1992-93**

Great Britain

Source: The Henley Centre for Forecasting

10.2 Time use in a typical week: by employment status and sex, 1992-93

Great Britain   *Hours*

| | Full-time employees | | Part-time female employees | Housewives | Retired | |
	Males	Females			Males	Females
Weekly hours spent on:						
Employment and travel[1]	47.1	42.2	20.8	0.4	0.5	0.6
Essential cooking, shopping and housework	13.0	25.5	32.5	38.1	17.0	33.0
Essential childcare, personal hygiene and other shopping	13.2	20.0	25.2	29.4	10.0	14.0
Sleep[2]	49.0	49.0	49.0	49.0	49.0	49.0
Free time	45.7	31.4	40.6	51.1	91.5	71.4
Free time per weekday	5.0	3.0	4.7	6.6	12.8	9.7
Free time per weekend day	10.3	8.2	8.5	9.0	13.8	11.5

1 Travel to and from place of work.
2 Seven hours per night.

Source: The Henley Centre for Forecasting

Availability of leisure time

Not surprisingly retired people have around twice the amount of free time of those in full-time employment. In 1992-93 retired men enjoyed over 90 hours of free time per week - 20 hours more than retired women **(Chart 10.1)**. Similarly, amongst people in full-time employment men enjoyed more free time than women - 46 hours per week for men compared with 31 hours for women **(Table 10.2)**. Women have less free time than men because they spend more time looking after the children, cleaning, cooking and shopping.

Home-based leisure activities

Watching the television and visiting or entertaining friends or relatives have remained the most popular home-based leisure activities **(Chart 10.3)**. Certain of these activities are more popular with men than women. Not surprisingly, the greatest difference between men and women was in participation in dressmaking, needlework or knitting - 41 per cent of women, but only three per cent of men, had done some of this in the previous four weeks. Although other differences were much smaller, women were also more likely than men to have visited or entertained friends and to have read books. On the other hand, men were more likely than women to have done some DIY or gardening, or to have listened to the radio or records and tapes.

10.3 Participation in home-based leisure activities, 1990

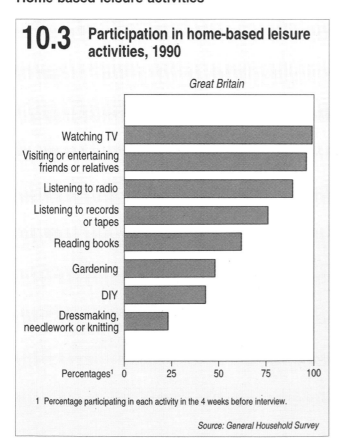

Great Britain

Watching TV
Visiting or entertaining friends or relatives
Listening to radio
Listening to records or tapes
Reading books
Gardening
DIY
Dressmaking, needlework or knitting

Percentages[1]   0   25   50   75   100

1 Percentage participating in each activity in the 4 weeks before interview.

Source: General Household Survey

10.4 Television viewing: by social class

United Kingdom   Hours and minutes and percentages

	1986	1991	1992
Social class[1]			
(hours:mins per week)			
AB	19:50	18:51	19:56
C1	23:05	23:56	25:08
C2	26:00	26:57	27:30
DE	33:35	31:56	31:54
All persons	26:32	26:04	26:44
Reach[2]			
(percentages)			
Daily	*78*	*79*	*82*
Weekly	*94*	*94*	*95*

1 See Appendix, Part 5: Social class.
2 Percentage of the United Kingdom population aged 4 and over who viewed TV for at least three consecutive minutes.

Source: Broadcasters' Audience Research Board; British Broadcasting Corporation; AGB Limited; RSMB Limited

10.5 Radio and television audiences[1] throughout the day, 1992[2]

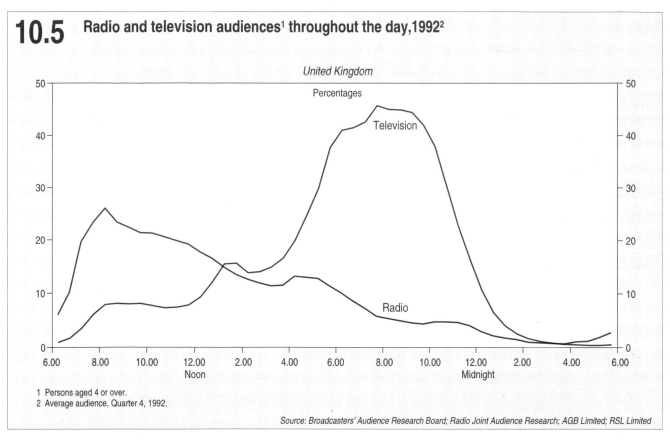

1 Persons aged 4 or over.
2 Average audience, Quarter 4, 1992.

Source: Broadcasters' Audience Research Board; Radio Joint Audience Research; AGB Limited; RSL Limited

People watched more television in 1992 than in each of the past five years, at around 26 and three quarter hours per week **(Table 10.4)**. People in the lowest social class group watched the most television - nearly 32 hours per week in 1992, 12 hours more than those in the highest social class group.

10.6 Video cassette recorders and hiring of pre-recorded tapes

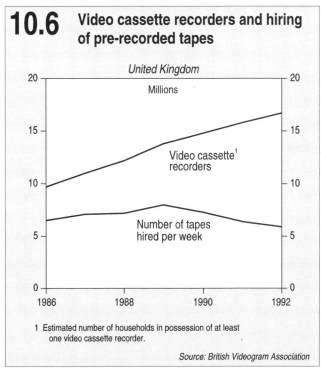

1 Estimated number of households in possession of at least one video cassette recorder.

Source: British Videogram Association

On average nearly half the population aged four and over watched TV between 7.30 and 8.00 in the evening in the fourth quarter 1992 **(Chart 10.5)**. This is traditionally the time that the soaps, Coronation Street and EastEnders, are scheduled. Despite the advent of breakfast television several years ago, people still prefer to listen to the radio with their cornflakes. Just over a quarter of people tuned into the radio between 8.00 and 8.30 in the morning.

Television has seen a number of changes during 1992. The most notable of these was the implementation of the new Independent Television franchises following the competitive tendering process. Three companies, Thames, Television South and Television South West, lost their franchises to be replaced from 1 January 1993 by Carlton, Meridian and West Country TV. The breakfast television company TV-AM also lost in favour of GMTV. Towards the end of 1993 satellite TV was boosted by the arrival of a further nine channels on the Astra satellite. The viewing figures for television in this chapter take account of these developments, and include viewing from satellite, cable and video.

The number of domestic video recorders in the United Kingdom increased to nearly 17 million in 1992 **(Chart 10.6)**, but the annual rate of increase is less than half that of five years ago. The number of video tapes hired has declined for the past three years.

10.7 BBC network radio output: by programme type

United Kingdom — Percentages

	1970-71	1980-81	1990-91	1991-92
Music	61.9	60.3	53.6	56.6
Features, documentaries, current affairs	15.5	15.0	22.6	22.3
News	6.9	5.9	6.7	5.5
Sport	2.2	3.5	5.3	5.0
Drama	4.8	3.0	2.9	2.9
Light entertainment	2.2	2.1	2.0	1.8
Continuity	1.1	2.0	1.5	1.5
Religion	1.8	1.6	1.4	1.3
Schools	1.9	1.4	1.8	1.2
Children's	..	0.9	1.1	1.1
Open University	0.2	3.3	0.6	0.5
Continuing education	1.5	1.0	0.4	0.3

Source: British Broadcasting Corporation

Music, features, documentaries and current affairs accounted for over three quarters of BBC radio output in 1991-92 **(Table 10.7)**. Music dominated radio output, though its share was around five percentage points lower than 20 years ago.

The compact disc or CD has revolutionised the way we listen to music. In 1992, for the first time, there were more CDs sold in the United Kingdom than cassettes **(Chart 10.8)**. In addition sales of LPs continued to fall in 1992 accounting for only a tenth of the sales they did in 1981.

The Radio Times celebrated its 70th anniversary in 1993. It was launched because of the reluctance of the national press to publish programme listings. This situation has been reversed dramatically over the

10.8 Trade deliveries of LPs, cassettes, compact discs and singles

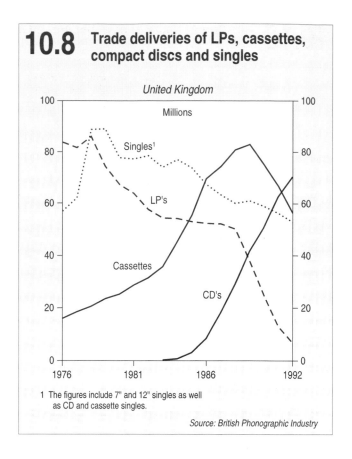

United Kingdom

1 The figures include 7" and 12" singles as well as CD and cassette singles.

Source: British Phonographic Industry

years, culminating in March 1991 when the BBC's monopoly over publishing its own listings ended. Many national newspapers today carry comprehensive weekly, as well as daily, listings and in addition a number of magazines have been established to rival the existing Radio Times and TV Times. These new magazines have become more popular and as a result

10.9 Reading of the most popular magazines: by sex and age, 1992

Great Britain

	Percentage of adults reading each magazine in 1992			Percentage of each age group reading each magazine in 1992				Readership[1] (millions)		Readers per copy (numbers)
	Males	Females	All adults	15-24	25-44	45-64	65 and over	1971	1992	1992
General magazines										
Reader's Digest	14	12	13	9	12	17	14	9.2	5.9	3.9
Radio Times	13	12	12	14	12	13	12	9.5	5.7	3.6
TV Times	11	11	11	15	10	11	9	9.9	5.0	4.5
Viz	14	5	10	29	11	2	-	.	4.3	1.0
TV Quick	5	8	6	9	8	5	3	.	2.9	..
What's on TV	6	7	6	9	7	4	5	.	2.8	1.9
Women's magazines[2]										
Bella	3	14	9	10	11	8	7	.	3.3	..
Woman's Own	3	14	9	10	10	8	7	7.2	3.4	4.9
Take a Break	4	13	8	12	10	8	4	.	3.0	..
Woman	2	11	6	6	7	6	5	8.0	2.6	3.8
Woman's Weekly	2	10	6	3	4	7	11	4.7	2.4	3.2
Best	2	10	6	7	7	6	3	.	2.3	3.9

1 Defined as the average issue readership and represents the number of people who claim to have read or looked at one or more copies of a given publication during a period equal to the interval at which the publication appears.
2 The age analysis for women's magazines includes male readers.

Source: National Readership Surveys Ltd

10.10 Reading of national newspapers: by sex and age, 1992

Great Britain

	Percentage of adults reading each paper in 1992			Percentage of each age group reading each paper in 1992				Readership[1] (millions)		Readers per copy (numbers)
	Males	Females	All adults	15-24	25-44	45-64	65 and over	1971	1992	1992
Daily newspapers										
The Sun	24	19	21	28	23	20	15	8.5	9.7	2.7
Daily Mirror	19	15	17	18	16	18	17	13.8	7.8	2.8
Daily Mail	10	10	10	8	9	11	11	4.8	4.5	2.6
Daily Express	9	8	8	7	6	10	11	9.7	3.8	2.5
The Daily Telegraph	6	5	6	4	4	7	7	3.6	2.5	2.4
Daily Star	7	4	5	8	6	5	2	.	2.4	3.0
Today	4	3	3	4	4	3	2	.	1.5	2.9
The Guardian	3	2	3	3	4	3	1	1.1	1.3	3.1
The Independent	3	2	2	2	3	2	1	.	1.1	2.9
The Times	3	2	2	2	2	3	1	1.1	1.0	2.7
Financial Times	2	1	1	1	2	1	-	0.7	0.6	3.6
Any national daily newspaper[2]	65	56	60	59	57	64	62	..	27.3	..
Sunday newspapers										
News of the World	29	26	28	35	31	26	19	15.8	12.5	2.7
Sunday Mirror	20	18	19	22	20	20	16	13.5	8.8	3.2
The People	14	13	13	13	12	15	14	14.4	6.1	2.9
The Mail on Sunday	13	13	13	14	14	14	9	.	5.8	2.9
Sunday Express	11	11	11	10	8	13	14	10.4	4.9	2.8
The Sunday Times	9	7	8	9	9	8	4	3.7	3.5	3.0
Sunday Telegraph	4	4	4	3	4	5	5	2.1	1.8	3.2
The Observer	4	3	4	4	4	4	2	2.4	1.7	3.1
Sunday Sport	5	1	3	7	3	1	-	.	1.3	4.1
Independent on Sunday	3	2	3	4	4	2	1	.	1.3	3.2
Any Sunday newspaper[3]	71	67	69	71	68	72	66	..	31.3	..

1 Defined as the average issue readership and represents the number of people who claim to have read or looked at one or more copies of a given publication during a period equal to the interval at which the publication appears.
2 Includes the above newspapers plus the Daily Record, Sporting Life and Racing Post.
3 Includes the above newspapers plus the Sunday Post, Sunday Mail and Scotland on Sunday.

Source: National Readership Surveys Ltd

the Radio Times lost over half a million readers between 1992 and 1993 and is no longer the most widely read magazine **(Table 10.9)**.

Some magazines vary widely in the age and sex of their readership. Viz, for example, is read by well over a quarter of people aged 15 to 24, but is hardly read at all by the over 45s. The most popular women's magazines are read by younger people, with about 1 in 10 reading the top three: Bella, Woman's Own and Take a Break. The only popular magazine not to follow this trend was Women's Weekly, which was read by 11 per cent of those aged over 65.

The Sun remained the most popular daily newspaper in Great Britain in 1992 **(Table 10.10)**, though the number of readers had fallen by 200 thousand since 1991. It was read by nearly a quarter of men and nearly a fifth of women. The majority of daily newspapers showed a

small increase in readers per issue in 1992. The Daily Mail and Daily Express had the largest increases, around 200 thousand readers per issue. Like magazines, some newspapers show a variation in readership according to age. For example more than a quarter of those aged 15 to 24 read the Sun, compared with only 15 per cent of those aged over 65.

The most popular Sunday newspaper in 1992 was the News of the World with over 12 million readers per issue. The top three Sunday newspapers all lost around 300 thousand readers per issue between 1991 and 1992. The paper to gain the most readers was the Independent on Sunday, launched in January 1990, whose readership increased sixfold, although it still had the lowest readership. The Sunday Sport had virtually the same number of readers, but they were predominantly men: 1 in 20 men read it compared with only 1 in 100 women.

Social and cultural activities

Nearly two thirds of adults spend their leisure time reading books **(Chart 10.3)** and over 50 per cent of men and women belong to a library according to results published by The Policy Studies Institute. **Table 10.11** looks at the provision of library facilities which are available to the general public. Between 1980 and 1992 the overall number of libraries fell by six per cent. However the number open 45 hours per week or more has dropped by almost a third. Mobile libraries which are used to reach isolated rural communities or those areas without proper facilities have remained almost constant in number. Over the same period there has been a drop in the number of books borrowed by the public of about two books per head of population in all areas of the United Kingdom. In 1992 the least books were borrowed in Greater London, at 9.3 per head, while the greatest number were borrowed in the English counties and Scotland, at 10.1.

10.11 Public libraries

United Kingdom	Percentages and numbers			
	1980	1990	1991	1992
Open 45 hours per week or more	21	17	17	16
Open 30-44 hours per week	27	31	31	31
Open less than 30 hours per week	40	38	39	40
Mobile libraries	13	14	14	13
All libraries (= 100%) (numbers)	5,590	5,353	5,283	5,253

Source: Policy Studies Institute

The cinema remains most popular with the young, with almost nine out of ten people in the 7 to 24 age group visiting the cinema in 1992 **(Table 10.12)**. This age group are twice as likely to visit the cinema as people aged 45 and over. But even they are three times more likely to visit the cinema today than they were back in 1984. The United Kingdom's most popular film of all time is 'Jurassic Park'; over 12 million people went to see it in 1993 breaking the previous record of 11 million held by 'E.T. The Extra Terrestrial' for the past 10 years.

10.12 Cinema attendance[1]: by age

Great Britain					Percentages
	1984	1986	1990	1991	1992
Age					
7-14	73	87	85	80	87
15-24	59	82	87	88	89
25-34	49	65	79	70	73
35-44	45	60	70	70	63
45 and over	13	25	41	39	39
All aged 7 and over	38	53	64	61	62

1 Percentage claiming to 'ever go' to the cinema.
Source: Cinema and Video Industry Audience Research

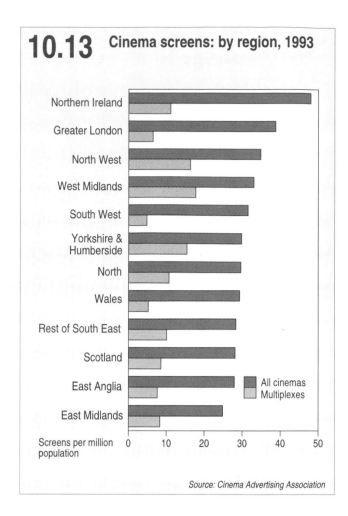

10.13 Cinema screens: by region, 1993

Source: Cinema Advertising Association

The increase in the numbers visiting the cinema has coincided with the development of multiplexes. These are purpose-built centres, often in out of town sites containing up to 14 screens, offering a wide choice of the latest films. The region with the largest number of multiplexes per person in 1993 was the West Midlands **(Chart 10.13)**. Overall Northern Ireland had the largest number of cinema screens per person, whilst the region with the smallest number was the East Midlands. The Cinema Advertising Association estimates that there were nearly 103 million visits to the cinema in 1992, which they forecast will rise to nearly 110 million in 1993, the highest for 14 years.

The recent increase in popularity of the cinema has to be seen in the context of the long-term downward trend in visits per head of population over the last 35 years **(Chart 10.14)**. The number of visits made in the United Kingdom in 1992 represented only eight per cent of the visits made in 1956. All the other countries shown in the chart have experienced a fall in the rate of attendances, though none as great as the United Kingdom. At 3.8 attendances per head of population in 1992 the USA had the highest attendance of the countries in the chart.

10.14 Cinema attendance in selected countries

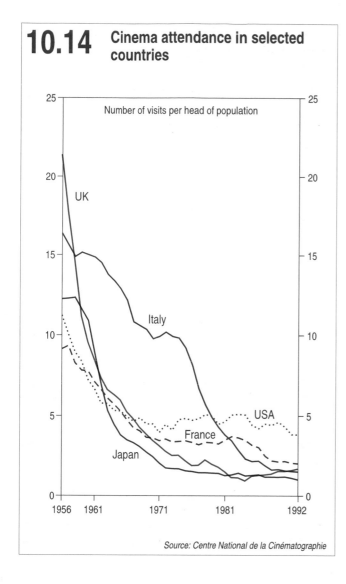

Number of visits per head of population

Source: Centre National de la Cinématographie

The number of West End theatre attendances in 1992 remained constant at around 11 million (Table 10.15). A half of these people went to see modern musicals. Five years ago this proportion was only three out of ten. In the same period the proportion attending traditional musicals has declined by nine percentage points.

10.15 Attendances at West End theatres: by type of performance

Percentages and millions

	1987	1990	1991	1992
Modern musicals	28	41	46	51
Modern drama	13	12	9	10
Traditional musicals	17	10	10	8
Classical plays	7	8	9	8
Comedy	15	11	7	7
Opera/operetta	7	6	6	6
Ballet/dance	4	4	4	4
Thrillers/others	3	2	3	3
Revue/variety	2	4	4	2
Children's shows/pantomime	3	2	2	1
Total (= 100%) (millions)	11	11	11	11

Source: City University Research for the Society of West End Theatres

10.16 Attendances at selected events

Thousands

	1981	1986	1991	1993
Wimbledon	358	400	354	393
Grand National	56	53	56	50
The Derby	50	47	26	27
Varsity Rugby Match	28	38	57	66
The Open Golf Championship	112	134	192	140
Royal Tournament	280	284	266	235
Edinburgh Military Tattoo	205	192	198	210
National Eisteddfod	..	126	164	132
Biggin Hill Air Fair	57	87	61	64
London International Boat Show	243	233	232	185
Southampton International Boat Show	..	98	110	104
London Motor Show	229	.	280	363
Ideal Home Plus	871	752	627	551
Crufts	74	79	77	79

Source: Organisations concerned

Around 393 thousand spectators attended Wimbledon fortnight in 1993, 11 per cent more than in 1991 (Table 10.16). Spectators at both the Grand National and the Derby have fallen in the last 12 years, the Derby by nearly a half. Amongst the other events the number of spectators watching the Edinburgh Military Tattoo rose by six per cent between 1991 and 1992, whilst the number watching the Royal Tournament fell by twice this amount. Some attendances at national events are limited by the number of seats available. For example, the FA Cup final each year attracts a capacity crowd of 80 thousand at Wembley. Detailed records are not kept for other events; the Chelsea Flower Show, for example, attracted around 180 thousand visitors in total in 1993 over the four days of the show.

Visiting friends and relations remained the most popular reason for day trips in Great Britain in 1991-92. Nearly 30 per cent of visits were for this purpose, virtually the same proportion as in 1988-89. The most popular period for day trips was between July and September,

10.17 Main purpose of leisure day vists: by time of year

Great Britain — Percentages

	Jan to March	April to June	July to Sept	Oct to Dec	Total
Visit attraction	11	31	41	18	100
Theatre, bingo, etc	30	27	21	22	100
Pub, restaurant	25	21	26	28	100
Dancing	26	21	17	36	100
Vist friends	28	26	25	22	100
Outdoor activity	18	25	41	16	100
Sport	24	30	27	20	100
Shopping	22	24	20	35	100
Exhibitions	24	32	21	24	100
All visits[1]	22	26	30	23	100

1 Includes other purposes not shown separately.

Source: Department of National Heritage

when almost a third of all trips were made (Table 10.17). The most popular destinations for day trips were London and the North West of England.

The most popular tourist attraction in Great Britain over the last ten years has been Blackpool Pleasure Beach (Table 10.18). The British Museum remains the second most popular attraction with the number of visitors increasing by nearly a quarter between 1991 and 1992 and more than doubling since 1981. Both these attractions do not charge for admission. The Strathclyde Country Park remains the most popular free tourist attraction outside England.

The top attraction charging for admission in England was Alton Towers; it saw over a quarter more visitors pass through its gates in 1992 than in 1991. The Natural History Museum remains the most popular museum to charge for admission; visitors have increased by eight per cent between 1991 and 1992, reversing the decline following the introduction of admission charges in 1987. Outside England, Edinburgh Castle was the most popular attraction charging for admission, with nearly one million visitors.

10.18 Attendances at the most popular tourist attractions

Great Britain			Millions
	1981	1991	1992
Attractions with free admission			
Blackpool Pleasure Beach	7.5	6.5	6.5
British Museum	2.6	5.1	6.3
National Gallery	2.7	4.3	4.3
Strathclyde Country Park	..	4.2	4.2
Palace Pier, Brighton	..	3.5	3.5
Pleasure Beach, Great Yarmouth	..	2.5	2.3
Pleasureland, Southport	..	1.8	2.0
Tate Gallery	0.9	1.8	1.6
Bradgate Park	1.2	1.3	1.3
Frontierland, Morecambe	..	1.3	1.3
Victoria and Albert Museum	1.4	1.1	1.2
Attractions charging admission			
Alton Towers	1.6	2.0	2.5
Madame Tussaud's	2.0	2.2	2.3
Tower of London	2.1	1.9	2.2
Natural History Museum[1]	3.7	1.6	1.7
St Paul's Cathedral[2]	..	1.5	1.4
Tower World, Blackpool	.	1.3	1.3
Science Museum[3]	3.8	1.3	1.2
Chessington World of Adventures	0.5	1.4	1.2
Thorpe Park	0.6	0.9	1.0
Royal Academy	0.6	0.8	1.0

1 Admission charges were introduced in April 1987.
2 Admission charges were introduced in April 1991.
3 Admission charges were introduced in 1989.

Source: British Tourist Authority

10.19 Attendances at the most popular preserved steam railways

Great Britain			Thousands
	1983	1991	1992
North Yorkshire Moors	..	250	250
Severn Valley	174	243	195
Bluebell	185	205	180
Ffestiniog	200	184	177
Keighley & Worth Valley	133	200	175
Paignton & Dartmouth	..	160	148
Romney, Hythe and Dymchurch	..	..	140
Lakeside & Haverthwaite	168	140	130
Snowdon Mountain	83	125	130
North Norfolk	..	125	125
Ravenglass & Eskdale	112	135	121
Midland Railway Trust	50	130	120

Source: British Tourist Authority

One of the tourist attractions which bring the past to life are preserved steam railways, the majority of which are run, largely by volunteers, on old British Rail tracks. The most popular preserved railway, in terms of visitors in 1992, was the North Yorkshire Moors Railway (Table 10.19). The railway is one of the longest private lines, running a distance of 18 miles from Grosmont to Pickering in North Yorkshire. The first preserved line was the Bluebell Railway in Sussex which opened in 1960.

Table 10.20 shows that there were around 900 bingo clubs in Great Britain in 1992-93 - nearly half the number in 1971. Conversely the number of gaming machines requiring a licence doubled over the 20 years to 1991-92, to more than 225 thousand.

10.20 Gambling: betting offices, clubs and gaming machines

Great Britain			Thousands and numbers	
	Betting offices[1] (thousands)	Bingo clubs[2] (thousands)	Casino gaming clubs (numbers)	Gaming machines[3] (thousands)
1971	14.5	1.7	115	110.1
1976	13.9	1.6	121	114.1
1981	12.0	1.5	126	162.3
1986	10.4	1.1	115	200.4
1987-88	10.3	1.0	116	233.7
1988-89	10.2	1.0	116	226.7
1989-90	10.2	1.0	119	226.8
1990-91	10.2	1.0	120	234.0
1991-92	10.1	1.0	120	225.2
1992-93	9.9	0.9	118	..

1 The number of licences.
2 The number of clubs operating, except for 1971 where the number of licences in force is shown.
3 Only machines requiring a licence are shown.

Source: Home Office; HM Customs and Excise

Sporting Activities

10.21 Participation in the most popular sports, games and physical activities: by age, 1990

Great Britain   Percentages and numbers

	16-19	20-24	25-29	30-44	45-59	60-69	70 and over	All aged 16 and over	Median age of partic-ipants
Percentage in each group participating in each activity in the 12 months before interview									
Walking	72	70	73	73	69	61	37	65	41
Swimming	70	65	63	58	35	20	6	42	34
Snooker, pool, billiards	56	46	37	25	13	7	3	22	29
Keep fit, yoga	31	35	31	23	14	9	5	19	33
Cycling	41	23	22	22	13	8	4	17	35
Darts	29	26	21	15	10	4	2	13	31
Golf	21	19	18	15	11	7	2	12	35
Tenpin bowls, skittles	26	26	19	15	7	2	1	11	30
Running, jogging	30	20	18	13	3	1	-	9	28
Soccer	33	23	18	9	2	-	-	9	25
Weightlifting, training	27	24	20	10	3	-	-	9	27
Badminton	32	18	13	10	4	1	-	9	27
Tennis	29	16	11	9	3	1	-	7	27
Squash	15	15	15	8	2	-	-	6	27
Fishing	11	7	8	8	6	3	1	6	36

Source: General Household Survey

The most popular sport or physical activity in 1990 was walking **(Table 10.21)**. Amongst the over 70s people were six times more likely to participate in walking than the next most popular activity, swimming. Britain's so-called national sport, football, was played by only nine per cent of all adults, though a third of those aged 16 to 19 played.

The creation of the Football Association Premier League has failed to bring the spectators back to the terraces **(Table 10.22)**. In the first season of the new league the average attendance per match was about two per cent lower than for the old Division One in 1991-92. Attendances at Scottish League Premier Division matches also fell in 1992-93 as did attendances in the Rugby Football League Premier Division. However the Football League Division One, the erstwhile Division Two, recorded a modest increase in spectators.

The benefit of swimming is recognised by doctors and it is now included on the National Curriculum for school children. **Chart 10.23** (overleaf) illustrates the provision of facilities across the United Kingdom. The region with the best provision is the North West with one centre for every 22 thousand people, whilst the worst is Greater London with almost three times as many people per centre.

The other half of the chart shows, for comparison, the number of sports centres. The North West again emerged as the region with the best provision of facilities.

10.22 Average attendances at football and rugby league matches

Great Britain   Numbers

	Football Association[1] Premier League[2]	Football League[1] Division One[3]	Scottish Football League Premier Division[4]	Rugby Football League Premier Division
1961/62	26,106	16,132	11,178	.
1966/67	30,829	15,701	8,683	.
1971/72	31,352	14,652	5,228	.
1976/77	29,540	13,529	11,844	.
1981/82	22,556	10,282	9,467	.
1986/87	19,800	9,000	11,720	4,844
1987/88	19,300	10,600	13,949	5,826
1988/89	20,600	10,600	15,708	7,292
1989/90	20,800	12,500	15,576	6,450
1990/91	22,681	11,457	14,424	6,420
1991/92	21,622	10,525	11,970	6,511
1992/93	21,125	10,641	11,520	6,170

1 League matches only until 1985/86. From 1986/87, Football League attendances include promotion and relegation play-off matches.
2 Prior to 1992/93, Football League Division One.
3 Prior to 1992/93, Football League Division Two.
4 Prior to 1976/77, Scottish League Division One.

Source: Football Association Premier League; Football League; Scottish Football League; Rugby Football League

10.23 Provision of sports facilities, 1993

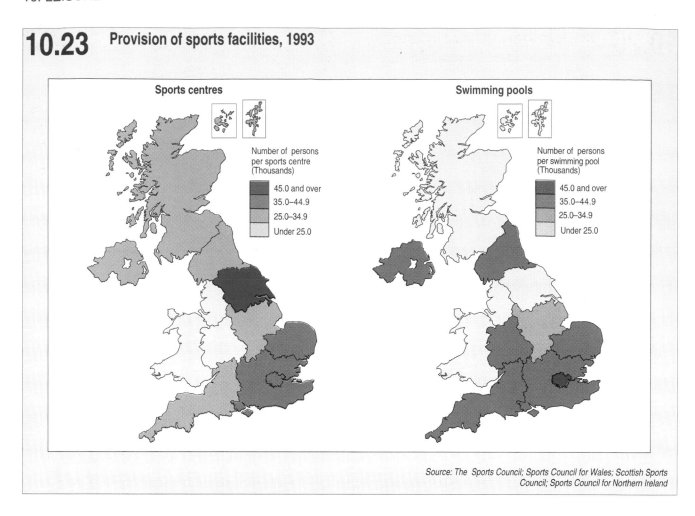

Source: The Sports Council; Sports Council for Wales; Scottish Sports Council; Sports Council for Northern Ireland

Holidays

10.24 Holidays[1]: by number taken per year by Great Britain residents

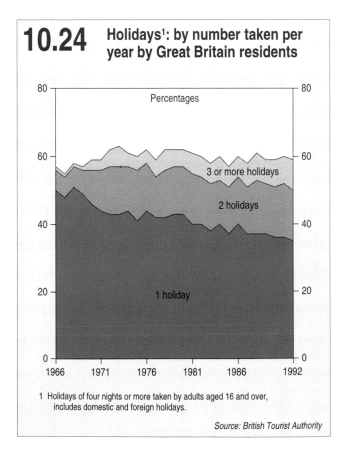

1 Holidays of four nights or more taken by adults aged 16 and over, includes domestic and foreign holidays.

Source: British Tourist Authority

The proportion of adults taking at least one holiday in 1992 was almost identical to the proportion over 25 years ago **(Chart 10.24)**. However the proportion taking two or more has increased from seven per cent in 1966 to 24 per cent in 1992. August remains the most popular month for holidays - 19 per cent of all trips start then.

Almost a quarter of holidays of four nights or more taken in Great Britain in 1992 by British residents were taken in the West Country **(Chart 10.25)**. The most popular type of location remains the seaside, and the most common form of transport is the car - more than three quarters of holiday makers travelled to their destination by car.

The number of holidays taken in Great Britain by Britons stood at 32 million in 1992, a decline of around 20 per cent on the peak of about 41 million in 1974. The number of foreign holidays taken by British residents has more than quadrupled in the last 25 years and in 1992 stood at almost 22 million - the highest number ever **(Chart 10.26)**. The destination abroad which saw the largest increase in British visitors, over the past ten

10.25 Holidays[1] taken at home by Great Britain residents: by destination, 1992

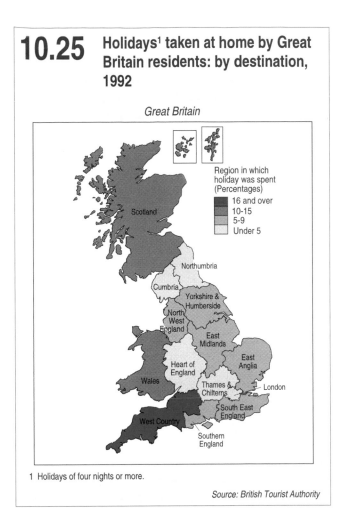

Great Britain

Region in which holiday was spent (Percentages)

- 16 and over
- 10-15
- 5-9
- Under 5

1 Holidays of four nights or more.

Source: British Tourist Authority

10.26 Holidays[1] taken by Great Britain residents: by destination

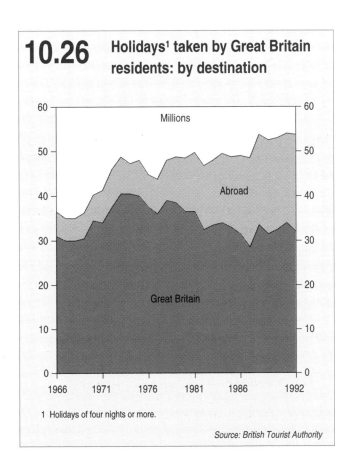

1 Holidays of four nights or more.

Source: British Tourist Authority

years, was the United States of America. Within the European Community the largest increase was recorded by Portugal.

More recent results from the *International Passenger Survey* for the 12 months to July 1993 indicate the rise is set to continue; the number of United Kingdom residents going abroad has increased by two per cent to 33.9 million. Futhermore spending overseas by United Kingdom residents increased by eight per cent over the same period.

In 1992 the age group most likely to holiday abroad were those aged 35 to 44, whilst the age group most likely to holiday in the United Kingdom were those aged 65 and over **(Table 10.27)**.

10.27 Holiday-makers: by age and destination, 1982 and 1992

	Great Britain[1]		Abroad[2]	
	1982	1992	1982	1992
16-24	13	13	21	17
25-34	17	16	18	16
35-44	20	19	19	21
45-54	14	15	17	18
55-64	18	14	16	17
65 and over	18	23	10	11
All aged 16 and over	100	100	100	100

Percentages

1 Holidays of four or more nights.
2 Holidays of one or more nights.

Source: British Tourist Authority

Resources

The Arts Councils of Great Britain and Northern Ireland were established to develop and improve the knowledge, understanding and practice of the arts, to increase their accessibility to the public and to advise and co-operate with government departments, local authorities and other organisations. They receive an annual grant from Government which they distribute to arts organisations.

Total expenditure of the Arts Council of Great Britain amounted to almost £222 million in 1992-93 **(Table 10.28 overleaf)**. Over a quarter of this went to the National Companies (theatre, ballet and opera). However, the proportion going to the regional arts associations has nearly doubled since 1981-82 to 20 per cent. Total expenditure by the Arts Council of Northern Ireland was nearly £7 million in 1992-93.

10.28 Arts Council expenditure

Great Britain	Percentages and £ thousand		
	1981-82	1991-92	1992-93
Scottish and Welsh Arts			
Councils	19	15	16
National companies[1]	27	33	28
Regional arts associations	11	18	20
Combined arts	.	1	1
Dance	3	4	4
Drama and mime	13	9	9
Film, video and broadcasting	.	1	1
Literature	1	1	1
Music	7	7	7
Touring	6	5	5
Visual arts	4	2	2
Other funding[2]	5	2	2
Management and services	4	4	4
Total (= 100%) (£ thousand)	80,821	208,881	221,758

1 Excludes South Bank Centre in 1981-82 as it was not funded at that time by the Arts Council of Great Britain. Data for 1991-92 include supplementary Grant-in-Aid of £10.8 million provided to enable English National Opera to purchase the freehold of the Coliseum theatre.
2 Data for 1981-82 include architecture, training, cross-disciplinary initiatives, incentive funding, external relations and Housing the Arts scheme.

Source: Arts Council of Great Britain

The proportion of the average weekly household budget spent on leisure items in the United Kingdom amounted to nearly 17 per cent in 1992 **(Table 10.29)**. The largest proportion of this expenditure was on holidays, where just over £11 a week was spent on average; this has increased in real terms by nearly a half since 1986.

10.29 Household expenditure in real terms[1] on selected leisure items

United Kingdom	£ per week at 1992 prices[1] and percentages		
	1986	1991	1992
Alcoholic drink consumed away			
from home	8.40	7.85	7.79
Meals consumed out[2]	6.19	6.24	6.10
Books, newspapers, magazines,			
etc	3.86	3.80	3.84
Television, video and audio			
equipment			
Purchases	4.14	4.77	5.20
Rentals, including licence			
fees	2.81	2.31	2.39
Home computers	0.23	0.54	0.61
Purchase of materials for home			
repairs, etc	4.33	4.07	3.96
Holidays	7.61	10.21	11.21
Hobbies	0.09	0.13	0.07
Cinema admissions	0.14	0.19	0.19
Theatre, concert, etc admissions	0.41	0.53	0.55
Subscription and admission			
charges to participant sports	1.01	1.10	1.50
Spectator sports admissions	0.16	0.19	0.24
Sports goods (excluding clothes)	0.52	0.45	0.52
Other entertainment	0.70	0.84	0.88
Total weekly expenditure on			
above	40.61	43.24	45.04
Expenditure on above items as a percentage of total household expenditure	*16.1*	*16.1*	*16.6*

1 Adjusted to real terms using the retail prices index.
2 Eaten on the premises, excluding state school meals and workplace meals.

Source: Central Statistical Office

REFERENCES AND FURTHER READING

The following list contains selected publications relevant to Chapter 10: Leisure. Those published by HMSO are available from the addresses shown on the back cover of *Social Trends*.

Annual Reports of the Sports Council, Sports Council for Northern Ireland, Sports Council for Wales, and the Scottish Sports Council, available from the individual Councils

Arts Council of Great Britain Annual Report and Accounts, Arts Council of Great Britain

Arts Council of Northern Ireland Annual Report and Accounts, Arts Council of Northern Ireland

BBC Handbook, BBC

BPI Statistical Handbook, British Phonographic Industry

Business Monitor MQ6 - Overseas Travel and Tourism, HMSO

Cinema and Video Industry Audience Research, CAA

CNC info, Centre National de la Cinématographie

Cultural Trends, Policy Studies Institute

Day visits in Great Britain 1991/92, HMSO

Digest of Tourist Statistics, British Tourist Authority

Employment Gazette, Harrington Kilbride

Family Spending - A report on the 1992 Family Expenditure Survey, HMSO

Film and Year Book, British Film Institute

General Household Survey, HMSO

Independent Broadcasting Authority Annual Report and Accounts, IBA

Leisure Futures, The Henley Centre for Forecasting

The UK Tourist - Statistics 1991, Tourist Boards of England, Northern Ireland, Scotland and Wales.

Visits to Tourist Attractions, British Tourist Authority and National Tourist Boards

Chapter 11: Participation

Charity

- In 1992-93 the top 25 fund raising charities in the United Kingdom collected nearly £800 million through voluntary contributions. Over a third of this amount went to charities concerned either with cancer or children.   *(Table 11.2)*

Voluntary sector

- Membership of both the Mothers' Union and the National Union of Townswomen's Guildshalved between 1971 and 1992.   *(Chart 11.6)*

Religion

- Only 15 per cent of the population of the United Kingdom are active church members - a lower proportion than in many other European countries.   *(Chart 11.9)*

Politics

- Over three quarters of those eligible voted at the last General Election.   *(Table 11.11)*

- Less than half the people in the United Kingdom think that membership of the EC is a good thing - the lowest proportion in any EC country.   *(Table 11.13)*

Other participation

- Only 38 per cent of the civilian workforce in the United Kingdom were members of a trade union in 1991 compared with 53 per cent in the peak year of 1978.   *(Table 11.14)*

- Over 1,200 complaints were received by the Health Service Commissioners in 1992 - more than double the number in 1976.   *(Table 11.17)*

- Between 1980-81 and 1992-93 the number of enquiries to the Citizen's Advice Bureaux relating to social security matters more than doubled to around 1.8 thousand.   *(Table 11.19)*

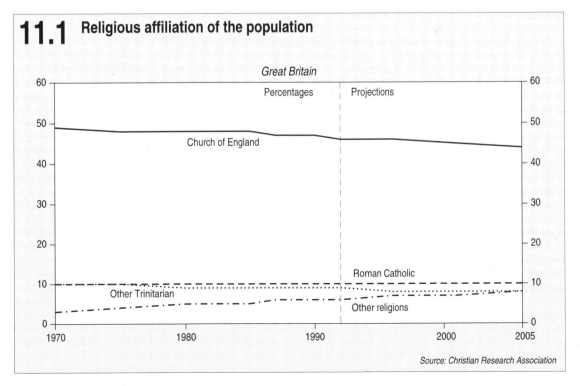

11.1 **Religious affiliation of the population**

Great Britain

Percentages | Projections

Church of England

Roman Catholic

Other Trinitarian

Other religions

Source: Christian Research Association

Participation

This chapter looks at how people participate in the life of the community. Participation can take various forms such as: supporting charities, membership of organisations, voting at elections and voluntary work.

Charity

Table 11.2 looks at the top 25 fund raising charities in the United Kingdom. For accounting years ending between April 1992 and March 1993 their total voluntary income was £793 million while the corresponding figure

11.2 Real[1] income of selected charities[2], 1981 and 1992-93

United Kingdom	£ million in real terms[1] and percentages			
	1981	1992-93		
	Voluntary income	Total income	Voluntary income	Voluntary as % of total
Save the Children Fund	17.4	99.6	70.4	71
National Trust	18.2	132.4	65.2	49
Royal National Lifeboat Institution	21.2	62.3	55.8	90
Oxfam	23.6	73.3	53.3	73
Imperial Cancer Research Fund	22.6	53.0	47.5	90
Cancer Research Campaign	22.9	44.7	40.9	92
Barnardos	20.3	75.5	34.5	46
Royal Society for the Prevention of Cruelty to Animals	9.1	38.9	33.0	85
Salvation Army	18.6	64.5	31.4	49
Help the Aged	14.1	33.2	29.0	87
British Red Cross Society	14.9	60.7	28.0	46
National Society for the Prevention of Cruelty to Children	9.6	34.1	27.9	82
Christian Aid	14.4	42.1	26.4	63
British Heart Foundation	8.6	31.4	25.7	82
Guide Dogs for the Blind Association	8.8	35.8	25.2	70
Royal National Institute for the Blind	13.5	47.0	24.9	53
Cancer Relief Macmillan Fund	2.7	30.3	24.9	82
ActionAid	8.9	32.9	23.1	70
Royal Society for the Protection of Birds	6.2	27.8	21.9	79
Spastics Society	13.2	56.6	21.5	38
Tear Fund	6.8	19.7	18.7	95
Marie Curie Cancer Care	10.0	26.6	18.1	68
People's Dispensary for Sick Animals	7.9	20.3	16.1	79
WWF UK	0.7	19.0	15.0	79
Institute of Cancer Research	5.0	20.7	14.8	72

1 1981 data has been adjusted to March 1993 prices using the retail prices index.
2 Top 25 fund raising charities in 1992-93. Figures for 1981 relate to 12 month accounting periods ending (in the main) between December 1980 and December 1981 and those for 1993 to periods ending between April 1992 and March 1993.

Source: Charities Aid Foundation

11.3 Real[1] income and expenditure of the top 200 charities[2], 1981 and 1992-93

United Kingdom	£million in real terms[1]	
	1981	1992-93
Income		
Voluntary		
Legacies	190.8	485.6
Covenants	16.4	103.5
Donations	} 378.4 {	635.4
Fund raising		105.1
Charity shops		42.5
Other voluntary income		11.7
Total voluntary income	585.5	1,383.8
Other		
Trading	37.0	28.8
Rents, investments, etc	115.3	201.7
Sales of goods and services	} 323.6 {	231.7
Government and EC grants		487.9
Other		81.0
Total other income	475.9	1,031.1
Total income	1,061.4	2,414.9
Expenditure		
Charitable	794.4	1,896.1
Fund raising	61.1	195.6
Administrative	61.1	127.0
Other	36.9	28.2
Total expenditure	953.5	2,246.9

1 1981 data has been adjusted to March 1993 prices using the retail prices index.
2 Top 200 charities in each year. Figures for 1981 relate to 12 month accounting periods ending (in the main) between December 1980 and December 1981 and those for 1993 to periods ending between April 1992 and March 1993.

Source: Charities Aid Foundation

for the same charities for accounting years ending between December 1980 and December 1981, after allowing for inflation, was around £320 million. In the later period, voluntary donations accounted for two thirds of the total income of these charities. This proportion, however, varied considerably from one charity to another; the Cancer Research Campaign, for example, raised over nine tenths of its income through voluntary contributions while the Spastics Society raised less than two fifths of its income in this way. Over a third of the voluntary income of the top 25 charities in 1992 went to organisations concerned with either children or cancer.

Table 11.3 is based on the 200 charities with the largest total income. For accounting years ending in the year to March 1993, their total income was £2,415 million - over double in real terms that for accounting years ending in the year to December 1981. For the later period, almost a half of total income was accounted for by donations and legacies. Total expenditure also more than doubled in real terms between the two periods to £2,247 million in 1992-93. Around five sixths of expenditure in both periods was used directly for charitable purposes, while around six per cent was spent on administration.

Further information on giving to charities is available from the 1992 Individual Giving Survey which was commissioned by the Charities Aid Foundation. Over three quarters of respondents to the survey said that they had made a donation to a charity within the previous month; £3 was the median donation of all respondents. Just over a fifth of respondents had given nothing while just over a quarter had given over £10.

Voluntary sector

Many people find that they can best help others by belonging to an established voluntary organisation. **Table 11.4** gives the membership of a selection of such organisations. There appears to be no discernable overall trend over the years shown; membership of Pensioners' Voice in 1992 was just a fraction of what it was 21 years earlier while that of the National Federation of Gateway Clubs increase fivefold over the same period.

The Charities Aid Foundation's 1992 Individual Giving Survey not only measured how much money people donated to help others, but also how much time they gave. Almost three quarters of the survey respondents

11.4 Membership of selected voluntary organisations

Great Britain			Thousands
	1971	1981	1992
Age Concern England[1]	..	..	180
British Red Cross Society	172	112	90
Lions Clubs International[2]	8	20	21
National Association of Leagues of Hospital Friends[1]	250	475	350
National Association of Round Tables of Great Britain and Ireland[2]	29	30	20
National Federation of Gateway Clubs	8	32	40
Pensioners' Voice	600	113	25
PHAB (Physically Disabled and Able Bodied)	2	..	20
Rotary International in Great Britain and Ireland[2]	50	59	65
Royal British Legion	750	..	679
Royal Society for Mentally Handicapped Children and Adults	40	50	55
Royal Society for the Prevention of Cruelty to Animals[3]	..	36	21
St John Ambulance Brigade[4]	91	77	50
Toc H	15	..	5

1 Figures refer to volunteers.
2 Includes Republic of Ireland.
3 England and Wales only.
4 England and Northern Ireland only. Excludes over 20 thousand members of youth organisations.

Source: Organisations concerned

11.5 Membership of selected organisations for young people

United Kingdom			Thousands
	1971	1981	1992
Cub Scouts[1]	265	309	349
Brownie Guides[2,3]	376	427	418
Scouts[4]	215	234	191
Girl Guides[3,5]	316	348	224
Sea Cadet Corps	18	19	18
Army Cadet Force	39	46	39
Air Training Corps	33	35	35
Combined Cadet Force	45	44	40
Boys Brigade	140	154	100
Girls Brigade	97	94	73
Methodist Association of Youth Clubs	115	127	60
NABC - Clubs for Young People	164	186	198
Youth Clubs UK - Boys	179	430	397
- Girls	140	341	318
National Federation of Young Farmers' Clubs[6]			
- Males	24	28	16
- Females	16	23	14
Young Men's Christian Association[7]			
- Males	35	36	46
- Females	13	19	34
Rotaract Clubs	1	10	10

1 Includes Beaver Scouts (6-8 years).
2 Includes Rainbow Guides (4 or 5-7 years).
3 Includes Guides in the Channel Islands, Isle of Man and British Guides in foreign countries.
4 Includes Venture Scouts (15.5-20 years).
5 Includes Ranger Guides (14-18 years) and young leaders (15-18 years).
6 Figures relate to England, Wales and the Channel Islands and to young people aged between 10 and 25 in 1971 and 10 and 26 in 1981 and 1992.
7 Figures relate to registered members aged under 25.

Source: Organisations concerned

had undertaken no voluntary work during the month prior to interview while ten per cent had given over ten hours.

Some organisations cater for the interests and needs of young people. Trends in the numbers joining such organisations are obviously affected by the size of the population in the relevant age groups. As 1964 was a peak year for births in the United Kingdom, the late 1970s and 1980s saw a rise in the number of teenagers. This appears to be reflected in the membership of many of the organisations shown in **Table 11.5** where numbers are generally higher in 1981 than in either 1971 or 1992.

The Duke of Edinburgh's Award is also aimed at young people. This is not an organisation, but a programme of activities for 14 to 25 year olds. Over two and a quarter million young people in 59 countries have taken part since the scheme began in 1956. In 1992, the scheme had 200 thousand participants of whom 40 thousand

11.6 Membership of selected women's voluntary organisations

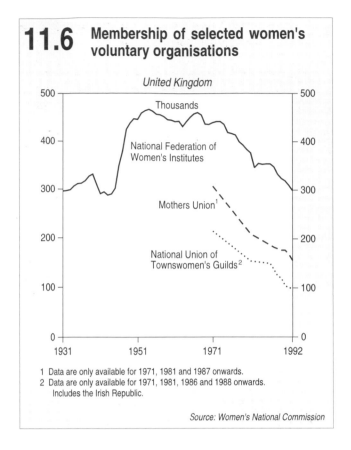

United Kingdom

1 Data are only available for 1971, 1981 and 1987 onwards.
2 Data are only available for 1971, 1981, 1986 and 1988 onwards.
  Includes the Irish Republic.

Source: Women's National Commission

gained a bronze, silver or gold award. In 1971 there were only 122 thousand participants of whom 28 thousand gained one of these awards.

There are a number of voluntary organisations specifically for women. Membership of many of them has fallen noticeably over the last two decades. Membership of the National Federation of Women's Institutes, for example, rose from 296 thousand in 1931 to 467 thousand in 1954 since when it fell to 299 thousand in 1992 **(Chart 11.6)**. Membership of both the Mothers Union and the National Union of Townswomen's Guilds halved between 1971 and 1992.

11.7 Voluntary rescue work

Numbers

	1971	1981	1992
Royal National Lifeboat Institution			
(United Kingdom)			
Voluntary crew members	5,000	5,000	5,678
Launches on service	2,789	3,017	5,522
Lives rescued	1,438	1,076	1,400
Mountain Rescue Committee of			
Great Britain			
Volunteer team members	2,340	2,804	3,355
Callouts	227	485	1,127
Persons assisted	207	541	1,450
British Cave Rescue Council			
Volunteer team members	..	900	900
Callouts	21	48	62
Persons assisted	66	101	102

Source: Organisations concerned

A number of organisations for women including the three mentioned above are represented on the Women's National Commission - an advisory committee to the government set up in 1969. It consists of 50 women elected or appointed from national organisations which have a large and active female membership. Groups represented include political parties, voluntary organisations, trade unions and professional and business organisations.

Some people not only give up their leisure time for others but also put their own lives at risk. In 1992 almost ten thousand people were members of either the Royal National Lifeboat Institution, the Mountain Rescue Committee of Great Britain or the British Cave Rescue Council **(Table 11.7)**. The Royal National Lifeboat Institution dealt with over five and a half thousand incidents in 1992 - double the number in 1971. Between the same years there was a fivefold increase in the number of callouts requiring the assistance of the Mountain Rescue Committee of Great Britain and a threefold increase in incidents requiring the attendance of the British Cave Rescue Council.

Religion

Chart 11.1, at the beginning of the chapter, shows the religious affiliation of the population. In 1992 just over 70 per cent of people in the United Kingdom expressed some form of religious affiliation - virtually the same proportion as in 1970. The proportion of the population who said that their religion was Church of England fell slightly from 49 per cent in 1970 to 46 per cent in 1992 while a constant ten per cent said that they were Roman Catholic. Overall, in 1992, 65 per cent of people said that they were allied to the Trinitarian churches - that is a belief in the unison of the Holy Trinity in one Godhead.

Actual enroled adult membership of the Trinitarian churches, however, at 6.7 million in 1992 **(Table 11.8)** represented only 15 per cent of the United Kingdom population aged 16 and over. Membership of the Trinitarian churches fell by 16 per cent between 1975 and 1992. However, the change in adult membership varied considerably between the different denominations. For example, the Presbyterian and Methodist Churches saw membership fall by almost a quarter over the period while that of the Orthodox Church actually increased by two fifths. Over the same period overall membership of the non-Trinitarian churches rose by just over a third while that for the other religions nearly doubled. Again, however, there are considerable variations in membership changes. On the one hand, the numbers of Spiritualists fell by a third while the numbers of Muslims and Sikhs more than doubled.

11.8 Church membership[1]

United Kingdom			Millions
	1975	1980	1992
Trinitarian Churches			
Anglican	2.30	2.18	1.81
Presbyterian	1.64	1.51	1.24
Methodist	0.60	0.54	0.46
Baptist	0.24	0.24	0.23
Other Free Churches	0.51	0.52	0.66
Roman Catholic	2.52	2.34	2.04
Orthodox	0.20	0.20	0.28
All Trinitarian churches	8.00	7.53	6.72
Non-Trinitarian Churches			
Mormons	0.10	0.11	0.15
Jehovah's Witnesses	0.08	0.08	0.13
Spiritualists	0.06	0.05	0.04
Other Non-Trinitarian	0.10	0.11	0.14
All Non-Trinitarian churches	0.34	0.35	0.46
Other Religions			
Muslims	0.20	0.31	0.52
Sikhs	0.12	0.15	0.27
Hindus	0.10	0.12	0.14
Jews	0.11	0.11	0.11
Others	0.04	0.05	0.08
All Other religions	0.57	0.74	1.12

1 Adult members.

Source: Christian Research Association

In October 1989, a detailed census of the churches in England was organised by MARC Europe (now the Christian Research Association). This showed that church attendance varied according to ethnic origin.

11.9 Active church membership: European comparison, 1990

Percentages[2] 0 20 40 60 80 100

1 French speaking area.
2 Of adult population.

Source: Christian Research Association

For example, less than a tenth of the White population attended while a sixth of the Afro-Caribbean population did so. The census also showed that notably fewer people in the 15 to 19 age range were attending church compared with a decade earlier, though the proportion of children under 15 attending remained constant.

Comparing church membership between different countries is difficult since not all churches have a list of members. In Finland, for example, 'active' members has been taken as those who vote in the Church Council elections; for Roman Catholics the number attending mass is used. Based on the available information, **Chart 11.9** shows that 'active' church membership varies widely between countries. Of the countries shown in the chart, the United Kingdom had the lowest level of active membership amongst adults - just 15 per cent in 1990. The Irish Republic was the highest at 81 per cent.

Politics

An annual poll by MORI asks people in Great Britain a number of questions about their political activity in the 'last two or three years'. **Table 11.10** shows that a third of those interviewed in 1993 had helped with fund-raising for a political purpose. Almost a fifth had urged someone outside their family to vote and the same proportion had urged someone to contact a local councillor or Member of Parliament. Less than 1 in 20 had taken an active part in a political campaign.

11.10 Political participation[1]

Great Britain			Percentages
	1982	1991	1993
Voted in the last election[2]	69	67	77
Helped on fund-raising drives	31	31	33
Urged someone outside my family to vote	17	19	19
Urged someone to contact a local councillor or MP	17	18	19
Presented my views to a local councillor or MP	13	15	17
Made a speech before an organised group	14	15	14
Been elected an officer of an organisation or club	14	11	14
Written a letter to an editor	6	6	8
Taken an active part in a political campaign	3	3	4
Stood for public office	1	1	1
None of these	17	18	12

1 Respondents were asked which of these things they had done in the last two or three years.
2 1991 wording 'voted in the 1987 General Election'; 1993 wording 'voted in the last General Election'.

Source: MORI

11.11 Votes recorded in parliamentary General Elections and by-elections: by party

United Kingdom

	General Election 3/5/79	May 1979 to June 1983	General Election 6/6/83	June 1983 to June 1987	General Election 11/6/87	June 1987 to April 1992	General Election 10/4/92	April 1992 to Sept 1993
Number of by-elections	.	20	.	31	.	24	.	2
Turnout *(percentages)[1]*	76.1	61.2	72.7	62.4	75.3	57.6	76.3	72.7
Votes recorded by party *(percentage of all votes)*								
Conservative	43.9	23.8	42.4	16.0	42.3	23.8	41.8	29.0
Labour	36.9	25.7	27.6	14.9	30.8	38.9	35.2	2.3
Liberal Democrats[2]	13.8	9.0	13.7	15.0	12.8	19.1	17.0	63.7
Social Democratic Party[2]	0.0	14.2	11.6	5.6	9.7	3.2	-	-
Plaid Cymru	0.4	0.5	0.4	0.3	0.4	2.3	0.4	-
Scottish National Party	1.6	1.7	1.1	.	1.3	4.8	1.9	-
Northern Ireland Parties[2]	2.2	23.3	2.5	47.4	2.2	3.7	2.1	-
Green Party[3]	0.1	0.3	0.2	-	0.3	1.8	0.6	-
Others	1.1	1.6	0.5	0.8	0.2	2.5	1.1	4.9
Total (= 100%)(thousands)	31,221	715	30,671	1,979	32,530	877	33,275	111

1 Estimated by dividing the number of votes cast by the number of people on the electoral registers in force at the time of the elections.
2 See Appendix, Part 11: Parliamentary elections and political parties.
3 Known as the Ecology Party before 1987.

Source: Home Office

Almost a quarter of those eligible did not vote at the last General Election in the United Kingdom, which was held on 10 April 1992 **(Table 11.11)**. The outgoing Government was returned with 42 per cent of the votes cast and an overall majority of 65 seats - a reduction of more than a third on the 1987 results. Labour won 271 seats with 35 per cent of the votes cast while the Liberal Democrats won only 20 seats although it had 17 per cent of the votes. Between April 1992 and December 1993 there were only two by-elections (Newbury and Christchurch), the turnout for which, at 73 per cent, was notably higher than the overall turnout for by-elections during any inter-General Election period since the mid 1970s. The voting in these by-elections saw a significant swing away from both the Conservative and Labour parties in favour of the Liberal Democrats.

The highest intake of women Members of Parliament (MPs) at a General Election was in 1992, when 60 women were elected to Parliament. **Chart 11.12** shows that there was a wide variation in the proportion of women MPs among the European Community (EC) countries at their last general election. The lowest proportions were found in Greece and France with just six per cent; in the United Kingdom nine per cent of MPs elected in 1992 were women. The country with the highest proportion was Denmark where a third of the members elected were women. This comparatively high percentage of women being elected is also reflected in the other Scandinavian countries: a third of those elected in Sweden were also women while the proportion in Norway and Finland was even higher at almost two fifths.

11.12 Women elected to Parliament[1] at the most recent general election: EC comparison

United Kingdom

Denmark
Netherlands
Germany
Irish Republic
Spain
Luxembourg
Portugal
Belgium
United Kingdom
Italy
Greece
France

Percentages 0   10   20   30   40

1 Lower House in bicameral Parliaments.

Source: House of Commons Library; Embassies of respective countries

In Autumn 1993 only 43 per cent of people in the United Kingdom thought that membership of the EC was a good thing - the lowest proportion in any EC country **(Table 11.13)**. In the Netherlands four fifths of people believed that it was beneficial. However, just over a third of those in the United Kingdom were not sure, hence only just over a fifth actually thought that EC membership was a bad thing. The proportion who

11.13 Attitude towards EC membership: EC comparison, Autumn 1993

	A good thing	A bad thing	Percentages Not sure
Netherlands	80	5	15
Greece	73	4	23
Irish Republic	73	8	19
Luxembourg	72	6	23
Italy	68	7	24
Belgium	59	9	32
Portugual	59	12	30
Denmark	58	22	19
France	55	14	31
Spain	54	14	32
Germany[1]	53	12	34
United Kingdom	43	22	35
EUR 12	57	13	30

1 As constituted since 3 October 1990.

Source: Commission of the European Communities

believed that membership of the EC was good fell in every country except Greece between the Summer and Autumn surveys.

Other participation

Based on the Certification Officer's annual returns from the trade unions, union membership in the United Kingdom fell by over a quarter between its peak in 1978 and 1991 **(Table 11.14)**. At the same time, the number of unions fell by nearly two fifths - this was, in part at least, due the merger of a number of unions. Since 1989 data on trade union membership has also been collected in the Labour Force Survey (LFS) by the Employment Department. This shows that union membership varies according to a number of factors. For example, in 1991, 37 per cent of employees were union members compared with only ten per cent of the self-employed and seven per cent of those on government training programmes. Of all employees, 42 per cent of men and 32 per cent of women were union members. Full-time employees were almost twice as likely to be union members as part-time employees. It should be noted that data collected in the LFS are not directly comparable with those obtained from the Certification Officer's annual returns.

There is also some variation in trade union membership according to ethnic origin. **Chart 11.15** shows that in Great Britain in Autumn 1992, overall a third of employed men were union members although the proportion of those of Pakistani or Bangladeshi origin was only 19 per cent. For women the contrast was more marked: 43 per cent of Black women were union members compared with less than one per cent of those of Pakistani or Bangladeshi origin. Only in the Black ethnic group was the proportion of members higher amongst women than men.

11.14 Trade Unions[1]: numbers and membership

United Kingdom

		Total membership		
	Number of unions	Millions	As a percentage of civilian workforce in employment[2]	Percentage change in membership since previous year
1976	473	12.4	50.6	+3.0
1977	481	12.8	52.4	+3.7
1978	462	13.1	53.1	+2.1
1979	453	13.3	53.0	+1.3
1980	438	12.9	51.8	-2.6
1981	414	12.1	50.4	-6.5
1982	408	11.6	49.2	-4.2
1983	394	11.2	48.2	-3.1
1984	375	11.0	45.4	-2.2
1985	370	10.8	44.5	-1.6
1986	335	10.5	43.0	-2.6
1987	330	10.5	41.4	-0.6
1988	315	10.4	39.8	-0.9
1989	309	10.2	38.1	-2.1
1990	287	9.9	37.7	-2.1
1991	275	9.6	37.7	-3.6

1 See Appendix, Part 11: Trade Union membership.
2 Mid-year estimates up to 1983, end-year from 1984 onwards.

Source: Employment Department

The Commission for Racial Equality (CRE) was set up in 1977 under the *Race Relations Act 1976.* It gives advice to people who believe they have been discriminated against because of their race and provides legal representation in courts or at industrial tribunals

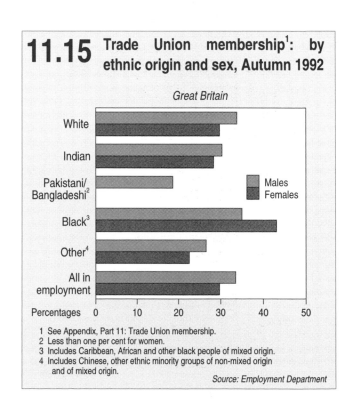

11.15 Trade Union membership[1]: by ethnic origin and sex, Autumn 1992

Great Britain

1 See Appendix, Part 11: Trade Union membership.
2 Less than one per cent for women.
3 Includes Caribbean, African and other black people of mixed origin.
4 Includes Chinese, other ethnic minority groups of non-mixed origin and of mixed origin.

Source: Employment Department

11.16 Cases referred to the Commission for Racial Equality

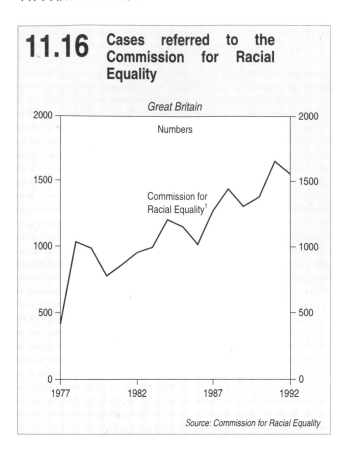

Great Britain

Source: Commission for Racial Equality

As well as discrimination on grounds of race, it is also possible to be treated unfairly on grounds of sex or marriage. The Equal Opportunities Commission is a statutory body established to work towards the elimination of such discrimination and to promote equal opportunities between men and women and to review equality legislation. The Commission deals with enquiries and provides assistance under *Section 75 of the Sex Discrimination Act 1975*. Between 1990 and 1992 casework enquiries or complaints rose from 3,254 to 6,868. In 1992 the Commission received 38 thousand enquiries.

Those who believe that they may have been subject to unjust treatment by a government department, the National Health Service, a local authority or various financial institutions can complain to an ombudsman. The number of complaints received by the Parliamentary Commissioner for Administration - the ombudsman who deals with complaints about government departments - rose to 945 in 1992 **(Table 11.17)**; in 1991 it was 801. However, in only 11 per cent of the cases looked at during 1992 was maladministration leading to injustice found.

The Health Service Commissioners (HSC) deal with complaints about the services and administration within the National Health Service. The number of complaints made to the HSC is on a generally upward trend and in 1992 it received 1,227 complaints - over double the number in 1976. Maladministration leading to injustice was found in almost a quarter of the complaints dealt with in 1992.

as well as promoting equal opportunities and good race relations. The number of cases dealt with peaked at 1,655 in 1991 and then fell back just slightly to 1,557 in 1992 **(Chart 11.16)**.

11.17 Complaints to Ombudsmen[1]

Great Britain

Numbers

	1976	1981	1986	1991	1992
Parliamentary Commissioner for Administration					
Received during the year	815	917	719	801	945
Dealt with during the year[2]	863	929	719	769	857
of which:					
Maladministration leading to injustice found	139	104	82	87	103
Health Service Commissioner[3,4]					
Received during the year	582	686	883	1,176	1,227
Dealt with during the year[2]	546	699	831	1,142	1,176
of which:					
Containing failures in service/ maladministration leading to injustice found	61	152	290	243	287
Commissioners for Local Administration[3]					
Received during the year[5]	1,335	3,293	5,159	14,057	15,432
Dealt with during the year[2]	1,057	3,028	4,889	12,392	15,505
of which:					
Maladministration leading to injustice found	143	203	266	330	392

1 See Appendix, Part 11: Parliamentary Commissioner for Administration, Health Service Commissioner, Commissioners for Local Administration.
2 Some complaints will have been received during the previous year.
3 The Health Service Commissioner and the Commissioner for Local Administration report annually from April to the following March.
4 From 1981 the figures refer to the number of individual grievances rather than reports issued.
5 In Wales includes complaints brought forward from previous year because complaint accepted for investigation but report not issued or complaint under consideration.

Source: The Parliamentary Commissioner for Administration; The Health Service Commissioner; The Commissioners for Local Administration in England, Wales and Scotland

11.18 Selected advisory and counselling services[1]

United Kingdom   Numbers and thousands

	Branches/centres (numbers)				Clients (thousands)			
	1971	1981	1991	1992	1971	1981	1991	1992
Al-Anon Family Groups	135	612	1,090	1,092	1	7	13	13
Alcoholics Anonymous	420	1,550	2,800	3,051	6	30	45	45
Catholic Marriage Advisory Council	63	68	82	82	2	3	17	20
Childline	.	.	3	4	.	.	69	79
Citizens Advice Bureaux	512	914	1,462	1,517	1,500	4,515	8,278	8,378
Cruse Bereavement Care	13	73	185	193	5	9	22	22
Disablement Information and Advice Lines	.	44	100	100	.	40	75	184
Law Centres Federation	1	41	60	55	1	155	452	500
Leukaemia Care Society	1	21	75	83	-	2	6	7
Relate	141	178	133	130	22	38	70	76
Samaritans	127	180	185	189	89	315	470	436
Terence Higgins Trust	.	.	1	1	.	.	..	4
Turning Point	..	..	30	32	..	..	7	8
Youth Access[2]	..	55	125	160	..	30	113	250

1 For details of coverage of individual organisations see Appendix, Part 11: Selected advisory and counselling services.
2 Formerly Young People's Counselling and Advisory Services.

Source: Organisations concerned

Complaints against local authorities are dealt with by the Commissioners for Local Administration. In 1992 this body received over 15 thousand complaints - almost a twelvefold increase on the number received in 1976. However, in less than three per cent of cases was maladministration leading to injustice found.

As already mentioned, there are also ombudsmen dealing with the activities of the various financial institutions. In 1992 the ombudsmen for banking, building societies and insurance companies received over 17 thousand complaints. Around three in ten of the complaints dealt with in respect of building societies and insurance companies were found wholly or partly in favour of the complainant.

In addition to the ombudsmen, there are also a number of regulatory bodies which deal with complaints about the services of the providers of energy, water and telephone services. In 1992 the bodies dealing with complaints about the supply of electricity (OFFER), water (OFWAT) and telecommunication services (OFTEL), dealt with over 73 thousand complaints.

The United Kingdom has a wide range of counselling and advisory services. Some of them have been set up comparatively recently to deal with problems such as child abuse and AIDS. All of the organisations shown in **Table 11.18** saw a large increase in the numbers of clients during the 1970s and 1980s - a trend which has continued in to the 1990s for most of them. Alcoholics Anonymous, for example, saw a more than sevenfold increase in the number of people who requested their services between 1971 and 1991.

Of all the organisations shown in the table, the one with the largest number of clients in 1992 was the Citizens Advice Bureau. **Table 11.19** looks at this organisation in more detail. In 1992-93 almost a quarter of its inquiries were concerned with consumer, trade and business problems; social security matters accounted for almost the same proportion. Between 1980-81 and 1992-93, the number of queries about holidays, travel and leisure fell by three fifths while those dealing with matters relating to social security more than doubled.

11.19 Citizens Advice Bureaux: by type of enquiry

England & Wales   Percentages and thousands

	1980-81	1991-92	1992-93
Consumer, trade and business[1]	18.6	23.4	23.4
Housing, property and land	15.8	10.1	9.4
Social security	9.7	22.7	22.9
Family and personal	14.8	9.0	8.7
Employment	10.0	11.3	11.2
Taxes and duties	2.7	5.1	5.0
Administration of justice	8.5	6.7	6.2
Holidays, travel and leisure	4.6	2.0	1.7
Health	3.6	2.1	1.9
Other	11.7	7.7	9.5
All enquiries (= 100%) (thousands)	4,016	7,484	7,748

1 Includes consumer debt.

Source: National Association of Citizens Advice Bureaux

REFERENCES AND FURTHER READING

The following list contains selected publications relevant to Chapter 11: Participation. Those published by HMSO are available from the addresses shown on the back cover of *Social Trends*.

Annual Report of the Commission for Local Administration in England
Annual Report of the Commission for Local Administration in Wales
Annual Report of the Commissioner for Local Administration in Scotland
Annual Report of the Council on Tribunals, HMSO
Annual Report of the Equal Opportunities Commission, HMSO
Annual Report of the Parliamentary Commission for Administration, HMSO
Annual Report of the Registrar General for Northern Ireland, HMSO
Annual Report of the Registrar General for Scotland, General Register Office (Scotland)
British Electoral Facts 1832-1987, Dartmouth
British Social Attitudes Survey, SCPR
Britain Votes, C. Rallings and M. Thrasher
Charity Commissioner's Report, HMSO

Individual Giving and Volunteering in Britain (6th Edition), Charities Aid Foundation
Charity Trends, Charities Aid Foundation
Christian England, MARC Europe
Eurobarometre, Commission of the European Communities
Marriage and Divorce Statistics (Series FM2), HMSO
Men and Women in Great Britain, HMSO
Official Handbook to the European Parliament, The European Parliament
Prospects for the Nineties, MARC Europe
Report on Voluntary Work, HMSO
The Lifeboat Service: Annual Report and Accounts, RNLI
Television Advertising Complaint Report (Monthly)
UK Christian Handbook, Christian Research Association
Women's Organisations in the United Kingdom, WNC

Chapter 12: Crime and Justice

Offences
- Recorded offences in England and Wales have risen from around three million in 1981 to 5.6 million in 1992.

  (Table 12.2)

- The value of property stolen but not recovered in England and Wales in 1992 was £2.7 billion   *(Table 12.5)*

Victims
- Afro-Caribbean people were twice as likely to be victims of burglary in England and Wales in 1991 than White people.

  (Table 12.9)

Offences cleared up
- Three quarters of sexual and violent offences against the person recorded in England and Wales in 1992 were cleared up.

  (Table 12.15)

Offenders
- In 1992 around five per cent of boys aged 14 in England and Wales were known to have committed an indictable offence.

  (Chart 12.16)

Police and courts action and sentencing
- Men over 21 committing an indictable offence in England and Wales were seven times more likely to receive a caution in 1992 than in 1971.

  (Table 12.21)

Prisons and probation service
- The United Kingdom had the second highest number of prisoners per head of population in the EC in 1991 with 92 prisoners per 100 thousand population.

  (Chart 12.30)

Resources and legal aid
- Since 1971 the number of police officers in Great Britain has increased by nearly a third while the number of police civilian staff increased by three fifths.

  (Table 12.35)

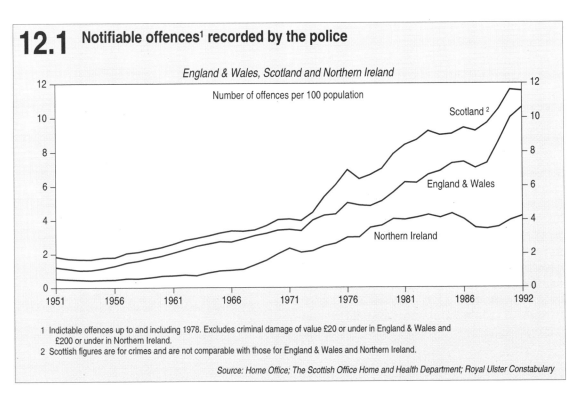

12.1 **Notifiable offences[1] recorded by the police**

England & Wales, Scotland and Northern Ireland

Number of offences per 100 population

Scotland [2]

England & Wales

Northern Ireland

1951 1956 1961 1966 1971 1976 1981 1986 1992

1 Indictable offences up to and including 1978. Excludes criminal damage of value £20 or under in England & Wales and £200 or under in Northern Ireland.
2 Scottish figures are for crimes and are not comparable with those for England & Wales and Northern Ireland.

Source: Home Office; The Scottish Office Home and Health Department; Royal Ulster Constabulary

12.2 Notifiable offences[1] recorded by the police: by type of offence

England & Wales, Scotland and Northern Ireland

Thousands

	England & Wales			Scotland			Northern Ireland		
	1981	1991	1992	1981	1991	1992	1981	1991[2]	1992[2]
Violence against the person	100.2	190.3	201.8	8.0	15.5	16.5	2.9	4.0	4.1
Sexual offences,	19.4	29.4	29.5	2.1	3.1	3.3	0.3	0.9	1.0
of which: rape	1.1	4.0	4.1	0.3	0.5	0.5	-	0.1	0.1
Burglary	718.4	1,219.5	1,355.3	95.7	116.1	113.2	20.5	16.6	17.1
Robbery	20.3	45.3	52.9	4.2	6.2	6.8	2.7	1.8	1.9
Drug trafficking	..	11.4	13.8	1.6	3.3	4.1	-	-	0.1
Theft and handling stolen goods,	1,603.2	2,761.1	2,851.6	201.1	284.3	270.8	25.4	32.0	34.3
of which: theft of vehicles	332.6	581.9	585.5	32.5	44.3	47.4	5.1	8.4	9.4
theft from vehicles[3]	379.6	913.3	961.3	..	..	97.1	6.5	7.2	7.1
Fraud and forgery	106.7	174.7	168.6	21.4	26.4	27.7	2.6	4.8	5.4
Criminal damage[4]	386.7	821.1	892.6	61.7	89.7	92.2	5.2	2.4	2.5
Other notifiable offences	8.9	23.2	25.6	12.4	48.1	55.0	2.8	1.0	1.2
Total notifiable offences	2,963.8	5,276.2	5,591.7	408.2	592.8	589.6	62.5	63.5	67.5

1 Includes attempted offences. Scottish figures of 'crime' have been recompiled to approximate to the classification of notifiable offences in England & Wales and Northern Ireland. However, because of differences in the legal system, recording and counting practices and classification problems, Scottish figures are not comparable with those for England & Wales and Northern Ireland.
2 These figures no longer include assault on police and communicating false information regarding a bomb hoax. These offences have been removed from the categories 'Violence against the person' and 'Other notifiable offences'.
3 In Scotland, data have only been collected from January 1992. The figures include theft by opening lockfast places from motor vehicles and other theft from vehicles.
4 In Northern Ireland, the figures exclude criminal damage valued at £200 or less.

Source: Home Office; The Scottish Office Home and Health Department; Royal Ulster Constabulary

In this chapter England and Wales, Scotland and Northern Ireland are often shown separately because of their different legal systems.

In England and Wales there was an offence recorded for every ten people in 1992. This compares with one offence for every 29 people in 1972 **(Chart 12.1)**. It is important to bear in mind that this is an increase in

Offences

The first three items in this chapter cover notifiable offences recorded by the police, a measure of the number of crimes the police are trying to solve. It does not measure the real level of crime: many offences are not reported to the police and cannot, therefore, be recorded, while some others are not recorded by them because the complainant may decide not to proceed, or the police may decide there is not enough evidence of an offence having been committed. Crime recorded by the police is only a partial picture of crime committed. Crime recording starts when someone reports to the police that an offence has been committed, or when the police themselves discover an offence.

The offences covered by the term notifiable offences have remained more or less the same over the years, despite changes to the name of the series. A list of the offences is published in the annual Home Office publication *Criminal Statistics: England and Wales*. The figures for Northern Ireland are broadly compatible with notifiable offences. In Scotland there is a difference between crimes and offences: crimes are more serious, and are roughly comparable with notifiable offences. Although there is some common ground, United Kingdom comparisons should only be made with care.

12.3 Notifiable offences recorded by the police: by type of offence, 1992

England & Wales and Northern Ireland

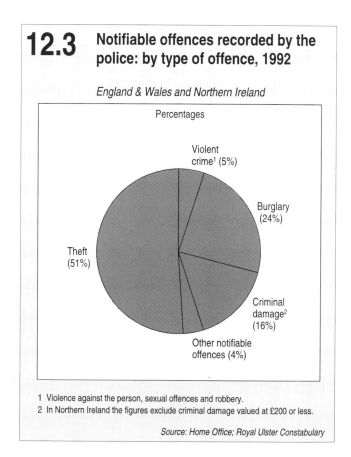

Percentages

Violent crime[1] (5%)

Burglary (24%)

Theft (51%)

Criminal damage[2] (16%)

Other notifiable offences (4%)

1 Violence against the person, sexual offences and robbery.
2 In Northern Ireland the figures exclude criminal damage valued at £200 or less.

Source: Home Office; Royal Ulster Constabulary

offences recorded and not necessarily an increase in crimes actually committed. The British Crime Survey, (BCS) which relies on interviews with the public, gives a fuller count of the number of offences than the number recorded by the police. It also shows that police figures are misleading with regards to trends, as readiness to report varies.

Recorded offences are on the increase. In England and Wales alone, the number has risen from around one million in 1961 to over five and a half million in 1992 (Table 12.2). Although offences recorded have risen across the United Kingdom, the rate of increase has varied between the countries. Since 1981 England and Wales has witnessed an 89 per cent rise, Northern Ireland an eight per cent rise and Scotland a 44 per cent rise. However, because of differences in the legal system, recording and counting practices and classification problems, Scottish figures are not directly comparable with those for England and Wales and Northern Ireland

Violent crime accounted for only 1 in 20 of all recorded offences in England and Wales and Northern Ireland in 1992 (Chart 12.3). Despite the overall increase in recorded offences, this proportion has stayed roughly constant since 1971. This does not indicate that the country is becoming a more violent place in which to live; indeed the BCS shows little increase in violence

throughout the 1980s. Other countries and areas are much more violent, for example, New York, which has a murder rate 16 times higher than London.

Chart 12.4 uses information from the BCS to show the proportion of offences actually recorded by the police. Crimes against organisations rather than people, such as company fraud and shoplifting, and so-called victimless crimes (eg drug abuse) are not covered by the survey. The most recent survey in England and Wales was in 1992 which provides estimates of crimes committed in 1991.

In 1991, 93 per cent of motor vehicle theft was recorded by the police, double the proportion for burglary and nearly three times that of theft from vehicles. Reasons for not reporting crimes varied from the incident being too trivial, to a belief that the police would not have been able to do anything about the incident.

Theft and burglary accounted for three quarters of all recorded offences in England and Wales in 1992. Property valued at £2.7 billion, stolen as a result of either offence in 1992, was not recovered (Table 12.5). Northern Ireland has a slightly higher recovery rate than England and Wales for theft from shops, at 39 per cent, and a lower rate, at 37 per cent, for theft of motor vehicles.

12.4 Percentage of offences recorded by the police: by type of offence, 1991

England & Wales

1 Excludes attempted offences.

Source: Home Office

12.5 Notifiable offences of theft and burglary recorded by the police - value of property stolen and recovered, 1992

England & Wales

	Property stolen		Property recovered	
	Offences (thous-ands)	Total value (£ mill-ion)	Total value (£ mill-ion)	% of total value stolen
Theft				
From the person of another	39	6	-	4
In a dwelling[1]	43	14	1	6
By an employee[2]	15	613	2	-
From shops	289	20	6	32
Of pedal cycles	222	48	2	3
From vehicles	961	243	11	5
Of motor vehicles	586	1,772	994	58
Burglary				
In a dwelling	708	601	24	4
In other building	647	455	40	9
Total theft and burglary	3,510	3,771	1,080	29

1 Other than from automatic machine or meter.
2 Includes one case where the value of property stolen was £557 million.

Source: Home Office

12.6 Offences currently[1] recorded as homicide: by sex of victim and apparent method of killing

United Kingdom	Male victims		Female victims	
	1982	1992	1982	1992
Sharp instrument	31	39	32	27
Hitting, kicking, etc	13	20	10	20
Shooting	19	18	4	8
Blunt instrument	10	8	13	9
Strangulation[2]	7	5	31	22
Burning[3]	6	3	2	6
Other	14	7	8	9
Total offences (= 100%) (numbers)	431	590	312	280

Percentages and numbers (column header)

1 As at August 1993. Figures are subject to revision as cases are dealt with by police and courts, or as further information becomes available.
2 Includes asphyxiation and, in Scotland, drowning.
3 Includes all homicides which occurred in fires, whatever the actual cause of death.

Source: Home Office; The Scottish Office Home and Health Department; Royal Ulster Constabulary

A total of 870 homicides were recorded in the United Kingdom in 1992. **Table 12.6** sets out the various ways in which the offences were committed. Whereas shooting accounted for two thirds of the homicides in Northern Ireland in 1992, it only accounted for eight per cent in England and Wales and less than four per cent in Scotland. Since 1982, there has been a 17 per cent increase in the overall number of homicides in the United Kingdom; homicides with a male victim increased by 37 per cent while female homicides fell by ten per cent. Since homicides are relatively uncommon, considerable year to year variation is to be expected both in the number and types of homicides recorded.

The percentage of people failing or refusing to take breath tests in England and Wales has fallen substantially over the last 20 years **(Chart 12.7)**. Although the actual numbers failing or refusing the test have increased by 40 per cent since 1971, there has been a more than fivefold increase in the number of tests taken over the same period. In 1992 over half a million tests were carried out resulting in 87 thousand positive or refused outcomes.

Victims

Chart 12.8 contradicts the popular image that it is the old who are at most risk from a burglary in their home. Indeed, in Great Britain in 1991 a burglary was nearly twice as likely to happen in a household headed by a 16 to 29 year old (56 per thousand households) than in one headed by someone aged 65 and over (29 per thousand). There also appears to be a relationship between the likelihood of being burgled and housing tenure. Results from the 1991 General Household Survey indicate that people living in rented property have a burglary rate 40 per cent higher than owner occupiers. Age was also a factor in the value of goods stolen. Amongst households with heads in the 16 to 29

12.7 Percentage of positive or refused breath tests

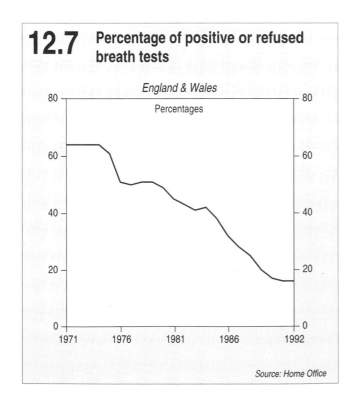

England & Wales

Source: Home Office

12.8 Burglary rate: by age of head of household[1], 1991

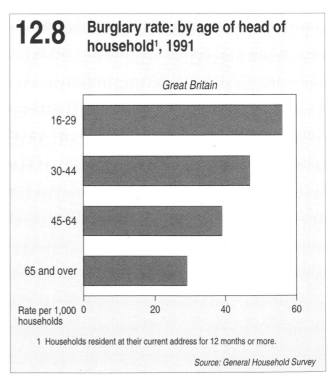

Great Britain

1 Households resident at their current address for 12 months or more.

Source: General Household Survey

12.9 Victims of one or more crimes[1]: by ethnic origin and type of offence, 1991

England & Wales			Percentages
	Ethnic origin of victim		
	White	Afro-Caribbean	Asian
Percentage who were victims of each offence			
Assault	3	5	4
Threats	3	3	4
Robbery/theft from the person	1	3	3
Burglary	6	12	9
Other household theft[2]	7	6	4
Household vandalism	4	4	5
Vehicle (owners)			
Vandalism	9	11	10
All thefts[3]	20	28	22
Bicycle (owners) theft	6	10	7

1 Based on incidents occurring over the full recall period.
2 Includes theft from a dwelling.
3 Includes theft of, and from, vehicles and attempted theft.

Source: Home Office

Information from the British Crime Survey on the ethnic origin of victims of crime is shown in **Table 12.9**. Social and demographic factors, particularly the areas in which they live, help to explain why ethnic minority groups are more at risk than the White population for many types of crime. For example, the proportion of Afro-Caribbeans in England and Wales who were victims of burglary in 1991 was twice that of Whites.

Nearly 0.9 million insurance claims were made in 1992 as a result of theft from domestic property, resulting in payouts totalling £750 million **(Chart 12.10)**. In real terms the costs have more than doubled since 1989, whilst at current prices the figure shows an increase of just over £470 million.

Results from the International Crime Survey, conducted by the Dutch Ministry of Justice, indicate that car owners in England and Wales are more likely to be a victim of theft from a car than in most other developed countries. **Chart 12.11** shows that nine per cent of car owners were victims of theft in England and Wales compared with six per cent in Germany and only two per cent in Switzerland.

age range, 30 in every thousand experienced a burglary of property worth more than £200, compared to just 11 in every thousand for those with heads aged 65 and over. The equivalent rates for burglaries of under £200 were 26 and 17 per cent respectively.

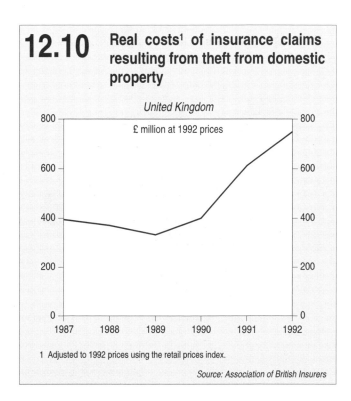

12.10 Real costs[1] of insurance claims resulting from theft from domestic property

1 Adjusted to 1992 prices using the retail prices index.

Source: Association of British Insurers

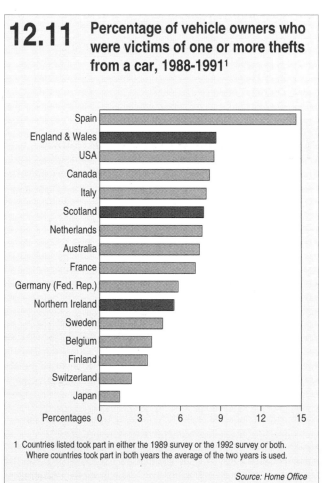

12.11 Percentage of vehicle owners who were victims of one or more thefts from a car, 1988-1991[1]

1 Countries listed took part in either the 1989 survey or the 1992 survey or both. Where countries took part in both years the average of the two years is used.

Source: Home Office

12.12 Criminal injuries compensation

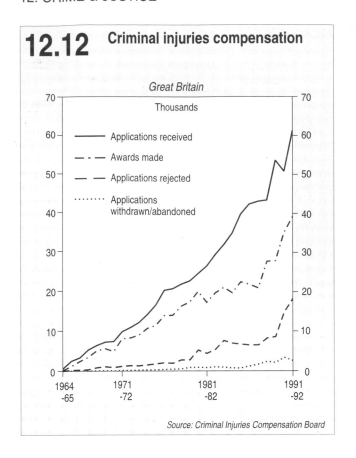

Source: Criminal Injuries Compensation Board

12.13 Notifiable offences cleared up as a percentage of those recorded by the police

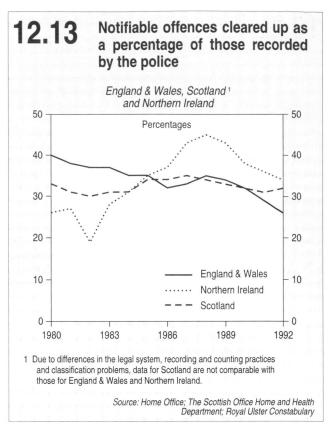

1 Due to differences in the legal system, recording and counting practices and classification problems, data for Scotland are not comparable with those for England & Wales and Northern Ireland.

Source: Home Office; The Scottish Office Home and Health Department; Royal Ulster Constabulary

Applications for criminal injury compensation in Great Britain have more than doubled since 1981-82, to 61 thousand in 1991-92 **(Chart 12.12)**. In the same ten year period there has been a fourfold increase in the number of applications rejected.

Offences cleared up

An offence can be cleared up by the police in a number of ways, such as if a person is charged, summonsed, warned or cautioned for the offence, if the offence is admitted and is taken into consideration by the court (not in Scotland), or if there is sufficient evidence to charge a person but the case is not proceeded with.

The proportion of recorded notifiable offences cleared up in England and Wales has declined steadily over the last 12 years from 40 per cent in 1980 to 26 per cent in 1992 **(Chart 12.13)**. This compares with a peak of 45 per cent in Northern Ireland in 1988, although this fell to 34 per cent by 1992. Throughout this period, the rate for Scotland has remained fairly stable at around 32 per cent. However, it is not possible to make a direct comparison between the figures for Scotland with those for England and Wales and Northern Ireland.

Some of the regional variation shown in the clear-up rates in **Chart 12.14** may be due to the differing use of secondary measures such as interviewing convicted prisoners. Primary methods accounted for over two

12.14 Clear up rates for recorded notifiable offences: by police force area, 1992

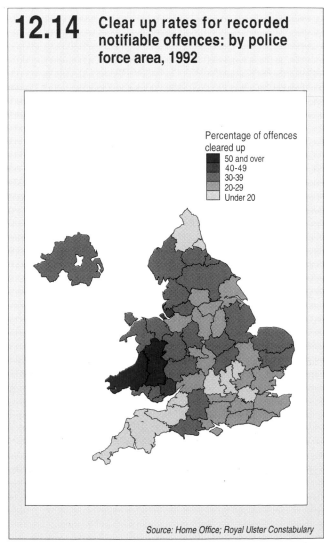

Source: Home Office; Royal Ulster Constabulary

12.15 Clear-up rates for notifiable offences[1]: by type of offence

England & Wales, Scotland and Northern Ireland — Percentages

	England & Wales			Scotland			Northern Ireland		
	1981	1991	1992	1981	1991	1992	1981	1991[2]	1992[2]
Violence against the person	75	77	76	83	81	78	47	62	64
Sexual offences,	73	76	75	65	77	76	71	87	80
of which: rape	68	76	75	74	79	73	45	80	80
Burglary	30	23	20	20	15	14	22	22	19
Robbery	25	23	22	26	27	25	15	17	19
Drug trafficking	..	97	98	99	100	100	100	82	95
Theft and handling stolen goods,	38	28	24	28	23	23	27	34	32
of which: theft of vehicles	28	24	20	26	21	19	14	29	28
theft from vehicles[3]	23	19	15	..	..	11	12	12	9
Fraud and forgery	70	55	53	78	70	73	66	67	61
Criminal damage[4]	27	19	17	22	19	19	17	32	34
Other notifiable offences	91	96	94	90	98	98	33	79	83
All notifiable offences	38	29	26	31	31	32	27	36	34

1 Includes attempted offences. Scottish figures of 'crime' have been recompiled to approximate to the classification of notifiable offences in England & Wales and Northern Ireland. However, because of differences in the legal system, recording and counting practices and classification problems, Scottish figures are not comparable with those for England & Wales and Northern Ireland.

2 These figures no longer include assault on police and communicating false information regarding a bomb hoax. These offences have been removed from the categories 'Violence against the person' and 'Other notifiable offences'.

3 In Scotland data have only been collected from January 1992. The figures include theft by opening lockfast places from motor vehicles and other theft from motor vehicles.

4 In England & Wales excludes criminal damage valued at £20 or less. In Northern Ireland, the figures exclude criminal damage valued at £200 or less.

Source: Home Office; The Scottish Office Home and Health Department; Royal Ulster Constabulary

thirds of all clear ups in 15 of the police force areas shown. Only five areas in England and Wales had a better clear up rate for 1992 compared with 1991. The highest clear up rate in 1992 was in Dyfed-Powys, at 53 per cent, while the Metropolitan Police force area was, as in 1991, the least successful area, at 16 per cent.

Despite the fall in the overall clear-up rate in England and Wales, three quarters of both offences of violence against the person and sexual offences are still cleared up in both England and Wales and Scotland **(Table 12.15)**. Theft from vehicles remains one of the offences that the police are less likely to clear up.

Offenders

By the age of 14, five per cent of males in England and Wales are known offenders (that is, they have been either cautioned or found guilty of an indictable offence) **(Chart 12.16)**. This rises to a peak of 11 per cent by the age of 18 while for females it peaks at age 15. In Scotland the peak age for being convicted of a crime for both sexes is 18; in Northern Ireland offenders tend to be slightly older (19 for men and 20 for women). Differences between parts of the country will reflect differences in the way young offenders are dealt with.

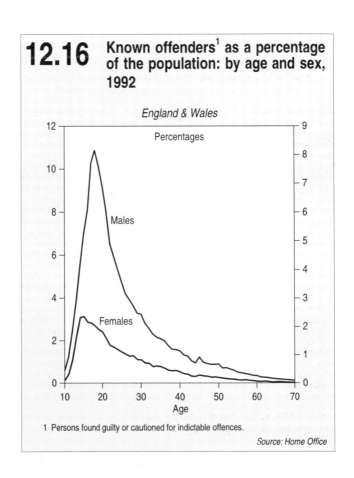

12.16 Known offenders[1] as a percentage of the population: by age and sex, 1992

England & Wales

1 Persons found guilty or cautioned for indictable offences.

Source: Home Office

12.17 Offenders found guilty of, or cautioned for, indictable offences: by sex, age and type of offence, 1992

England & Wales										Percentages and thousands
	Males					Females				
	10-13	14-16	17-20	21 and over	All aged 10 and over	10-13	14-16	17-20	21 and over	All aged 10 and over
Theft and handling stolen goods	64	53	40	39	43	86	76	69	67	71
Violence against the person	8	12	11	15	13	7	14	9	9	10
Burglary	18	19	16	9	13	4	4	3	1	2
Drug offences	1	5	14	11	10	-	2	7	6	5
Criminal damage	5	3	3	3	3	1	1	1	1	1
Sexual offences	1	2	1	2	2	-	-	-	-	-
Robbery	2	2	1	1	1	-	1	-	-	-
Other indictable offences	2	5	14	20	15	1	3	11	15	11
All indictable offences (= 100%) (thousands)	24.7	58.0	109.9	245.2	437.9	8.5	19.2	20.5	52.9	101.1

Source: Home Office

Young offenders are more frequently involved in theft offences than any other type of offence. Males aged 10 to 13 are eight times more likely to commit theft than offences of violence against the person **(Table 12.17)**. In general, violence increases with age while theft falls; males aged 21 and over are only two and a half times more likely to commit theft as they are violence against the person. Offenders aged under 21 commit 45 per cent of all known indictable offences.

The total number of drug offences committed continues to rise **(Table 12.18)**, although the rise had slowed to under three per cent between 1991 and 1992.

12.18 Drug offences - persons found guilty, cautioned or dealt with by compounding[1]: by type of offence

United Kingdom				Numbers
	1981	1986	1991	1992
Unlawful production[2]	1,603	944	664	756
Unlawful supply	1,000	1,876	2,133	2,189
Possession with intent to supply unlawfully	699	1,858	2,782	3,203
Unlawful possession	14,850	20,052	42,575	43,492
Unlawful import or export	1,357	1,525	2,136	2,034
All drug offences[3]	17,921	23,905	47,616	48,927

1 Includes H.M. Customs and Excise cases dealt with by the payment of a penalty in lieu of prosecution.
2 Includes offences of cultivation of cannabis plants.
3 As the same person may appear in more than one category, rows cannot be added together to produce totals or sub-totals.

Source: Home Office

Police and courts action and sentencing

In Scotland the Procurator Fiscal decides what action to take with alleged offenders. The Fiscal can prosecute, issue a warning, a conditional offer of a fixed penalty notice (for some motoring offences) or a fiscal fine (for minor common law offences), divert the case over to other agencies (eg social work) or decide not to proceed. The number of fixed penalty notices issued has increased by almost 55 per cent between 1981 and 1991 **(Table 12.19)**.

The options available to the police in England and Wales on the detection of an alleged offender are: to take no action; issue a formal caution; or refer the case to the Crown Prosecution Service, who will then decide whether to prosecute. No action is taken where the offender is below the age of criminal responsibility (ten years of age) or if there is insufficient evidence.

12.19 Persons proceeded against or given fixed penalty notices

Scotland				Thousands
	1981	1986	1991	1992
Crimes	59	70	60	65
Motoring offences:				
Persons proceeded against	103	67	76	72
Fixed penalty notices[1]	401	491	618	621
Other offences[2]	84	67	55	60

1 Includes conditional offers of a fixed penalty by the Procurator Fiscal introduced in 1983. Number of notices, not persons.
2 From January 1988 Procurator Fiscal made conditional offers of a fixed penalty for some minor offences.

Source: The Scottish Office Home and Health Department

12.20 Defendants proceeded against and persons cautioned, given written warnings or fixed penalty notices

England & Wales   Thousands

| | Indictable offences | | Summary offences | | | | | |
| | | | Motoring offences | | | Other offences | | |
	Defendants proceeded against	Persons cautioned	Defendants proceeded against[1]	Persons given written warnings	Fixed penalty notices[1]	Defendants proceeded against	Persons cautioned
1978	470	107	1,185	..	..	438	35
1981	523	104	1,299	253	4,317	472	50
1986	463	137	1,199	208	5,059	508	77
1990	469	166	846	154	6,298	577	103
1991	489	180	893	160	5,676	573	99
1992	490	216	938	136	5,077	601	105

1 For notices issued up to 1 October 1986 some persons were prosecuted following non-payment of a fixed penalty. The extended fixed penalty system was introduced on 1 October 1986. It allowed the police to issue fixed penalty notices for a much wider range of offences than hitherto, and to register fines automatically in the event of non-payment without the need for court proceedings.

Source: Home Office

An indication of the split between serious (indictable) and less serious (summary) offences is given in **Table 12.20**. It shows that three times as many people are proceeded against for summary offences, of which the largest component is motoring offences, than for indictable offences. However, by far the most common action taken by the police following a motoring offence such as speeding, is to issue a fixed penalty notice. The number of notices issued fell in 1991 and in 1992, but still stood at over five million.

The increase in the use of cautioning in England and Wales (issued by a senior police officer after an admission of guilt) is evident in **Tables 12.20 and 12.21**. The numbers cautioned for indictable offences in England and Wales doubled between 1981 and 1992. Cautioning is most frequently used for young offenders. However, in 1992, males aged 21 and over were over five times more likely to be cautioned than in 1981. Cautioning rates for females have always been higher but these have also increased. In 1992 over three fifths of all females found guilty or cautioned for indictable offences were cautioned. Home Office figures suggest that 87 per cent of people cautioned in 1985 had not been convicted of an indictable offence within two years of the caution.

When the Crown Prosecution Service decides to prosecute a case, it will be heard at a magistrates court, or a Crown Court for the most serious offences. Following a conviction, the judge or magistrate will pass sentence based on the severity of the crime. Magistrates can only impose custodial sentences of up to six months, but can refer the case to the Crown Court for a longer sentence.

12.21 Persons cautioned for indictable offences: by sex and age

England & Wales   Thousands and percentages

| | Found guilty or cautioned (thousands) | | | | | Percentage cautioned | | | | |
	1971	1981	1986	1991	1992	1971	1981	1986	1991	1992
Males										
10-13	45.4	47.3	32.4	23.3	24.7	60	68	81	90	91
14-16	64.2	94.9	81.3	58.2	58.0	31	35	54	70	73
17-20	74.9	117.3	109.4	111.1	109.9	5	3	10	25	32
21 and over	148.8	213.5	207.3	232.2	245.2	3	4	9	18	22
All males aged 10 and over	333.3	473.0	430.4	424.8	437.9	17	16	21	31	35
Females										
10-13	8.4	13.3	9.2	6.5	8.5	80	87	94	97	98
14-16	10.8	18.8	18.6	17.0	19.2	53	60	80	87	90
17-20	8.6	15.5	16.2	18.6	20.5	6	5	21	45	55
21 and over	33.1	46.8	44.2	48.2	52.9	11	11	25	39	46
All females aged 10 and over	60.9	94.3	88.2	90.5	101.1	27	31	43	53	60

Source: Home Office

12.22 Offenders sentenced for indictable offences: by type of offence and type of sentence, 1992

England & Wales

Percentages and thousands

Offences	Discharge	Probation /super- vision	Community service order	Fine	Fully suspended sentence	Immediate custody Under 5 years	5 years and over	Other	Total sentenced (=100%) (thousands)
Violence against the person	24	9	10	26	7	16	1	8	43.6
Sexual offences	10	21	2	17	8	29	10	3	4.9
Burglary	12	20	17	12	6	27	-	6	44.3
Robbery	4	12	5	1	2	54	15	7	5.1
Theft and handling stolen goods	28	12	9	35	5	8	-	3	127.8
Fraud and forgery	25	10	12	27	10	12	-	3	20.1
Criminal damage	27	18	9	22	3	10	-	11	9.9
Drug offences	15	6	5	53	5	14	2	1	22.7
Motoring	5	5	7	68	3	13	0	1	10.7
Other	16	4	6	55	4	11	-	4	35.5
All indictable offences	21	11	10	34	5	14	1	4	324.6

Source: Home Office

Twice as many offenders in England and Wales are fined than receive custodial sentences for all indictable offences (Table 12.22). However, for robbery, custody is the most frequently used sentence with nearly 70 per cent of offenders sentenced for robbery receiving an immediate custodial sentence. In Scotland almost three times as many offenders are fined than receive custodial sentences for crimes. For non-sexual crimes of violence, custody is more frequently used than a fine in Scotland,

in particular for offenders convicted of homicide and robbery where the use of custody in 1992 was 88 per cent and 66 per cent respectively.

Since 1981, the use of community based sentences (Chart 12.23) has increased for all offences. Around 41 per cent of people sentenced for burglary received a community based sentence in 1992. However, the rate is quite low for drug offences, where there is a far greater use of fines. The use of community based sentences for sexual offenders fell between 1985 and 1989, but has now risen again to above the 1985 level.

Prisons and probation service

Over 90 thousand people began criminal court order supervision by the probation service in England and Wales in 1992. Table 12.24 also shows that for the first time community service orders were used more than probation orders. Part of the fall in probation orders can

12.23 Percentage of offenders receiving community based sentences: by selected indictable offence

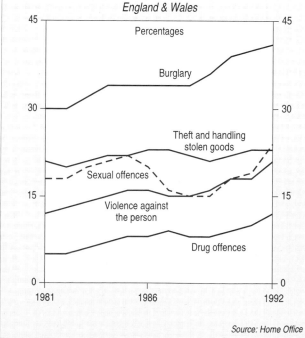

Source: Home Office

12.24 Persons commencing criminal supervision by the probation service: by selected type of supervision

England & Wales

Thousands

Type of supervision	1982	1986	1991	1992
Probation	36.8	39.7	45.4	41.4
Community service order	30.9	34.7	41.8	43.4
Under Children and Young Persons Act[1]	11.0	6.0	2.4	2.0
Money payment orders	5.9	4.8	5.9	4.5

1 Supervision under the Children and Young Persons Act 1969.

Source: Home Office

12.25 Receptions under sentence[1] into prison service establishments[2]

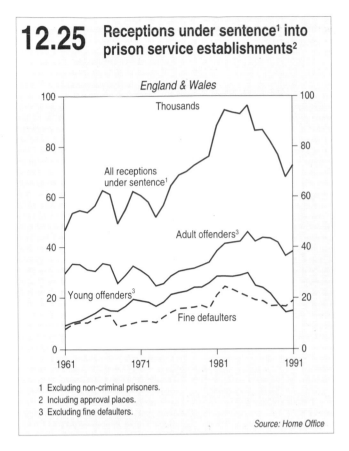

England & Wales

1 Excluding non-criminal prisoners.
2 Including approval places.
3 Excluding fine defaulters.

Source: Home Office

12.26 Average population in custody[1]: by type of prisoner

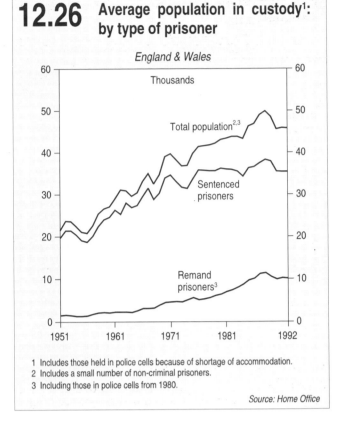

England & Wales

1 Includes those held in police cells because of shortage of accommodation.
2 Includes a small number of non-criminal prisoners.
3 Including those in police cells from 1980.

Source: Home Office

be explained by the introduction of a new combination order (a combination of probation and community service) in the *Criminal Justice Act 1991*. In the first three months after combination orders were introduced some 1,400 commenced.

There were about 72 thousand receptions under sentence into prison service establishments in England and Wales in 1991 **(Chart 12.25)**. Young offenders accounted for a fifth (15 thousand) of receptions compared with a third in 1980.

The average population in custody was almost 46 thousand in England and Wales in 1992. Since January 1993, the prison population has risen from 42 thousand to just under 47 thousand in November, on a seasonally adjusted basis, just over the certified accommodation.

Over the last forty years remand prisoners have made up an increasing proportion of the prison population, 22 per cent in England and Wales in 1992 compared with only seven per cent in 1951 and 12 per cent in 1971**(Chart 12.26)**. An average of 1,100 prisoners were held in police cells in 1992, much the same number as in 1991.

Table 12.27 gives details of prisoners in the United Kingdom. It shows that the number of untried prisoners has fallen by one thousand since 1986, but they still represent a sixth of the total prison population. In line with the fall in receptions, the number of sentenced young offenders has nearly halved since 1981. Prisons are still largely a male preserve with males accounting for 96 per cent of all prisoners.

12.27 Population[1] in custody in prison establishments

United Kingdom				Thousands
	1981	1986	1991	1992
Average population				
Males	48.9	52.5	49.7	50.0
Females	1.6	1.8	1.7	1.8
Total	50.5	54.3	51.4	51.8
Remand prisoners				
Untried prisoners	5.9	9.6	8.6	8.6
Convicted prisoners awaiting sentence[2]	2.3	1.7	2.0	2.1
All remand prisoners	8.2	11.3	10.6	10.7
Sentenced prisoners				
Adults	29.3	32.0	33.7	34.3
Young offenders[3]	12.6	10.7	6.8	6.5
Other sentences	-	-	0.1	0.1
All sentenced prisoners	41.9	42.7	40.6	40.9
Non-criminal prisoners	0.4	0.2	0.3	0.3

1 Annual averages. Excludes prisoners held in police cells in England and Wales.
2 Includes persons remanded in custody while social and medical inquiry reports are prepared prior to sentence. Prisoners in Northern Ireland are not committed for sentence but are sentenced at the court of conviction.
3 See Appendix, Part 12: Young offenders.

Source: Home Office; The Scottish Office Home and Health Department; Northern Ireland Office

12.28 Prison population[1] rates: by ethnic origin

England & Wales	Rate per 10,000 population[2]		
	Males	Females	All
White	19.4	0.5	9.6
West Indian, Guyanese, African	144.0	9.9	76.7
Indian, Pakistani, Bangladeshi	24.3	0.4	12.4
Other/not disclosed	72.1	5.4	38.3
All ethnic origins	22.0	0.7	11.0

1 On June 30 1992.
2 Aged 14 and over.

Source: Home Office; Office of Population Censuses and Surveys

People from ethnic minority groups are over represented in prisons in England and Wales compared with those of White origin **(Table 12.28)**. However the younger age structure of the ethnic minority population and the offences for which they are imprisoned play an important role in explaining the imbalance. For example, a high proportion of West Indian, Guyanese and African females in the prison population are foreign nationals convicted of drug importation offences.

Between 1986 and 1991 there was a 53 per cent rise in the number of male offenders in the United Kingdom with prison sentences of over four years but less than life, but the numbers then fell by over 800 in 1992 **(Table 12.29)**. For females there was an increase of

12.30 Prison population[1]: EC comparison, 1991

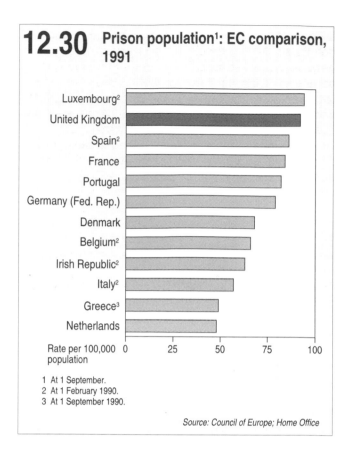

Rate per 100,000 population

1 At 1 September.
2 At 1 February 1990.
3 At 1 September 1990.

Source: Council of Europe; Home Office

160 per cent between 1986 and 1991, followed by a small fall in 1992. The number of male young offender life sentences has fallen steadily and in 1992 was 144, just under half the 1986 figure.

12.29 Sentenced prisoners[1]: by sex and length of sentence

United Kingdom						Numbers
	1986	1988	1989	1990	1991	1992
Males						
Prisoners aged under 21 serving[2] :						
Up to 18 months	6,789	5,235	4,213	3,682	3,540	3,392
Over 18 months and up to 4 years	2,732	3,172	2,839	2,522	2,189	2,271
Over 4 years less than Life	646	889	849	804	712	633
Life sentences	271	227	212	207	169	144
Prisoners aged 21 and over serving:						
Up to 18 months	11,388	10,268	9,442	8,309	8,941	10,550
Over 18 months and up to 4 years	9,900	11,255	11,606	10,058	9,634	9,517
Over 4 years less than Life	6,779	9,000	9,877	10,294	10,670	9,933
Life sentences	2,670	3,022	3,189	3,279	3,397	3,486
All sentenced male prisoners[3]	41,175	43,067	42,227	39,154	39,253	39,925
Females						
Prisoners of all ages serving:						
Up to 18 months	810	613	558	532	497	559
Over 18 months and up to 4 years	355	480	453	398	331	329
Over 4 years less than Life	134	227	295	336	348	330
Life sentences	80	89	97	102	106	105
All sentenced female prisoners[3]	1,379	1,410	1,404	1,369	1,281	1,323

1 As at 30 June each year for England & Wales and annual averages for Scotland and Northern Ireland.
2 For Scotland includes detention centre sentences which were abolished on 1 November 1988.
3 Excludes prisoners held in police cells in England and Wales.

Source: Home Office; The Scottish Office Home and Health Department; Northern Ireland Office

Differences in sentencing policy, detection rates and definitions make comparisons of prison populations between countries difficult. A country with a high prison population may not have a high crime rate, just a tougher sentencing policy. One way to make comparisons is to look at the number of prisoners per head of population **(Chart 12.30)**. By this method the United Kingdom had the second highest rate of all the countries in the European Community in 1991 with 92 prisoners per 100,000 population, second only to Luxembourg.

In 1991, The National Prison Survey (NPS) of some four thousand prisoners in custody in England and Wales was conducted for the first time. The survey was carried out for the Home Office by the Office of Population Censuses and Surveys with the aim of getting an insight into prison life from the prisoners' perspective. The survey was designed to help the Prison Service to develop more positive prison regimes.

The NPS found that 30 per cent of prisoners said they regularly played truant while at secondary school **(Chart 12.31)**. This compares to separate Office of Population Censuses and Surveys figures which indicate the figure for the general population to be just three per cent. Care must be taken when comparing the percentage of the prison population who played truant with those of the general population as 96 per cent of the prison population are male and males are more likely to play truant than females.

12.32 Prisoners'[1] assessment of reimprisonment as very or fairly likely: by main offence

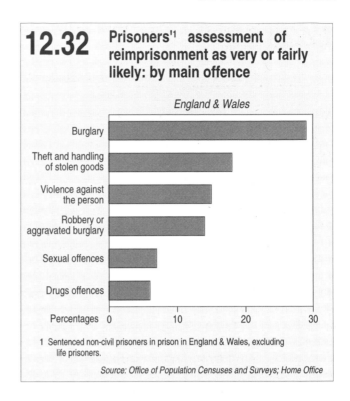

England & Wales

1 Sentenced non-civil prisoners in prison in England & Wales, excluding life prisoners.

Source: Office of Population Censuses and Surveys; Home Office

Prisoners' views on the likelihood of reimprisonment are shown in **Chart 12.32**. Nearly three in ten convicted burglars considered it very, or fairly, likely they would return to prison.

Resources and legal aid

Almost £15 billion of public expenditure was spent on justice and law in 1992 **(Table 12.33)**. At nearly six per cent of total general government expenditure this is the same proportion as in 1991 but two percentage points higher than in 1986. Expenditure on the law courts

12.31 Truancy rates[1], whilst at school of prisoners[2] compared with the general population

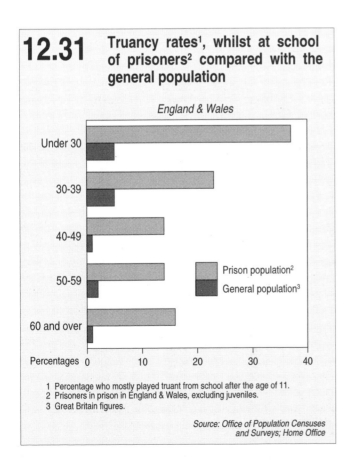

England & Wales

1 Percentage who mostly played truant from school after the age of 11.
2 Prisoners in prison in England & Wales, excluding juveniles.
3 Great Britain figures.

Source: Office of Population Censuses and Surveys; Home Office

12.33 Public expenditure on justice and law[1]

United Kingdom		£ million and percentages		
	1982	1986	1991	1992
Police	2,780	3,691	6,448	7,116
Law courts	825	1,219	3,207	3,591
Prisons	635	1,071	1,770	1,726
Legal aid	211	345	754	1,056
Parliament	324	530	798	871
Probation	109	148	262	321
Total	4,884	7,004	13,239	14,681
As a percentage of general government expenditure	*3.8*	*4.3*	*5.8*	*5.8*

1 Costs are not included for social work staff employed in Scotland on aspects related to the criminal justice system which in England and Wales are undertaken by the probation service.

Source: Central Statistical Office

12.34 Criminal legal aid[1]: applications granted[2]

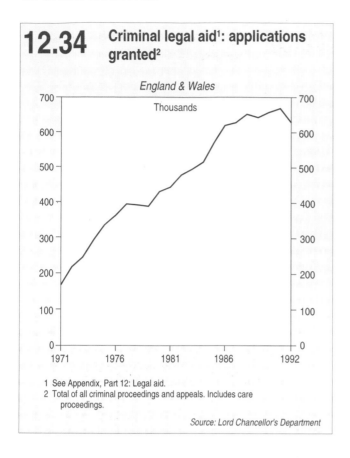

England & Wales

Thousands

1 See Appendix, Part 12: Legal aid.
2 Total of all criminal proceedings and appeals. Includes care
  proceedings.

Source: Lord Chancellor's Department

made up almost a quarter of the total in 1992 compared with almost 17 per cent in 1982, whereas expenditure on the police has fallen from 57 per cent of the total in 1986 to 48 per cent in 1992.

The Legal Aid scheme aims to provide legal advice, assistance and representation to people who can least afford to pay for such a service. In England and Wales 629 thousand applications for criminal legal aid were granted in 1992 **(Chart 12.34)**. A further 21 thousand applications were granted in Northern Ireland. There were 78 thousand applications granted for criminal legal aid in Scotland in 1992-93 and 295 thousand grants of advice and assistance.

Total police and prison service manpower **(Table 12.35)** stood at almost 240 thousand people in Great Britain in 1992. The number of police officers has increased by nearly a third since 1971, whilst the number of civilian staff has increased by three fifths over the same period. Around 15 thousand people make up the total police manpower in Northern Ireland, half of whom are police regulars, with reservists making up a further 30 per cent. The number of probation officers in England and Wales has doubled since 1971.

12.35 Employment in the criminal justice system[1]

Great Britain				Thousands
	1971	1981	1991	1992
Police				
Police	107.6	132.7	141.1	142.1
Civilian staff[2]	36.0	45.0	55.3	57.9
All police	143.6	177.7	196.4	200.1
Prison service[3]				
Prison officer class[4]	13.4	19.2	28.2	30.3
Governor class	0.6	0.6	1.0	1.0
Other non-industrial staff	3.2	4.3	5.2	5.6
Industrial staff	2.0	2.4	2.6	2.7
All prison service	19.2	26.5	37.1	39.7
Probation service[5]				
Probation officers[6]	3.8	5.7	7.5	7.8
Ancillaries	..	1.0	2.0	2.0
Other staff[7]	..	5.9	8.3	8.5
All probation service	..	12.5	17.7	18.4

1 As at 31 December each year.
2 Includes traffic wardens, clerical and technical staff. Scottish data for 1992
  is recorded as full time equivalents. Excludes special constables.
3 Excludes headquarters staff. Part-time staff are counted as half.
4 Excludes trainees.
5 England and Wales only, whole plus part time numbers.
6 For 1981 onwards the figures include a small number of trainees. All
  figures include a small number of temporary officers.
7 Excludes non-probation officer grade hotel staff.

*Source: Home Office; The Scottish Office Home and
Health Department*

12.36 Average number of inmates per prison officer[1]

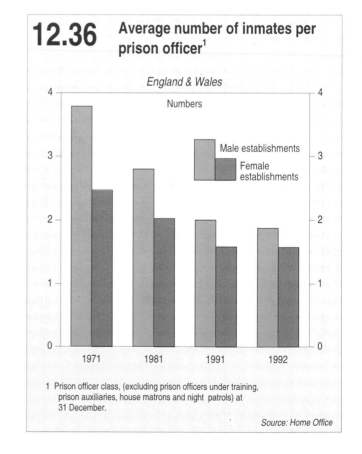

England & Wales

Numbers

Male establishments
Female establishments

1 Prison officer class, (excluding prison officers under training,
  prison auxiliaries, house matrons and night patrols) at
  31 December.

Source: Home Office

Of the 142 thousand police in Great Britain in 1992, only 12 per cent were female, compared with nearly two thirds of the civilian staff. In Northern Ireland about ten per cent of the police force are women. Around one per cent of all police officers in England and Wales come from ethnic minorities.

One result of the increase in the number of prison officers is shown in **Chart 12.36**. Despite a general increase in the prison population over the period the number of inmates per officer has fallen from nearly four male inmates per officer in 1971, to just under two in 1992.

Northern Ireland

Between 1969 and 1992, 3,027 people had been killed as a result of the security situation in Northern Ireland, of which 2,104 were civilians **(Chart 12.37)**. In addition, 35 thousand people had been injured. In 1992 there were 85 deaths, nine of which were members of the security forces, the lowest number since 1970; 1,066 people were injured.

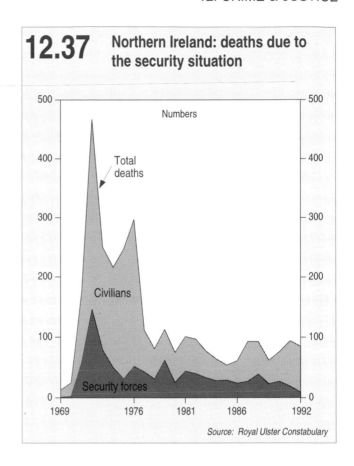

12.37 **Northern Ireland: deaths due to the security situation**

Source: Royal Ulster Constabulary

REFERENCES AND FURTHER READING

The following list contains selected publications relevant to Chapter 12: Crime and Justice. Those published by HMSO are available from the addresses shown on the back cover of *Social Trends*.

Annual Report of the Law Society of Scotland on the Legal Aid Scheme, HMSO

Annual Report of the Scottish Legal Aid Board, SLAB

Civil Judicial Statistics, Scotland, HMSO

Chief Constables's Annual Report, Royal Ulster Constabulary

A Commentary on Northern Ireland Crime Statistics, HMSO

Digest of Information on the Northern Ireland Criminal Justice System 1992, HMSO

Crime in Scotland, findings from the 1988 British Crime Survey, The Scottish Office

Crime and the quality of life: public perceptions and experiences of crime in Scotland, The Scottish Office

Criminal Injuries Compensation Board Report and Accounts, HMSO

Criminal Statistics, England and Wales, HMSO

Criminal Statistics, Scotland, HMSO

Criminal Victimisation in the Industrialised World: Key Findings of the 1989 and 1992 International Crime Survey, The Hague, Ministry of Justice

Crown Prosecution Service, Annual Report, HMSO

Digest 2: Information on the Criminal Justice System in England and Wales, Home Office

General Household Survey 1991, HMSO

Home Office Statistical Bulletins Series, Home Office

Judicial Statistics, England and Wales, HMSO*Legal Aid Annual Reports, (England and Wales)*, HMSO

Legal Aid Reports, (Northern Ireland), HMSO

Northern Ireland Prison Service Annual Report, HMSO

National Prison Survey, HMSO

Police Statistics, England and Wales, CIPFA

Prison Statistics, England and Wales, HMSO

Prisons in Scotland Report, HMSO

Probation Statistics, England and Wales, Home Office

Report of the Parole Board for England and Wales, HMSO

Report of the Parole Board for Scotland, HMSO

The Scottish Office Statistical Bulletins Series, The Scottish Office

Statistics of the Misuse of Drugs: Seizures and Offenders Dealt With, United Kingdom, Home Office

Ulster Year Book, HMSO

Victim Support: Annual Report, Home Office

The Work of the Prison Service, HMSO

Chapter 13: Transport

Transport - general

● People in Great Britain travel, on average, almost 200 kilometres a week. *(Table 13.2)*

● Between 1981 and 1993 rail, bus and coach fares increased by over 130 per cent while motoring costs increased by just over 80 per cent. *(Table 13.7)*

● Only seven per cent of freight in Great Britain went by rail in 1992 compared with almost six times that proportion in 1952. *(Chart 13.10)*

● United Kingdom residents made 24 million visits to other EC countries in 1992 - ten million more than in 1981. *(Table 13.5)*

Road

● Between 1985-86 and 1992-93 the annual distance operated by local buses increased by a fifth while the number of passenger journeys decreased by the same proportion. *(Chart 13.14)*

Rail

● The number of journeys made on British Rail was 27 per cent lower in 1992-93 than in 1961. *(Chart 13.15)*

Air

● Almost 57 million international passengers arrived at, or departed from, London's Heathrow and Gatwick Airports in 1992 compared with just under 18 million in 1971. *(Table 13.19)*

Transport casualties

● In 1992 there were just over four thousand deaths from road accidents in Great Britain - well below the record of over nine thousand in 1941. *(Chart 13.1)*

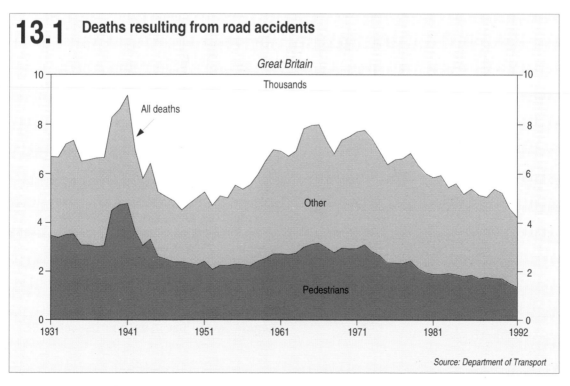

13.1 **Deaths resulting from road accidents**

Great Britain

Thousands

All deaths

Other

Pedestrians

Source: Department of Transport

13.2

Distance travelled[1] per person per week: by purpose[2] and age, 1989-1991

Great Britain   Kilometres

	Aged under 16	Aged 16-29		Aged 30-59		Aged 60 and over	All persons
		Males	Females	Males	Females		
Commuting	0.8	83.1	46.9	101.0	30.9	7.3	39.0
Business	0.6	39.6	8.8	72.6	11.6	5.0	21.6
Education	12.7	9.5	7.3	1.2	1.1	0.1	4.7
Escort - commuting	1.6	2.1	1.6	3.8	2.0	0.8	2.0
Escort - education	1.3	0.3	1.2	2.2	4.4	0.4	1.8
Shopping	11.5	18.6	23.9	23.9	31.3	23.2	22.1
Personal business[3]	20.2	30.3	25.3	36.3	29.6	18.1	26.0
Social/entertainment	43.8	73.4	65.0	59.5	53.8	35.9	51.8
Holiday/other	24.5	24.2	26.7	28.6	29.5	27.9	27.2
All purposes	116.9	281.3	206.8	329.1	194.2	118.8	196.1

1 Excludes all journeys under one mile.
2 See Appendix, Part 13: Journey purpose.
3 Includes other escort journeys.

Source: Department of Transport

Transport - general

The British are travelling around the country more than ever. Results from the National Travel Survey in **Table 13.2** show that over the period 1989 to 1991 each person in Great Britain travelled an average of around 200 kilometres per week (excluding journeys under one mile), the equivalent of around 10,200 kilometres a year - nearly 75 per cent more than in 1965. This increase is almost entirely due to increased ownership, and use, of the car. In 1989-1991, as in 1985-86, commuting and social/entertainment journeys were the most important in terms of distance; together they accounted for 46 per cent of distance travelled in 1989-1991. The average time taken to travel to work was 54 minutes for those working in Central London, half an hour longer than the Great Britain average of 24 minutes. Amongst commuters in general, 64 per cent travelled by car, although for those working in Central London it was only 18 per cent.

Chart 13.3 shows that the total distance travelled by road or rail each year in Great Britain more than doubled from 283 billion passenger kilometres in 1961 to 681 billion passenger kilometres in 1990; since then it has fallen slightly. Since 1961 there has been a significant increase in the amount of travel by private motor vehicles and a corresponding fall in that by public transport. In 1961 around 40 per cent of the total distance travelled was by public transport compared with just 12 per cent in 1992. The greatest fall was in travel by bus and coach which accounted for over a quarter of the distance travelled in 1961 but only six per cent in 1992.

Table 13.4 compares overland passenger traffic for 1981 and 1991 in selected countries. The amount of traffic is obviously heavily dependant upon the population of each country. All the countries shown have experienced an increase in total passenger travel over the decade, although the extent varies considerably from country to country. Portugal experienced the biggest increase in percentage terms, 46 per cent, followed by Great Britain and Japan, each with a 42 per cent increase. In all three of these countries travel by cars, light vans and taxis increased by over half between the two years. The smallest increase in distance travelled was in Spain - just 13 per cent between 1981 and 1991.

13.3

Road and rail passenger transport use

Source: Department of Transport

13.4 Passenger transport[1] - by mode: international comparison, 1981 and 1991

Billion passenger kilometres

	Cars, light vans and taxis		Buses and coaches		Rail excluding metro systems		All modes	
	1981	1991	1981	1991	1981	1991	1981	1991
Great Britain[2]	388.0	586.0	49.4	44.0	34.0	38.0	471.4	668.0
Belgium[3]	62.7	75.0	9.1	10.0	7.1	6.5	78.9	91.5
Denmark	37.4	53.3	7.4	9.3	4.5	4.9	49.3	67.5
Germany[4,5]	..	681.0	93.1	68.0	64.8	57.0	..	806.0
France	466.3	599.0	38.5	43.0	55.7	62.1	560.5	704.1
Greece	..	..	5.8	5.3	1.5	2.0	..	..
Italy[6]	335.8	494.0	85.4	85.0	40.1	45.5	461.3	624.5
Netherlands	110.5	133.9	11.4	13.5	9.2	12.0	131.2	159.5
Portugal	42.5	67.0	8.6	10.5	5.9	5.7	57.0	83.2
Spain	131.8	145.4	28.3	38.6	15.5	15.0	175.6	199.0
Austria[6]	49.9	65.2	13.6	13.8	7.3	8.6	70.8	87.6
Czechoslovakia	..	..	34.7	43.1	13.7	19.3	..	..
Finland	34.6	46.4	8.5	8.1	3.3	3.2	46.4	57.7
Norway[6]	28.0	40.1	4.3	4.1	2.3	2.2	34.5	46.4
Sweden[6]	67.0	93.0	7.9	10.0	7.1	6.1	82.0	109.1
Japan	347.6	570.0	89.5	110.0	316.2	387.5	753.5	1,067.5
USA[7]	3,275.7	4,273.8	43.6	66.4	17.7	22.0	3,337.0	4,362.2

1 National vehicles on national territory except where otherwise stated.
2 Includes foreign cars, light vans and taxis.
3 Excludes taxis.
4 As constituted since 3 October 1990.
5 Excludes firms with fewer than six buses or coaches.
6 Includes foreign vehicles.
7 Intercity buses and coaches only.

Source: Department of Transport

Between 1981 and 1992 the number of visits made to the United Kingdom by other European Community (EC) residents increased by two thirds **(Table 13.5)**.

13.5 Travel[1] between the United Kingdom and the rest of the EC[2]: by mode

Percentages and millions

	1981	1986	1991	1992
Visits to the UK by EC visitors[3]				
Air	41	44	52	53
Sea[4]	59	56	48	47
All (=100%)(millions)	6.0	6.9	9.4	10.0
Visits to the EC by UK residents[3]				
Air	49	59	57	60
Sea[4]	51	41	43	40
All (=100%)(millions)	14.0	19.1	22.7	24.3

1 Anyone entering or leaving more than once in the same period is counted on the occasion of each visit.
2 As currently constituted.
3 See Appendix, Part 13: EC visitor.
4 Includes passengers travelling across the land border between the United Kingdom and the Irish Republic.

Source: Department of National Heritage

An increasing proportion of journeys were made by air; these amounted to just over half of all visits in 1992. An analysis of journeys by purpose (excluding travel from the Irish Republic) shows that in 1992 over two fifths of EC visitors to the United Kingdom came for a holiday, while almost a quarter came on business. Visits to other EC countries by United Kingdom residents also increased by around three quarters between 1981 and 1992, with three fifths of visits being made by air in 1992. Almost three quarters of United Kingdom residents who visited other EC countries went there on a holiday and only 14 per cent were on business - noticeably different to the proportions for inward visitors. When the channel tunnel is opened to passenger trains, now planned for early summer 1994, the proportions travelling by sea and air are likely to be reduced.

Consumers' expenditure per person on transport increased in real terms by 78 per cent between 1971 and 1989 and then fell by 15 per cent between 1989 and 1991, since when it has increased slightly **(Table 13.6)**. There are marked differences between the various categories of expenditure on transport. Between 1971 and 1992 overall expenditure on motor vehicles increased by a half while expenditure on bus and coach fares fell by just over two fifths. Just over a tenth of our

13.6 Expenditure per head[1] on transport

United Kingdom					£ per week at 1990 prices and percentages		
	1971	1976	1981	1986	1989	1991	1992
Net purchase of motor vehicles, spares and accessories	3.56	3.41	4.01	5.40	6.95	4.92	4.79
Maintenance and running of motor vehicles	1.50	1.99	2.05	2.22	2.68	2.74	2.76
Railway fares[2]	0.66	0.60	0.64	0.74	0.73	0.70	0.69
Bus and coach fares[2]	1.36	1.24	0.95	0.87	0.86	0.78	0.76
Other travel and transport[3]	0.86	1.04	1.61	2.08	2.94	2.87	3.08
All transport and vehicles	7.94	8.28	9.26	11.31	14.16	12.01	12.08
Expenditure on transport and vehicles as a percentage of total consumers' expenditure	*11.3*	*10.7*	*11.0*	*11.3*	*12.2*	*10.6*	*10.7*

1 Average weekly expenditure per head of population.
2 Includes purchase of season tickets.
3 Includes purchase and maintenance of other vehicles and boats.

Source: Central Statistical Office

total expenditure is on transport - a proportion which has remained broadly unchanged for the last two decades.

Table 13.7 shows that between 1981 and 1993 bus and coach and rail fares increased by over 130 per cent - well above the rate of inflation. Motoring costs, on the other hand, increased by only 83 per cent. An analysis of local bus service fares shows that between 1982 and 1991-92 there were marked regional differences in fare increases. In Scotland, for example, fares increased by just over half, while in the English Metropolitan areas they more than doubled.

In 1992-93, £5.9 billion was spent on road and rail infrastructure **(Chart 13.8)**. Investment in roads increased by 45 per cent in real terms between 1981-82 and 1992-93 while investment in rail tripled over the same period. Since 1987-88 some private capital has been used in the construction of roads and in 1992-93 this accounted for £134 million out of total road investment of £4.2 billion. Projects funded by private

capital were the Dartford-Thurrock Bridge, the second Severn River Crossing and the Skye Road Bridge. Similarly, since 1986-87 some investment in rail infrastructure has been privately funded, namely that by Eurotunnel Plc. In 1992-93, at £596 million, this accounted for 35 per cent of the total investment in rail infrastructure.

Details of the numbers employed in transport are collected by the Employment Department in the Census of Employment. **Table 13.9** shows that in June 1993 there were almost 900 thousand workers (excluding the self-employed) in transport in the United Kingdom - nine per cent fewer than in 1981. The largest component of this fall was in rail where the number of employees fell by just over 50 thousand, while the biggest percentage decrease occurred in sea transport where

13.7 Passenger transport prices[1]

United Kingdom		Retail prices indices		
	1981	1986	1991	1993
Fares and other travel costs	100	135	186	211
Bus and coach fares	100	139	198	236
Rail fares	100	137	201	231
Other	100	107	136	149
Motoring costs	100	131	163	183
Purchase of vehicles	100	116	144	151
Maintenance of vehicles	100	138	195	231
Petrol & oil	100	145	156	175
Vehicle tax and insurance	100	146	220	288
Retail prices index (all items)	100	137	185	196

1 At January each year.

Source: Central Statistical Office

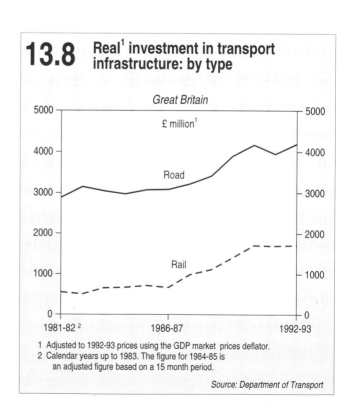

13.8 Real[1] investment in transport infrastructure: by type

Great Britain

£ million[1]

1 Adjusted to 1992-93 prices using the GDP market prices deflator.
2 Calendar years up to 1983. The figure for 1984-85 is an adjusted figure based on a 15 month period.

Source: Department of Transport

13.9 Employment in transport[1]: by type

United Kingdom				Thousands
	1981	1986	1991	1993
Railways[2]	177.4	143.2	133.2	125.5
Other inland transport	418.9	395.3	410.7	400.7
Sea transport	65.9	33.8	32.4	31.2
Air transport	55.5	51.9	70.1	67.7
Other[3]	269.0	253.8	266.0	271.4
All transport	986.6	878.0	912.5	896.5

1 At June each year.
2 Excludes urban railways which are included in 'Other inland transport'.
3 Supporting services to transport and miscellaneous transport and storage.

Source: Employment Department; Department of the Environment, Northern Ireland

the number halved. The number of employees in air transport increased by over a fifth during the same period. While, in Great Britain, the overall number of employees in transport has fallen, the number of women has risen - from 167 thousand in 1981 to 204 thousand in 1992. In addition to those people directly employed by transport operators, almost an equal number are employed in transport related activities such as the distribution and repair of motor vehicles. Employment levels in these related industries fell by almost a quarter between 1981 and 1991.

Between 1952 and 1992 the amount of freight moved (excluding air traffic) within Great Britain increased by three fifths from 1,203 million tonnes to 1,923 million tonnes. Over the same period, the average distance over which goods were moved also increased. Hence, when both weight and distance are taken into account,

freight traffic more than doubled over the forty years. On this basis, over three fifths of freight in Great Britain in 1992 was moved by road compared to just over a third in 1952 **(Chart 13.10)**. Conversely, rail accounted for 42 per cent of freight traffic in 1952 but only seven per cent in 1992. Domestic air freight carried by United Kingdom airlines is fairly insignificant and accounted for only 28 million tonne kilometres in 1992. As with passenger traffic, these proportions may well change with the opening of the channel tunnel to freight traffic which is planned for Spring 1994.

Road

In 1961 only three in ten households had the regular use of a car **(Chart 13.11)**. Following a sharp increase in this proportion during the 1960s, and a steady increase during the 1970s and 1980s, only three in ten households were without the use of a car in 1991. Indeed, in 1991 almost a quarter of households had two or more cars compared with just two per cent in 1961. The rise in car ownership, as would be expected, has been reflected in the number of new registrations each year. This figure rose steadily from 0.7 million in 1961 to 2.5 million in 1989 and then fell back sharply to just under 1.7 million in 1992. The total number of cars and light vans on the road, however, has continued to increase having risen from 6.2 million in 1961 to 22.3 million in 1992.

13.10 Goods moved[1]: by mode

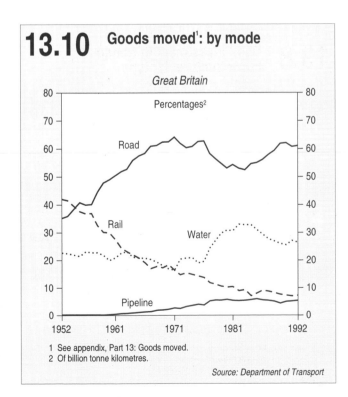

Great Britain

Percentages[2]

1 See appendix, Part 13: Goods moved.
2 Of billion tonne kilometres.

Source: Department of Transport

13.11 Households with regular use of a car[1]

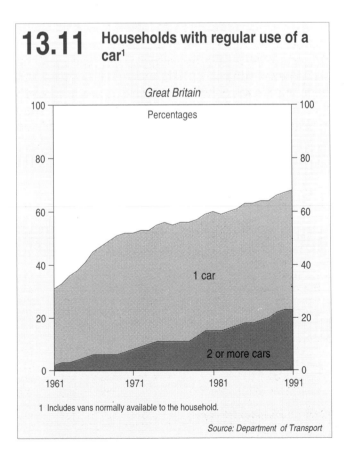

Great Britain

Percentages

1 Includes vans normally available to the household.

Source: Department of Transport

13.12 Cars[1] and car ownership: by region, 1981 and 1991

United Kingdom   Percentages and cars per 1,000 population

| | Percentage of households without the regular use of a car | | Percentage of households with regular use of | | | | Cars per 1,000 pop. | |
| | | | One car only | | Two or more cars | | | |
	1981	1991	1981	1991	1981	1991	1981	1991
United Kingdom	40	32	45	45	15	23	277	361
North	48	41	41	45	10	14	227	299
Yorkshire & Humberside	46	38	43	44	12	17	245	324
East Midlands	37	28	47	47	15	25	273	351
East Anglia	31	25	51	49	18	26	321	420
South East	36	28	46	44	19	28	316	391
Greater London	45	38	42	42	14	20	287	347
Rest of South East	30	22	48	45	22	33	337	417
South West	31	24	51	47	18	29	329	412
West Midlands	38	31	46	44	16	24	290	391
North West	45	37	42	44	13	20	250	336
England	39	31	45	45	16	24	288	371
Wales	38	33	47	46	15	22	271	344
Scotland	49	42	40	42	11	16	217	300
Northern Ireland	40	34	46	46	14	20	238	298

1 Includes cars and vans normally available to the household.

Source: Department of Transport

There are marked regional differences in the level of car ownership **(Table 13.12)**. Over two fifths of households in Scotland and the North were without the use of a car in 1991 compared with just over a fifth in the South East outside Greater London. A third of households in the latter region owned two or more cars in 1991 - a 50 per cent increase since 1981. The highest levels of car ownership per head of population are found in East Anglia, the South West and the South East outside Greater London, all of which had over four cars for every ten people in 1991.

The increase in both private motoring and the carriage of freight by road has led to an increase in the volume of traffic on the roads. **Table 13.13** shows how the average daily flow of traffic increased on different classes of road. Motorways experienced the greatest increase - 76 per cent between 1981 and 1991, before falling slightly in 1992. In comparison, the length of motorways in Great Britain increased by 19 per cent between 1981 and 1992 to 3.1 thousand kilometres.

13.13 Average daily flow of motor vehicles[1]: by class of road

Great Britain   Thousands

	1981	1986	1991	1992
Motorways[2]	30.6	38.3	53.9	52.9
Built up roads				
Trunk	13.6	16.5	18.5	18.3
Principal	12.3	12.8	15.2	14.9
Non built-up roads				
Trunk	9.0	11.5	15.0	15.0
Principal	4.5	5.5	6.8	7.0

1 Flow at an average point on each class of road.
2 Includes principal road motorways.

Source: Department of Transport

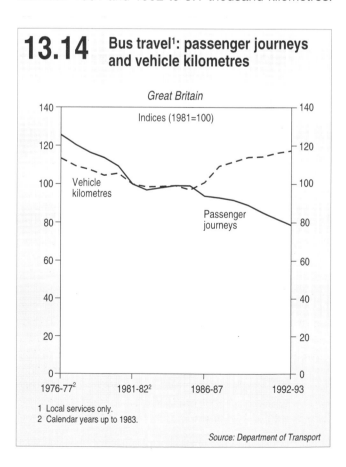

13.14 Bus travel[1]: passenger journeys and vehicle kilometres

Great Britain

Indices (1981=100)

1 Local services only.
2 Calendar years up to 1983.

Source: Department of Transport

The total length of all roads increased by just six per cent to 362.3 thousand kilometres. In 1992-93, 647 lane kilometres of motorway and trunk roads were completed in England at an average cost of £790 thousand per lane kilometre.

Chart 13.14 shows that while the number of passenger journeys on local buses continues to fall, since 1985-86 the mileage operated by local buses has actually risen. In 1950, 16.4 billion passenger journeys were made by local bus or tram but by 1992-93 this had fallen to just 4.5 billion. Between 1950 and 1985-86 the distance operated by local buses fell from 3.4 billion to 2.1 billion kilometres, but between 1985-86 and 1992-93 it increased by over a fifth. This increase is linked to the move to smaller vehicles and to the deregulation of buses outside London in October 1986 which encouraged greater competition in the provision of local bus services. The overall increase in provision, however, has failed to halt the decline in the number of journeys made by bus. The declining numbers of passengers encouraged the move to smaller vehicles; between 1985-86 and 1992-93 the number of vehicles with between 17 and 35 seats increased more than fourfold to over 13 thousand. At the same time there was a fall in the number of traditional single and double deck vehicles.

Local bus travel is particularly important in built-up areas. The National Travel Survey found that in 1989-1991 those living in English Metropolitan areas made about 120 bus trips per year, compared with only about 50 trips per year by those living in the English shire counties and in Wales.

Rail

The number of journeys made by British Rail passengers fell unevenly from 1,025 million in 1961 to a trough of 630 million in 1982; in 1992-93, 745 million journeys were made **(Chart 13.15)**. The figure for 1982 was affected by a series of two-day strikes early in the year. Passenger journeys on the London Underground also fell from 675 million in 1961 to a low point of 498 million in 1982; in 1992-93, 728 million journeys were made - much the same number as were made by passengers on British Rail. The London Underground figure for 1982 would have been affected by the 91 per cent fares increase in March of that year which followed the decision in the House of Lords that the GLC could not use rate income to support fares and also by some industrial action. The subsequent introduction of the Travelcard (a zone-based ticket valid on London's buses and the underground) together with a 27 per cent fare reduction in 1983, the introduction of the Capitalcard (which added travel on British Rail to the Travelcard

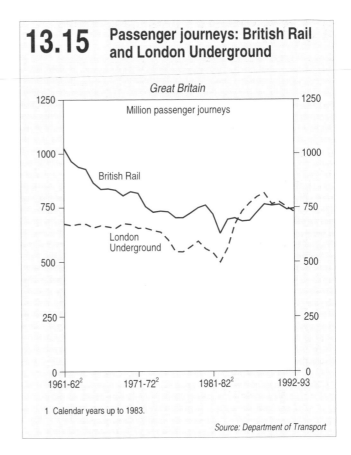

13.15 **Passenger journeys: British Rail and London Underground**

Great Britain

Million passenger journeys

1 Calendar years up to 1983.

Source: Department of Transport

scheme) in 1985 and a fall in the level of unemployment all helped to boost travel on the underground during the second half of the 1980's. In 1985-86, for the first time, the number of journeys on the underground exceeded the number on British Rail.

For public transport to be an attractive option the customer must be able to expect a certain standard of service. This standard is now formally documented by both British Rail and London Transport in a Passenger's Charter. The British Rail charter specifies targets and standards in respect of punctuality and reliability, waiting times at ticket offices, the provision of timetable information, and facilities for the disabled, and keeping the customer informed as to how these targets and standards are being met. It also specifies circumstances under which refunds will be offered when the quality of service has fallen below specified levels.

The London Underground charter includes targets for performance, the provision of service information on trains and stations, lifts and escalators in service and cleanliness. **Table 13.16** shows performance indicators for the railways. In 1992-93 all sectors of British Rail met their punctuality targets except InterCity. In terms of reliability, neither InterCity nor Regional Railways met their targets. The performance of London Underground is measured against a number of criteria including 'trains in peak time customer service'. On this basis for the four week period ending 9 October 1993,

13.16 Railway performance indicators[1]

Great Britain

Percentages

	Trains arriving within punctuality target				Trains cancelled[2]			
	1986-87	1990-91	1991-92	1992-93	1986-87	1990-91	1991-92	1992-93
British Rail								
InterCity	85	84	84	85	0.8	2.8	2.3	1.7
Network SouthEast	91	90	91	91	1.6	2.0	1.2	1.5
Regional								
Express and long rural	91	90	92	91	0.7	1.6	1.8	1.1
Urban and short rural	89	89	89	91	1.5	2.8	1.6	1.6
London Underground	88	85	88	88	2.9	5.0	3.2	3.3
Docklands Light Railway	..	..	..	..	..	6.0	15.7	2.3

1 See Appendix, Part 13: Railway performance indicators.
2 Percentage of services run for British Rail and scheduled kilometres operated for London Underground.

Source: Department of Transport

the level of service was just 0.1 per cent below the target of 98 per cent - the first time since May that the target figure had not been met. The Docklands Light Railway does not yet have performance targets.

Water

The arrival and departure of passenger carrying cars at British ports from overseas destinations increased by almost three quarters between 1981 and 1992 **(Table 13.17)**. In 1992, around two and a half times the number of vehicles went to, or from, France by ship compared with 1981. Car movements by hovercraft between Great Britain and France have halved in the last six years and in October 1991 the service was withdrawn for a short period. In addition to the carriage of cars to, and from, other countries, 1,256 thousand cars crossed between the mainland and such destinations as Northern Ireland, the Isle of Man, the Channel Islands and the Scottish islands. Coaches as

13.17 Passenger car arrivals at and departures from British ports: by overseas country

Thousands

	1981	1986	1991	1992
By ship				
France	1,402	1,944	3,329	3,594
Belgium	591	478	514	463
Netherlands	259	325	399	413
Germany	22	21	34	35
Irish Republic	378	345	611	577
Denmark	112	45	44	39
Scandinavia and Baltic		67	56	52
Spain and Portugal	20	27	47	40
All overseas routes	2,784	3,252	5,034	5,213
By hovercraft				
France	287	218	189	109
All overseas routes	3,071	3,470	5,223	5,322

Source: Department of Transport

well as cars are, of course, transported by sea. In 1992 there were 208 thousand coach arrivals and departures to, or from, overseas destinations - more than double the number in 1980.

Air

In 1992 there were 0.9 million international aircraft arrivals and departures at United Kingdom airports - double the number in 1976 **(Chart 13.18)**. The number of scheduled international flights increased every year throughout the last decade except for 1991 when air transport activity was reduced due to the effects of the conflict in the Gulf. In 1992 scheduled flights accounted

13.18 Landings or take-offs at United Kingdom airports[1]: by type of service

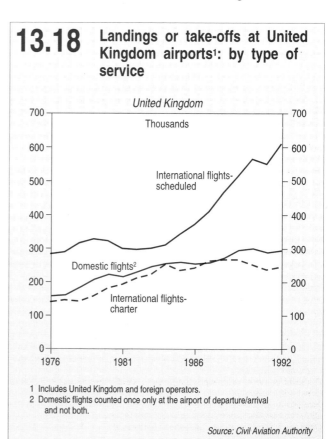

1 Includes United Kingdom and foreign operators.
2 Domestic flights counted once only at the airport of departure/arrival and not both.

Source: Civil Aviation Authority

for nearly three quarters of all arrivals and departures. The number of international charter flights rose slightly between 1991 and 1992 to reach 246 thousand flights

which was still lower than the peak of 268 thousand in 1988 and 1989. There were almost twice as many domestic flights in 1992 as there were in 1976.

13.19 International air passengers[1] : by selected airport

United Kingdom				Thousands
	1971	1981	1991	1992
Heathrow	13,437	22,543	33,531	38,257
Gatwick	4,143	9,714	17,679	18,690
Manchester	1,419	3,729	8,196	9,748
Birmingham	553	1,091	2,526	2,912
Glasgow	415	839	1,865	2,343
Stansted	475	253	1,432	2,056
Luton	2,668	1,938	1,748	1,758
Newcastle	155	564	983	1,358
East Midlands	172	518	802	956
Bristol	150	202	641	869
Aberdeen	-	515	703	812
Cardiff	141	232	457	589
Belfast	68	170	384	513
Other	1,332	1,423	1,839	2,089
All airports	25,128	43,731	72,786	82,950

1 Includes British government/armed forces on official business and travel to/from oil rigs.

Source: Civil Aviation Authority

Almost seven in ten international air passenger movements in the United Kingdom in 1992 arrived at, or departed from, London's Heathrow or Gatwick airports **(Table 13.19)**. A further 12 per cent used Manchester Ringway airport. However, it is Newcastle which saw the greatest increase, almost ninefold, in the number of international passengers between 1971 and 1992. Of the airports shown in the table, only Luton recorded a decrease in international passengers over the same period. Three fifths of all international passengers to, or from, United Kingdom airports in 1992 flew with United Kingdom operators.

Transport casualties

Table 13.20 shows casualty rates by type of travel. When taking the distance travelled into account, air transport is the safest form of transport while travel by motorcycle carries the highest risk. With the exception of pedal cyclists, the casualty rates shown in the table were lower in 1991 than in 1981. However, the intermittent occurrence of major disasters continues to cause year to year fluctuations. The higher rate for rail

13.20 Passenger casualty rates: by mode of transport

United Kingdom								Rate per billion passenger kilometres
								Average
	1981	1983	1986	1988	1989	1990	1991	1981-1991
Air[1]								
Deaths	0.2	0.3	0.5	0.0	0.4	0.0	0.0	0.2
Total casualties	0.4	0.6	0.7	0.0	1.0	0.1	0.0	0.4
Water[2]								
Deaths	0.4	0.9	0.5	0.5	23.2	0.4	0.0	8.9
Total casualties	..	..	..	..	..	..	..	..
Rail[3]								
Deaths	1.0	0.8	0.8	1.7	0.8	0.9	1.4	1.0
Total casualties	70	72	72	83	76	72	68	74
Bus or coach[3]								
Deaths	0.3	0.7	0.5	0.3	0.4	0.4	0.6	0.5
Total casualties	189	204	192	194	205	204	183	196
Car or van[3,4]								
Deaths	5.9	5.0	4.9	4.1	4.3	4.1	3.6	4.7
Total casualties	379	322	347	325	324	328	309	335
Two-wheeled motor vehicles[3,4]								
Deaths	116	107	100	102	105	108	93	105
Total casualties	7,075	7,172	6,881	6,495	6,562	6,402	5,204	6,775
Pedal cyclists[3,5]								
Deaths	57	51	50	43	56	49	47	50
Total casualties	4,644	4,792	4,786	4,944	5,473	5,033	4,797	4,781
Foot[3,6]								
Deaths	76	78	75	71	68	68	60	72
Total casualties	2,475	2,514	2,464	2,369	2,411	2,410	2,151	2,426

1 World passenger carrying services of United Kingdom airlines for fixed and rotary wing craft over 2,300 kilograms. Passenger kilometres relate to revenue passengers only.
2 Domestic and international passenger services of United Kingdom registered vessels.
3 Great Britain only.
4 Includes drivers.
5 Distance travelled is used as 'passenger kilometres'.
6 Distance walked is used as 'passenger kilometres'.

Source: Department of Transport

13.21 Fatal and serious road accidents, 1981 and 1992

United Kingdom   Numbers and rates

	1981			1992			
	Total	Per 100,000 population	Per 100,000 vehicles	Total	Per 100,000 population	Per 100,000 vehicles	Per 10,000,000 vehicle kilometres[1]
United Kingdom[2]	70,539	125	357	46,791	81	184	0.89
North	3,002	96	341	2,134	69	189	0.75
Yorkshire & Humberside	6,032	123	385	4,231	85	204	1.00
East Midlands	5,822	151	426	3,388	84	192	0.89
East Anglia	2,931	185	359	2,247	108	204	0.90
South East	21,474	126	325	14,797	84	181	0.96
Greater London	6,916	102	287	6,575	95	239	2.23
Rest of South East	14,558	143	348	8,222	77	152	0.61
South West	7,176	164	386	3,425	73	141	0.66
West Midlands	6,832	132	366	4,137	79	166	0.83
North West	5,765	89	286	4,250	66	165	0.79
England	59,034	126	348	38,609	80	178	0.87
Wales	3,426	122	367	2,033	70	165	0.84
Scotland	7,875	152	564	4,696	95	247	1.08
Northern Ireland[2]	204	13	47	1,453	91	251	..

1 Major roads only.
2 Northern Ireland data exclude serious accidents in 1981 and are excluded altogether from accidents 'per 10,000,000 vehicle kilometres' in 1992.

Source: Department of Transport; Welsh Office; The Scottish Office Environment Department; Department of the Environment, Northern Ireland

deaths in 1988, for example, was due to the 35 deaths in the multiple rail crash near Clapham Junction in December of that year. The sinking of the pleasure boat *Marchioness* with the loss of 51 lives in August 1989 similarly inflated the rate for water fatalities in that year. Although the casualty rate for air travel is substantially lower than for other types of travel, a much higher proportion of casualties result in death.

Chart 13.1, at the beginning of this chapter, shows that deaths resulting from road accidents peaked in 1941 at 9.2 thousand, fell to 4.5 thousand in 1948 and then rose gradually to just under eight thousand in 1966. The peak in 1941 is attributed to the blackout restrictions imposed during the war years and an influx of inexperienced drivers of armed services vehicles. By 1992, despite the rapid increase in car ownership in the 1960s and 1970s, the number of road deaths had fallen to 4.2 thousand. Throughout the 1930s and 1940s pedestrians accounted for around half of all road accident deaths but by the early 1980s this proportion had fallen to about a third. Deaths of car drivers and their passengers as a proportion of all road deaths has been increasing and in 1992 accounted for almost half of road deaths. Over one in ten deaths in 1992 were motorcyclists or their passengers.

The risk of a fatal or serious road accident varies considerably between regions **(Table 13.21)**. For example, in 1992 the risk (based on head of population) of a fatal or serious road accident was over one and a half times greater in East Anglia than in the North West. Based on the number of vehicles, the chance of a

serious or fatal accident was 75 per cent more likely to occur in Scotland than in the South West. Between 1981 and 1992 the number of such accidents fell in every region. The South West had the largest proportional fall, with the number of such accidents more than halving between the two years.

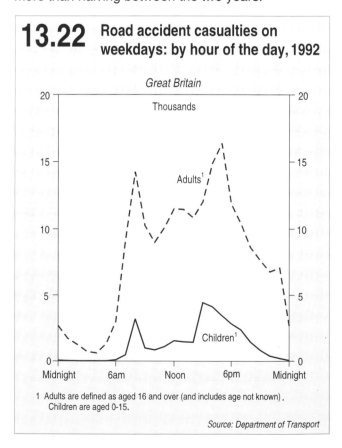

13.22 Road accident casualties on weekdays: by hour of the day, 1992

Great Britain

1 Adults are defined as aged 16 and over (and includes age not known). Children are aged 0-15.

Source: Department of Transport

As would be expected, the number of road casualties peaks during the weekday morning and evening rush hour periods **(Chart 13.22)**. The morning peak for both adult and child casualties occurs between 8am and 9am. However, in the afternoon, due to the earlier school finishing times, the peak for child casualties occurs slightly earlier than that for adults. At weekends the peak times for both child and adult casualties is between midday and 6pm. Among adult casualties there is also a second lesser peak between 11pm and 1am.

The timing of road accidents is, of course, affected by factors other than simply the number of people on the roads. The consumption of alcohol, for example, obviously increases the risk of being involved in an accident. The numbers failing breath tests begin to rise after 1pm and peaks in the evening between 11pm and midnight. Accidents caused by a lack of sleep are also time related. A pilot study by the *Sleep Research Laboratory* amongst people driving on Midlands' motorways in August 1991 found that sleep related accidents were clustered in three periods of the day: midnight to 2am, 4am to 6am (the most likely time) and 2pm to 4pm.

Table 13.23 shows three ways of measuring road deaths for comparative purposes - per head of population, per motor vehicle and in relation to distance travelled. Whichever method is used, in 1991 the United Kingdom had one of the lower rates of all the countries shown.

13.23 Road vehicles, road deaths[1] and car user deaths: international comparison, 1991

		Rate of road deaths		Rates Rate of car user deaths per billion car kilo-metres[2]
	Motor vehicles per 1,000 population	Per 100,000 population	Per 100,000 motor vehicles	
United Kingdom	390	8	21	8
Belgium	418	19	43	36
Denmark	341	12	35	11
France	473	18	39	18
Germany (Fed. Rep.)[3]	586	13	22	11
Greece	201	20	74	..
Irish Republic	245	13	52	22
Italy[4]	616	12	21	..
Luxembourg[4,5]	519	18	31	..
Netherlands	414	8	21	16
Portugal[4,5]	313	32	86	..
Spain	686	23	65	61
Austria	463	20	43	24
Finland	417	13	30	14
Germany (Dem. Rep.)[3,5]	420	19	45	33
Hungary	213	20	96	..
Norway	433	8	18	8
Sweden	427	9	20	8
Switzerland	562	12	21	23
Japan[6]	441	12	19	16
USA	597	16	27	10

1 See Appendix, Part 13: Road deaths.
2 United Kingdom figure relates only to Great Britain.
3 1990 data.
4 1989 data for rate of road deaths.
5 The number of road vehicles and deaths per 100,000 motor vehicles exclude mopeds.
6 1990 data for rates of road deaths and car user deaths.

Source: Department of Transport

REFERENCES AND FURTHER READING

The following list contains selected publications relevant to Chapter 13: Transport. Those published by HMSO are available from the addresses shown on the back cover of *Social Trends*.

Annual Vehicle Census Great Britain, Department of Transport

Bus and Coach Statistics Great Britain, HMSO

Car and Driver: Injury Accident and Casualty Rates Great Britain, HMSO

International Comparisons of Transport Statistics, Parts I, II and III, HMSO

International Passenger Survey, Employment Department

International Passenger Transport, HMSO

London Traffic Monitoring Report, HMSO

Merchant Fleet Statistics, HMSO

Motor Vehicle Registrations, Department of Transport

National Road Maintenance Condition Survey Report, HMSO

National Travel Survey, HMSO

Overseas Travel and Tourism, HMSO

Ports Statistics, Department of Transport

Quarterly Transport Statistics, Department of Transport

Regional Trends, HMSO

Road Accidents Great Britain - The Casualty Report, HMSO

Road Accidents, Scotland, Scottish Office

Road Accidents Statistics English Regions, HMSO

Road Accidents: Wales, Welsh Office

Road Casualties Great Britain, Department of Transport

Road Lengths in Great Britain, HMSO

Scottish Transport Statistics, Scottish Office

Statistics of Road Traffic Accidents in Europe, United Nations

Traffic in Great Britain, Department of Transport

Transport of Goods by Road in Great Britain, HMSO

Transport Statistics for London, HMSO

Transport Statistics Great Britain, HMSO

UK Airports - Annual Statement of Movements, Passengers and Cargo, Civil Aviation Authority

Welsh Transport Statistics, Welsh Office

ajor surveys used in *Social Trends*

	Frequency	Sampling frame	Type of respondent	Location	Set sample size (most recent survey included in *Social Trends*)	Response rate (percentages)
ricultural Census	Annual	Agricultural lists	Occupiers of agricultural holdings	UK	242,000 individuals	87
nsus of Population	Decennial	Detailed local	Household head	UK	Full count	100
tish Social Attitudes Survey	Annual	Electoral Register	Adult in household	GB	4,402 addresses	64
tish National Travel Survey - Yearly[1]	Annual	Electoral Register	Individual adult	GB	4,440 individuals[2]	55
tish Crime Survey	Intermittent	Electoral Register	Adult in household	EW	11,400 addresses	77
arity Household Survey	Annual	Quota sample	Individual in household	GB	1,000 individuals	[3]
ntinuous Household Survey	Continuous	Rating valuation list	All adults in household	NI	4,500 addresses	71
y Visits Survey[4]	Intermittent	Postcode Address	All adults in household	GB	12,000	74
mily Expenditure Survey	Continuous	Postcode Address File	Household	UK	11,693 addresses	72[6]
neral Household Survey	Continuous	Postcode Address File	All adults in household	GB	11,858	83
ernational Passenger Survey	Continuous	International passengers at ports and airports	Individual traveller	UK	191,000 individuals	86
bour Force Survey	Continuous File	Postcode Address	All adults in household[7]	GB	60,000 addresses	83[8]
tional Food Survey	Continuous File	Postcode Address	Housewife	GB	12,238 addresses	59
tional Readership Survey	Continuous	Electoral Register	Individual in home	GB	28,319 individuals	65
tional Travel Survey	Continuous File	Postcode Address	Individual in household	GB	5,000 households per year	80
w Earnings Survey	Annual records	Inland Revenue PAYE	Employee[9]	GB	[9]	[9]
rvey of Personal Incomes	Annual	Inland Revenue	Individuals[10]	UK	80,000 individuals	98
are Survey	Annual	Stock Exchange and companies	Share holders	UK	80,000 shareholders[11] 220 companies	
ort term surveys	Monthly	Employment Department Register	Employers	GB	30,000	83
noking among secondary school children	Biannual	DFE and SOED[12] records	School pupils (aged 11 - 15)	GB	9,728 pupils	87
uth Cohort Study	Irregular	DFE schools records	Young people aged 16 - 19	EW	23,000 individuals	84

1 Previously known as the British Tourism Survey, yearly.
2 Basic sample only; in 1989 a further 4,302 individuals were contacted in connection with holidays abroad.
3 Not applicable; quota sample.
4 Trailer to the General Household Survey.
5 Effective sample only. Set sample includes ineligible households.
6 Response vote refers to GB.
7 Includes some proxy information.
8 Response rate to first wave interviews quoted. Response rate to second to fifth wave interviews 96% of those previously accepting.

9 In the New Earnings Survey employers supply data on a 1 per cent sample of employees who are members of PAYE schemes. 226 thousand were selected for the 1991 sample and there was a 95.5 per cent response but some 44 thousand returned questionnaires did not contain data.
10 In the Survey of Personal Incomes local tax offices supply data on individuals to a central point in Inland Revenue.
11 Taken from Share Registers.
12 Department for Education and The Scottish Office Education Department.

e **Census of Population** is described in the article 'The 1991 Census of eat Britain: plans for content and output' in *Social Trends 21* (page 13).

e first **British Social Attitudes Survey** was conducted in 1983 by Social d Community Planning Research. Technical details of the survey, which conducted annually, were contained in the Appendix to the article 'Recent ends in Social Attitudes' in *Social Trends 19* (page 22).

description of the **British Crime Survey** was contained in the Appendix Social Trends 21 (page 213)

description of the **General Household Survey** was contained in the pendix to *Social Trends 12* (page 253). In 1984 the sampling frame of e General Household Survey was changed from the Electoral Register to e Postcode Address file. The **Continuous Household Survey** in rthern Ireland is a similar survey to the General Household Survey in eat Britain.

description of the **Labour Force Survey** was contained in the Appendix Social Trends 16 (page 204).

A description of the **National Food Survey** was contained in the Appendix to *Social Trends 12* (page 255). In 1984 the sampling frame of the National Food Survey changed from the Electoral Register to the Postcode Address File, selecting the sample by means of a stratified random sampling scheme from 52 local authority districts.

A description of the 1985-86 **National Travel Survey (NTS)** was contained in the Appendix to *Social Trends 18* (page 197).

Descriptions of these surveys were contained in the Appendix to *Social Trends 12* (pages 253, 255 and 256).
British National Travel Survey
Family Expenditure Survey
International Passenger Survey
New Earnings Survey
National Readership Survey

APPENDIX: Definitions and Terms

PART 1: POPULATION

Population and population projections

The estimated and projected populations of an area include all those usually resident in the area, whatever their nationality. Members of HM forces stationed outside the United Kingdom are excluded. Students are taken to be resident at their term-time addresses. Figures for the United Kingdom do not include the population of the Channel Islands or the Isle of Man.

The population estimates at mid-1991 for England and Wales and Scotland are final figures based on the 1991 Census of Population. Mid-1991 estimates for Northern Ireland are provisional, based on early 1991 Census results. Mid-1991 estimates are not fully comparable with those for earlier years, which were based on 1981 Census results with allowance for subsequent births, deaths and migration. The estimates for 1982 to 1990 will be revised in due course to remove the discontinuity.

Population projections for the United Kingdom are based on the provisional estimates of the populations of England and Wales, Scotland and Northern Ireland at mid-1991, again based on early 1991 Census results.

Further details of the 1991 - based projections were published in *National Population projections: 1991-based* (*series PP2 no. 18*, HMSO). Subnational projections are also made.

Due to definitional changes, there are minor discontinuities for Scotland and Northern Ireland between the figures for 1971 and earlier years. At the United Kingdom level these discontinuities are negligible.

International Passenger Survey migration estimates

The International Passenger Survey (IPS) data do not provide information on all migrants to the UK. Respondents to the survey state the length of time for which they intend to stay in the UK or abroad (the qualifying period is twelve or more months). Migrants to and from the Irish Republic are excluded as are diplomatic and military personnel. It is also highly likely that the IPS migration figures exclude persons seeking asylum after entering the country and short term visitors granted extensions of stay. Adjustments need to be made to the data to give a better estimate of actual net migration. These range from about ten thousand in 1981 to 50 thousand in 1992, ie an average of approximately 20 thousand a year.

Asylum

The basis for recognition as a refugee and hence the granting of asylum is the 1951 United Nations Convention relating to the Status of Refugees, extended in its application by the 1967 Protocol relating to the Status of Refugees. The United Kingdom is party to both. The Convention defines a refugee as a person who 'owing to a well-founded fear of being persecuted for reasons of race, religion, nationality, membership of a particular social group or political opinion, is outside the country of his nationality and unable or, owing to such fear, is unwilling to avail himself of the protection of that country'. In addition, the United Kingdom is prepared to grant, to applicants who do not meet the requirements of the Convention, exceptional leave to stay here for an appropriate period, if it would be unreasonable or impracticable, in all the circumstances, to seek to enforce their return to their country of origin.

PART 2: HOUSEHOLDS AND FAMILIES

Households

A household: a person living alone or a group of people who have the address as their only or main residence and who either share one meal a day or share the living accommodation.

Size of household: is commonly referred to as household size and counts those people who are usually resident in the household irrespective of whether or not they are present on census night. In the General Household Survey the size of the household is the number of people who normally live there.

Families

A family: is a married couple, either with or without their never-married child or children (of any age), or a lone parent together with his or her never-married child or children. A lone parent (in the Census) is a married parent whose spouse does not reside in the same household, or any single, widowed, or divorced parent.

A lone parent family (in the General Household Survey): consists of a lone parent, living with his or her never-married dependent children, provided these children have no children of their own. Married lone mothers whose husbands are not defined as resident in the household are not classified as lone parents because evidence suggests the majority are separated from their husband either because he usually works away from home or for some other reason that does not imply the breakdown of the marriage (see OPCS's *GHS Monitor 82/1*). Couples describing themselves as married (or common-law married) but who are in fact co-habiting are coded and counted as married.

Children: are never-married people of any age who live with one or both parent(s). They also include step-children and adopted children (but not foster children) and also grandchildren (where the parents are absent).

Dependent children: in the 1961 Census, dependent children were defined as children under 15 years of age, and persons of any age in full-time education.

In the 1971 Census, dependent children were defined as never-married children in families who were either under 15 years of age, or aged 15-24 and in full-time education. However, for direct comparison with GHS data, the definition of dependent children used for 1971 in Table 2.6 has been changed to include only never-married in families who were either under 15 years of age, or aged 15-18 and in full-time education.

In the 1991 Census and the GHS, dependent children are never-married children in families who are aged under 16, or aged 16-18 and in full-time education.

PART 3: EDUCATION

Main categories of educational establishments

Educational establishments in the United Kingdom may be administered and financed in a number of ways:

Public sector: by local education authorities, which form part of the structure of local government;

Assisted: by governing bodies which have a substantial degree of autonomy from public authorities but which receive grants direct from central government sources;

Grant Maintained: since 1988 all local education authority maintained secondary, middle and primary schools can apply for self governing (Grant Maintained) status and receive direct grants from the Department for Education. The governing body of such a school is responsible for all aspects of school management, including the deployment of funds, employment of staff and provision of most of the educational support services, staff and pupils. In January 1993 there were 75 primary and 266 secondary self governing schools in England and Wales;

Non-maintained: by the private sector, including individuals, companies, and charitable institutions;

Further Education Funding Councils (FEFCs): From 1993 all colleges in the FEFC sector and further education courses in other establishments have been funded by an FEFC.

Higher Education: since April, publicly-funded HE courses in the United Kingdom have been funded by the HE Funding Councils, the FE Funding Councils of England and Wales, The Scottish Office Education Department and the Department of Education, Northern Ireland;

Local Management of Schools (LMS): Under LMS, which was introduced in Northern Ireland in 1991, all public sector and assisted secondary schools have delegated responsibility for managing their school budgets and staff numbers, and this delegation is being extended to primary schools in these sectors.

Stages of education

There are three stages of education: primary (including nursery), secondary, and further (including higher) education. The first two stages are compulsory for all children between the ages of five and sixteen years (fifteen before 1972/73). Both nursery and primary schools may include 'rising fives', that is, pupils aged four at 31 August who will be five by 31 December. The transition from primary to secondary education is usually made between ten and a half and twelve years but is sometimes made via middle schools (see below) after age twelve. The third stage of education is voluntary and includes all education provided after full-time schooling ends.

Primary education

Primary education includes three age ranges: nursery, under five years of age; infant, five to seven or eight years; and junior, seven or eight to eleven or twelve years. The majority of public sector primary schools take both boys and girls in mixed classes. In Scotland the distinction between infant and primary schools is generally not made. The pattern for nursery and primary education in Northern Ireland is nursery education (age three to four) and primary schools (age four to eleven). Nursery education is provided in either nursery schools or nursery classes in primary schools. It is compulsory for children who attain the age of four on or before 1 July to commence primary school the following September.

The usual age for transfer to secondary is eleven as in England and Wales. In Scotland it is twelve.

Middle Schools

In England and Wales middle schools take children from first schools and generally lead on, in turn, to comprehensive upper schools. They cover varying age ranges between eight and fourteen. Depending on their individual age range they are deemed either primary or secondary.

Secondary education

Provision of maintained secondary schools in an area may include any combination of types of school. The pattern is a reflection of historical circumstance and of the policy adopted by the local education authority. Comprehensive schools normally admit pupils without reference to ability and aptitude, and cater for all the children in a neighbourhood; but in some areas they co-exist with modern, grammar, and technical schools.

In Northern Ireland secondary education normally begins when pupils reach the age of eleven. Under current transfer arrangements from primary to secondary education parents have the choice as to whether or not their children take the Transfer Procedure tests which are compiled and marked by the Department of Education. The *Education Reform Order 1989* introduced new open enrolment arrangements whereby all secondary schools are required to admit pupils who have indicated a preference for the school, provided there is room at the school. Where schools receive more applications for admission than places available then pupils must be admitted on the basis of published criteria prepared by the schools.

Special schools

Special schools, either day or boarding, provide education exclusively for children who are so seriously handicapped, physically or mentally, that they cannot profit fully from education in normal schools.

Further Education

The term 'further education' may be used in a general sense to cover all non-advanced education after the period of compulsory education. More commonly it excludes those staying on at secondary school, and those studying higher education at universities, polytechnics and some other colleges. The figures in Chart 3.8 cover all further education courses taken in publicly funded educational establishments; those in chart 3.9 include courses in schools and further education colleges.

Higher education

The term 'higher education' as used in Table 3.10 covers all courses in universities, further and higher education colleges leading to qualifications above General Certificate of Education A level, Scottish Certificate of Education H grade and BTEC National Diploma/Certificate or their equivalents. The figures in Table 3.14 cover all first degree students whose destination is known and who attended publicly funded United Kingdom HE institutions.

Educational attainment

Tests for seven and fourteen year olds (England and Wales)

In 1992 the second report on pupils achievements under the National Curriculum was produced. It related to tests given to seven year olds in respect of English, mathematics, science and technology and in Wales, Welsh and Welsh as a second language. All seven year olds in public sector schools were included with the exception of a small number with special educational needs. The tests were not mandatory for those in non-maintained schools but over two thousand seven year olds sat them.

In 1992 all schools with 14 year olds were invited to participate in the pilot tests for assessing 14 year olds. The invitation was taken up by 80 per cent of maintained secondary schools, 51 per cent of independent schools and 45 per cent of special schools. Overall, 72 per cent of all schools with 14 year olds participated. The tests covered mathematics and science.

In Wales, Welsh as a subject was also assessed although not on a statutory basis. The results were published by the Welsh Office.

The assessment of both seven and fourteen year olds were made against a common scale of Attainment Targets. These targets are based on what is considered a realistic and challenging level of achievement for pupils of ten specified ages. Hence, a typical five year old is expected to have reached the target set at level one, a seven year old the target for level two and so on up to level ten. The tests for 14 year olds were set so that a typical child of that age would have mastered the target for a 13 year old (level five) and be on the way to achieving that for a 15 year old (level six).

Some seven year olds and some fourteen year olds were recorded as not having attained a graded result. In the case of 14 year olds, the examination papers were banded so that the more able pupils would not be faced with too many questions below their capabilities and those who were less able with too many questions they could not answer. A pupil given a paper covering bands three to six who did not reach level three would not, therefore, be recorded at level one or two although they may have been capable of achieving that level. In the overall results for mathematics, 6.0 per cent of boys and 6.8 per cent of girls fell into this ungraded category. These pupils are excluded from the results shown in Chart 3.17

School leaving qualifications

In England, Wales and Northern Ireland, the main examination for school pupils at the minimum school leaving age is the General Certificate of Secondary Education (GCSE) which is taken in a wide range of subjects. This examination replaced the GCE O level and CSE examinations in 1987 (1988 in Northern Ireland). The GCSE examination is awarded at grades A to G. GCSE grades A to C are equivalent to O level grades A to C or CSE grade one.

The GCE is also offered at A level and usually taken after a further two years of study in a sixth-form, or equivalent. The results of candidates who have passed at A level are graded from A (the highest) to E (the lowest).

Secondary schooling in Scotland starts at age eleven and a half to twelve and a half years approximately. In 1986 the first phase of the new Standard Grade examinations was introduced and this is now the main certification for fourth year pupils. These examinations, which are aimed at a wider ability range, have replaced O grades.

From 1973 to 1985 O grades were awarded in a five-band, A to E, structure; awards in bands A to C correspond to what were previously rated passes. Since 1986 Standard grades have been awarded on a one to seven scale, with O grades being awarded on a comparable one to five scale; grades one to three, in total, are approximately equivalent to the previous A-C. The examination of the Higher (H) grade requires, basically, one further year of study and may be taken at the end of the fifth or sixth year. For the better H grade candidates, the range of subjects covered may be almost as wide as for the O grades - it is not unusual for candidates to study five or six subjects spanning both arts and science. The breadth of study inevitably means that an individual subject in the H grade course is not taken to the same depth as the more specialised GCE A level course.

Pupil/teacher ratios
The pupil/teacher ratio within schools is the ratio of all pupils on the school register to all teachers employed in schools on the day of the annual count. Part-time teachers are included on a full-time equivalent basis, with part-time service calculated as a proportion of a full-time school week. Part-time pupils are counted as 0.5 (except in Scotland where they are counted on a full time equivalent basis in nurseries and as 1.0 in other sectors).

PART 4: EMPLOYMENT

Labour force
The civilian labour force includes people aged 16 and over who are either in employment (whether as an employee, self-employed, on work-related government employment and training programmes or doing unpaid family work, but excluding those in HM armed forces) or unemployed. The ILO definition of unemployment refers to people without a job who were available to start work within two weeks and had either looked for work in the previous four weeks or were waiting to start a job they had already obtained. Estimates on this basis are not available before 1984, as the Labour Force Survey did not then collect information on job search over a four week period. The former GB/UK Labour Force definition of unemployment, the only one available for estimates up to 1984, counted people not in employment and seeking work in a reference week (or prevented from seeking work by a temporary sickness or holiday, or waiting for the results of a job application, or waiting to start a job they had already obtained), whether or not they were available to start (except students not able to start because they had to complete their education).

Workforce
Workforce in employment plus claimant unemployed.

Workforce in employment
This measure comprises employees in employment, self-employed, participants on work-related government training programmes and HM armed forces. The first three of these component series differ from their Labour Force Survey counterparts, being derived in a variety of different ways, as set out below.

The *employees in employment* component comes from employer surveys which count jobs held by civilians paid by employers who run a PAYE scheme.

The *self-employed* component is based on the 1991 Census of Population, updated using rates of change shown by annual Censuses of Agriculture and Labour Force Surveys.

The *work-related government training programme participants* component is derived from clerical and computer records of persons participating in programmes which provide an element of work-experience. The series is adjusted to exclude such persons who have a contract of employment and who are therefore counted in the employees in employment component.

Ethnic groupings
From the Spring 1992 survey, the Labour Force Survey data are based on an ethnic grouping which follows the classification developed for the 1991 Census of Population.

Occupational classification
From 1991 the Labour Force Survey has used the Standard Occupational Classification 1990 (SOC) which has replaced the old Classification of Occupations and Directory of Occupational Titles (CODOT).

Redundancies
These are based on the responses of people interviewed in the Labour Force Survey who reported that they had been made redundant in the three months before the interview. The regional redundancy rate is calculated as the number of redundant employees per thousand employees in the region, using the LFS estimate of employees.

Labour disputes
Statistics of stoppages of work caused by labour disputes in the United Kingdom relate to disputes connected with terms and conditions of employment. Small stoppages involving fewer than ten workers or lasting less than one day are excluded from the statistics unless the aggregate number of working days lost in the dispute exceeds 100. Disputes not resulting in a stoppage of work are not included in the statistics.

Workers involved and working days lost relate to persons both directly and indirectly involved (unable to work although not parties to the dispute) at the establishments where the disputes occurred. People laid off and working days lost at establishments not in dispute, due for example to resulting shortages of supplies, are excluded.

There are difficulties in ensuring complete recording of stoppages, in particular near the margins of the definition; for example short disputes lasting only a day or so, or involving only a few workers. Any under-recording would affect the total number of stoppages much more than the number of working days lost.

The unemployed
Definitions of unemployment - claimant count
People claiming benefit (that is unemployment benefit, income support, or national insurance credits) at Employment Service local offices (formerly Unemployment Benefit Offices) on the day of the monthly count, who on that day state that they are unemployed and that they satisfy the conditions for claiming benefit. (Students claiming benefit during a vacation and who intend to return to full-time education are excluded.)

Unemployment rates - claimants
Unemployment rates, available down to the level of travel-to-work areas, are calculated by expressing the number of unemployed claimants as a percentage of the mid-year estimate of the total workforce (the sum of employees in employment (Employer survey-based measure), unemployed claimants, self employed, HM armed forces and participants on work-related government training programmes).

Narrower rates (as a percentage of employees in employment (Employer survey-based measure) and the claimant unemployed only) are also available down to the level of travel-to-work areas.

Definition of unemployment and unemployment rates - ILO/OECD concepts
The unemployment figures used in these standardised rates are estimated by the OECD to conform, as far as possible, with the definition of unemployment in the guidelines of the International Labour Organisation (ILO), and the rates are calculated as percentages of the total economically active, again as defined in the ILO guidelines. According to these guidelines the unemployed covers all persons of working age who, in a specified period, are without work, who are available for work in the next two weeks, and who were seeking employment for pay or profit in the last four weeks or are waiting to start a job already obtained. The total labour force consists of civilian employees, the self-employed, unpaid family workers, professional and conscripted members of HM armed forces, and the ILO unemployed. The standardised rates will therefore differ from the unemployment rates published in national sources whenever the national definition of unemployment differs from that indicated above, or the denominator used to calculate the national rates is other than the total economically active.

GHS definition of unemployed
Until 1990; the unemployed consist of those who, in the week before interview, were looking for work, would have looked for work if they had not been temporarily sick, or were waiting to take up a job they had already obtained. In this context temporary sickness refers to illness

lasting 28 days or less. These definitions apply whether or not the person was registered as unemployed or claiming unemployment benefit. In 1991 the GHS introduced the ILO definition of unemployed. From 1985 full-time students were classified according to their own reports of what they were doing in the reference week; in previous years they were classified as 'inactive'. Also, from 1985 people on the Youth Training Scheme were classified as 'working' if they were with an employer providing work experience in the reference week and as 'inactive' if they were at college. From 1989 all those on schemes YTS/YT, ET and JTS were classified as 'working'.

Employment and training measures

Government employment and training programmes comprise all people aged 16 and over participating in Youth Training, Youth Credits, Training for work together with those on similar programmes administered by the Training and Enterprise Councils in England and Wales, the Local Enterprise Companies in Scotland and the Employment Services Agency.

Current Employment Department schemes and programmes include:
- Community Industry
- Youth Training
- Youth Credits
- Training for work (replaces Employment Training and Employment Action)
- Business Start Up Scheme (replaces Enterprise Allowance)
- Learning for work
- TEC challenge
- Workstart
- Community Action

Past schemes and programmes
- Community Industry
- Employment Training
- Employment Action
- Enterprise Allowance Scheme
- Temporary Short-Time Working Compensation Scheme, which replaced the Short-Time Working Compensation Scheme in the textiles, clothing, and footwear industry.
- Temporary Employment Subsidy
- Small Firms Employment Subsidy
- Adult Employment Subsidy
- Job Release Scheme (full-time and part-time schemes)
- Young Workers Scheme
- New Workers Scheme
- Youth Employment Subsidy
- Youth Training Scheme
- Youth Opportunities Programme
- Job Creation Programme
- Special Temporary Employment Programme
- Job Introduction Scheme
- Work Experience Programme
- Training in Industry
- Community Programme
- Voluntary Projects Programme
- Old Job Training Scheme
- New Job Training Scheme
- Training for Enterprise
- Job-Share Scheme
- Jobstart
- Access to Information Technology
- Local Grants to Employers
- Wider Opportunities Training Programme
- Open Technology Programme
- National Priority Skills Service
- Industrial Language Training Service
- Training Opportunities Program

PART 5: INCOME AND WEALTH

The household sector

The household sector includes private trusts and individuals living in institutions as well as those living in households. It differs from the personal sector, as defined in the national accounts, in that it excludes unincorporated private businesses, private non-profit-making bodies serving persons, and the funds of life assurance and pension schemes. More information is given in an article in *Economic Trends*, September 1981.

Household disposable income is equal to the total current income of the household sector *less* payments of United Kingdom taxes on income, employees' national insurance contributions, and contributions of employees to occupational pension schemes. It is revalued at constant prices by a deflator implied by estimates of total household expenditure at current and constant prices. This deflator is a modified form of the consumers' expenditure deflator.

Regional Accounts

Estimates of household income by region and county were published in *Economic Trends* (May 1993), together with brief notes on changes to sources and methods. A full description of sources and methods was published in *Economic Trends* (July 1989).

Groups of beneficiaries

Group	Benefits included
Elderly people	Retirement Pension Non-contributory Retirement Pension Christmas Bonus paid with Retirement Pension and other non-disability benefits Principal income-related benefits and Social Fund payments to people over 60[1]
Long-term sick and disabled people	Invalidity Benefit Attendance Allowance Mobility Allowance Disability Working Allowance Industrial Disablement Benefit Other Industrial Injuries Benefits Severe Disablement Allowance Invalid Care Allowance War Pensions Independent Living Fund Motability Christmas Bonus paid with disability benefits Principal income-related benefits and Social Fund payments to disabled people and people sick for more than six months[1]
Short-term sick people	Statutory Sick Pay Sickness Benefit Principal income-related benefits and Social Fund payments to people who are sick up to six months and who do not receive a disability benefit[1]
Families	Child Benefit One Parent Benefit Family Credit Family Income Supplement Statutory Maternity Pay Maternity Allowance Maternity Grant Social Fund Maternity Payments Principal income-related benefits and Social Fund payments to lone-parent families[1] Housing and Community Charge Benefits paid to people in work
Unemployed people	Unemployment Benefit Principal income-related benefits and payments from the Social Fund to unemployed people and their families[1]
Widows and other	Widows' benefits War widows' pensions Guardians' Allowance and Child's Special Allowance Death Grant Industrial Death Benefit

Social Fund Funeral payments

Income Support/Supplementary Benefit paid to people between 50 and 60 who have not had contact with the labour market for over ten years

1 Principal income-related benefits are Incone Support, Housing Benefit and Community Charge Benefits

Social security benefits

The National Insurance Fund provides insurance against loss of income in the event of unemployment, sickness and invalidity, widowhood or retirement. These are generally known as contributory benefits. Non-contributory benefits include income-related support to people or families with low income (income support and family credit). Payments, often in the form of loans, may also be made from the social fund to assist people with exceptional expenses which they would find difficult to pay out of their regular income. Non-income-related support is available through child benefit and, for the long-term sick or disabled, through severe disablement allowance, attendance allowance and disability living allowance and the various industrial injury benefits. A separate war pensions scheme pays benefit to people widowed or disabled as a result of wars, or service in HM armed forces, since 1914.

For the purpose of the *Social Security Act 1975* there are five classes of contribution to the National Insurance Fund. Class 1 is payable by employed earners and their employers, from 1991/92 Class 1A contributions are payable by employers on the benefit of cars and car fuel provided to their employees, Class 2 and Class 4 are payable by the self-employed, and Class 3 is payable on a voluntary basis by those who are neither employed nor self-employed but who wish to maintain their contributions record. Class 1 contributions are wholly earnings-related, Class 1A contributions are assessed according to the scale rate charges used by the Inland Revenue and Class 4 contributions are related to the level of profits or gains. Class 2 and Class 3 contributions are flat-rate. In general, unemployment benefit and industrial injuries benefits are only payable to Class 1 contributors.

The weekly standard rates of benefits and personal allowances for income support are:

Rates of benefits, April 1993　　　　　　　　　　　　　　　£

	Standard rate	Adult depen ant	Each child
Retirement pension (single pension)	56.10	33.70	10.95[3]
Widow's pension	56.10		10.95[3]
Unemployment benefit	44.65		27.55
eldest child			9.80[2]
subsequent child			10.95[2]
Invalidity pension	56.10	33.70	10.95[3]
Industrial disablement benefit (100%)	91.60		
Invalidity allowance[1]			
Age 40	11.95		
Age 50	7.50		
Age 60 (men) (55 women)	3.75		
Sickness benefit	42.70	26.40	
Child benefit			
first child			10.00
subsequent child			8.10
One-parent benefit (first or only child of certain lone persons)	6.05		

1 Payable with Invalidity pension when incapacity began before each age shown.

2 Child dependency only payable where beneficiary is over pension age.

3 The child dependency increase in respect of a child for whom the higher rate of Child Benefit is in payment will be reduced by £1.15.

Income support personal allowances, April 1993　　　　£

Couple	One aged 18 or over	69.00
	Both under 18	52.40
Single claimant	Aged 25 or over	44.00
	18-24	34.80
	under 18	26.45
	under 18 higher rate	34.80
Lone parent	Aged 18 or over	44.00
	under 18	26.45
	under 18 higher rate	34.80
Dependent	Child under 11	15.05
	11-15	22.15
	16-17	26.45
	18	34.80

Income support is income-related and non-contributory. From September 1988 it has not normally been available to people aged below 18. People in full-time education or working more than 16 hours are also excluded. Couples (whether married or not) and any dependent children are assessed as a unit. Claimants with one or more dependent children also receive a family premium of £9.65. Certain 'client groups' are entitled to additional payments.

Additional payments, April 1993　　　　　　　　　　£

	Single	Couple
Disability premium	18.45	26.45
Pensioner premium	17.30	26.25
Enhanced pensioner premium	19.30	29.00
Higher pensioner premium (80 or over or disabled 60-79)	23.55	33.70
Lone parent premium	4.90	
Family premium	9.65	
Carer	11.95	

It is not possible to receive more than one of these premia, except for the carer premium. There is also a severe disability premium of £33.70 and a child disability premium of £18.45.

Independent Taxation

Since the introduction of Independent Taxation on 6 April 1990 all taxpayers are taxed separately on their own incomes and take responsibility for their own tax affairs.

Under Independent Taxation every individual taxpayer is entitled to a personal allowance which can be set against any type of income. A married man is entitled to claim the married couple's allowance in addition to his personal allowance. If his total net income is too small to use the whole of the married couple's allowance he can transfer the unused allowance to his wife. In 1993-94 a couple may choose to allocate the whole married couple's allowance to the wife or to split it equally between them.

In 1991-92 taxpayers aged 65 and over are entitled to claim the aged personal allowance and the aged married couple's allowance. The amount of the aged personal allowance depends on the age of the individual taxpayer while the amount of the married couple's allowance depends on the age of the elder of the husband or wife. These aged allowances are subject to an income limit, and for incomes in excess of this limit, the allowances are reduced by £1 for each additional £2 of income until the basic levels of the personal and married couple's allowances are reached.

Households Below Average Income (HBAI)

Information on the distribution of income is provided in the Department of Social Security (DSS) publication *Households Below Average Income: 1979 to 1988/89*. This gives a comprehensive statistical analysis of income relating principally to the lower half of the income distribution; and explains the methodology used to derive the figures from the Family Expenditure Survey (FES).

Redistribution of income (ROI)
Estimates of the incidence of taxes and benefits on household income, based on the FES, are published by the Central Statistical Office in *Economic Trends*. The article covering 1991 appeared in the issue of May 1993, and contains details of the definitions and methods used.

Difference between Households Below Average Income and Redistribution Of Income series
There are two separate and distinct income series based on the FES, produced by two different government departments. Each series has been developed to serve the specific needs of that department. The DSS series, called "Households Below Average Income" (HBAI), provides estimates of patterns of personal disposable income in the United Kingdom and of changes over time; as the name suggests, it concentrates on the lower part of the income distribution and shows disposable income before and after housing costs (where disposable income is after deduction of income tax and National Insurance). The CSO series, called "Redistribution Of Income" (ROI), shows how Government intervention through the tax and benefit system affects the income of households; it covers the whole income distribution and includes the effects of indirect taxes like VAT and duty on beer, as well as estimating the cash value of benefits in kind (eg from state spending on education and health care). The ROI results are designed to show the position in a particular year rather than trends in income levels over time, although trends in the distribution of income are given. An important difference between the two series is that HBAI counts individuals (not households as in ROI).

Equivalence scales
Both HBAI and ROI use McClements equivalence scales to take into account variations in the size and composition of households. This reflects the common sense notion that a household of five adults will need a higher income than a single person living alone to enjoy a comparable standard of living. An overall equivalence value is calculated for each household by summing the appropriate scale values for each household member. Equivalised household income is then calculated by dividing household income by the household's equivalence value. The scales conventionally take a married couple as the reference point with an equivalence value of 1; equivalisation therefore tends to increase relatively the incomes of single person households and (since their incomes are divided by a value of less than 1) and to reduce relatively incomes of households with three or more persons. For further information see *Households Below Average Income, A Statistical Analysis*, HMSO.

The HBAI analyses use both before and after housing costs scales, whilst ROI only use before housing costs scales.
McClements equivalence scales:

Household member	Before housing costs	After housing costs
First adult (head)	0.61	0.55
Spouse of head	0.39	0.45
Other second adult	0.46	0.45
Third adult	0.42	0.45
Subsequent adults	0.36	0.40
Each dependent aged:		
0-1	0.09	0.07
2-4	0.18	0.18
5-7	0.21	0.21
8-10	0.23	0.23
11-12	0.25	0.26
13-15	0.27	0.28
16 or over	0.36	0.38

Distribution of personal wealth
The estimates of the distribution of the marketable wealth of individuals relate to all adults in the United Kingdom. They are produced by combining estimates of the distribution of wealth identified by the estate multiplier method with independent estimates of total personal wealth derived from the Central Statistical Office personal sector balance

sheets. The methods used were described in an article in *Economic Trends* (October 1990) entitled "Estimates of the Distribution of Personal Wealth".

Net wealth of the personal sector
Balance sheet estimates of the net wealth of the personal sector are published in the *United Kingdom National Accounts*, 1993 edition. These figures exclude the stock of consumer durables which are no longer available. Quarterly estimates of net financial wealth (excluding tangible and intangible assets) are published in *Financial Statistics*.

Social class: Institute Practitioners in Advertising (IPA) definition
Social class categories are based on head of household's occupation as follows:

Class A	Higher managerial, administrative, or professional
Class B	Intermediate managerial, administrative, or professional
Class C1	Supervisory or clerical, and junior managerial, administrative, or professional
Class C2	Skilled manual workers
Class D	Semi and unskilled workers
Class E	State pensioners or widows (no other earners), casual or lowest grade workers, or long term unemployed.

PART 6: EXPENDITURE

Retail prices
The General Index of Retail Prices measures the changes month by month in the level of the commodities and services purchased by all types of households in the United Kingdom, with the exception of certain higher income households and households of retired people mainly dependent on state benefits. These households are:

(a)   the four per cent (approximately) where the total household recorded gross income exceeds a certain amount (£925 a week in 1991/92).

(b)   those in which at least three-quarters of the total income is derived from state pensions and benefits and which include at least one person over the national insurance retirement age.

The weights which are used to calculate the index are based on the pattern of household expenditure derived from the continuing Family Expenditure Survey. Since 1962 the weights have been revised in February of each year.

Expenditure patterns of one-person and two-person pensioner households differ from those of the households upon which the General Index is based. Separate indices have been compiled for such pensioner households since 1968, and quarterly averages are published in the CSO *Business Monitor MM23 (Retail Prices Index)*. They are chain indices constructed in the same way as the General Index of Retail Prices. It should, however, be noted that the pensioner indices exclude housing costs.

A brief introduction to the RPI is given in the February 1993 issue of CSO *Business Monitor MM23 (Retail Prices Index)*, also available as a booklet from HMSO. Each month's edition of the RPI *Business Monitor* contains further articles of interest, covering topics such as reweighting, indicator items and the constructing of the new foreign holidays index.

Household expenditure
The national accounts definition of household expenditure, within consumers' expenditure, consists of: personal expenditure on goods (durable and non-durable) and services, including the value of income of kind; imputed rent for owner-occupied dwellings; and the purchase of secondhand goods less the proceeds of sales of used goods.

Excluded are: interest and other transfer payments; all business expenditure; and the purchase of land and buildings (and associated costs). In principle, expenditure is measured at the time of acquisition rather than actual disbursement of cash. The categories of expenditure include that of non-resident as well as resident households and individuals in the United Kingdom.

For further details see the article entitled 'Consumers' expenditure' in *Economic Trends*, September 1983.

Household saving
Household saving is the balance of income and expenditure on the current account of households, and is derived from the personal sector account, mainly by subtracting the income and expenditure (and hence saving) of the other parts of the personal sector. The household savings ratio is household saving expressed as a percentage of household disposable income.

Household income comprises:
> Wages and salaries, and forces' pay
> Self-employment income
> Rent, dividends, and interest
> Income in kind
> Pensions and benefits paid by life assurance
> and pension schemes
> Social security benefits
> Other current transfers

Household disposable income comprises:
> Household income less
> United Kingdom taxes on income
> Employees' contributions to occupational pension schemes

Household expenditure comprises:
> Interest payments
> Community charge
> Expenditure on goods and services
> Life assurance premiums etc paid by individuals
> Other current transfers

(Note: this definition of household expenditure does not accord with that for national accounts purposes - see above.)

PART 7: HEALTH AND PERSONAL SOCIAL SERVICES

Expectation of life
The expectation of life at birth, shown in Chart 7.1 for the years 1921 to 2001 is the average number of years which a new-born baby could be expected to live, if its rates of mortality at each age were those experienced in that calendar year.

The mortality rates which underlie the expectations of life figures in Chart 7.1 are based, up to 1992, on total deaths occurring in each year, and in the case of subsequent years on the mortality rates assumed for those years in the Government Actuary's mid-1991 based population projection.

Death Certificates
On 1st January 1986, a new certificate for deaths within the first 28 days of life was introduced in England and Wales. It is not possible to assign one underlying cause of death from this certificate. In Table 7.3 for the sake of consistency, the United Kingdom figures for 1991 exclude deaths at ages under 28 days. In Table 7.22 the 1991 and 1992 figures for England and Wales exclude deaths under 28 days.

Cot deaths
Cot deaths relates to infant deaths (babies aged under one year) where Sudden Infant Death Syndrome (SIDS, ICD 9th revision, 798.0) is identified.

Standardised mortality rates
The mortality rates used in Chart 7.5 have been directly standardised - that is, for each year they were calculated by applying observed age-specific rates to a standard population. The standard population used was for the United Kingdom in 1981.

Drinking
A unit of alcohol is 8 grams of pure alcohol, approximately equivalent to a half pint of ordinary strength beer, a pub measure of spirits or a glass of wine.

Notified Addicts
Doctors are required to send to the Chief Medical Officer at the Home Office particulars of persons whom they consider to be addicted to any of 14 controlled drugs (mainly opiates).

Accidental deaths
The data in Table 7.22 exclude deaths where it was not known whether the cause was accidentally or purposely inflicted, misadventure during medical care, abnormal reactions and late complications.

In-patient activity
In Table 7.23 in-patient cases treated for 1981 are hospital discharges and deaths taken from the SH3 return. From 1991-92 these are Finished Consultant Episodes (FCE) from the KP70 return. A FCE is a completed period of care of a patient using a bed, under one consultant, in a particular District/Special Health Authority. If a patient is transferred from one consultant to another within the same hospital, this counts as an FCE not a hospital discharge. Conversely, if a patient is transferred from one consultant to another within the same district without changing consultant, this counts as a hospital discharge but not as an FCE. The KP70 includes healthy live born infants whereas the SH3 returns did not.

Discharges from mental illness and learning disability hospitals and units
A major change in data collection affected hospital activity statistics from 1 April 1987. Up to 1986 the data for Chart 7.27 were collected through the Mental Health Enquiry (MHE) which covered mental illness and learning disability hospitals and units and was based on the calendar year. Since April 1 1987 the data has come from the Hospital Episode Statistics (HES system) which covers all NHS hospitals and is based on the financial year. Any interpretation of the data should take into account serious deficiencies in both quality and coverage of HES data in its first year (1987-88) as well as differences in coverage of the two systems.

Hospice beds
The classification of hospice beds used in Chart 7.34 refers to the management of each hospice bed and not funding. Almost all hospices receive some funding from the National Health Service. Other major sources of funding are the Cancer Relief Macmillan Fund, Sue Ryder and Marie Curie.

Unrestricted principals
An unrestricted principal is a medical practitioner who provides the full range of general medical services and whose list is not limited to any particular group or persons. In a few cases (about 20), he may be relieved of the liability to have patients assigned to him or be exempted from liability to emergency calls out-of-hours from patients other than his own. Doctors may also practise in the general medical services as restricted principals, assistants or trainees.

Persons employed in health and personal social services
The total of Health Authorities' staff and family practitioners would contain an element of duplication, since some practitioners have been counted under more than one of the categories shown. Figures relate as closely as possible to 30 September, except those for ophthalmic family practitioner staff which refer to 31 December. Figures for Northern Ireland before 1991 relate to 31 December, except those for family practitioner staff which relate to 31 July.

Staff of the Post Graduate Special Health Authorities and those Family Health Service Authority staff on health authority payrolls are included in Regional and District Health Authorities' staff, as are Common Services Agency staff in Scotland. In 1982, due to the restructuring of the NHS in England and Wales, Area Health Authorities were removed and their functions devolved to District Health Authorities.

The figures for medical and dental staff in Regional Health Authorities, District Health Authorities and NHS Trusts include permanent paid and honorary staff in hospital and community health services, hospital practitioners and part-time medical/dental officers, but exclude locum staff in Great Britain. Northern Ireland figures include all community sessional staff.

Figures for family health staff include General Medical Practitioners (principals, assistants and trainees), General Dental Practitioners (principals and assistants) and staff of the General Ophthalmic Service.

PART 8: HOUSING

Dwellings
Estimates of the stock of dwellings are based on data from the censuses of Population, with adjustments for enumeration errors and for definitional changes. The figures include vacant dwellings and temporary dwellings occupied as a normal place of residence. Privately rented dwellings include those rented from housing associations, private owners and other tenures; including dwellings rented with farm or business premises and those occupied by virtue of employment.

Bedroom standard
This concept is used to estimate occupation density by allocating a standard number of bedrooms to each household in accordance with its age/sex/marital status composition and the relationship of the members to one another. A separate bedroom is allocated to each married couple, any other person aged 21 or over, each pair of adolescents aged 10-20 of the same sex, and each pair of children under 10. Any unpaired person aged 10-20 is paired, if possible with a child under 10 of the same sex. If that is not possible, they are given a separate bedroom, as in an unpaired child under 10. This standard is then compared with the actual number of bedrooms (including bedsitters) available for the sole use of the household, and deficiencies or excesses are tabulated. Bedrooms converted to other uses are not counted as available for the sole use of the household, and deficiencies or excesses are tabulated. Bedrooms converted to other uses are not counted as available unless they have been noted as bedrooms by the informant; bedrooms not actually in use are counted unless uninhabitable.

The mixed adjusted series
The house prices are based on the BS4 monthly return of dwellings purchased with building society mortgages at approval stage. The series (1990=100) is based on building society mortgages at completion stage from the 5 per cent sample survey. The mix (type, size, location and age of dwelling) changes through time, a house price series that takes account of this provides a better measure of true house price movements than an index based on the simple average price where variations in mix are not taken into account.

Housing standards
The English House Conditions Survey 1991, the fifth in a quinquennial series undertaken by the Department of the Environment. The survey provided three measures of dwellings in poor condition; dwellings lacking basic amenities, unfit dwellings and dwellings in a state of serious disrepair. Basic amenities were those which qualified for a mandatory grant under the *Local government and Housing Act 1989*. These were a kitchen sink, a bath or shower in a bathroom, a wash hand basin, each with hot and cold water supply and an indoor WC. An unfit dwelling is one which is unsuitable for human habitation as defined in the *Housing Act 1989*. To be classified unfit, the dwelling must be so far defective in one or more of nine specified ways as to be unsuitable for occupation. The requirements of the standard are: repair, stability, freedom from damp, internal arrangement, natural lighting, ventilation, water supply, drainage and sanitary conveniences and facilities for the preparation and cooking of food and for the disposal of waste water. There is no statutory definition of dwellings in a state of serious disrepair.

PART 9: ENVIRONMENT

Quality of bathing water
Directive (76/160/EEC) concerning the quality of bathing water sets the mandatory values for bacteriological parameters:
- for total coliforms   10,000 per ml; and
- for faecal coliforms   2,000 per ml
In determining compliance with the coliform standards the following method has been used:
     a.   where 20 or more samples are analysed, 95 per cent of coliform results must not exceed the mandatory

value;
     b.   where less than 20 but more than 11 samples are analysed, no more than 1 coliform result may exceed the mandatory value;
     c.   where 11 or fewer samples are analysed, no coliform result may exceed the mandatory value.

This method is applied separately to results for faecal coliforms and for total coliforms. If one of the bacteriological parameters fails to comply with its standard then the water is said to fail to comply with the coliform standards.

Farmland birds
Population changes are shown for all those farmland species for which it is possible to calculate a valid index from the farmland sample of British Trust for Ornithology Common Birds Census plots. Population changes were calculated as follows:- Quadratic regressions were fitted to log transformed population indices for each year from 1971 to 1991.

PART 11: PARTICIPATION

Church membership
Definitions of membership vary according to the church denomination or religious group in question. For the purpose of Table 11.8 adult church membership is defined as appropriate to each particular group, so that, for example the Electoral Roll (not to be confused with the Local Authority Electoral Roll) has been used for the Church of England, the Easter communicant figure has been used for the Church in Wales, while mass attendance has been used for the Roman Catholic churches.

Parliamentary elections and political parties
A general election must be held at least every five years, or sooner, if the Prime Minister of the day so decides. The United Kingdom is currently divided into 651 constituencies, each of which returns one member to the House of Commons. To ensure equitable representation, four permanent Boundary Commissions (for England and Wales, Scotland and Northern Ireland) make periodic reviews of constituencies and recommend any change in the number or redistribution of seats that may seem necessary in the light of population movements or for some other reason.

The Social Democratic Party (SDP) was launched on 26 March 1981. In the 1983 and 1987 General Elections the Liberals and SDP contested seats as the Liberal-SDP Alliance. In 1988 the Social and Liberal Democrats were formed, after which the Democrats and the SDP contested elections separately. In June 1990 the SDP disbanded.

On 17 December 1985 all 15 Ulster Unionist MPs resigned their seats and sought re-election as a protest against the Anglo-Irish agreement. The 15 by-elections were held on 23 January 1986.

Trade Union membership
Includes organisations described as staff associations. Thirty one organisations previously regarded as Trade Unions are excluded from 1975 onwards because they failed to satisfy the statutory definition of a Trade Union in Section 1 of the *Trade Union and Labour Relations (Consolidation) Act, 1992*.

Commissioners for Local Administration
The Commissioners investigate complaints from members of the public about injustice caused by maladministration in local government in England, Scotland and Wales.

Examples of faults or failures which the Local Commissioners have treated as maladministration are: neglect and unjustified delay; malice or bias or unfair discrimination; failure to observe relevant rules or procedures; failure to take relevant considerations into account; and failure to tell people of their rights. Commissioners have no power to question the merits of a decision taken without maladministration.

A complaint should be made in writing and may be sent direct to the Local Commissioner or to a member of the authority complained against with a request that it should be sent to the Local Commissioner.

Certain administrative actions are outside the jurisdiction of the Commissioners; these include matters where the complainant has a right of appeal to a tribunal or court of law, personnel matters, contractual and commercial transactions, complaints about public passenger transport, docks harbours, entertainment, industrial establishments and markets, and the internal affairs of schools and colleges. Where the complainant has the right of appeal to a tribunal, minister or court of law the Commissioner has a discretion to waive this restriction if he or she considers it not reasonable for the complainant to have exercised that right.

If a report by a Local Commissioner finds that injustice has been caused by maladministration, the Council must consider in the report and tell the Local Commissioner what action they propose to take. A Local Commissioner cannot force a Council to act if they decide not to. Since 1 January 1985, the statistical records of the Local Commissioner for Wales relate to all complaints, not only to formally referred complaints as hitherto.

Health Service Commissioners
The function of the Health Service Commissioners, who are statutory independent Officers appointed by the Crown, is to investigate complaints of failure in provision or in execution of a service provided by a health authority, or maladministration by or on behalf of these authorities. The authorities concerned include Regional Health Authorities, District Health Authorities, Family Health Service Authorities and NHS Trusts. A complaint may be made directly to the appropriate commissioner, but only after it has been brought to the attention of the relevant health authority and an adequate opportunity given to that authority to investigate it and reply. Matters outside jurisdiction include action taken in the Commissioner's opinion solely in the exercise of clinical judgement and any action taken by family doctors, dentists, pharmacists and opticians who provide services under contract to a health authority.

There are three Health Service Commissioners: one each for England, Scotland and Wales. At present all three posts and that of Parliamentary Commissioner, are held by the same person. The Commissioners report annually to Parliament for the year to 31 March from April to the following March and otherwise as they see fit.

Parliamentary Commissioner for Administration
The Parliamentary Commissioner is a statutory independent officer appointed by the Crown. His function is to investigate complaints of maladministration referred to him by Members of Parliament on behalf of members of the public. His powers of investigation extend to actions taken by central government departments and certain non-departmental public bodies in the exercise of their administrative functions, but not to policy (which is the concern of Government) or legislation (which is the concern of Parliament).

Certain administrative actions are, however, outside his jurisdiction; these include matters affecting relations with other countries, contractual matters, hospitals (but see the note on the Health Service Commissioners) and personnel questions of the armed forces and the civil service. The Commissioner cannot investigate any matter where the complainant has exercised a right of appeal to a tribunal or court of law. However, he may at his discretion conduct an investigation if such a right of appeal exists and it is held that the complainant has, with good reason, not resorted to that right. In the performance of his duties, the Parliamentary Commissioner has the power to require the production of evidence, including official papers, and the attendance of witnesses. He reports his findings to the Member of Parliament who presented the case. The Commissioner reports annually to Parliament and may submit such other reports as he thinks fit. An all-party Select Committee considers his reports.

Selected Advisory and counselling services
Al-Anon Family Groups: Includes Irish Republic.
Alcoholics Anonymous: Includes branches in the Channel Isles. The 1981 and 1990 figures exclude Northern Ireland.
Catholic Marriage Advisory Council: Figures relate to Great Britain.
Citizens Advice Bureaux: The figures given for 'Clients' represent new enquiries in 1971, and new plus repeat enquiries thereafter.
Cruse: Cruse Bereavement Care. Figures given for clients exclude many short-term contracts.
Leukaemia Care Society: Figures for 'Clients' represent numbers of families.

Relate: Includes England, Wales, N Ireland, Channel Isles and Isle of Man. Marriage Guidance Scotland is excluded. Up to 1991, figures given for 'Clients' represented numbers of families (based on new cases during the year). From 1992 it represented the number given reception interviews and those entering councelling.

PART 12: CRIME AND JUSTICE

Criminal courts in England and Wales
The courts of ordinary criminal jurisdiction in England and Wales are the magistrates' courts, which try the less serious cases and the Crown Court which deals with the more serious cases. Prior to 1 October 1992, almost all offenders under 17 were dealt with in juvenile courts, which were a special form of magistrates' court. The *Criminal Justice Act 1991*, which came into effect on 1 October 1992, brought offenders aged 17 within their jurisdiction and renamed them youth courts. The Crown Court was established by the *Courts Act 1971*, which came into effect on 1 January 1972. From that date the former courts of assize and quarter sessions were abolished.

Part III of the *Criminal Law Act 1977*, which came into effect on 17 July 1978, redefined offences according to three new modes of trial, namely:

    i.   offences triable only on indictment
    ii.   offences triable either on indictment or summarily, but which are triable summarily only with the consent of the accused
    iii. offences triable only summarily

For statistical purposes the figures for court proceedings and for police cautioning for 1979 onwards are shown in two groups; the first group is a combination of i. and ii. above which has been called 'indictable' and covers those offences which may be tried by jury in the Crown Court and the second group, 'summary' offences, covers iii. above and are usually only tried at magistrates' courts.

Criminal courts in Scotland
The courts exercising criminal jurisdiction in Scotland are the High Court of Justiciary, the Sheriff Court and the District Court.

The High Court is Scotland's supreme criminal court, and deals with the most serious cases and with all appeals. There is no appeal from it to the House of Lords. All cases in High Court are tried by a judge and jury (referred to as "solemn procedure" or "on indictment").

The Sheriff Court has both solemn and summary jurisdiction and deals with less serious cases. Most prosecutions are dealt with by summary procedure (ie before a sheriff and without a jury). The sentencing powers of the Sheriff Court are more limited than those of the High Court, but where a case merits more severe penalties the sheriff may remit it to the High Court for sentence.

The District Courts were established in 1975 by statute to replace the former Burgh Courts. The District Courts are presided over by lay justices and deal summarily with minor offences. The sentencing power of the District Court is more limited than that of the Sheriff Court, except where it is presided over by a stipendiary magistrate, when it has the same jurisdiction and powers as a sheriff sitting summarily.

Prosecutions in Scotland are brought by procurators fiscal who act in the public interest on behalf of the Lord Advocate. It is the procurator fiscal, advised in serious cases by Crown Counsel, who decides in each case whether to proceed, and if so, in which court to prosecute.

Criminal courts in Northern Ireland
Courts of criminal jurisdiction in Northern Ireland, like England and Wales, include magistrate's courts and Crown Courts with similar distinctions in treating offences of varying seriousness. However, since 1973 a special procedure has been developed for dealing with serious offences relating to terrorism. The majority of these offences are also tried in the Crown Court on indictment but they are tried by a judge without a jury, the judge alone deciding all issues of fact as well as law and passing sentence after conviction. The special non-jury

Crown Courts are often referred to as 'Diplock' courts (as they are based on recommendations of a Commission under Lord Diplock).

The offences triable in this way are listed in Schedule 1 of the Northern Ireland Emergency Provisions Act 1991 and are referred to as scheduled offences. Some of the offences listed may be de-scheduled by the Attorney-General in particular cases. They should be de-scheduled if no element of terrorism was involved in their commission. An example of an offence which could be de-scheduled is murder, where it occurs in a domestic setting and is clearly unconnected with terrorist activity.

Support for victims of crime
The Criminal Injuries Compensation Scheme provides lump sum compensation based on common law damages for victims of violent crime in Great Britain where the injury is assessed as worth £1000 or more. The ex-gratia scheme applies to anyone criminally injured within Great Britain or on a British registered ship or aircraft.

Sentences and orders
The following are the main sentences and orders which can be imposed upon those persons found guilty in 1991 and 1992. Some types of sentence or order can only be given to offenders in England and Wales in certain age groups. Under a new statutory framework for sentencing contained in the Criminal Justice Act 1991, the sentence must reflect the seriousness of the offence. Custody may also be justified by the need to protect the public from serious harm from a violent or sexual offender. Where custody is not justified, a court may pass a community sentence which may consist of one or more community orders, as well as a fine.

Absolute and conditional discharge
A court may make an order discharging a person absolutely or (except in Scotland) conditionally where it is inexpedient to inflict punishment and, before 1 October 1992, where a probation order was not appropriate. An order for conditional discharge runs for such period of not more than three years as the court specifies, the condition being that the offender does not commit another offence within the period so specified. In Scotland a court may also discharge a person with an admonition.

Attendance centre order
This sentence, available in England, Wales and Northern Ireland, involves deprivation of free time. The centres are mainly for boys between the ages of 10 and 16 found guilty of offences for which an adult could be sentenced to imprisonment. At the end of 1991, there were over 80 centres for boys aged 10 to 16, 18 of which also took girls in the same age group, as well as 26 centres for males aged 17 to 20. Attendance is on Saturday mornings or afternoons for up to three hours on any one occasion and for a total of not more than 36 hours and (normally) not less than 12. The activities include physical training and instruction in useful skills (eg first aid).

Probation orders
The *Criminal Justice Act 1991* states that a court may make a probation order where this is desirable in the interests of securing the rehabilitation of the offender or protecting the public from harm or preventing further offending. An offender placed on probation is under the supervision of a probation officer (social worker in Scotland), whose duty it is to advise, assist, and befriend him. A cardinal feature of the order is that it relies on the co-operation of the offender. In England and Wales probation orders may only be made on people aged 16 or over (17 or over prior to 1 October 1992). The *Criminal Justice Act 1991* also extended the use of supervision orders, previously limited to juveniles aged under 17, to include those aged 17. There is no age limit in Scotland, but children under 16 would normally be dealt with outside the criminal justice system. Probation orders may be given for any period between 6 months and 3 years inclusive.

Community service
An offender aged 16 or over who is convicted of an offence punishable with imprisonment may be required to perform unpaid work for not more than 240 hours, and not less than 40 hours. Prior to 1 October 1992 those aged 16 could be required to perform a maximum of 120 hours. In Scotland the *Law Reform (Miscellaneous Provisions) (Scotland) Act 1990* requires that community service can only be ordered where the court would otherwise have imposed imprisonment or detention. Probation and community service may be combined in a single order in Scotland.

Combination order
The *Criminal Justice Act 1991* introduced the combination order, which combines elements of both probation supervision and community service, and may be given to offenders aged 16 or over. The order may require the offender to perform between 40 and 100 hours unpaid work and to be supervised by a probation officer for a period between 12 months and 3 years.

Imprisonment
The custodial sentence for adult offenders is imprisonment or, in the case of mentally abnormal offenders, hospital orders with or without restrictions on when the offender may be discharged. Prior to 1 October 1992 in England and Wales a third of a prisoner's sentence, or one half for those serving sentences of 12 months or less, was remitted subject to good conduct and industry. Those serving sentences of over 9 months (18 months in Scotland) could be released under the parole scheme after serving 6 months (12 months in Scotland) or a third of the sentence, whichever was the longer. The *Criminal Justice Act 1991* abolished remission and substantially changed the parole scheme in England and Wales. Those serving sentences of under 4 years, imposed on or after 1 October 1992, are subject to Automatic Conditional Release and are released halfway through their sentence. Those serving sentences of four years or longer are considered for Discretionary Conditional Release after having served half their sentence, but are automatically released at the two-thirds point of sentence. All offenders serving a sentence of 12 months or more are supervised in the community until the three-quarter point of sentence. Additional days imposed for breaches of prison discipline can delay a prisoner's early release. A life sentence prisoner may be released on licence subject to supervision and is always liable to recall. Similar changes for Scotland came into effect in October 1993.

Fully suspended sentences of imprisonment and suspended sentences with supervision order
In England, Wales and Northern Ireland, sentences of imprisonment of two years or less may be fully suspended for a period of between one and two years. A court should not pass a suspended sentence unless a sentence of imprisonment would be appropriate in the absence of a power to suspend. The result of suspending a sentence is that it will not take effect unless during the period specified the offender is convicted of another offence punishable with imprisonment. The *Criminal Justice Act 1972*, which came into force on 1 January 1973, gave the courts power, on passing a suspended sentence of over 6 months, to impose a 'suspended sentence with supervision order' placing the offender under the supervision of a probation officer for a specified period not longer than the period of suspension. The *Criminal Justice Act 1991* provides that fully suspended sentences may only be passed in exceptional circumstances.

Partly suspended and extended sentences of imprisonment
Section 5 of the *Criminal Justice Act 1991* abolished the courts' power to pass a partly suspended sentence of imprisonment or to pass an extended sentence of imprisonment on a persistant offender, with effect from 1 October 1992.

Deferred Sentence
A court may decide to defer sentence after conviction for a period and on conditions determined by the court. At the end of this period the case is considered by the court at the deferred date. The court has the same powers of sentence as at conviction.

Young offenders institutions
The *Criminal Justice Act 1991* made a number of changes to the custodial sentencing arrangements for young offenders. A common minimum age of 15 for boys and girls was set for the imposition of a sentence of detention in a young offender institution, thus removing boys aged 14 from the scope of this sentence. From 1 October 1992 the minimum period for which those aged 15 to 17 may be detained is 2 months (previously 21 days for boys and 4 months for girls) and the maximum is 12 months. For offenders aged 18 and under 21 the minimum is 21 days and the maximum is the same as the adult maximum for the offence. A sentence of custody for life is mandatory for offenders convicted of murder aged 18 and under 21, and is also available for other grave offences. Young offenders serving determinate

sentences are eligible for early release (see below). In Scotland no person under 21 may be sent to prison. Children under 16 are dealt with by the children's hearings system, which is not part of the criminal justice system. For young offenders (aged 16-21) Borstal training was abolished in Scotland by the *Criminal Justice (Scotland) Act 1980*, and detention centres were abolished by the *Criminal Justice Act 1988* and replaced by detention in a young offenders institution.

Young Offenders Centres: Northern Ireland
On 1 June 1979 provisions in the *Treatment of Offenders (Northern Ireland) Act 1968* were brought into operation so that those under 21 years of age would no longer be sent to prison unless the court wished to impose a sentence of 3 years or more, but would be detained in a Young Offenders Centre.

Fines
The Criminal Justice Act 1991 introduced new arrangements for setting fines in magistrates' courts, the unit fine scheme, which required magistrates to calculate fines directly related to the means of the offender. The unit fine scheme was replaced by new arrangements applicable to both magistrates' courts and Crown Courts on 20 September 1993. The new provisions require courts to take into account an offenders financial circumstances but give more discretion to sentencers. The Act also introduced the power for courts to arrange deduction of fines from income benefit for those offenders receiving such benefits. Fines may be imposed with or without time to pay the fine. If the fine is not paid in the time allowed imprisonment or detention may result. In Scotland the *Law Reform (Miscellaneous Provision) (Scotland) Act 1990* introduced supervised attendance orders. These orders are intended to provide an alternative to custody for fine defaulters. The minimum number of hours is 10 and the maximum 60. Orders will comprise work of benefit to the community and/or sessions devoted to topics such as debt counselling and advice on alcohol abuse.

Compensation Orders
The *Powers of Criminal Courts Act 1973* and *Criminal Justice (Scotland) Act 1980* enable criminal courts to help the victims of crime, imposing compensation orders on those found guilty. The *Children Act 1989* abolished the courts' power to make care orders in criminal proceedings, with effect from 14 October 1991.

Legal aid
Advice and assistance provided by a solicitor, short of actual representation in court or tribunal proceedings, may be obtained free by those whose capital and income are within certain financial limits.

Assistance by way of representation covers the cost of a solicitor preparing a case and representing a client in court. It is available (either free or on payment of a contribution to those who are financially eligible) for some civil cases in the magistrates' court, for proceedings before Mental Health Review Tribunals', discretionary life prisoners before the parole board and disciplinary hearings before a prison governor, and for certain proceedings relating to the care of children and young people.

Legal aid in civil cases, such as county court and higher court proceedings, covers all work up to and including court proceedings and representing by a solicitor and a barrister, if necessary. Legal aid in these cases is available free or on a contributory basis to those whose capital and income are within certain financial limits. Applicants must show that they have reasonable grounds for asserting or disputing a claim. Certain types of action, including libel and slander, are excluded from this type of legal aid.

In the criminal courts in England and Wales a legal aid order may be made if this appears desirable in the interest of justice and the defendant's means are such that he requires financial help in meeting the costs of the proceedings in which he is involved. No limit of income or capital above which a person is ineligible for legal aid is specified, but the court must order a legally-aided person to contribute towards the costs of his case where his resources are such that he can afford to do so.

Advice and assistance and civil legal aid in Scotland operate on the same basis. In the case of advice by way of representation (ABWOR), however, this is granted mainly for summary criminal cases rather than civil cases and applies where a plea of guilty is made. Mental health appeals are also covered by ABWOR. Criminal legal aid, which is granted by the Scottish Legal Aid Board, for summary cases and for all appeals, and by the courts for solemn cases, is not subject to a contribution.

Civil courts in England and Wales
The main Civil Courts in England and Wales are the High Court and the county courts. Magistrates' courts have a very limited civil jurisdiction, for example, in some family proceedings. Most appeals in civil cases go to the Court of Appeal (Civil Division) and may go from there to the House of Lords.

Since July 1991, county courts have been able to deal with all contract and tort cases and actions for recovery of land, regardless of value. Cases are presided over by a judge who almost always sits without a jury. Jury trials are limited to specified cases, for example, actions for libel. Other types of matter dealt with by these courts include Equity (such as trusts and mortgages), bankruptcy and insolvency, and family proceedings (including divorce and adoption). Some courts will have jurisdiction to deal with all these types of work; others are designated to deal with only some.

Civil courts in Scotland
The Court of Session is the supreme civil court in Scotland. As a general rule it has the original jurisdiction in all civil cases and appellate jurisdiction (that is, the power to hear and give decisions on appeals) over all civil courts, unless such jurisdiction, original or appellate, is expressly excluded by statute. The Court is divided into two parts, the Inner House and the Outer House. The Inner House exercises appellate jurisdiction on reclaiming motions from the Outer House and on appeals from the inferior courts. Appeals from the Court of Session may go to the House of Lords.

The Sheriff court is the principal local court of civil, as well as criminal, jurisdiction in Scotland. Its civil jurisdiction is comparable with that of the county courts in England and Wales but is more extensive in certain directions. These is no limit to the sum which may be sued for in the Sheriff court. The Sheriff's jurisdiction now includes actions of divorce, but does not extend to actions of declarator of marriage, or to certain other actions; but, with these exceptions, the civil jurisdiction of the court is generally similar in scope to that of the Court of Session. In addition, the Sheriff deals with a mass of quasi-judicial and administrative business, some of which is similar to that dealt with in county courts in England and Wales, but of which a large part is particular to the Scottish system.

CHAPTER 13: TRANSPORT

Journey purpose
The purpose of a journey is taken to be the activity at the destination, unless that destination is 'home' in which case the purpose is defined by the origin of the journey. A journey is defined as a one-way course of travel having a single main purpose.

To and from work: journeys to a usual place of work, or from work to home.

In course of work: personal journeys in course of work. This includes all work journeys by people with no usual place of work (eg site workers) and those who work at or from home.

Education: journeys to school or college etc, excluding part-time non-vocational courses.

Escort for work/education: used when the traveller has no purpose of his own, other than to escort or accompany another person to a place of work or education. All other escort purposes are included with the purpose of the person being escorted.

Shopping: all journeys to shops or from shops to home.

Personal business: visits to services eg hairdressers, launderettes, solicitors, churches etc and for medical consultations/treatment, and eating and drinking unless the main purpose was entertainment/social.

Social and entertainment: meeting friends etc, travelling to all types of entertainment, voluntary work, non-vocational evening classes etc.

Holidays and day trips: journeys (within Great Britain) to or from any holiday (including stays of 4 nights or more with friends or relatives) or journeys for pleasure (not otherwise classified as social or entertainment) within a single day.

EC Visitor

'EC' visitor means a person who, being permanently resident outside the United Kingdom, visits the United Kingdom for a period of less than 12 months. United Kingdom citizens resident in the EC for 12 months or more coming home on leave are included in this category. Visits to the EC similarly are visits for a period of less than 12 months by people permanently resident in the United Kingdom (who may be of foreign nationality.)

Goods Moved

Rail. Up to 1962, figures for rail traffic include departmental traffic (eg ballast) on revenue earning trains. Figures are for financial years with effect from 1991-92.

Water. Up to 1972, includes only Great Britain coastwise traffic and internal traffic on BWB waterways. From 1972, includes all United Kingdom coastwise and one-port freight movements by sea and inland waterway traffic.

Pipeline. The increase between 1989 and 1990 is largely due to changes in coverage .

Railway performance indicators

As a part of its Passenger's Charter, British Rail has specified the following punctuality and reliability targets:

	Percentage of trains arriving within time shown[1]	Percentage of services to run
Intercity	90%/ 10 mins	99
Regional Railways		
Express & long rural	90%/ 10 mins	99
Urban & short rural	90% / 5 mins	99
Network SouthEast[2]	80-90% / 5 mins	97-99

1 Monday to Saturday measured at the end of the route.
2 Targets vary between groups of services.

London Underground has a number of performance targets including 'trains in peak hour service' for which the current target is 85 per cent. There is no target based on 'kilometres run' as used in Table 13.16.

Road deaths

Road deaths are normally counted as those which occur within 30 days of the accident. Figures for countries whose road deaths do not meet this definition have been standardised using the factors below:-

Country	Death within	Correction (per cent)
Austria	3 days	+12
France	6 days	+9
Greece	3 days	+12
Italy	7 days	+7
Japan	24 hours	+30
Portugal	At scene	+35
Spain	24 hours	+30
Switzerland	1 year	-5

Index

The references in this index refer to table and chart numbers, or entries in the Appendix.

International comparison (continued)
        education,
                16 to 18 year olds 3.12
                public expenditure 3.29
        external purchasing power of the pound 6.11
        fertility rates 1.19
        hours worked 4.14
        infant mortality 1.19
        life expectancy 1.19
        migration 1.15, 1.16
        passenger transport 13.4
        personnel income taken by direct taxes 5.14
        population 1.19
        prices, consumer 6.12
        prison population 12.30
        road accidents 13.23
        road vehicle ownership 13.23
        transport casualties 13.23
        unemployment rates 4.19
Investment, real, in transport infrastructure 13.8

Job related training 4.26
Job search methods 4.24
Journeys, number of, by purpose 13.2

Labour force, App. Pt 4
        civilian 4.4, 4.5
        economic activity rates 4.5, 4.6
Land
        use 9.14
        agricultural 9.15
        designated as Green Belt, National Parks
        or Areas of Outstanding Natural Beauty 9.18
Learning disability, daily available beds 7.28
Lecturers 3.25
Legal aid, App. Pt 12
        criminal 12.34
Leisure
        Arts Council expenditure 10.28
        availability of leisure time 10.1, 10.2
        cassette sales 10.8
        cinema 10.12, 10.14
        day visits 10.17
        holidays 10.24, 10.25, 10.26
        home-based activities 10.3
        household expenditure 10.29
        magazine readership 10.9
        newspaper readership 10.10
        radio 10.3, 10.7
        sport
                participating 10.21
                spectating 10.22
        television viewing 10.3, 10.4
        theatre, West End attendances 10.15
        time 10.1
        tourist attractions 10.18
                see also 'Holidays'
        video cassette
                recorders, households with 6.7
                tapes, hiring of 10.6
Libraries 10.11
Life expectancy 1.19, 7.1, App. Pt 7

Local authorities
        children's welfare 7.35, 7.36
        dwellings 8.1, 8.4
        homeless, provision for 8.12, 8.13, 8.14
Lone mothers 2.8, 2.9
Lone parents 2.8
Low cost home ownership App. Pt 8

Magazine readership 10.9
Manpower
        education 3.25
        health and personal social services 7.30 App. Pt
        7
        police 12.35
        prison service 12.35
        probation service 12.35
Marriage 2.1, 2.11, 2.12
Maternities 2.17
Maternity leave 2.23
Medical insurance, private 7.32
Medicine, alternative 7.33
Membership
        of churches by religion 11.8
        of environmental organisations 8.4
        of Trade Unions, 11.14
        voluntary rescue teams 11.7
        women's organisations 11.6
        young people's organisations 11.5
Migration
        acceptances for settlement 1.17
        applications for asylum 1.18
        international 1.15, 1.16
        UK, inter regional 1.14
Mortality
        see 'Deaths'
Mortgage
        building societies, balances, arrears and
        repossessions 8.20, 8.21, 8.22
        interest rates 8.19
        interest tax relief 8.23
        repayment 8.16
Motorcycles
        casualties 13.20
Motoring and fares 6.2, 6.6, 13.7
Motor vehicles, average daily flow of 13.13

National events
        attendances at 10.16
National Federation of Women's Institutes 11.6
National insurance contributions
        effect on earnings 5.12
        percentage of income 5.3, 5.12
Natural gas
        production 9.22
        reserves 9.21
Nature conservation 9.16
Newspaper readership 10.10
Night work 4.15
Northern Ireland
        deaths due to the security situation 12.37
        notifiable offences, recorded 12.1, 12.2
                clear up rates 12.15

Central
Statistical
Office

SNAPSHOT OF BRITAIN

Do you need economic and social statistics on different parts of the United Kingdom? If so, there are few better sources than Regional Trends.

Here's what the press have said about this famous publication ...

'... provides a fascinating insight into the differing lifestyles of particular regions...'- *Financial Times*

'... essential to Government planners, scientific researchers or businessmen seeking a profile of an area in which to test their market...'- *Daily Telegraph*

'... includes district statistics... providing an intriguing insight into small pockets of the country...' *The Times*

'... the definitive reference book on how parts of Britain differ...'- *Daily Telegraph*

'...Regional Trends' 200 pages provide a highly readable snapshot of social and economic conditions in Britain...'- *Daily Star*

'... myths exploded by the latest statistics from Regional Trends...' - *The Guardian*

'...contains some information to confirm stereotyped images of lifestyle around Britain's regions-but also some to challenge them...'- *Financial Times*

From HMSO and through good booksellers.

Regional Trends

Published for the Central Statistical Office by HMSO.
Price £26 net
ISBN 0 11 620 596 2